THE LETTERS OF
THOMAS BABINGTON MACAULAY

VOLUME I

MACAULAY IN 1833
Portrait in oil by Samuel W. Reynolds, Jr, 1833.
Given by Macaulay to his sister Margaret and
now in the possession of
Mrs Lancelot Errington
(photo: Thomas Errington)

THE LETTERS OF
THOMAS BABINGTON
MACAULAY

EDITED BY

THOMAS PINNEY
PROFESSOR OF ENGLISH
POMONA COLLEGE, THE CLAREMONT COLLEGES
CLAREMONT, CALIFORNIA

VOLUME I
1807–FEBRUARY 1831

DULCE·PERICULUM

CAMBRIDGE UNIVERSITY PRESS
1974

Published by the Syndics of the Cambridge University Press
Bentley House, 200 Euston Road, London NW1 2DB
American Branch: 32 East 57th Street, New York, N.Y.10022

© Cambridge University Press 1974

Library of Congress Catalogue Card Number: 73–75860

ISBN: 0 521 20201 9

First published 1974

Printed in Great Britain
at the University Printing House, Cambridge
(Brooke Crutchley, University Printer)

The title-page device is
the Macaulay coat of arms, taken from Macaulay's seal
on a letter of 17 December 1833;
it was later the basis of Macaulay's arms as Baron Macaulay.
Acknowledgement is made to the Master and Fellows of
Trinity College, Cambridge.

CONTENTS

INTRODUCTION

I

Macaulay's letters have the same virtues as his other writings: their language is clear and energetic; their perceptions distinct and confident. They abound in passages of rapid and vivid description. Like all that he wrote, they have a strong rhetorical cast, arguing, instructing, persuading. And they show, without ostentation but naturally and habitually, the rich store of wide-ranging learning that Macaulay's quick impressibility and firm memory kept ready for his use, to be poured out at need. The letters are thus excellent reading. They are also limited in the same way that Macaulay's public writings are, having the overemphatic opinions, the liking for violent contrast, and the sometimes mechanical or superficial effects of their assertive manner. Critics do not exactly agree as to what the general defect is, but it is not misleading to say that Macaulay has no meditative, speculative tendency whatever, so that the pleasures of a shifting point of view, of the sudden opening out of an unexpected perspective, with the consequent effect of ironic self-doubt or of touching the region of the mysterious and hidden, are nowhere to be found in his writing. The absence of any directly personal element is also a notable feature of the essays and the *History*; as G. O. Trevelyan put it, 'the most ardent admirers of Macaulay will admit that a minute study of his literary productions left them, as far as any but an intellectual knowledge of the writer himself was concerned, very much as it found them.' But it is far otherwise with the letters. They are not carefully studied compositions like those of the great eighteenth-century letter writers, but are spontaneous letters written to family or friends, or practical messages written to answer a question or to state an opinion. They thus reveal Macaulay, so far as one can judge long after the writer is dead, directly and honestly.

The full publication of Macaulay's letters will not materially alter the impression created by the *Life and Letters of Lord Macaulay* published in 1876 by Macaulay's nephew, George Otto Trevelyan. But the letters deepen and confirm our understanding of Macaulay and will, I hope, persuade their readers of the truth of Carlyle's judgment: 'A man of thorough honesty, withal, and of sound human sense in regard to all practical matters, and of a most affectionate, tender and equitable nature.' Carlyle was writing of his response to Trevelyan's *Life*, and, correctly, concludes that the person there presented exhibits 'a placid and complete satisfaction with his lot.' On this point, the letters will make a difference, for they show that Macaulay's emotional dependence upon his two youngest sisters was more extravagant – at least in some of the forms of its expression – than, naturally enough, Trevelyan was prepared to demonstrate in 1876. In other relations, too, the letters make clear that Macaulay's life was hardly one of placid self-satisfaction. It is tempting, and would be easy, to draw a portrait of Macaulay from the materials provided by the letters which would present an exact antithesis to Trevelyan's – dark not bright, moody not placid, susceptible not self-sufficient, violently unstable, not equable. Such a picture would embody all the distortions of over-correction, but it would also have its truth. For Macaulay was a sensitive man, and therefore vulnerable. It is not his habit to dwell on suffering or to speculate on the mystery of life; but a sympathetic reader will not miss the evidence in the letters of a sensibility that could not live in the world with undisturbed satisfaction.

Besides their record of the personality of a great Victorian, striking and complicated though that is, the letters have much else in them to interest anyone who cares to know something about the life of England in the first half of the nineteenth century. Macaulay may or may not have been the pre-eminent Victorian, as S. C. Roberts has called him, but he certainly touched Victorian life at an extraordinary number of points. His experiences among the Evangelicals of Clapham, his careers at Cambridge, on circuit, as contributor to the *Edinburgh Review*, in the agitation for the Reform Bill, as a candidate at Leeds and Edinburgh, in the administration of India, in high Whig society, and as the most honored of English writers in his time, are all set down vividly in the letters. The information that they incidentally provide about domestic, political, and literary life in the first fifty years of the century is a large and interesting contribution to the social history of England.

In G. O. Trevelyan's judgment, not much of Macaulay's real personality is evident in his letters up to 1830. To that point, most of his correspondence is with his parents and elders, and

may be characterised as belonging to the type of duty letters, treating of politics, legal gossip, personal adventures, and domestic incidents, with some reticence and little warmth or ease of expression. The periodical insertion on the son's part of anecdotes and observations bearing upon the question of Slavery reminds the reader of those presents of tall recruits with which at judiciously chosen intervals Frederic the Great used to conciliate his terrible father (*Life*, 1, 35).

This is an amusing and not unfair description, as any quick comparison of the letters before 1830 and those of the early 1830s written to Hannah and

Margaret Macaulay will readily show. But the earlier letters do have their
own positive interest. Even when he wrote guardedly, Macaulay never
wrote dully, for he always has something to say. And as Trevelyan himself
observes at an earlier point in the *Life*, 'Macaulay was by nature so in-
capable of affectation or concealment that he could not write otherwise
than as he felt...so that we may read in his letters, as in a clear mirror, his
opinions and inclinations, his hopes and affections, at every succeeding
period of his existence' (1, 4).

The earliest letters, most of them written from school, show Macaulay's
almost unmatched appetite for reading already established, and are full of
references to his progress through the classics, continental literature, history, and English poetry. His own literary ambition, though he never talks
about it, can be felt even in his dutiful production of translations and imi-
tations as schoolboy tasks. He had the itch to write in the strongest degree
and from the earliest age. Occasionally, we are made to feel something of
his own excitement in imaginative discovery, as in the extensive passage he
translates from Sismondi on the decline of nations in the letter of 14 May
1816: the long vista of time and the melodramatic contrast of past and
present were just what he liked most, and though they are presented in his
published writings mostly to enforce the idea of progress, we must not
forget that the other direction of the cycle was included in the vision. The
delight in teaching, which made him such an admirable elder brother and
to which he added such a brilliant power of exposition, also appears clearly
in the early letters and is part of their attractiveness. What he learned he
wished at once to impart, an impulse that has much to do with the success
of the essays he wrote later. We also see in these schoolboy letters how
natural it was for Macaulay to take an interest in great public affairs: topics
such as the changes of ministries, the abolition of slavery, or the Christian-
izing of India are as familiar in them as the examinations at Preston's
school or the prospects of the summer holidays.

'Lord Macaulay,' as Matthew Arnold dryly observed, 'had, as we
know, his own heightened and telling way of putting things, and we must
always make allowance for it.' The letters show how quickly that 'heightened and telling way' was formed and how habitual it was to Macaulay
even when he had no thought of a public audience in mind. A trivial but
revealing instance is his telling, in a letter of 24 October 1817, an anecdote
of the savages of the Pelew Islands, who, on first seeing European tools,
'gazed upon the kettle and tongs...with astonishment; and almost worshipped the bellows': here Macaulay cannot resist adding, what is not said
in his source, that the sacred bellows 'had a broken spout and a cracked
side.' 'Heightened and telling,' indeed: one wonders at times whether
Macaulay himself knew what his favorite form of statement did to the

truth. When he writes of Lady Holland, for example, that she is 'sceptical and superstitious, afraid of ghosts and not of God, – would not for the world begin a journey on a Friday morning, and thought nothing of running away from her husband' (10 June 1833), we are pleased by the art of such rapid, pointed paradox but may be perplexed to know just where the artist stands. The instance is a broad one, but it points towards what is, after all, the central critical question in Macaulay's serious work, whether, as someone has said, it be possible to tell the truth in such a style. Whatever may be concluded, the letters prove, if proof were needed, that the style was the boy as well as the man.

If rhetorical heightening has its dangers, it also provided the means through which Macaulay could express some of the strongest elements in his imagination and personality: the love of classical tradition, the patriotic enthusiasm for his own country's achievements, the histrionic imagining of his own role in public affairs, were genuine forces in him, and one may see them united in the rhetoric of, for example, the verses on Albion (28 November 1817), conventional school exercise though it is. As G. M. Young has observed in writing of Macaulay,

The patriotism of early Victorian England was at heart a pride in human capacity, which time had led to fruition in England; and in the great humanist, who brought all history to glorify the age of which he was the most honoured child, it heard its own voice speaking....*Il a son orgueil d'homme.* Taine's fine saying of Macaulay is true of his whole age.[1]

The letters from Cambridge record Macaulay's growing sense of independence from the standards of Clapham, an independence that Macaulay had somehow to assert while yet retaining a willing deference to the prejudices of his parents. The task could not have been easy; there were repeated crises over politics, literature, and personal values, yet Macaulay always managed to avert a break. At the same time we see that the parents come more and more to consult their son for his advice; though the relation was not easy, especially between father and son, it was kept intact by mutual respect.

It may be that having to justify himself so often and emphatically as he did helped develop in Macaulay one of his notable powers as a writer, the ability to state a case. Whether it be a question of academic instruction (May? 1828), of the value of literature (5 February 1819), of the style appropriate to periodical writing (25 January 1830), or of the wisdom of interrupting a public career in order to accept appointment in India (to Lansdowne: 5 December 1833), he is a master of putting, *currente calamo*, the considerations that determine a course of action, and this in the clearest, most forceful, and persuasive manner.

Victorian England: Portrait of an Age, N.Y., 1954, p. 21.

This readiness takes another form in the letters that touch on historical, literary, or biographical topics. When he pleases, Macaulay can dilate almost at will on a given topic – even in a mere catalogue, such as the list of English actors in 28 September 1833, we get a glimpse of the remarkable power of development that made him both so formidable and fascinating as a talker. As Trevelyan says of some of the letters to Macvey Napier, editor of the *Edinburgh Review*, they have a 'picturesque amplitude of literary detail' that makes them 'as readable as so many passages from Saint Beuve' (II, 353).

The most attractive of Macaulay's letters are certainly those that he wrote to his two youngest sisters, Hannah and Margaret, beginning in 1830 and swelling to a flood in the years from 1831 through 1833. In these he is without any constraint, free to range through all subjects and all tones. In them, he gives rein to his native playfulness, punning, making bad jokes, talking folly, and pouring out abundant doggerel by the 'Judicious Poet.' He displays his keen mimic ability, particularly in mocking the language of Quakers and of other sects that Macaulay regarded with a wholly Augustan contempt for singularity. He reports on the life that he leads in the great world from a peculiarly fascinating domestic point of view – what people wear, how rooms are furnished, what is served at table, what commonplace things that Lords and Ladies say. All this is of course adapted to his audience, two young girls living quietly in a modest Evangelical home; but it also says something of Macaulay's own sense of himself as a sort of traveller into the great world who is always aware of himself as a stranger, at home only in a different style of manners.

The letters to Hannah and Margaret will be most striking and curious for their amorous language and their evidence of Macaulay's almost complete dependence for emotional satisfaction upon his relation to these two girls. At times, these letters seem strongly self-pitying, almost maudlin, as though Macaulay were indulging in them every obscure and unacknowledged impulse he had ever felt. At other times sentimental indulgence is set off in sharp contrast against perfectly judicious self-awareness or almost jaunty matter-of-factness. The effect is not ironic but contradictory, or so I conclude. Even allowing for the very different conventions governing the language between brothers and sisters then, and for the evident tendency of the Macaulay children to present themselves in very dramatic language, these letters are perplexing. It is very difficult to venture a confident opinion about them; all the more so since it seems doubtful that, on the evidence of the letters alone, the case can be adequately diagnosed. Macaulay himself, so far as I can judge, never betrays the least consciousness that his relation to his sisters was latently incestuous; to suppose that it was ever overtly so, I think absurd. There was, unquestionably, a need in Macaulay to have someone whom he could exalt without reservation. In his younger years it was his two sisters whom he converted, in his imagination, into paragons of womanly virtue. In later years he discovered an equivalent in the person of his niece, Margaret Trevelyan, for whom he could not find praise high enough and for whom he could not perform favors enough to satisfy his wish to please her. 'I respect her more than any other human being,' he wrote in his Journal for 12 June 1851; 'more, I am sure, than I ever respected my father. She is goodness, truth, noble-ness personified' (IV, 135–6). I think it very likely, at least, that Macaulay's imaginative transformation of his niece sheds a retrospective light on his relationship to Hannah and Margaret in the 1830s. Both the sisters in his youth and the niece in his middle age provided objects upon whom he could concentrate all his power of affection and idealization, without any of the risks of marriage.

The letters that Macaulay wrote in unrestrained freedom to his sisters belong to the time when he had achieved some standing as a public man and had entered the best literary and political Whig society. The different voices that these different relations required from him make an amusing counterpoint in the letters of the early 1830s: the high pretension in the public voice of the statesman (e.g., 2 August 1832) is answered by the easy cynicism of his letter to Napier, summarizing his campaign at Calne as 'speaking, eating, drinking, hallooing, and so forth' (19 June 1832). Meantime, in speaking as a brother to his admiring sisters, he betrays a genuinely excited sense of being caught up in high public destiny and an equally genuine longing for the private satisfactions of domestic life. Hard, stern, ambitious, unsparing in public life; anxiously tender, strongly filial, emotionally susceptible in private life, Macaulay may seem in these letters very nearly one of his own antithetical characterizations. Whatever else, they have that mixture of various tones that Macaulay himself felt was the chief element in the popularity of his essays. But they have, too, the unity imparted by a strong individuality.

II   PREVIOUS PUBLICATIONS OF THE LETTERS

The first significant publication of Macaulay's letters is George Otto Trevelyan's *Life and Letters of Lord Macaulay*, 2 vols., 1876, a delightful work, one of the very few really first-rate nineteenth-century literary bio-graphies; it has been deservedly popular since its publication, and, after having passed through some revision and many editions during the long life of its author, remains in print today. Trevelyan, the son of Macaulay's beloved sister Hannah, had access to all of Macaulay's family letters and to a good many of those written to Macaulay's friends and political acquaintance. From the considerable body available to him he selected all or part of about five hundred for the *Life*. They appear there treated according to the usual biographical practice of the time. One or two may be printed pretty much as Macaulay wrote them; the rest have been adapted and altered in a variety of ways, some of them familiar enough from other Victorian Lives and Letters but some of them less so. Trevelyan of course suppressed names, freely altered spelling and punctuation, and made large omissions of matter irrelevant to his narrative or too personal or circumstantial for general interest. In order to achieve a uniformly interesting text Trevelyan made other sorts of changes besides those just mentioned: he added sentences of his own, changed Macaulay's language, and, most striking of all, conflated extracts from two, three, or sometimes four different letters under a single date. The letter that Trevelyan prints on pp. 346–8 of his first volume will do as a notable but by no means extreme example of his editorial practice. It is dated 5 December 1833, and, though there *is* a Macaulay letter of that date, Trevelyan's text contains nothing from it. The first paragraph is from a letter of 6 December. The first sentence of the next paragraph is from 22 November; the rest of the paragraph is from 31 October. In the last sentence 'is' is altered to 'may be.' The first sentence of the third paragraph is supplied by Trevelyan, whose changes have made an explanatory, transitional sentence necessary. The rest of the letter is from 26 November, with many substantial omissions and some minor alterations. The 'letter' is thus a blend of four different letters and the date from a fifth, the whole slightly but steadily modified by the smoothing hand of the editor. There is no question that, in point of evenness and sustained interest, Trevelyan's synthetic texts are an improvement over Macaulay's originals, being all wine and no lees. But it is presumably not necessary to argue that the original texts are what is wanted in a scholarly edition such as this. Fortunately, not many letters – a total of twenty-one – in this edition have had to be printed from the texts in Trevelyan: most of those are to his publisher, Longman, the MSS of which were destroyed in the German bombing of London.

After Trevelyan, the only considerable printing of Macaulay's letters is in the *Selection from the Correspondence of Macvey Napier*, 1879, edited by Macvey Napier the younger. This volume, which is not a very common one, prints all or part of some 128 letters from Macaulay to the elder Napier, editor of the *Edinburgh Review*, between 1829 and 1846. The letters are of great interest for their record of Macaulay's connection with the *Review* in those years. The editorial procedure is much more direct than in Trevelyan, letters appearing with omissions and slight changes in punctuation but otherwise unaltered. The originals from which the editor worked are now all in the British Museum among the Napier papers.

In the more than a century since Macaulay's death many single letters or small groups of his letters have been printed in newspapers, magazines, and books. Not many years go by without some new one making its appearance, and the total thus produced in this scattered way is by now quite large. It has been possible, though, to trace a MS for the larger part of these printed letters, so that this edition does not heavily depend on the vagaries of many varying editorial practices. Inevitably, though, many letters remain that are known only in a printed version.

III   SOURCES AND SCOPE OF THIS EDITION

The correspondence of an eminent Victorian is like a great monument from which, over a period of years, the public has been chipping away fragments, to carry off to their scattered homes as trophies of greatness. The process continues until changing fashion or declining interest turns the public attention elsewhere, and the monument, now much diminished and mutilated, is left in peace, a large part of it reduced to chips and splinters either obscurely displayed in souvenir collections or carelessly thrown away. So with Macaulay's letters. The analogy is not exact, since Macaulay's correspondence was never intact in one place; but the comparison will suggest the way in which letters are dispersed in time. As Dr A. N. L. Munby has shown in his authoritative study, the cult of the autograph letter is among the many inventions of the nineteenth century. Macaulay, as a great man flourishing in the middle of that century, inevitably attracted the interest of his contemporaries in his letters as objects to be preserved; the process of collecting them in small groups or simply of adding one to a general collection began even in his lifetime, and was greatly intensified in the two generations after his death. The twofold consequence is first, that much has been saved, and second, that single letters or small groups of letters are to be found everywhere and in every sort of place, likely or unlikely. There is nothing remarkable in this, but an editor may be allowed to make the point as an explanation in advance of the certainty that letters unknown to him are going to turn up.

By far the largest collection of letters is that at Macaulay's own Trinity College, Cambridge, a collection that began with the gift of the letters to Thomas Flower Ellis, Macaulay's closest friend, and was then multiplied several times over by the rich gifts of Macaulay's great-nephew, G. M. Trevelyan, Master of Trinity. The letters in Trevelyan's possession were family letters, including almost all of those used by G. O. Trevelyan for the *Life*; with the Ellis letters, then, Trinity has the great bulk of the most personal part of Macaulay's surviving letters. Also in the Trevelyan gift were the eleven volumes of Macaulay's MS Journal, mostly written in the last decade of his life. I have been allowed to make use of this incomparable source of detailed biographical information through the courtesy of Trinity and especially of Dr R. Robson, who has undertaken the heroic labor of preparing the Journal for publication. The Trinity collection, already of unchallenged pre-eminence, continues to grow: it has been quite recently augmented by the acquisition of the Macaulay letters among the papers of R. M. Milnes, Lord Houghton, and of the splendid personal collection formed by Dr A. N. L. Munby. I am grateful to the Master and Fellows of Trinity for permission to publish the materials in their care, a permission which is the enabling condition of this work.

The letters to Macvey Napier, two hundred in number, now in the British Museum, have already been mentioned; the Museum, as one would expect, has other, smaller but interesting groups of letters to Lord and Lady Holland, to Gladstone, to Leigh Hunt, to Hobhouse, and a few other of Macaulay's acquaintance and associates. Apart from the Museum, most of the great institutional libraries of England and America have collections of varying sizes, some of them quite valuable but none challenging those at Trinity and the British Museum. A most substantial, interesting, and useful collection, not of Macaulay's letters (though it includes some good ones) but of Macaulay family papers is now in the Huntington Library. It contains many letters, extending over nearly a century, to and from Macaulay's parents, sisters, brothers, and from a number of the family's relatives and close friends. I have found it of essential service in documenting especially Macaulay's earlier and hence less public years.

Though most of the family letters are now in libraries, many interesting letters remain in the possession of living members of the Macaulay family, notably Mrs Lancelot Errington and Mrs Humphry Trevelyan. The valuable letters to Charles Macaulay and other family papers until recently in the hands of Mrs Margaret Booth Ritchie are now, through her gift, in the library of the University of London, whose first student was Macaulay's brother Charles.

What is the size of the body of material still extant in libraries and in private hands? This edition, at the time that the introduction is being written, is expected to contain about 2,500 letters. The number is large, but not particularly impressive if measured against the 9,500 letters of the Carlyles, the 12,000 or more of Dickens, or the nearly uncountable number of Ruskin's letters, to name a few among the more notable epistolary *Nachlässe* bequeathed by Macaulay's fellow Victorians. There is no reliable way of estimating how large a proportion of the letters that Macaulay wrote is represented by the 2,500 of this edition, but it is naturally only a fragment of the whole. From the evidence of the journal that he kept in the last decade of his life and from references in extant letters I have compiled a list of well over a thousand letters known to have been written but as yet untraced. This edition excludes, except for a very few selected items, the many hundreds of official letters sent out over Macaulay's name from the various offices – Secretary to the Board of Control, Member of the Supreme Council of India, Secretary at War, Paymaster General – that he held between 1832 and 1848. We also know that some parts of Macaulay's correspondence have been destroyed. The letters to Longman have already been mentioned. Perhaps most to be regretted are the letters that Macaulay wrote to Francis Jeffrey, a correspondence that certainly began as early as 1824 and continued until Jeffrey's death in 1850. This would uniquely document Macaulay's early connection with the *Edinburgh Review* and reveal the special quality of Macaulay's relation to a man whom he admired beyond all others among contemporary literary men. On Jeffrey's death, his papers went to his son-in-law William Empson, and on Empson's death the heirs returned to their writers the letters saved by both Jeffrey and Empson. Macaulay does not state that he destroyed the letters thus returned to him, but the chance that he did is a strong probability, amounting almost to a certainty. All that we have left is the tantalizing entry in Macaulay's Journal for 4 February 1854 that he spent the day reading his old letters, 'some so far back as 1825. I could do nothing but read them till I had finished them all. They interested me very deeply, sometimes painfully.'. The loss of the letters to Empson is almost as much to be regretted as the loss of those to Jeffrey. Empson was a genuine and open admirer of Macaulay, who, for his part, appreciated the friendship and seems in return to have written unreservedly to Empson. Nothing of all this remains except for a few brief and impersonal notes that, presumably, Empson was willing to give to collectors and that thus escaped the general fate. The letters to Empson in the 1820s, when Macaulay was living in ambitious obscurity, might have given an unmatched view of his hopes, fears, and plans at a period in his life about which we now know relatively little. No doubt letters to other correspondents have been destroyed – those to Sydney Smith and Sir Henry Holland, for example, probably were – but without making quite so lamentable a gap as the Jeffrey/Empson letters. Macaulay himself was a determined letter-destroyer. When Gladstone, in 1839, wrote to thank him for his review of Gladstone's book, Macaulay kept the letter, 'a compliment,' says G. O. Trevelyan in the *Life*, 'which, except in this single instance, he never paid to any of his correspondents' (II, 53). This is not strictly true: a few other letters to Macaulay, especially letters from his family in his earlier years, survive. But it is true enough for practical purposes. In a letter to Lord Rosebery, written forty-five years after the publication of the *Life*, Trevelyan repeated that 'Macaulay left *no* letters addressed to himself at any period of his life. It was his habit to keep in the breast pocket of his coat the *last* letter he received from some two or three people; and then, when another came, he destroyed the former one' (2 October 1921: MS, Dr A. N. L. Munby). The consequence is that there is no question of printing both sides of Macaulay's correspondence in this edition, for, except in rare instances, only one side exists. Despite the losses occasioned by time, accident, and design, a considerable and various body of letters still remains. Though I hope that there will be a few readers who will wish the work longer, I suspect that with most the opposite will be true. Apart from the exclusion, already mentioned, of most of Macaulay's official correspondence, I have printed all of the letters known to and available to me. I do so knowing that the principle inevitably means that some chaff will be included, but believing that the proportion of interesting substance in Macaulay's letters is very high and that completeness, where possible, should be sought in scholarly work of this kind.

IV MACAULAY AND HIS CORRESPONDENTS

Though he was born in the Midlands and though his first home was in the heart of the City of London, the true symbol of Macaulay's early years is Clapham. In the early part of the last century Clapham was still a village, but a village distinguished as the residence of a notable band of religious philanthropists and reformers, the so-called Clapham Sect. The distinguishing mark of this group was its combination of worldly success, Evangelical zeal, and activity in the reform of manners and morals; the Claphamites, as Christian men of affairs, were out to make a difference in things, and to an impressive degree they succeeded. The origin and center of the group at Clapham was William Wilberforce, the voice of Evangelical concern in Parliament for many years, the public leader of the abolition movement, and the apostle of Christian earnestness among the wealthy and powerful. With him at Clapham, or associated with him in Parliament or in the myriad religious societies generated by Evangelical energy, were the families of Thornton, Venn, Grant, Stephen, Shore, and Macaulay. The connection branched out to the West to include, at Bristol, its best-known literary figure, Hannah More, and to Cambridge, where several of the dominant personalities of the University – Simeon, Milner, and Scholefield especially – gave Clapham an immediate influence upon the young men of the families who counted. As Macaulay wrote to a sister on the appearance of Sir James Stephen's *Edinburgh Review* article of 1844 on the Clapham Sect, the group was worthy of the attention of history:

The truth is that from that little knot of men emanated all the Bible Societies and almost all the Missionary Societies in the world, the Prayer Book and Homily

Society, the African Institution, and the Antislavery Society. The whole organization of the Evangelical party was their work. The share which they had in providing means for the education of the people was great. They were really the destroyers of the Slave trade and of Slavery. Many of those whom Stephen describes were public men of the greatest weight. Lord Teignmouth governed India at Calcutta. Grant governed India in Leadenhall Street. Stephen's father was Percival's right hand man in the House of Commons. . . . It is needless to speak of Wilberforce. As to Simeon, if you knew what his authority and influence were, and how they extended from Cambridge to the most remote corners of England, you would allow that his real sway in the Church was far greater than that of any primate (10 July 1844).

The very special atmosphere of the Clapham in which Macaulay grew up is an influence whose importance in his life it would be difficult to over-emphasize. To set forth the full account of that influence would need a separate essay, but among its enduring effects were Macaulay's sense of his own fitness to play an important part in public affairs of great moment, his habit of emphatic moral judgment on writers and statesmen and a tendency towards something like self-righteousness, his sense of his party loyalty to the Whigs as of a loyalty to a Cause, his belief in the possibility of progress and reform, and his dislike for the merely frivolous or whimsical. Much of the man, especially of the public man, is in these things. Macaulay did not inherit the religious intensity of his father, but one can see again and again how Clapham, subdued and secularized, persists in his habits of thought and feeling.

It was the aim of Macaulay's parents to see that the Clapham influence was maintained and reinforced by all possible means. When, in 1813, he was sent away to school, his parents' fears of the immorality and worldliness of the public schools made it certain that he would be kept from them, though Westminster seems to have been briefly considered at one time. He was sent instead to the rigidly Evangelical Matthew Preston, who later married a wife out of Clapham, and the influence of the Evangelicals at Cambridge made it a foregone conclusion that, despite his distaste for the mathematics that were the specialty of the place, Macaulay would be sent there on leaving Preston's school.

But at Cambridge, though he lived with another young son of Clapham, Henry Thornton, was committed to the care of an Evangelical tutor, was watched over by such Evangelical powers as Milner, Farish, and Scholefield, and heard the word from the mouth of Simeon, Macaulay was free to follow his own bent. The delightfulness of his new situation – license to read without restraint and the company of bright, ambitious young men ready for argument in literature and politics – made an ineffaceable impression on him. He developed a strong romantic attachment to Trinity, and though he left the college for the great world his idea of a life to his taste was always modelled after the style that he had known there; the bachelor surrounded by his books in the sheltered quiet of the Albany was, as Macaulay said of himself, enjoying 'college life at the West end of London.'

As a more than ordinarily remarkable prodigy of youthful learning and fluency, Macaulay must have seemed to his parents a chosen being, perhaps a young Samuel. It is certain that both of his parents dreamed that their son might enter the church, but there is no evidence that they exerted any special pressure upon him towards a specific vocation. And, despite his dutifulness and his positive wish to please his parents, Macaulay seems never, after his earliest years, to have given any serious thought to the ministry or to have undergone even anything like a crisis of religious feeling. Instead, partly no doubt out of unacknowledged rebellion against his parents' religion, but even more, I think, from mere insensibility to the religious passion, Macaulay, on leaving the University, found himself headed directly towards worldly objects. A ready and confident writer, he aspired to literary fame; a voluble and exciting orator, he aspired to political fame. He would have to achieve both on his own, for his father, once prosperous, had fallen on hard times, and the son, who had always expected to be provided for as a gentleman's son, had now to provide for himself. In these circumstances, the bar was practically the only professional choice open to Macaulay, and he accordingly ate his dinners, received his call to the bar, joined the Northern Circuit, attended the Court of King's Bench, and kept chambers in Gray's Inn. His formal identity as a barrister does not appear to have affected Macaulay's own idea of himself, however; he neither got nor seemed to wish to have much business, and, whatever forms his ambition may have taken, the desire to be a Q.C. or a judge was not among them. His real life in these years was in his writing, first for *Knight's Quarterly* and then for the *Edinburgh Review*, in his friendships with old Cambridge companions such as Charles Austin and Winthrop Praed, or with new friends like William Empson, in the activities of John Stuart Mill's London Debating Society, in assisting in such enterprises as the anti-slavery agitation or launching the London University, and, always, in the circle of his immediate family.

The record of these years is relatively meager, especially the record of the intellectual and literary influences at work on Macaulay. Bentham and Scott were clearly among them, however. Political economy was what every bright young man of the time who hoped to make a mark went in for, and the current of Benthamite ideas was the headiest element in that mixture. Macaulay's relation to Utilitarianism was ambiguous, for his attraction to the prospect of reasonable and progressive reform was countered by his dislike of the doctrinaire systematizing among the brasher Utilitarians. Macaulay's zeal for reform is always modified by romantic conservatism, the tradition that runs from Burke through Scott. Besides that, both his sense of political practicality and his Augustan distaste for extremes made him sceptical of theoretical programs. Scott, all of whose novels Macaulay must have read as they appeared, revealed what may be called the democracy of history, the perception that great national movements rest on the broadest basis of popular life and that the details of that life are legitimate material for history. Already, in 1828, Macaulay was writing down his notions on this subject in his *Edinburgh Review* article on 'History' and planning a history of the Stuarts that would, as his friend Ellis reported, 'introduce, . . . with perfect security as to truth, characteristic anecdotes and speeches – giving for instance King James's broad Scotch verbatim' (see Appendix, [August? 1828]).

The years of preparation were fulfilled, with what in retrospect seems perfect timing, in 1830, when, on the eve of the great struggle for political reform in England, Macaulay was suddenly introduced into Parliament through the Whig magnate Lord Lansdowne's gift of the seat for the pocket borough of Calne. The debates on the Reform Bill in the next year instantly made Macaulay's reputation as a leading parliamentary orator, and his public and literary life from this point on is an almost unbroken series of success upon success. The ministry clearly did not know, at first, quite how to reward their brilliant young man – a 'parvenu' as he called himself – but at length found a minor place for him on the Board of Control. Shortly after, Macaulay was elected for the newly enfranchised Borough of Leeds, a fitting distinction for one who had so eagerly vindicated the political rights of the middle classes. Then came the appointment, at £10,000 per annum, to the Supreme Council of India.

The Indian years are the watershed years in Macaulay's life. If they did not quite put an end to his political ambition, they greatly reduced it. By making him financially independent they made it possible for him to devote himself to his work on the *History of England*, so that he had a genuine alternative to put in the place of his political life. The death of his sister Margaret while he was in India, and conscious of distance, separation, mortality, as never before, worked a profound emotional change in him: henceforth, his spirits are lower, his sense of possibility diminished, his dependence on books and on domestic relations in place of an active public life stronger and more frankly acknowledged. A full half of Trevelyan's *Life* is devoted to the twenty years that remained to Macaulay after his return from India, and that is no doubt a just proportion to allot to the external history. These were the years of his greatest accomplishment – the years in which he represented Edinburgh in the House of Commons and achieved cabinet office in his political life, and the years devoted to the writing and the triumphant publication of the *History* in his literary life. But they do not see much internal change; the *set* of the man is fully determined, and, except for the changes that inevitably accompany advancing years, there is little to say of spiritual and intellectual development in Macaulay after his return from India. This is far from saying that the interest of the letters ceases with the end of change in their writer, however; there is plenty of interest still in the variety of Macaulay's public and private relations and in the alert and positive mind displayed in the letters that are now, for the first time, presented at length.

The Babington family

When Macaulay accepted Palmerston's offer of a peerage in 1857 he wrote in his journal, 'It was necessary for me to choose a title off-hand. I determined to be Baron Macaulay of Rothley. I was born there; I have lived much there; I am named from the family which long had the manor; my uncle was Rector there' (Trevelyan, *Life*, II, 425). Rothley Temple, near Leicester, was the estate of *Thomas Babington* (1758–1837), an Evangelical country gentleman and M.P., whose connection with the Macaulay family began through his friendship with Aulay Macaulay, Zachary Macaulay's older brother. This in time led to Babington's marriage to Aulay's sister, Jean, in 1787, and, not long after, to Babington's decisive influence on Zachary Macaulay upon his return to England from Jamaica. In 1796 Babington presented Aulay Macaulay to the living of Rothley, so that the Macaulays were in both the manor and the manse of Rothley. The place continued to be a rallying-ground for the Macaulays through many years. But Babington died deeply in debt, partly through his investment in the affairs of Zachary Macaulay, and the place was bought by his son-in-law James Parker in 1845. Thomas Babington Macaulay, for all the intimacy of his connection with his birth place, does not seem to have had anything to do with Rothley after his return from India.

Thomas Babington, though he was one of Wilberforce's principal supporters in the abolition movement (there is a highly inaccurate monument to the formation of the campaign still standing in the grounds of the house), was not especially remarkable for his public achievements; he impressed people rather by what he was. In the epitaph that Thomas Babington Macaulay wrote for his uncle in 1851, now inscribed in the chapel at Rothley, the key terms are 'incorruptible probity,' 'winning courtesy,' 'childlike innocence,' and 'angelic temper' (see 24 September 1851).

His wife, Jean, was a complementary type, 'a clever, impulsive Macaulay,' according to the recollections of her granddaughter Eliza Conybeare.

The same granddaughter remembered that Mrs Babington ran her large household by sitting in her room, and, when some thought for action struck her, ringing a bell violently, startling uninitiated guests and sending servants flying.

Thomas Babington and his wife had ten children, who, with the nine Macaulay children, not to mention uncounted other relations, made a sufficiently large cousinhood. The eldest son, *Thomas Gisborne Babington* (1788–1871), had an unhappy importance for the Macaulays. Zachary Macaulay took him into partnership, creating the firm of Macaulay and Babington, around 1810. When Macaulay determined in 1823 to devote most of his time to the anti-slavery movement, he turned over the direction of the business to his nephew, who proceeded very swiftly to ruin it through the combination of ambitiousness and incompetence.

The only Babington cousin for whom Thomas Babington Macaulay seems to have felt not merely affection but something like admiration was *George* (1794–1856), a surgeon in London. George became one of Thomas Babington Macaulay's dearest friends in the years between his leaving the University and his departure for India, so dear that he could say of him that 'I love him like a brother – much more indeed than I ever loved any of my own brothers' (16 February 1834). Unluckily, George, who was no good at money matters, was one of Macaulay's agents in London while Macaulay was in India. His inadequacy in this position was so complete as, effectively, to destroy all further relations between the two men.

Thomas Flower Ellis

Ellis (1796–1861) was Macaulay's closest friend, indeed, his only close friend. The relation is Ellis's one claim to fame: though he is included in the *Dictionary of National Biography*, the brief, indistinct, and inaccurate entry there for him was evidently taken mostly from Trevelyan's *Life* and presents him mostly in his aspect as Macaulay's friend. From what little fresh evidence that I can find, Ellis appears as a man of quick intelligence, with a deep and strong interest in literature and scholarship. Macaulay and Ellis had some important things in common, not least the fact that both were graduates and Fellows of Trinity; they shared an abiding pleasure in the classics, and both had strong domestic feelings, so that their personal and intellectual tastes were very like. Besides distinguishing himself in classical study at Cambridge, Ellis had also studied, at various times, Italian, German, Spanish, and Hebrew. His daughter wrote of him that even after his professional work kept him constantly busy he continued to find time for study: 'But in truth study was his great relaxation; in the evening, as soon as his correcting the sheets of reports for the press was done, he would throw himself on the sofa with a Greek book, as another man might refresh himself with the newspaper' (Louisa or Marian Ellis, MS Memoir of T. F. Ellis: Trinity).

Ellis obviously lacked Macaulay's flamboyance; but, while he appreciated his friend's genius, he was no uncritical admirer. A letter from Ellis to Napier on Macaulay's essay on Bacon gives us a pretty clear notion of how the two men must have responded to each other, dissenting as well as assenting, but always with affection:

I have read over Macaulay's wonderful article on Bacon repeatedly and with increasing admiration. To say that I differ from him in numerous points is saying only what everyone must say, who thinks for himself, on an essay containing so great a variety of opinions so strongly urged. . . . It seems to me that Macaulay cannot quite rid himself of the effects of an early rhetorical education. If he contrasts two systems, he compares the strongest point of one with the weakest of the other: e.g., shoemaking, which is both necessary and perfectly done, with Seneca's chapter on Anger, which has been a by word ever since Fielding. I might as well say in answer, that I would not give Hamlet or the Phaedo for the sake of reviving the art of making cream tarts with pepper, which (as appears by the Persian tales) has perished from the circle of physical appliances. I long to see him. He sails in January. I had a letter about six weeks back' (2 November 1837: MS, British Museum).

Macaulay and Ellis must at least have been acquainted at Trinity, but their friendship begins in 1826, when Macaulay joined the Northern Circuit, of which Ellis was already a member. From that time, for as long as Macaulay remained on circuit, they travelled together when they could. In London they saw each other regularly and often. Ellis, four years older than Macaulay, had married immediately after leaving the University, very early for a professional man. He and his wife had seven children, in whom Macaulay, especially after the death of Mrs Ellis in 1839, came to take much interest. Ellis enjoyed substantial but not remarkable professional success, holding appointments to various special commissions and being made Recorder of Leeds and Attorney-General to the Duchy of Lancaster. He collaborated on the editing of three major series of law reports, 1835–61. For many years Ellis was very active in the work of the Society for the Diffusion of Useful Knowledge, for which he wrote a few things as well as performing much editorial work. He also wrote occasionally for the *Edinburgh Review*.

Macaulay's death, Ellis wrote to Sir Charles Trevelyan, was 'the end of a friendship of more than thirty years, more affectionate and confidential than that of brothers, uninterrupted, to the best of my recollection and belief, by a single unkind word or thought' (20 February 1860: MS, Trinity).

The Macaulay family

Zachary Macaulay (1768–1838): Macaulay's father was the son of a Scottish minister at Inveraray. At the age of sixteen he had been sent to Jamaica, where he worked as an under-manager on a sugar plantation. He remained in Jamaica for five years, acquiring a hatred of slavery that determined the main work of his life in the cause of abolition. On his return to England he underwent a conversion through the influence of his brother-in-law, the Evangelical Thomas Babington. He then accepted an appointment in the administration of the colony of Sierra Leone, on the west coast of Africa, and spent most of the years 1790–9 there, the last five of them as governor of the colony. Sierra Leone had been founded by Evangelical philanthropists, Wilberforce among them, in 1786, as a place of settlement for freed slaves. The colony did not prosper under the management of the Sierra Leone Company, the English group who had chartered the colony and whose employee Macaulay was, and in 1808 the colony passed from the company's administration to the crown. Zachary Macaulay's years there had at least shown of what tough stuff he was made. He had had to face loneliness, disease, harassment from native tribes and foreign slavers, civil disorder, and all the cares of an administrator who was also judge, policeman, legislator, and preacher to his community. In 1794, Freetown, the capital of the colony, was bombarded and sacked by ships of the revolutionary French navy. Through all this Macaulay showed extraordinary energy and unfailing presence of mind. G. O. Trevelyan's summary is a just one: 'To a rare fund of patience, and self-command, and perseverance, he united a calm courage that was equal to any trial' (*Life*, I, 12). So great indeed was his self-command that he seemed to be hardly aware of anxieties that would have unnerved almost anyone else.

In 1799 Macaulay returned permanently to England, married, and settled in London as secretary to the Sierra Leone Company. Nine children were born to him and his wife between 1800 and 1813. About 1803 he had moved his family to Clapham, where he could be near his patron, Henry Thornton, to Wilberforce, and to others of the sect. He had entered business on his own account, trading, apparently, to the East and West Indies as well as to Africa, even before the winding up of the affairs of the Sierra Leone Company in 1808 put an end to his secretaryship. After that, in partnership with a nephew, he enjoyed for some years a substantial prosperity through what seems to have been an effective monopoly of the trade with Sierra Leone.

Macaulay, though evidently an excellent businessman, devoted his best efforts to the chief enterprises of the Clapham Sect, above all else to the campaign to abolish the slave trade, and, later, to free the slaves in

British possessions. The first object was achieved in 1807, and Macaulay then turned his energies to the work of the Bible Society, the Church Missionary Society, the African Institution, and other Evangelical groups. He had already, so long ago as 1802, taken on the editorship of the Evangelical *Christian Observer* and continued in that demanding position to 1816. The final work of his life began in 1823, when he founded the London Anti-Slavery Society, only the second such group then established, and took on a large, perhaps the greatest, part of the labor of the campaign to emancipate the slaves. In the next ten years the struggle to enact an anti-slavery bill took almost all of Macaulay's time; he founded and single-handedly wrote the *Anti-Slavery Monthly Reporter* and mastered in encyclopaedic detail the history of the subject to make himself the unquestioned authority on all the disputed points that perplexed it. His business, meanwhile, left to the incompetent hands of his nephew, had collapsed; on the passage of the anti-slavery bill in 1833, Zachary Macaulay found himself, in broken health, a ruined man. Macaulay had religiously avoided all publicity for himself in his reforming work, with the result that, even now, after the sympathetic accounts of him in Trevelyan's *Life of Lord Macaulay* and in his granddaughter, Lady Knutsford's, *Life and Letters of Zachary Macaulay* (1900), his role in the movement for emancipation is not yet properly understood and recognized.

In his relations with his children Zachary Macaulay was strict but not tyrannous; he was too astute a man to think that he could mold his children exactly after his heart's desire. What he could and did do was to hold them to his own austere standard of hard work, seriousness, and self-abnegation: they did not like it, but they never forgot the lesson.

Zachary Macaulay being one of a large family, a numerous company of aunts, uncles, and cousins in various degrees figures dimly in the letters. But of these only one, apart from Mrs Thomas Babington, was at all a familiar part of the Clapham family. This was Zachary's older brother *Colin* (1760–1836). He had entered the East India Company's military service in 1777, had been assigned to civilian work, and, in 1810, had returned to England a major-general. The General never married, and, after his return, 'spent the remainder of his life peacefully enough between London, Bath, and the Continental capitals' (Trevelyan, *Life*, 1, 36–7). He sat briefly in Parliament, and took a modest part in Evangelical organizations. On his death he left £10,000 to Thomas Babington Macaulay, his major heir.

Selina Mills Macaulay (1767–1831), wife of Zachary and mother of Thomas, was the daughter of a Quaker bookseller in Bristol, Thomas Mills. Mills did not bring up his children as Quakers, and Selina became a protégée of the Evangelical Hannah More and her sisters at their boarding school for young ladies in Bristol. On the More sisters' retirement in 1790, Selina Mills and her sisters took over the school. Her connection with Hannah More eventually led to her meeting Zachary Macaulay, whom she married in 1799. Her history thereafter is wholly domestic. The surviving letters from her show a sensible, good-natured, affectionate, and intelligent woman, but, from her very strong dislike of society and from the streak of irritability in some of her children, it is possible to suspect some strain of nervousness in her.

Selina Macaulay (1802–58), the oldest daughter, grew into confirmed invalidism while still in her twenties and does not figure importantly in Macaulay's family relations. The nature of her illness is only vaguely indicated in the contemporary references, but one of its symptoms was migraine headache. Selina never married, and, after her father's death, she lived with her sister Fanny; for the last decade of her life she resided in Brighton, on an income supplied by her brother Thomas.

Jean (or Jane) Macaulay (1804–30), like Selina, is not a very distinct figure. Her health, almost from the time we first hear of her, was weak – presumably she was tubercular – so that she could not participate fully in normal life. She died unmarried.

John Macaulay (1805–74) was evidently a quiet and retiring person. Destined for a business life, he entered his father's counting house in 1823 but did not take to the work. He was then sent to Queens' College, Cambridge, graduated B.A. in 1829, took orders, and thereafter led the quiet life of a country clergyman at various livings obtained through family influence. For the last twenty-five years of his life he held the living of Aldingham, Lancashire. John married in 1834 and had seven children.

Henry William Macaulay (1806–46) was the liveliest and most attractive of Macaulay's brothers. He attended the Charterhouse, worked in James Cropper's mercantile house in Liverpool, and then went out to Sierra Leone following the wreck of his father's affairs there to see what could be salvaged. In 1832 he was appointed a Commissioner of Arbitration at Sierra Leone, a position worth more than whatever remained of the family firm. Though he endangered his standing at the Colonial Office by fighting a succession of duels, he was made a Judge of the Mixed Court at Sierra Leone in 1835. In 1841 he married Margaret Denman, daughter of Lord Denman. In 1843 he was made Commissioner at Boa Vista, where he died of fever in 1846. His wife, by whom he had two surviving children, later married Edward Cropper, widower of Margaret Macaulay: there are thus two Margaret Macaulays, both of them wives of Edward Cropper. Henry apparently was not notable for good sense, but his spirited and affectionate nature made him well liked.

Frances Macaulay (1808–88), always called Fanny, was the solid, reliable sister, whose life was devoted to the service of her family – she was the paragon daughter, sister, and aunt, naturally looked to when help was needed. When her mother died, Fanny took charge of the household; when her brother and sister went to India, Fanny remained behind to take care of her aging father and her invalid sister Selina; when her sister Margaret died, Fanny took care of her orphaned nephew. Perhaps appropriately, she survived all of her brothers and sisters. It was Fanny who saved many of the letters and papers, and laboriously copied many more, that were put at the service of her nephew George Otto Trevelyan for the *Life of Macaulay*. She is described in 1860 as having 'a strong, thoughtful face, with a good deal of humor in it and much tenderness' (Caroline Fox, *Memories of Old Friends*, 2nd edn, Philadelphia, 1882, p. 353). Fanny never married.

Hannah Macaulay (1810–73) was, with her sister Margaret, Macaulay's favorite, on whom he concentrated most of his emotional life. It is not clear just when Macaulay recognized that he loved his two youngest sisters better than anyone else in the world; they were mere babies when he left home for school and college. When he left Cambridge in 1824 to return to his London home and take up the study of law, Hannah was fourteen and Margaret twelve. In her *Recollections*, Margaret states that 'I think I was about twelve when I first became very fond of him,' that is, at the time when her brother returned to the family, and this is most likely when the special relation between Macaulay and his sisters began to develop. It is fully established by 1830, when, having emerged into public life, he begins to keep up a steady correspondence with them. Hannah seems to have resembled her brother intellectually and personally more closely than anyone else in the family: she was a voracious reader, had a powerful memory, and something of Macaulay's nervous susceptibility: they even shared a slight lisp in their speech. In 1838, the youthful Emily Shore, whose Indian friends were full of Hannah, wrote: 'I have heard of her, and her wonderful memory, and how she can repeat Pollok's "Course of Time" all through' (*Journal of Emily Shore*, 1891, p. 268: 'The Course of Time,' a favorite of pious households, extends through more than 8,000 blank verse lines). Hannah accompanied her brother to India in 1834 – had she not, it is probable that he would have refused the appointment, so unable was he to bear separation from her. In India she married Charles Trevelyan, a civil servant in the East India Company's administration; but Macaulay so arranged matters that the Trevelyans lived with him, accompanied him back to England, were provided for there, and continued to live with him until late 1840. The Trevelyans then moved to Clapham, where Macaulay could easily think of them as still part of his world. There, and when they moved back into London, Macaulay visited them almost daily. Years later, in 1859, when Trevelyan had gone back out to India and Hannah was preparing to join him, the prospect of the separation from her seems to have destroyed Macaulay's will to live and thus contributed directly to his death in that year, shortly before Hannah's departure. Macaulay's love for Hannah included her three children as well: Margaret ('Baba'), later Lady Knutsford; George Otto, statesman and historian as well as his uncle's biographer; and Alice, later Mrs Stratford Dugdale. Hannah's words on her brother's death do not seem exaggerated: 'We have lost the light of our home, the most tender, loving, generous, unselfish devoted of friends. What he was to me for fifty years how can I tell? What a world of love he poured out upon me and mine!' (Trevelyan, *Life*, II, 479).

Margaret Macaulay (1812–34) was the universal favorite among the Macaulay children, attractive, sweet-tempered, with less of Hannah's irritability and more of balanced good sense. The *Recollections* of her brother that she wrote in 1831–2 as an exercise in Boswellizing show a charming mixture of affection, quickness of observation, and naive enthusiasm; she is occasionally but not essentially extravagant. The impression that Hannah and Margaret made on a Fellow of Trinity in 1832, on their visit to the University in company with their brother, is recorded thus: 'Breakfast to Macaulay & his 2 sisters (agreeable girls with sweet voices: not pretty but clever and conversible & very young)' (J. P. T. Bury, ed., *Romilly's Cambridge Diary 1832–1842*, Cambridge, 1967, p. 20). In 1832 Margaret married a family friend, the wealthy Liverpool merchant Edward Cropper. Her death in 1834 of scarlet fever, while Macaulay was in India, was a devastating blow from which he never entirely recovered. Margaret's one child, Charles, died, aged thirteen, in 1847.

Charles Macaulay (1813–86) attended the Charterhouse and then entered the new London University to prepare for the study of medicine. He spent several years thereafter studying surgery; he even practised for a while, but, it would seem, without enthusiasm. On his brother's appointment as Secretary at War in 1839, Charles became his private secretary. He was called to the bar in 1840 and went out to Mauritius in the civil service in 1841, remaining there until 1848. Back in England, he was Secretary to the Board of Health, 1850–4, to the Board of Audit, 1854–66 (Gladstone's appointment), and Commissioner of Audit, 1866–7. Charles is remembered as a large, likeable, witty man. After his retirement in 1867 he ventured into print behind the pseudonym of 'Conway Morel' with *Authority and Conscience: A Free Debate on the Tendency of Dogmatic Theology, and on the Characteristics of Faith*, 1871. In 1841 Charles married Mary Potter, by whom he had three children. He and his older brother were always on good terms but were not close.

Hannah More

Hannah More (1745–1833), the dramatist, religious writer, teacher, and chief publicist of Evangelical causes, was a sort of tutelary deity to the Macaulay family. Selina Mills was her pupil, friend, and successor in the Bristol school founded by the More sisters; it was on a visit to Hannah More that Zachary Macaulay met his wife to be, and though the Mores at first obstructed the marriage the Macaulays remained good friends with them. Hannah More, who earlier in life had enjoyed fame as a playwright, had been the intimate friend of Garrick, and on good terms with Dr Johnson and Walpole, was a sharp and lively woman who retained her gaiety even after giving up eighteenth-century London for the retirement of her house at Cowslip Green and, later, at Barley Wood, both near Bristol. Here she devoted herself to setting up Sunday schools, to writing tracts, narratives, and treatises of Evangelical morality, and to receiving a stream of right-thinking visitors attracted to her retreat. She took a particular interest in Macaulay as a child, and, as the *Letters of Hannah More to Zachary Macaulay* (1860) show, did much to encourage his precocious literary talent. Some part of Macaulay's special affection for eighteenth-century literature and particularly for the age of Johnson may be explained by his personal link to it through Hannah More.

In 1810 Zachary Macaulay named the daughter born to him then after Hannah More, and for years he acted uncomplainingly as her agent in many troublesome dealings with her London publishers. Until Macaulay went to school he seems to have spent part of most summers at Hannah More's, a custom that Selina Mills Macaulay herself kept up until her death. In his life of Hannah More in the *DNB* Leslie Stephen says of her relation to Macaulay that 'she gave him his first books, and after her death he showed his affection by refusing to write about her in the "Edinburgh Review."' This is witty but unfair. In her old age, grown timid and reactionary, Hannah More revoked the legacy of her library to Macaulay, but, as he laconically wrote, 'I kept her regard as long as she kept her wits.' He had no resentment but always thought affectionately of her.

V   EDITORIAL PROCEDURES

1   *Transcription*

Macaulay's letters present few eccentricities of form: most are clearly dated; their format is reasonably consistent; their spelling, with very few exceptions, virtually indistinguishable from modern practice. Their punctuation only is at all striking, for Macaulay, like many other Victorians, was fond of using the dash for terminal as well as for internal punctuation.

It would be possible, then, to attempt a very close style of transcription, aiming at the fidelity of facsimile so far as the inevitable modifications introduced by turning autograph into type would allow. But I have chosen a different policy, thinking that, since the originals are so very little different from modern conventions, it does them no real injury to make the few adaptations needed to bring them even closer to our practice, and that the advantage to the reader's convenience in doing so much outweighs whatever disadvantages the procedure may entail. I have therefore aimed at providing an accurate text without attempting an exact transcription. The reader may see at once what kinds of changes I have made by comparing the facsimile opposite, of the letter of 30 July 1831, with the printed text. An analytic account of the more important of these changes is provided by the following rules.

Contractions and abbreviations: sh^d, w^d, y^e, y^t, &, and similar contractions are silently expanded. So also are such forms as *govt.*, *Parlt.*, *Ld*, and *no.* A very few abbreviations of proper names are silently expanded: *ER* and *HC*, for example, become *Edinburgh Review* and House of Commons. As a rule, abbreviated proper names are expanded in brackets thus: H[annah]; W[estbourne] T[errace], though only on the abbreviation's first appearance if it recurs throughout a letter.

Superscript letters are lowered, with a period after them to indicate Macaulay's sense that he is using an abbreviation.

Punctuation: Macaulay's frequent dashes are treated as convenience requires: at the end of a sentence, the dash becomes a period; after the salutation or close, a comma; but within a sentence, I have left it alone. I have also retained the dash that he sometimes puts *after* a period. I have silently supplied quotation marks, parentheses, and commas enclosing parenthetic elements where Macaulay has provided one such mark but not the other. In almost every other detail of punctuation – e.g., his omitting periods between the initials of his signature – I have followed Macaulay.

Capitalization: I have followed Macaulay, but in doubtful cases I have preferred modern usage.

Spelling: in this matter I have followed Macaulay exactly, except that incontestably inadvertent misspellings – *think* for *thing* or *that* for *than* – have been silently corrected. I have allowed misspelled proper names – e.g., Jane Austin – to stand unreproved by [*sic*]. The reader thus should

Reduced facsimile of Macaulay's letter to his sister Hannah, 30 July 1831. The concluding lines have been circled and the word 'omit' written over them by G. O. Trevelyan, who used a part of the letter in his *Life of Macaulay*, 1, 238.

repaired to the smoking room. Shall
I describe it Edger? A large, square,
wainscotted, uncarpeted, place, with
tables covered with green baize and
writing materials. On a full night
it is generally thronged toward
twelve o'clock with smokers. It is then
a perfect cloud of tobacco fume —
there have I seen — (tell it not to
the West Indians —) Buxton blowing
fire out of his mouth. My father
will not believe it. He holds smoking,
eating underdone meat, liking high
game, — lying late in a morning, — as
all the things which give pleasure
to others and none to himself to be

absolute sins. — Is not that an undutiful reflection?

At present, however, our smoking room is pure enough from smoke to suit my father himself — All the doors and windows are open; — officers of the house and strangers are seen passing to and fro through the surrounding passages — Benne the Member for Wiltshire is writing at one table — O'Connell & I at another — But I must stop — Here comes Sir William Ingilby to say that Burdett is up — Get Blackwood's new number there is a description of me in it. What do you think he says that

I am — "a little, play booted, ugly, dumpling of a fellow: with a mouth from ear to ear" — Conceive how such a charge must affect a man

London
Miss Macaulay
Rothley Temple
Mountsorrel
Leicestershire

J.B. Macaulay

so enamoured of his own beauty as I am. Farewell, my darling — Kindest love both at Rothley, and warmest congratulations on the happy event which has taken place there. Ever yours, my love, Will

assume that an eccentric spelling is Macaulay's. Among the most frequently occurring are the old-fashioned *sate*, *chuse*, and *agreable*; TBM remained constant to the first two but gave up the last in the 1840s in favor of *agreeable*.

The treatment of word-division has been more troublesome. Macaulay is consistent about *to day* and *to morrow*, and I have retained his style. Where such divisions as *any thing* or *every one* are clear I have retained them. But they frequently are not clear, and I have then preferred modern usage. The result is inconsistent, but so was Macaulay. The effect, I think, is not one that affects the reader's convenience.

Lineation: to save space, I have run all but the last line of formal closings and all dates of more than one line into one, indicating the original lineation by oblique lines. I have placed the salutation of all letters on the line immediately above the body of the letter, though Macaulay often runs on in the same line from salutation to body.

Overscored passages: though these are almost always recoverable, I have, except in rare instances, omitted them. Typically, they show Macaulay revising the structure of his sentence or changing his choice of word, but, though they are interesting, they do not affect the substance of what is said.

Editorial additions are bracketed. The usual occasions are in supplying omitted places, conjectured dates, words or phrases conjecturally restored or inadvertently omitted.

2   *Description and annotation*

Headnote: As well as giving the location of the MS or source of text I have given the place of first publication, where ascertainable; in a few cases, this is interpreted to mean place of first *full* publication as opposed to excerpts published earlier. If no previous publication is specified, then so far as I have been able to find the letter is now first published. I have transcribed the address and frank if the letter includes these. My rule has been to transcribe what Macaulay wrote and to omit whatever the cover or the envelope may include of different origin. I have thus excluded from the headnote the description of many marks that old letters can accumulate: the seal, the postal charges written by the postman, the readdressings, endorsements, and notes that it may have acquired as it passed through different hands. I have, with some trepidation, also excluded postmarks from the description. It is the convention to include them, but no one has been able to give me a reason why, so I do not. Of course if any of these things contains information worth noting, it is noted. An exception to the rule of 'what Macaulay wrote' is the inclusion of addresses and franks in other hands.

Footnotes: in references to books, London is assumed to be the place of publication unless otherwise stated. In biographical and bibliographical notes, the general rule may be expressed thus: the less familiar the reference, the fuller the explanation. This is bound to create some illogical results, since quite unimportant details may require a good deal more explanation than world-historic events; but it is practically, if not logically, a good rule. In annotating the more obscure or unpublicized events of Macaulay's life I have been deliberately copious, since such notes are original contributions to biography. In biographical notes I have tried, where possible, to emphasize the subject's relation to Macaulay.

Cross-references have been made by date of the letter in question. When more than one letter exists for that date, then the recipient's name is added to the reference. Cross-references should be understood to include footnotes as well as text.

I have not thought it worth while to correct all of Macaulay's quotations in the notes. Readers are warned, then, that despite his legendary memory Macaulay often introduces changes into the passages he quotes.

Finally, I have made no effort, in citing Trevelyan's *Life* as the place of first publication of a Macaulay letter, to describe Trevelyan's treatment of it. If the reader will make the experiment of comparing almost any letter in this edition with its form in Trevelyan he will find many changes. But it would not be very profitable to document the fact in detail.

ACKNOWLEDGEMENTS

The person who has helped most in the long labor of searching, transcribing, annotating, checking, and proofing for this edition is my wife, Sherrill Ohman Pinney. I make this acknowledgement not as a conventional form but because it is simply true. That the edition appears at all is in large measure owing to her steady, cheerful, indispensable assistance. Despite the frequent tediousness of editorial drudgery protracted over many years, I have enjoyed the work; I hope that she has too.

At a time when it seemed that the edition could not be carried out, the support of Mrs Mary Moorman, daughter of G. M. Trevelyan, and herself the distinguished biographer of Wordsworth, was decisive. I am happy to be able to express my gratitude to her here.

One of the pleasantest parts of an editor's experience must be the discovery that the community of scholarship does exist. I have met almost everywhere with assistance and encouragement, almost nowhere with obstruction. Since a work of this kind is always a collaboration, whether it be done by an actual committee, or, as in this case, nominally at least by one person, its achievement depends on that community. No one who has not been at the center of such work can easily comprehend how complete is that dependence or how impossible it is to acknowledge effectively and justly the extent of the collaboration that has actually gone on. One is tempted, out of a keen sense of one's own inadequacies, to begin acknowledgements more or less *gemino ab ovo*. But I will restrict myself to naming those who have had an immediate and personal part in the work. Two enthusiastic and learned students of Macaulay, John Clive of Harvard and Dr A. N. L. Munby of King's College, Cambridge, have been of essential assistance to me in every sort of way; it is a pleasure to me to recall what I have received from them. Alan Bell, of the National Library of Scotland, has directed me to letters that I should otherwise have missed and has suggested many fruitful places of inquiry. I suspect that all editors of Victorian texts have reason to appreciate his expert knowledge, freely given: I know that I have. I want particularly to acknowledge my debt to my teacher and friend Gordon S. Haight, whose work has done so much to secure the good name of Victorian studies and whose edition of George

Eliot's letters has served, so far as I have been able to imitate it, as a model for my own. For their goodwill, knowledge, and encouragement I am grateful to F. R. Cowell, Joseph Hamburger, Dr G. Kitson Clark, Jane Millgate, and Dr R. Robson, good Macaulayites all. For their help on particular questions, I wish to thank Mr E. E. Smith, who gave me the benefit of his encyclopaedic knowledge of Clapham history; Richard Ormond, who clarified the subject of Macaulay's portraits; and Alistair Elliot, who was my guide through the Trevelyan papers at the University of Newcastle and through the library at Wallington.

Among the members of Macaulay's family, Sir William Dugdale, Mrs Lancelot Errington, Mrs Mary Moorman, the late Mrs Margaret Booth Ritchie, and Mrs Humphry Trevelyan have made available to me the letters in their possession and some of the traditions of Macaulay family history. Mr Bernard Babington-Smith has given me interesting information about Macaulay's Babington cousins.

A fellowship from the John Simon Guggenheim Memorial Foundation in 1967 and a grant from the American Philosophical Society in 1969 helped make it possible for me to carry on essential research in England. My own institution, Pomona College, has given me very generous assistance, including a summer fellowship in 1968, a grant from its Humanities Fund towards the expenses of a sabbatical year in 1969–70, and several grants to cover material expenses. To each of these institutions I am grateful for vital assistance and for their practical expression of confidence in my work.

To the authorities of the following institutions I gratefully acknowledge permission to publish the letters in their possession and my thanks for the information they have supplied about them:

American Philosophical Society; American School of Classical Studies, Gennadius Library; University of Amsterdam; Auckland Public Libraries; National Library of Australia.

Bavarian State Library, Munich; University of Bergen; Berlin State Library, Preussischer Kulturbesitz; Bodleian Library; Bonn University; Boston Public Library; British Museum; Buffalo and Erie County Public Library.

University of California, Berkeley; University of California, Los Angeles; University Library, Cambridge; University of Chicago; Christ Church, Oxford; Church Missionary Society, London; Colby College; Columbia University; Cornell University; Corpus Christi College, Cambridge.

Royal Library of Denmark; Devon County Record Office; Duke University; University of Durham.

Edinburgh Central Public Library; Edinburgh University.

Fitzwilliam Museum, Cambridge.

University of Glasgow.

Harvard University; Haverford College; Hessische Landesbibliothek, Darmstadt; Henry E. Huntington Library and Art Gallery.

India Office Library; Indiana University; Iowa Historical Library; University of Iowa; National Library of Ireland.

Kent County Council; King's College, Cambridge; Knox College.

Leeds City Libraries; Brotherton Library, University of Leeds; Liverpool City Libraries; Corporation of London Records Office; University College, London; University of London.

McGill University; Manchester Central Library; Massachusetts Historical Society; University of Michigan; Mitchell Library, Sydney; Pierpont Morgan Library.

National Portrait Gallery, London; National Register of Archives; General State Archives, the Netherlands; University of Newcastle; New College, Oxford; New York Public Library; New York University; Northumberland County Council; University of Nottingham.

Osborn Collection, Yale University.

Historical Society of Pennsylvania; Carl H. Pforzheimer Library; Free Library of Philadelphia; Princeton University; Public Record Office, London.

Royal Archives, Windsor Castle; Royal College of Surgeons; Royal Library, The Hague; John Rylands Library.

National Library of Scotland; Scottish Record Office; The Sorbonne; Stanford University; Swarthmore College.

University of Texas; Trinity College, Cambridge; Alexander Turnbull Library, Wellington.

State Library of Victoria; Victoria Memorial Hall, Calcutta.

National Library of Wales; University of Washington; Westminster City Library; Dr Williams's Library.

Yale University.

I am indebted to the following private owners of MSS for permission to publish letters in their possession:

Lady Hermione Cobbold; Mr F. R. Cowell; Sir William Dugdale; Mrs Lancelot Errington; the Executors of the late E. M. Forster; the Earl of Halifax; Mr Joseph Hamburger; Mr D. C. L. Holland; Viscount

Knutsford; the Marquess of Lansdowne; Mr Walter Leuba; Longmans, Green and Company; Mr C. S. Menell; the Hon. Mrs John Mildmay-White and her Trustees; Mrs Michael Millgate; Dr A. N. L. Munby; Mr W. Hugh Peal; Mr Gordon N. Ray; Dr Howard R. Seidenstein; Mr E. E. Smith; the Earl Spencer; the Trustees of the Chevening Estate (Stanhope Papers); Brigadier A. C. Swinton; Mrs Humphry Trevelyan.

BIOGRAPHICAL CHRONOLOGY

1800 October 25
TBM born, Rothley Temple,
Leicestershire
1802 or 1803
Family moves from London to
Clapham
1806?
Sent to day school, Clapham
1807 July
At Hannah More's, Barley Wood
1809 Summer
In Brighton
1810, 1811, 1812
Summer visits to Barley Wood
1813 February 2
Leaves Clapham for the Rev.
Matthew Preston's school, Little
Shelford, Cambridgeshire
– April 19
Visits Dean Milner, Queens'
College, Cambridge
1814 April
Guest of Dean Milner again
– Summer
In Brighton with family
– August
Preston's school moves to Aspen-
den Hall, Hertfordshire
1815 July
At Barley Wood
1816 Summer
In Brighton with family: severe
illness?
1817 Summer
Tours Scotland with father and
mother

1818 Spring?
Serious illness
– Early October?
Family leaves Clapham for
Cadogan Place, London
– October 17
TBM leaves for Trinity College,
Cambridge. Resides in Jesus Lane
1819 May
In first class, Trinity preliminary
(i.e., freshman) examinations
– July 5
Recites prize poem, 'Pompeii,' in
Senate House on occasion of royal
visit to University
– Summer
In Clapham with Stainforth
studying for scholarship exam
1820 April
Wins Trinity Scholarship
– October
Wins Latin Declamation Prize
1821 February 12
Goes into rooms in college
– March 6
Wins Craven University Scholarship
– June 9
Wins Chancellor's English Verse
Medal for 'Evening'
– July 11–late September
On reading party, Llanrwst,
North Wales
1822 January 19
Takes B.A. without honors,
having given up on mathematical
examination

– January 25
Admitted student of Lincoln's
Inn
– February 5
First record of TBM's speaking at
Cambridge Union. He remains an
active speaker until 14 December
1824
– April–mid June
In London and at Brighton with
family
– June
Returns to Cambridge
– July
Engages to take two pupils
1823 May
At Rothley Temple
– June
First contribution to *Knight's
Quarterly Magazine* published.
Continues to contribute through
November 1824
– Late July
Leaves Rothley Temple for
London
– August 16
Returns to Cambridge
– October 1
Sits, unsuccessfully, for Trinity
Fellowship
– Late Fall
Family moves to 50 Great
Ormond Street, Bloomsbury
1824 June 25
Speech to Anti-Slavery Society,
Freemasons' Hall, London
– October 1
Elected to Trinity Fellowship
– December
Leaves Cambridge: does not again
reside there
1825 January
First article in *Edinburgh Review*:
'West Indian Slavery.' Studying
law in London. Joins London
Debating Society

– August
'Milton,' *ER*
1826 February
'The London University,' *ER*
– February 9
Called to the bar
– March 8
Joins Northern Circuit at
Lancaster
– May 23–June 25
In Leicester as counsel to William
Evans in contested election
– July 8–August 21
On circuit
– October 17–27
Attends West Riding Quarter
Sessions
1827 March
'Machiavelli' and 'Social and
Industrial Capacities of Negroes,'
ER
– March 10–April 12
On circuit
– April 23–27
Attends West Riding Quarter
Sessions
– June
'The Present Administration,' *ER*
– July 9–September 15
At West Riding Sessions and on
Northern Circuit. Receives his
first brief
– [October 16–26]
Perhaps attends West Riding
Quarter Sessions
1828 January
'Dryden,' *ER*
– January 15–23
Attends West Riding Quarter
Sessions
– January 18
Appointed a Commissioner of
Bankrupts by Lord Lyndhurst
– April 8–[13]
Visits Francis Jeffrey at Craig-
crook

– April 14–18
Attends West Riding Quarter
Sessions
– May
'History,' *ER*
– July 15–August 30
At West Riding Sessions and on
Northern Circuit
– September
'Hallam's Constitutional History,'
ER
– October 14–22
Attends West Riding Quarter
Sessions
1829 January 13–22
Attends West Riding Quarter
Sessions
– March
'Mill's *Essay on Government*,' *ER*
– March 7–April 4
On circuit
– June
'Bentham's Defence of Mill,' *ER*
– August 1–September 14
On circuit
– October 14
Finishes 'Utilitarian Theory of
Government' (*ER*, October)
Late 1829–early 1830
Takes chambers in Gray's Inn;
leaves Great Ormond Street
1830 January 25
Finishes 'Southey's *Colloquies on
Society*' (*ER*, January)
– February 8
Goes to Bowood, to stand for

election at Calne on Lord Lans-
downe's invitation
– February 15
Elected M.P. for Calne
– February 18
Takes seat in Parliament
– March 6–early April
On circuit for last time
– April 5
Maiden speech: on Jewish
disabilities
– April 29
Returns proofs of 'Montgomery's
Poems' (*ER*, April)
– June 12
Elected to Athenaeum
– July 10
Returns proofs of 'Sadler's *Law of
Population*' (*ER*, July)
– August 2
Re-elected for Calne, following
dissolution of Parliament
– September 1
Leaves for Paris
– September 22
Death of sister, Jean
– September 30
Leaves Paris for London
– December 17
Finishes 'Civil Disabilities of the
Jews' (*ER*, January 1831)
– December 18
Elected to Brooks's
– December 25
Finishes 'Sadler's Refutation,
Refuted' (*ER*, January 1831)

ABBREVIATIONS

Boase

Frederick Boase, ed., *Modern English Biography...1851–1900*, 6 vols., Truro, 1892–1921; reprinted London, 1965

DNB

Dictionary of National Biography

ER

Edinburgh Review

Hannah Trevelyan, Memoir of TBM

MS Memoir of TBM, written *c.* 1863 by Lady Trevelyan for her family, now at Trinity. The MS was used extensively by Trevelyan in the *Life*

Huntington

In the footnotes, refers to the collection of Macaulay family papers in the Henry E. Huntington Library

Journal

TBM's MS Journal, 11 vols., 20 October 1838–15 May 1839; 18 November 1848–23 December 1859, at Trinity College

Margaret Macaulay, *Recollections*, 1881 and 1864

Recollections by a Sister of T. B. Macaulay, in [J. B. Macaulay], *Memoirs of the Clan 'Aulay,'* Carmarthen, privately printed, 1881; also, *Recollections by a Sister of T. B. Macaulay, 1834*, London, privately printed, 1864. The *Recollections* were written by Margaret Macaulay in 1831–2; the MS, now lost, was in the hands of Margaret Denman Macaulay Cropper, Henry Macaulay's widow and third wife of Edward Cropper, who had it printed in 1864 in a very small edition. The 1881 reprint omits a few passages from 1864, but it is slightly more available, and I have therefore usually quoted from that text

OED

Oxford English Dictionary

Selina Macaulay, Diary

Selina Macaulay's MS Diary, 10 May 1826–3 June 1833, in the Huntington Library

TBM

Thomas Babington Macaulay, in all references to him in the notes to this edition

Trevelyan
George Otto Trevelyan, *The Life and Letters of Lord Macaulay*, 2 vols., 1876

Trevelyan, 2nd edn
idem, 2 vols., 1877. A number both of additions to and subtractions from the first edition have been made in this

Trevelyan, 1908
idem, 1 vol., 1908. The final version, incorporating some new material

Trinity
In the footnotes, refers to the collection of Macaulay MSS – letters, journals, papers – and to related material in the library of Trinity College, Cambridge

THE LETTERS

CLAPHAM AND SCHOOL
1807–1818

1800 October 25
  TBM born, Rothley Temple, Leicestershire
1802 or 1803
  Family moves from London to Clapham
1806?
  Sent to day school, Clapham
1807 July
  At Hannah More's, Barley Wood
1810, 1811, 1812
  Summer visits to Barley Wood
1813 February 2
  Leaves Clapham for the Rev. Matthew Preston's school, Little Shel-
  ford, Cambridgeshire
– April 19
  Visits Dean Milner, Queens' College, Cambridge
1814 April
  Guest of Dean Milner again
– Summer
  In Brighton with family
– August
  Preston's school moves to Aspenden Hall, Hertfordshire
1815 July
  At Barley Wood
1816 Summer
  In Brighton with family; severe illness?
1817 Summer
  Tours Scotland with father and mother
1818 Spring?
  Serious illness

TO KENNETH MACAULAY,[1] 4 APRIL 1807

MS: British Museum. *Address:* [Kennet]h[2] Macaulay (in Zachary Macaulay's hand).

Clapham, 4th. April, 1807.

My dear Kenneth,

There are now four of us besides myself, Selina, Jane, John, and William Henry.[3] How do you do? I will tell you that the Slave trade is abolished.[4] I have read Homer, Virgil, and Pindar. Papa and Mamma are very well. Kenneth[5] is at School with Schuler,[6] and Henry Daly.[7] I am reading Rollin,[8] the sixth Volume. How does Uncle Colin[9] do? Henry Daly says that in India there are no silly boys, nor foolish ones. I went to School when I was five years old.[10] I am learning "As in præsenti"[11] and make Latin Exercises. I am in Arithmetic, at long Division. Frederic Schuler is writing a letter also. You must excuse my not writing it in small hand, for I have not learned it. / I ever remain,

Your most affectionate Cousin,

Thomas Macaulay.

---

[1] The son of Zachary Macaulay's half-brother Hector, Kenneth Macaulay (1780?–1841) was in the Indian medical service, Madras Presidency.

[2] Part of the cover has been torn away.

[3] See Introduction.

[4] The act abolishing the English slave trade received the royal assent on 25 March.

[5] A second cousin of Zachary Macaulay: see 30 September 1811.

[6] Frederic Schuler, the son of a Mr Schuler in India. Like Henry Daly (next note), Schuler, while at school in England, was cared for by Zachary Macaulay. He returned to India as a cadet in the Bombay artillery, 1810.

[7] The son of a Colonel Daly in India. Zachary Macaulay had earlier written to Kenneth that 'my boy has formed a particular friendship for Henry Daly. Daly won his heart by telling him how elephants, and Tygers, and Camels, etc. etc. etc. are caught in India' (1 August 1806: MS, University of London).

[8] Charles Rollin, *Histoire ancienne des Egyptiens*, Paris, 1730–8. Zachary Macaulay wrote to Kenneth, 3 April 1807, that TBM's 'favourite books are Pope's Homer, Dryden's Virgil, Fox's book of Martyrs, Robinson Crusoe, The Pilgrim's progress, Rollin's antient History, and More's sacred Dramas. These he has read not by way of task, but of his own mere motion. He delights in them, quits them with regret and returns to them with avidity' (MS, University of London).

[9] See Introduction.

[10] TBM went to the schoool of William Greaves at Clapham until 1813. Greaves, whose school room in the garden of no. 3 Church Buildings stood until 1934, came to Clapham about 1804 to teach the twenty-five boys and girls that Zachary Macaulay had brought back with him from Sierra Leone in 1799. All but six of these had died by January 1806, when Greaves opened his school to the children of the Clapham Sect. There is some disagreement over the date of TBM's entering school; the likeliest date is the autumn of 1806.

[11] 'As in Præsenti, &c. or, The Rules for Verbs Construed,' a section heading in the Eton Latin Grammar.

TO ZACHARY MACAULAY, 7 JULY 1807

MS: Trinity College. *Address:* Mr. Macaulay (in Selina Mills Macaulay's hand).

[Barley Wood]¹

My dear Papa

I hope that y[ou]² will come to Barey wood M[rs.]² Hanah More taught me the na[mes]² of the birch mountain ash³

TO ZACHARY MACAULAY, [11? JULY 1807]⁴

MS: Harvard University. *Address:* Zachary Macaulay Esq / Sierra Leone House / Birchin Lane⁵ / Cornhill (in Selina Mills Macaulay's hand). *Partly published:* Viscountess Knutsford, *Life and Letters of Zachary Macaulay*, 1900, p. 279.

[Bristol]

My dear Papa

I am sorry that my writing did not please you. I hope that I shall improve in it.

¹ With her four sisters – Mary, Elizabeth, Sarah, and Martha ('Patty') – Hannah More (see Introduction) had been living since 1802 at her country residence, Barley Wood, near Bristol. TBM was introduced to the Mores in 1801, before his first birthday, when his mother took him to Bristol (Viscountess Knutsford, *Life and Letters of Zachary Macaulay*, 1900, p. 247). That was the first of a series of visits to Hannah More that continued for many summers.   ² Word cut off by mounting of MS.
: TBM's note, which ends thus for lack of room, is written at the end of a letter from Selina to Zachary Macaulay describing the way in which her son is treated by the sisters: 'he is in such request that I cannot have him at all, Mrs. More has just summoned him into the Kitchen Garden, Dear Miss H[annah] is teaching him the names of Shrubs, and Trees, and he is more admired than any thing I ever saw, he has been very cleaver and original in his remarks, and they all relate his sayings, and exclaim Wonderful! I never saw such a Child!...Miss H[annah] called me into her Room, and gave me a Letter to give to Tom, when he got Home...it contained a Bank Note of £10...She made him read to her out of St John, and she told me his remarks and discussions had quite overpowered her....' TBM remembered of this visit that it 'was a great event in my life. In parlour and kitchen they could not make enough of me. They taught me to cook; and I was to preach, and they got in people from the fields, and I stood on a chair, and preached sermons. I might have been indicted for holding a conventicle' (Trevelyan, 2nd edn, I, 35n).
⁴ Postmark of receiving post office dated 13 July.
⁵ Birchin Lane runs between Cornhill and Lombard Street in the heart of the City. The office of the Sierra Leone Company was there until 1808, at number 26; after that it was the office of the partnership of Macaulay and Babington. Zachary Macaulay's family lived in the rooms above the office until 1802 or 1803 (the date is uncertain) when they moved to Clapham. After a tour of Longman's warehouse on 2 April 1849 TBM wrote: 'The garrets and the view over the red tiles and dingy chimneys of the city reminded me of my very early days in Birchin Lane. I left Birchin lane at three years old. Yet it is strange how vivid my recollection of the place is – and of my childish walks – Draper's Garden – Moorfields – and Guildhall, then hung with pictures which have long disappeared' (Journal, I, 560). The site is now the headquarters of Messrs Williams Deacon's Bank, the descendant of the bank of which Henry Thornton was a director.

Selina is in the country, and I am going this evening.[1] All Mama's commands are readily and chearfully obeyed. The Miss Mores gave me a guinea, a bank note, and Selina a half guinea. She sends her love to you. I remain

your dutiful son,
Thomas Macaulay.

Virgo absque modestia est equa furiosa absque fræno. Advocatus egit causam meam Judice illo. Ivi cum fratre in agros ibique verberavi eum baculo.

to Zachary Macaulay, 1 June 1811

Text: Extracts in Sotheby's Catalogue, 4 April 1955, item 162, $2\frac{1}{2}$ pp. 4to: dated Clifton,[2] 1 June 1811, 'to his father.'

...I design as soon as possible to send you the tiresome sum which you sent me,[3] as for the Greek, I shall begin it very soon, Mamma must tell you how we have behaved. I am exceedingly sorry that Henry and John are not here to enjoy a spectacle, so congenial to their feelings, I need not say I mean that of soldiers....

...My Grandfather[4] took us yesterday to Mr. Danby's where we saw a droll little woman, called Mrs. Ricks,[5] or some such name, Mr. Walter Scott has written a new Poem intitled The vision of Don Roderick.[6]

---

[1] TBM was evidently at the house of his grandfather, Thomas Mills, in Bristol and was about to return to Barley Wood. A letter from Selina Mills Macaulay to Zachary Macaulay, 10 July 1807, is dated from Bristol (MS, Huntington).

[2] TBM, his mother, and his sister Selina were at Clifton in late May and June visiting Zachary Macaulay's brother Colin, who had returned from service in India the year before.

[3] Zachary Macaulay's letter to TBM, 30 May 1811, contains the following problem: 'A Merchant in London purchased 20 pipes of Madeira wine at Funchal, containing 2145 gallons for which he paid at the rate of £48 for every 110 gallons. He sent the wine to Jamaica, and paid freight for it at the rate of £4.2.6 per pipe and insurance at the rate of £3 per cent on what it cost at Madeira. When the wine came to Madiera [*sic*] it was found that 47 gallons had leaked out. The whole that remained was sold for 3 dollars a gallon each Dollar being worth 4/9d. A Commission of 5 per cent was also charged by the Agent who sold it, on the whole of the proceeds. Now I wish to know how much the Merchant gained by his adventure, and what was the total sum of money he had on hand after the sale?' (copy, Trinity College: the Greek passage referred to in TBM's letter is omitted from the copy). A week later, his father scolds TBM: 'I have seen no fruit of your labours' (6 June: MS, Huntington Library).

[4] Thomas Mills (1736?–1820), for many years a bookseller, stationer, and binder at various addresses in Bristol. He is described as 'a beautiful old man, talking incessantly of Jacob Behmen' in Hannah Trevelyan's MS Memoir of TBM, p. 3; though he was a Quaker, he apparently did not bring up his children in that sect.

[5] Mrs Ricks was no doubt the 'most extraordinary dwarf – a woman of forty' whom TBM recalls in 15 July 1852 as one of the sights of Clifton and Bristol in 1811.

[6] Published in July. I do not know how TBM knew of it at this time. The letter seems correctly dated.

TO KENNETH MACAULAY,[1] 30 SEPTEMBER 1811

Text: Extract in Anderson Galleries Catalogue, Howard K. Sanderson sale, 3 May 1916, item 547, 1 p. 4to: dated Clapham, 30 September 1811, 'To his cousin Kenneth, at Sierra Leone.'

Buonaparte is at present on the French Coast and has beheld the late defeat of his immense fleet at sea by the English.[2] Some French prisoners who designed to mutiny discovering that their design had been revealed to the English by one of their Sailors, tattooed him with these words "J'ai vendu mes freres aux Anglois á bord du Centaur," [...]

TO SELINA MILLS MACAULAY, 8 JULY 1812

MS: Trinity College. *Address:* Mrs. Macauley (in Hannah More's hand).

[Barley Wood]

Childe Hugh
and
the Labourer
a
pathetic ballad

There was in Somerset a Childe,
Lord of the west countrèe,
Fortune with gold his coffers fill'd,
And from him want did flee.

His wife he treated with respect,
As sure became a Knight;
Tho' shrewder neighbours did suspect
That all things were not right.

[1] Kenneth Macaulay (1792?–1829) was a second cousin of Zachary Macaulay, who provided for his education. In 1808, on the transfer of the Sierra Leone Colony from the Sierra Leone Company to the Crown, he was sent there as a government writer through Zachary Macaulay's influence. He was later Superintendent of Recaptured Slaves at Sierra Leone, agent for Zachary Macaulay's firm, and a Member of Council.

[2] Napoleon visited the coasts of France and Holland in the fall of 1811. At Boulogne, 20 September 1811, on the orders of and in the presence of the emperor, the Boulogne flotilla attacked an English frigate anchored offshore. The next day the English, reinforced by four more ships, captured a small French ship from the flotilla. No 'immense fleet' was involved.

And none could guess, and none could tell,
Where he his money found;
He had, if I remember well,
Six hundred thousand pound.

O may thy hands be smear'd with pitch,
And daub'd with tar thy head,
And may'st thou veil in lowly ditch
The glories of thy head.

A man in lowly vale there dwelt,
Contented with his lot,
Tho' hunger's stinging pangs he felt,
And scarce potatoes got.

He scarce could in him keep the life,
He was in hungry case,
And there were found upon his wife,
Nor silk, nor Brussel's lace.

And O! she had no necklace bright,
Nor jewel yet, nor broach,
And strange it is that this poor wight,
Had ne'er been known to poach.

[To][1] hunt with hound and horn, Childe Hugh
[One] morning bent his way
[O!] Samuel Stellard well may rue
[Th]e hunting of that day.

[T]he hare she jump'd with one high bound
Into a field of corn;
[Po]or Sam was walking it around,
With woeful looks forlorn.

And now as true as shaggy fur
Clothes back of mighty bear,
He there beheld a terrier cur
To tear a harmless hare.

And then this hare to save he fled,
Tho he was a poor man,

---

[1] Edge of sheet torn away, affecting this and five of the next six lines.

And thus with all his speed he sped,
But when he came, alas 'twas dead,
So he for nothing ran.

And then poor puss uplifted he,
And o'er his shoulders threw,
Alas! there chanced then to see
That barbarous Knight Childe Hugh.

The man thought they would him requite,
In this he judg'd amiss,
"I pray, Sir Childe, thou noble Knight!
I pray thee to take this."

Then spake Childe Hugh "Thou naughty knave,
Why dost thou plague me thus?
I'm sure enough of hares I have,
O thou ridiculus mus."[1]

Tho' grieved was that poor, poor, man,
For wife and children's sake,
He went unto the publican,
And asked him to take.

Then he too said; "I can't, I can't,
I cannot take from thee;
For if I did I soon should want,
Childe Hugh would angry be."

Then grieved was that poor, poor, man,
And tottered his knee,
That face of his waxed pale and wan,
That he a wretch should be;

And O! a wretch indeed he was,
That made that Childe his foe,
Who cruel was in every cause,
And mocked at tales of woe.

And, for now fell the evening shade,
Poor Sam he hied him home,
And there within his cottage staid,
Nor went abroad to roam.

[1] Horace, *Ars Poetica*, 139.

He told the story to his wife;
Which did her poor heart pierce;
She begg'd him not to go to strife,
With that Childe Hugh so fierce.

Then she "while fortune on thee smiles,
He could not hunt thee down:
Wert thou e'en like that sable Giles,
Who plunder'd widow Brown.

That man whose fame and name do grow
Among the west countrèe;
Who took her apples, and also
Stripp'd redstreak apple tree."

The words of all her eloquence,
(For eloquent she was),
Persuaded Samuel's innocence,
Tho' in a doubtful cause.

To bed they went on that same floor,
Nor thought of what might hap;
When suddenly came to the door,
Rat-tat-tat-tat-tat-tap. – .

"Who's there, who's there;" "Ho let us in:"
The men without replied,
"No:" answer'd boldly they within;
"You shall:" the others cried:

Then the poor children 'gan scream out,
And also 'gan to roar,
And then two doughty yeomen stout,
Broke ope the cottage door.

Then the poor wife she made a fuss,
And also made a riot;
Presenting then a blunderbuss,
One charg'd her to be quiet.

She screech'd, she scream'd, and thought she dream'd,
Alas no dream was it;
Her husband doom'd to death she deem'd;
And fell down in a fit.

Down fell the husband on his knee,
And said "an't this enough;"
The officers for what they see,
Care not a pinch of snuff:
But they began the poor Sammée
To batter and to cuff.

But yet one of these yeomen twain,
The most compassionate,
The woman on her bed had lain,
In pity of her fate.

Then vile Childe Hugh did them impel
Before the magistrate
To take unhappy Samuel,
The man whom he did hate.

Then rose the Mores fair sisters five,
And to Childe Hugh did hie,
To keep this poor, poor, man alive,
And eke his family.

Then Leeves arose that abbot old,
That Abbot old and gray,
Rector of Wrington's people bold,
And thither bent his way.

Childe Hugh not e'en to Abbot bow'd,
Thro' all the west countrèe,
Of all its knights and barons proud,
The proudest Knight was he.

"I come" he said "o noble knight!
Thy mercy for to call,
Towards a certain wretched wight,
Who's now at justice Hall."

When Samuel Stellard he 'gan say,
Childe Hugh's stern cheek grew hot,
"Abbot! why pray'st thou that I may,
I tell thee I will not."

Then woxe the Abbot hot with pride,
Since now was gone all hope,
He fearlessly the Childe defied,
As if he were the Pope.

Now shalt thou wish, thou knavish Knight,
Thine eyes the light ne'er saw,
Know for this poor forsaken wight,
Wrington will go to law.

From ruin Samuel to save,
The justices are willing;
They have decreed that thou shalt have,
No more than fifty shilling.

Fierce woxe the Knight and smote with rage,
His hand upon the table;
But all I know I now have wrote;
And all that I am able:
And now I shall draw in my boat,
Like Spenser with a cable.[1]

My dear Mamma

This incident really happened in our neighbourhood some little time ago: for particulars apply to Papa.

Key to the persons

Childe Hugh ——— Sir Hugh Smith[2]
Abbot Leeves ——— Rev Mr. Leeves[3] Rector of Wrington
The Yeomen ——— two Constables.

Miss Hannah More desired me to write a ballad upon this subject in which they have much interested themselves: I have begun to read Guiseppe riconosciuto a play of Metastasio's[4] to Miss Hannah More. I never saw

---

[1] No such passage is in Spenser.
[2] Sir Hugh Smyth (1772–1824), of Long Ashton, Somersetshire.
[3] William Leeves (1748–1828: *DNB*), Rector of Wrington, 1779–1828.
[4] Rome, 1776. A letter from Hannah More to Zachary Macaulay about this time describes TBM's life at Barley Wood: 'he goes on in the usual Pindaric style; much desultory reading, much sitting [flitting?] from bower to bower; Spenser, I think, is the favourite poet to-day. As his time is short, and health, I think, the chief object just now, I have not insisted on much system. He read in the sun yesterday and got a little headache....I do compel him to read two or three scenes of Metastasio every day, and he seems to like it' (Knutsford, *Zachary Macaulay*, p. 288: letter dated May 1810, but clearly 1812). TBM may have been

them in better health. My love to Papa, my brothers and sisters; finally / I ever remain

My dear Mamma your dutiful and affectionate son

Thomas B Macaulay

P.S. I would thank you to tell Papa that the Miss Mores would be very glad to have a sight of the parody on the Prince Regent's letter to Lords Grey and Grenville.[1]

July 8th AD 1812

TO SELINA MILLS MACAULAY, 3 FEBRUARY 1813

MS: Trinity College.

Shelford February 3d. 1813

My dear Mamma

I do not remember being ever more gloomy in my life than when I first left Clapham.[2] We got into the Cambridge Stage and at Chelmsford took a Post-Chaise which carried us on to Shelford where we arrived about 5 o'clock. Mr. Preston had put off the dinner hour till our arrival and here I met William Wilberforce[3] who came but the day before; after dinner I got a little acquainted with the boys and after tea arranged my books in my shelves put my clothes in the drawers and began to shift for myself.

After prayers I went very sorrowfully to bed and in the morning went down expecting to be called instantly to work, but Papa was so kind as to take me with him to Cambridge on Mr. Preston's horses.

recovering from illness this summer, as the reference to his health implies: in a letter of 6 Feburary 1813 Selina Mills Macaulay tells TBM that, though he may find himself behind the other boys at school, 'You have from uncontrollable circumstances nearly lost the last year' (copy, Trinity). But the 'uncontrollable circumstances' may mean something quite different.

[1] Grey and Grenville refused the Regent's invitation to them to join the government, conveyed in a letter written in February.

[2] TBM left Clapham, accompanied by his father, on 2 February to enter the private school opened in 1808 by the Reverend Matthew Morris Preston (1780?–1858: *Boase*) at Little Shelford, near Cambridge. Preston, a Fellow of Trinity, was an Evangelical, had been curate to Simeon (see p. 15, note 1), and had some connection with Clapham. A letter from Henry Thornton to Hannah More [*c.* 1813?] says that 'Tom Macaulay and William Wilberforce are going to Mr. Preston's near Cambridge.... Preston preached a sensible sermon at our church here, but not of a very striking kind' (MS, Thornton papers, Cambridge University Library). Preston was Vicar of Cheshunt, 1826–58. The house where Preston lived and kept his school at Little Shelford is, though much altered, still standing, opposite the church.

[3] Eldest son (1798–1879: *Boase*) of William Wilberforce; he entered Trinity but did not take a degree; was called to the bar but did not practise; was elected M.P. for Hull but was unseated; he ended his days 'excluded from respectable society' (Isabella Thornton Harrison to Hannah Trevelyan, in E. M. Forster, *Marianne Thornton*, New York, 1956, p. 213) and a convert to Roman Catholicism.

14

Of the boys only nine are come and there is but one more coming. William Wilberforce is as agreable and as mischievous. One boy at table was thought by Mr. Simeon[1] who dined here to day to be a striking resemblance of Harry Venn[2] upon which William as soon as dinner was over fastened the name of "Little master Wenn" upon him mimicking the boy's Cockney accent.

Added to the advantage of every boy's having a separate [room] is that Mr. Preston imposes a shilling fine upon every one who intrudes without leave into another boy's room. Give my kindest love to Selina Jane and John; tell Henry that I had rather be sitting by the fireside with him on my knee than seeing sights at Cambridge.

You cannot conceive with what pleasure I look forward to the holidays and in the mean time I ever remain

Your affectionate and dutiful Son
Thos. B Macaulay

TO SELINA MILLS MACAULAY, 6 FEBRUARY 1813

MS: Trinity College. *Address:* Mrs. Macaulay / 26 Birchin Lane / London.

February 6th. 1813 Shelford

My dear Mamma

I write again because tho' I never liked writing it seems to ease me now to write to you and I will write as often as I can. Do write to me sometimes for in the midst of the vexations which absence from home and the plagues of a school nothing would give me so much comfort. You cannot concieve how anxiously I wait for the postman.

We have not so much work as I expected to do here, yet we have enough. We work about half an hour in the morning two hours and a half in the forenoon an hour and a half in the afternoon and half an hour in the evening. The boys seem more pleasant than I thought on my first arrival there but then indeed I was melancholy and disposed to find fault with every thing.

Tell Papa that as to what he said about a newspaper Mr. Preston lends me his and there is no need of my subscribing for one with the boys.

---

[1] The Reverend Charles Simeon (1759–1836: *DNB*), Fellow of King's College and incumbent of Holy Trinity, Cambridge, was the leading Evangelical spirit at Cambridge; he was the master, in fact, of all the Evangelical clergymen in the generation after Wilberforce and, in fiction, of Charlotte Brontë's Mr Brocklehurst and George Eliot's Amos Barton. Simeon's approval of Preston (who published *Memoranda of Charles Simeon*, 1840) was a decisive reason for entrusting TBM to Preston's care (Hannah Trevelyan, Memoir of TBM, p. 14).

[2] Henry Venn (1796–1873: *DNB*), elder son of John Venn, Rector of Clapham.

We are at present about to establish a spouting club as the boys call it in other words a debating society such as we had at Mr. Greaves's. Mr. Preston is very kind to me and lends me such books as I want besides amusing books to read out of school hours.

I am very dull and do not like to play at games which I should have delighted in a month ago. The only games at which I have seen them play are throwing quoits and shooting the bow and arrow.

"Hope deferred maketh the heart sick,"[1] but nothing relieves mine more than looking forward to the holidays and counting the weeks and days and hours which are to pass before them. Four months and twelve days and I shall again see Clapham. But that is a long time tho' the other boys laugh at me who consider as an age what they esteem as a fortnight. Give my love to all the children. Tell Selina and Jane that if I can I will write to them in less than a week. Again, pray write to me sometimes. / I ever remain / My dear mamma

Your affectionate son
Thomas B Macaulay

TO SELINA MILLS MACAULAY, 12 FEBRUARY 1813

MS: Trinity College. *Address:* Mrs. Macaulay / Clapham.

February 12. 1813

My dear Mamma

I was delighted beyond measure at recieving your letter and Papa's. Mr. Preston before this letter arrived gave me the same advice as you have done concerning exercise. I believe he thinks it particularly necessary to me for every morning he dismisses me from school before breakfast and compels me to make the round of the shrubbery: he often goes with me himself and is very kind to me. I am tolerably well; I very seldom indeed cough and my eyes tho' they appeared a little inflamed the day before yesterday are now perfectly well and I hope that the new sort of diet on which I have just entered. that is to take as little butter and tea as possible.[2] Miss Preston has got a pair of socks for me which I wear above my stockings on a wet day and which keep my feet quite warm. I was rather too hasty in what I said about the newspaper for Mr. Preston does not make a regular point of lending it to the boys. As to my Latin and Greek, I am in the second class and stand with W Wilberforce as also in mathematics. We are still at the Ass's bridge in this branch of learning not having yet got over the 5th Proposition of Euclid at which we have been fagging for 3 days.

---

[1] Proverbs 13: 12.   [2] Thus in MS.

I present you here with a sketch of our employment. Before breakfast we say our Latin Exercises and Greek grammar which we prepare overnight and do two or three sums.

Breakfast being over we study Euclid and Greek till one o'clock dine at two and learn Cicero and Horace. We go into school at 4 o'clock and fag till six. Then we go into tea after which we prepare Exercises and Grammars against the next morning. After the evening work is done, we amuse ourselves as we like. I for my part read Charles the 5th.[1]

Give my kindest love to all at home. I shall most likely write to Papa to morrow.

I ever remain my dear Mamma

Your affectionate son

T B M

TO ZACHARY MACAULAY, 22 [FEBRUARY][2] 1813

MS: Trinity College. *Address:* Mr. Macaulay / 26 Birchin Lane / London. *Mostly published:* Trevelyan, I, 40–1.

Shelford. Monday October 22nd. 1813

My dear Papa

As this is a Whole Holiday I cannot find a better time for answering your letter, and with respect to my health, I am very well, and tolerably cheerful, as Blundell[3] the best and most clever of all the scholars is very kind and talks to me, and takes my part. He is quite a friend of Mr. Preston's. The other boys, especially Lyon, a Scotch boy, and Wilberforce are very goodnatured, and we might have gone on very well had not one Clayfield a Bristol fellow come here.[4] He is unanimously allowed to be a queer fellow, and is generally characterized as a foolish boy, and by most of us as an ill-natured one.

In my learning I do Xenophon every day, and twice a week the Odyssey; in which I am classed with Wilberforce, whom all the boys allow to be very clever, very droll, and very impudent. We do Latin verses twice a week and I have not yet been laughed at, as Wilberforce is the only one who hears them being in my class. We are exercised also once a week in English compositions and once in Latin composition, as letters from per-

[1] William Robertson, *The History of the Reign of the Emperor Charles V*, 3 vols., 1759.
[2] TBM wrote 'October' and was corrected by his father's reply: 'you have dated your letter *October* 22nd. Now this month happens not to be Oct. but Feb.' (25 February: MS, Trinity).
[3] Thomas Blundell (1796?–1819), the son of a Major Blundell of London. Matriculated at Trinity College, Cambridge, Michaelmas, 1813; B.A., 1818.
[4] I am unable to identify Lyon. Clayfield may be the James Ireland Clayfield who matriculated at Oriel College, Oxford, on 18 October 1821, aged seventeen, the second son of E. R. Clayfield of Bristol. If so, he was only nine years old in 1813.

sons renowned in history to each other. We get by heart Greek Grammar, or Virgil every evening. As for sermon writing, I have hitherto got off with credit, and I hope I shall keep up my reputation.

We have had the first meeting of our debating Society the other day, when a vote of censure was moved for, upon Wilberforce, but he getting up said, "Mr. President, I beg leave to second the motion" by this means he escaped. The kindness which Mr. Preston shows me is very great, he always assists me in what I cannot do, and takes me [to][1] walk out with him every now and then.[2] Miss Preston is very kind: she comes now and then into my room to get me to read to her. My room is a delightful, snug, little chamber, which nobody can enter as there is a trick about opening the door. I sit like a king, with my writing desk before me, for (would you believe it) there is a writing desk in my chest of drawers, my books on one side my box of papers on the other with my armchair, and my candle for ev'ry boy has a candlestick snuffers and extinguisher of his own. Being press'd for room I will conclude what I have to say [to][1] morrow and ever remain my dear Papa,

your affectionate Son
Thomas B Macaulay

TO ZACHARY MACAULAY, 26 FEBRUARY 1813

MS: Mr Gordon N. Ray. *Address:* Mr. Macaulay / Clapham.

Shelford February 26th. 1813

My dear Papa

I resume my pen to give you a little more insight into the fashions of the school: every half-year we have an examination, in which the boys after being examined in every thing that they learn are classed accordingly. This half year's examination will begin June 21st and will occupy as many days as Mr. Preston thinks fit, three at most; Blundell stood highest, last examination, for Stainforth[3] was not examined, and Blundell is generally

---

[1] Paper torn away with seal.

[2] The anonymous writer in [Eliza Rennie], *Traits of Character*, 1860, II, 8–9, says that TBM 'won quickly the affection and regard of his preceptor' and quotes Preston as saying that '"Tom Macaulay is an extraordinary young man; he has much classical and more miscellaneous reading, a vivid imagination, and a prodigious memory; nor do I, either in or out of Cambridge, know any one with whom I can converse more pleasantly, or would prefer as my companion in my rambles of a Saturday afternoon."'

[3] George Stainforth (1796–1820), matriculated at Trinity College, Cambridge, 1814; president of the Union, 1816; B.A., 1818. He was the son of Richard Stainforth, a banker and 'a member of the former Clapham coterie' (Knutsford, *Zachary Macaulay*, p. 338), and of Maria Stainforth, a daughter of the first Sir Francis Baring. Before his early death at the age of twenty-four, his kindness to TBM at Preston's school was confirmed by his services in tutoring him in 1818 and 1819.

esteemed his superior in Latin, Greek, Mathematics etc. tho' in Latin Verses Stainforth is generally classed first.

Wilberforce is very goodnatured indeed to me, and as he is a favourite with most of the big boys, he has often begged me off from a beating: Mr. Preston is sometimes forced to laugh at his jokes even when he is displeased, which does not often happen. We have just past the sixteenth proposition of Euclid and are very much fagged at it indeed; Mr. Preston reads one or two propositions to us every morning which we prepare for the next, and very hard things they are. I like them however a great deal better than I did at first, tho' there is but little comfort in drawing circles and angles without eather rule or compass.

I have just received your letter of the 25th and I am very sorry to hear that Mamma is ill; I wonder you mean that *that* Mr. Williams[1] whose combed locks turned half the female heads in the parish preach'd at Clapham on Sunday. Give Selina my love and my best compliments for Miss Harriett Dodd; I assure you that I shall make amends for my long silence by writing Jane a letter as soon as the post goes. Ask John if he remembers, Superus, high, superior higher or more high, supremus highest or most high. Tell Henry that his dreams do me honour but that my coat is not yet patched. As for the three little darlings, tell Fanny that I did not leave her the mumps intentionally, and Hannah that I think that Senna Tea is nasty but that it must be taken, and give Margeret a kiss. Give my Uncle Colin my love. I hope he will soon be well. / I ever remain / My dear Papa

Your Affectionate Son
Thomas Babington Macaulay

PS I got the newspapers the two first Saturdays but not last week.

---

[1] Zachary Macaulay to TBM, 25 February 1813 (copy, Trinity), reports: 'Your Mama has been poorly some days, but today is somewhat better. Her complaint has been occasioned by severe cold taken last Sunday evening when she went to hear Miss Williams preach.' 'Miss Williams' is Zachary Macaulay's joke. Theodore Williams (1787?–1875), Vicar of Hendon, preached at Holy Trinity, Clapham, on 28 June 1812 and 21 February 1813 (Preachers' Book, Holy Trinity Church, Clapham). A further extract from Zachary Macaulay's letter will explain what remains of TBM's: 'Selina is now recovered from her illness and begins again to think of joining her merry party in the village. Jane is meditating a second letter to you but thinks you very ungrateful for the first. John trudges to school by himself every morning, but not I hope like snail unwillingly. Henry is blundering through the multiplication table and dreaming that he sees you every night in a patched coat at Mr. Preston's. Fanny has just had the Mumps, Your legacy to her I suppose. The pensive Hannah hangs her head aside, and assures us all that she can't bear Senna tea. Margaret's noises become every day more interesting.' For Fanny, Hannah, and Margaret Macaulay, see Introduction.

TO SELINA MILLS MACAULAY AND SELINA MACAULAY,
2 MARCH 1813

MS: Trinity College. *Address:* Mrs. Macaulay / Clapham.

Shelford March 2nd 1813

My dear Mamma

I have this instant read your letter of the 26th, which I received to day, and I am very glad to hear that you are recovered from your illness, as also to inform you that I have very good health at present. I should be very much indeed obliged for a case of mathematical instruments of which I assure you I am very much in want, and which Mr. Preston I am told does not furnish, as also a mathematical pocket book, that is a red Morocco book about the size of your account book, with all the leaves blank, in which I can draw my Mathematical figures.

This is the second of March: it was on the second of February, exactly a month ago that I left dear Clapham. I am quite surprized at Mr. Preston's kindness: I never could have any conception of it for he leads me to walk out with him and talks to me quite familiarly.

I am determined to apply myself to mathematics with all my power, as I want very much to stand high in the examination, of which I gave an account in my letter to Papa. Mr. Preston has written to Papa and he will most likely receive the letter to day. I hope you will excuse my breaking off as I promised Selina a letter and must in conscience keep my word, / I ever remain / My dear Mamma

Your affectionate Son
T B Macaulay

Miss Selina Macaulay

Shelford March 2nd. 1813

My dear Selina

I have only room for a short letter now but I hope I shall soon be able to write you a longer one. I hope you will not be jealous of Jane and Papa and Mamma to whom I have written amply. Tell me particularly how you all are and especially my uncle Colin; I assure you I shall never be tired of hearing from you. My love to all at home; / I ever remain / My dear Selina

Your affectionate Brother
T B Macaulay

TO SELINA MILLS MACAULAY, 8 MARCH 1813

MS: Trinity College. *Address:* Mrs. Macaulay / Clapham. *Extract published:* Trevelyan, I, 41.

Shelford March 8th. 1813.

My dear Mamma

I received your letters yesterday, and am very much obliged to you for your kindness in procuring me the instruments. The only ones which I want are compasses, a scale, and a steel pen, with which I shall be able to prosecute my mathematical studies without any hindrance.

I have my time all employed, and hardly a single idle minute, of which I am glad, since it keeps me from being dull, which I am when I have nothing to do. We do here as much work in a day as at Mr. Greaves's in three; Latin Verses, instead of taking me a day to make a couple of lines, come as it were to the point of my pen, without any difficulty, and forty lines of Horace seem nothing at all after about a week. I have now been here a month and a week, a long time to be without seeing those whom I love best. Time is rolling away, and fourteen weeks will bring on the holidays, when I shall forget Latin, and Greek, and Euclid, by the fire-side at Clapham. Every night almost I dream of it, and every day I think of it. "Home is home, be it ever so homely."[1]

I received to day the newspaper. The Catholics seem to be getting on finely. I should not wonder if this Session of Parliament should gain them all the privileges for which they have been contending so long.[2] But really I hope the parliament will take cognizance of the Prince Regent's barbarous manner of treating his wife.[3] I cannot think that parliament will ever be so base as to consent to a divorce between them.

Our debate for Friday next, is whether Lord Wellington or Marlborough was the greatest general, and a very warm debate is expected.

My case of instruments must be sent by the Fly directed on an outside cover to Mr. Preston with the usual direction, and an inside cover to my unworthy self. I wonder whether the little ones have really got the measles. I should be glad to know particularly how all at home are. My kindest love to all. / I ever remain / My dear Mamma

Your affectionate Son
Thomas Babington Macaulay

[1] Proverbial: first recorded in John Clarke, *Paroemiologia Anglo-Latina,* 1639.
[2] On 25 February Henry Grattan, M.P. for Dublin, moved, as he had done almost annually since 1805, for a committee of inquiry into the question of relief from civil disabilities for Catholics. After extended debate, the motion passed on 2 March; it is to this event that TBM refers. The bill that Grattan brought in on 30 April for the removal of Catholic disabilities passed its second reading but was rejected on 24 May.
[3] The question between the Prince Regent and Princess Caroline at this point was her right of visiting their daughter, Princess Charlotte. A debate was raised on the matter in the Commons on 5 March, but came to nothing.

TO SELINA MILLS MACAULAY, 17 MARCH 1813

MS: Huntington Library. *Address:* Mrs. Macaulay / Clapham.

Little Shelford March 17. 1813

My dear Mamma

I received Papa's letter two days ago, and I am glad to say that I have not suffered from the cold. I had, indeed, a trifling cough but it went off with a few lozenges. You have not written to me for more than a week, and I am in a great hurry for a letter. I hope that you have not forgotten me; for indeed I have not forgotten you.

But I am now in very high spirits; we had an examination of Greek, in which, as I beat all the others in the class I am to receive a prize. The prizes that have this half-year been won are to be given out by Mr. Preston in a few days; they have been won by Blundell, Stainforth, Daintry,[1] the oldest boy in the school, and myself.

To day is a whole holiday, and I have employed it principally in taking notes for a speech which I shall deliver on Friday night before our assembly, and which will occupy at least half-an-hour in the delivery. The question is "whether the Crusades were or were not beneficial to Europe". I confess that I shall speak against my conscience in opposing the Crusades, but there are such a number of specious arguments against them that I shall be in no want of matter.

I, with the assistance of Stainforth Blundell and Wilberforce who are very kind to me, have dug a little garden which Mr. Preston gave me. I am going to fill it with flowers, and there are already in it, a great number of tulips and lilies of the valley. It is very shady, and there is a little secluded arbour in it, where I can sit as long as I like.

My love to all / I ever remain / My dear Mamma

Your affectionate son

T B Macaulay.

PS Mr. and Miss Preston send their kindest regards.

[1] Perhaps the John Daintry listed in Venn, *Alumni Cantabrigienses*, as having matriculated at Trinity College, Cambridge, at Michaelmas, 1812.

TO ZACHARY MACAULAY, 23 MARCH 1813

MS: Mr Gordon N. Ray. *Address:* Mr. Macaulay / No 26 / Birchin-Lane / London. *Extract published:* Knutsford, *Zachary Macaulay*, p. 309.

Little Shelford March 23. 1813

My dear Papa

I received your letter respecting the news-paper, which I carried according to your desire to Mr. Preston as soon as I saw him. I also received a letter from you, and another from Mamma a little before; – I received the instruments and I am very much obliged to you for them: they are a great convenience to me and very much facilitate my mathematical studies.

You ask how many there are in our class in Greek. There are five of whom Wilberforce is one. But you must not think that I beat them in Greek Translation: it was in repeating an immense quantity of Latin Rules for Greek Verbs. We are at present reading in Latin besides Horace Cicero's masterly Oration against Catiline. From what I have read of Cicero, I think that if he excels more in one thing than in another it is in the art of the Climax.

As for the debates on Friday Night, I was really in great doubt upon the subject, when I came to consider it carefully, for it is a fact that the Crusaders put to death 70,000 Mahometans in the streets of Jerusalem tho' they implored mercy on their knees.[1] A principal argument which I brought against the Crusades was that as they were undertaken from motives of superstition and served to confirm the minds of the People in it. Our next subject is on Catholic Emancipation. I do not much like political subjects, for they make the boys rather too warm in defence of this or that Party; especially when some of the boys have their fathers in the house of commons, they fight for their father's party, right or wrong.

My love to Mamma and all at home. I shall very soon write again. / I ever remain / My dear Papa

Your affectionate Son
T B Macaulay.

Mr. Preston desires to know whether you have seen Mr. Robert Hall's letter on the East India Question.[2]

---

[1] The First Crusade achieved the conquest of Jerusalem on 15 July 1099; of the massacre that followed, 'No one can say how many victims it involved; but it emptied Jerusalem of its Moslem and Jewish inhabitants' (Steven Runciman, *History of the Crusades*, Cambridge, I, [1953], 287).

[2] 'An Address to the Public on an Important Subject, Connected with the Renewal of the Charter of the East India Company,' Bristol, 1813.

TO SELINA MILLS MACAULAY, 30 MARCH 1813

MS: Trinity College. *Address:* Mrs. Macaulay / Clapham.

Little Shelford March 30. 1813.

My dear Mamma

I am very much obliged to you for your long letter which I have this instant read; I really was in great anxiety at not receiving one, and I am very glad at having got one.

You ask whether I feel my difficulties in mathematics increase as I go on. Quite the contrary. That there are difficulties and very many ones is true; but there must be difficulties in every science, especially in those which are like mathematics. I find, upon the whole, that to understand a proposition and to know it are the same thing or in other words, that if I can comprehend the meaning of what is to be proved I am very near being able to prove it myself.

Since I have been here it will be on Friday morning two months. It is to-day 8 weeks since I left the place which I can not even now think of but with mournfulness, except when I cast my eye forward to "my destined triumphs and my glad return." I am sure my return will be happy; I hope it will be triumphant; if I can get over my examination with credit it will; and that depends much on myself. The subjects will be given out for the examination in six weeks; I do not know whether I shall succeed or not, but if I am not up and fagging before five in the morning from the time they are given out till the holidays, you may say it was my fault. One of the boys, who stood very high last examination is, saving myself, the most bashful in the school, and when he took his seat to be examined; tho' he had studied very hard; he could not speak a word, and he trembled so, that the whole table at which he was sitting, shook. Nevertheless he stood second in that part of the examination which relates to knowledge of history.

As the house of commons have voted an address of condolence to the Prince Regent, on the death of the Duchess of Brunswick;[1] so I take the liberty of condoling with my dear Selina upon the banishment of one of the favourites of her *inconstant* heart and the imprisonment of the other. Give my love to Papa and to all at home. / I ever remain My dear Mamma

Your affectionate son

Thos. B. MACAULAY

[1] The Duchess of Brunswick, George III's sister and mother of the Princess Caroline, died on 23 March 1813. The next day the House of Commons voted an address of condolence to her son-in-law and nephew, the Prince Regent, though not before it had been suggested that the address might be more properly directed to the Princess Caroline.

TO SELINA MILLS MACAULAY, 12 APRIL 1813

MS: Trinity College. *Address:* Mrs. Macaulay / Clapham.

Little Shelford. April 12. 1813.

My dear Mamma

How time flies; I have been here exactly half the time which I trembled at on my first arrival. If I remember, I wrote to you a little while after my arrival to tell you that we should not meet again for four months and twelve days. That time has now dwindled to two months and 8 days.

I was very sorry as well as Mr. Preston, who I am sure takes a great interest in the state of all the family, to hear that Papa had been ill. Fortunately however the same letter brought me the news of his sickness and recovery.

I believe you will be pleased to hear that the instant Mr. Preston had read the enclosed Paper relative to the East India business, which I showed him, he rode off to Cambridge to canvass among the inhabitants of that abode of learning, and to vote for a petition to be sent up to Parliament. But I do not think you will be pleased to hear that that dilatory university have decreed to defer the consideration of it.[1]

I have already begun to season myself for working at the examination, the subjects for which will be given out in four weeks, by rising usually before six in the morning. The promised prize has at length been bestowed on me: it is "Pascal's thoughts" beautifully bound in Octavo; it is in a very beautiful type; but it is in French. Perhaps it might not be amiss, since I have named French, to desire you to send me a French dictionary of which I am in great want.

I will now inform you in what Classes I stand. In Euclid you will not be surprized to hear that I am in the last, which however comprises all who

---

[1] In his letter of 5 April 1813 to TBM Zachary Macaulay enclosed the form of a petition to Parliament in favor of the admission of missionaries to the British dominions in India and with it 'a paper which I drew up for spreading correct information on the subject through the country, and for inducing all good men to write in presenting similar petitions. About a hundred thousand of them will soon be circulated, and we expect petitions from all quarters' (Knutsford, *Zachary Macaulay*, p. 297).

When the renewal of the East India Company's charter came before Parliament in 1813, Wilberforce moved for the introduction of Christianity into India, an object that he and his Clapham associates had fought for and lost on the occasion of the last charter renewal, in 1793, and that Wilberforce himself regarded as an even greater cause than that of the abolition. After an unpromising debate on 22 March the Evangelicals, with Zachary Macaulay directing the effort, successfully undertook to raise petitions in favor of the cause throughout the kingdom. According to E. M. Howse, *Saints in Politics*, 1952, p. 92, '837 petitions, bearing more than half a million signatures,' had been presented by 22 June, when Wilberforce's resolution passed the House of Commons. It was the basis of the so-called 'pious clauses' of the Charter Act, by which the Church of England was established for the English community in India and the country opened to missionaries.

study Euclid except Stainforth, Blundell, and a Scotch boy named Lyon. In Greek of which there are four classes, I am in the third. In Latin there are three, and I am in the second; in Latin Verses, Exercises etc; I am in the second in every thing but Latin Verses, in which I am in the third, together with Wilberforce. In French, however, I stand in the first, for Mr. Preston hears us read French to him every Monday evening. And he did me the honour of saying that I read French better than any of the other boys. But whom am I to thank for that?

My love to my dear Papa and all at home. / I ever remain, my dear Mamma

Your affectionate son
Thos B Macaulay

TO SELINA MILLS MACAULAY, 19 APRIL 1813

MS: Trinity College. *Address:* Mrs. Macaulay / Clapham Common / Surry.

Little Shelford April 19. 1813.
My dear Mamma

I received your letter yesterday, and am very much amused with the accusation which John Babington[1] has thought fit to bring against me, upon the score of not taking exercise. I generally get up at six, and take a walk round the shrubbery before breakfast. Then after breakfasting off tea or milk with a dry roll and dry bread, for I do not touch butter, I very often contrive to get another walk before school. After dinner also I walk a great deal, but I take my principal walking exercise after tea, in the evening. To set you still more at rest, I am not only in the best health, but Mr. and Miss Preston say that I am so much grown since I came, that you would hardly know me again.

With regard to the dictionary, I left one at home when I came here, it was a very small one about the size, as near as I can guess from memory, of Denon's Travels.[2]

It is rather strange that Cambridge, the abode of learning and religion for so many years, should hesitate an instant to do her utmost, in order to promote Science and Christianity through such a vast tract of country.[3]

[1] John Babington (1791–1885), the second son of Thomas Babington, was at Magdalene College, Cambridge, while TBM was at Shelford.

[2] Vivant Denon, *Voyage dans la Basse et la Haute Égypte*, 2 vols., Paris, 1802. TBM presumably refers to the English translation published by Ridgway, 2 vols., 1802, 18mo.

[3] See 12 April 1813: Wilberforce's resolution aimed at 'useful knowledge' as well as 'religious and moral improvement,' for the Evangelicals regarded English education as the precondition of successful missionary work. The Charter Act of 1813 provided for an annual grant of 100,000 rupees for education.

We are now in our Easter holidays, that is Easter Monday; and Easter Tuesday; and as I have gone upon the plan of writing to you every whole holiday, you will receive two this week, and if I have time and anything to say I will send a third. Since my dear little John is also in his Easter holidays, could he not spend one morning in writing a letter to poor Tom, who is thinking of him every day and night.

Miss Hannah More is coming to Cambridge, or to a country seat of a friend very near it, as Mr. Simeon informed Mr. Preston, – who has promised to take me to see her if there is no danger of her thinking it an intrusion.[1] I can hardly believe that she is coming. My love to Papa and all at home. I ever remain my dear mamma

Your affectionate Son.

Thos. B Macaulay

Mr. and Miss Preston's best regards.

TO SELINA MILLS MACAULAY, 20 APRIL 1813

MS: Trinity College. *Address:* Mrs. Macaulay / Clapham / Common / Surry. *Mostly published:* Trevelyan, I, 41–2.

Little Shelford April 20th. 1813.

My dear Mamma

Pursuant to my promise I resume my pen to write to you with the greatest pleasure; Since I wrote to you yesterday, I have enjoyed myself more than I have ever done since I came to Shelford. Mr. Hodson[2] called about twelve o'clock yesterday morning with a poney for me, and took me with him to Cambridge. How surprized and delighted was I to learn that I was to take a bed at Queen's College in Dean Milner's[3] apartments.

---

[1] The meeting apparently did not take place: 'Only think of my being so near you as Cambridge and never seeing you!' (Hannah More to TBM [January 1814?]: MS, Huntington).

[2] George Hodson (1788–1855: *Boase*) was an Evangelical Fellow of Magdalene who married into the Stephen family. He became Archdeacon of Stafford, Canon and Chancellor of Lichfield Cathedral, and Vicar of St Mary, Lichfield. On an Easter in Lichfield, 1849, TBM heard Hodson preach: 'an old friend of mine. He was kind to me when I was a boy and once took me from Shelford to Cambridge on horseback to pass a day or two with Dean Milner. This was at Easter 1813 when I was only twelve years old' (Journal, I, 567: 8 April 1849).

[3] Isaac Milner (1750–1820: *DNB*), President of Queens' College, Cambridge, since 1788, and Dean of Carlisle since 1791, was one of the major Evangelical influences in Cambridge, a friend of Wilberforce, and, through him, of the Clapham Sect generally. According to Sir James Stephen, 'The Clapham Sect,' *ER*, LXXX (July 1844), 295, 'he talked with children (his chosen associates) inimitably. It was like a theological lecture from Bunyan, or a geographical discourse from DeFoe.' TBM's cousin Lydia Rose recalled that Milner used to send for TBM 'for the pleasure of his conversation' and said of him: '"Sir that boy is fit to stand before Kings and he will some day"' (Recollections of TBM: MS, Trinity).

Wilberforce arrived soon after, and I spent the day very agreeably; the dean amusing me with the greatest kindness. I slept there and came home on horseback to day just in time for Dinner. The dean has invited me to come again, and Mr. Preston has given his consent.

The books which I am at present employed in reading to myself are, in English Plutarch's lives, and Milner's Ecclesiastical History,[1] in French Fenelon's dialogues of the Dead.[2] I shall send you back the volumes of Madame de Genlis's Petits Romans[3] as soon as possible, and I should be very much obliged for one or two more of them.

Every thing now seems to feel the influence of Spring. The trees are all out. The lilacs are in bloom. The days are long, and I feel that I should be happy were it not that I want home. Even yesterday when I felt more real satisfaction than I have done for almost three months, I could not help feeling a sort of uneasiness, which indeed I have always felt more or less since I have been here, and which is the only thing that hinders me from being perfectly happy. This day two months will put a period to my uneasiness.

"Fly fast the hours, and dawns th'expected morn".[4]

Every night when I lie down I reflect that another day is cut off from the tiresome time of absence.

Mr. Hodson, the Dean, Mr. and Miss Preston send their best regards. My love to my Papa and all at home. / I ever remain, my dear Mamma

Your affectionate Son,

Thos B, Macaulay

TO ZACHARY MACAULAY, 26 APRIL 1813

MS: Mr Gordon N. Ray. *Address:* Mr. Macaulay / Clapham. *Partly published:* Trevelyan, I, 42–3.

Little Shelford. April 26th. 1813.

My dear Papa,

I received yesterday a letter from Mamma, and an enclosed one from John, to whom I enclose an answer, with which I hope he will be satisfied;

---

[1] Joseph Milner, *The History of the Church of Christ,* 5 vols., 1794–1809. Joseph Milner died in 1797, after publishing three volumes of his *History;* it was continued by his younger brother, the Dean, though the work had been a sort of collaboration between the two Milners from the first. TBM's mature judgment of the work was harsh: see Trevelyan, II, 284n.

[2] François Fénelon, *Dialogues des Morts,* Paris, 1700–18.

[3] Mme de Genlis published over eighty volumes, as popular in England as in France, among them *Adèle et Théodore,* 1782, *Les Veillées du Château,* 1784, and *Les Chevaliers du Cygne,* 1795.

[4] Cf. Pope, 'Messiah,' line 21.

I am glad that Mamma is satisfied with my defence on the topic of exercise; and I assure her that though the current opinion here is that I shall grow tall there is not much suspicion of my being thin.

I am very much concerned to hear of the death of old Mrs. More;[1] and I should be afraid it would put a stop to Miss H. More's intended journey. I am pleased however to hear of Mr. Venn's recovery;[2] and I should be glad to know what illness he was labouring under.

Since I have given you a detail of my routine of weekly duties, I hope you will be pleased to be informed of my Sunday's occupations. It is quite a day of rest here, and I really look to it with pleasure through the whole of the week;[3] after breakfast, we learn a chapter in the Greek Testament i.e. with the aid of our bibles, and without doing it with a dictionary etc. like other lessons. We then go to Church. We dine almost as soon as we come back, and we are left to ourselves till church-time; during this time I employ myself in reading; and Mr. Preston lends me any books for which I ask him, so that I am nearly as well off in this respect as at home, except for one thing; which though I believe it is useful is not very pleasant; I can only ask for one book at a time; therefore I am limited to one at a time; and cannot touch another till I have read it through; we then go to church, and after we come back I read as before till tea-time; after tea, we go in to sermon; and write it out as you were before told by Stainforth; I cannot help thinking that Mr. Preston uses all imaginable means to make us forget the sermon. For he gives us a glass of wine a-piece on Sunday, and on Sunday only, the very day when we want [to][4] have all our faculties awake; and some do literally go to sleep during the sermon, and look rather silly when they wake; I, however, have not fallen into this disaster.

My love to Mamma, and all at home. / I ever remain, My dear Papa

Your affectionate Son,

Thos. B. Macaulay

---

[1] The oldest of the More sisters, Mary, died on 18 April 1813, aged 75.

[2] John Venn (1759–1813: *DNB*), Rector of Clapham since 1792. He was suffering from dropsy and died on 1 July.

[3] Henry Thornton remembered TBM as saying that 'Mr. Preston's idea of keeping Sunday was to be in a bad temper' (Dorothy Alston, 'Some Personal Recollections of Lord Macaulay,' *London Mercury*, xviii [May 1928], 59).

[4] Paper torn away with seal.

TO ZACHARY MACAULAY, 8 MAY 1813

MS: Mr Gordon N. Ray. *Address:* Mr. Macaulay / Clapham. *Partly published:* Trevelyan, I, pp. 43–4.

Little Shelford May 8th. 1813.

My dear Papa

As on Monday it will be out of my power to write, since the examination subjects are to be given out then, I write to day instead to answer your kind and long letter.

I am very much pleased that the nation seem to take such interest in the Introduction of Christianity in India. My Scotch blood begins to boil at the mention of the 1750 names that went up from a single country parish.[1] Ask Mamma and Selina if they do not now admit my argument with regard to the superior advantages of the Scotch over the English peasantry?

I am glad to hear that my cousin Lydia has added another name to the genealogy of Olaüs.[2] The Macaulay family seems determined to exist, come what will. I am also pleased that it is a boy, for now Mr. Rose will be under no temptation to assassinate it; Perhaps you remember the old story of the man who threatened his wife to kill the next child she had if it was a girl. Unfortunately it was a girl, but the mother educated it as a boy, and prevailed on Diana to change it into one in reality.[3]

I have written to my Uncle Colin yesterday and dispatched the letter under a frank to my Uncle Babington. I meant to have added a letter for you, only I was afraid that it would not go in a frank.

The Don Cossack seems to be of all men the fittest for war.[4] I cannot comprehend his character. It is however easy to see that he kills men with the same indifference as he would crush a snail, and burns a city as if he were treading upon an ant hill.

As for my examination-preparations, I will, if you please, give you a sketch of my plan. On Monday, the day on which the examination subjects are given out, I shall begin. My first performance will be my verses and my declamation, two exercises which after I have done and corrected carefully, I shall show up immediately. I shall then translate the Greek and Latin;

[1] 'A single country parish in Scotland sent up 1750 names, and we expect that scarcely a parish in that part of the Kingdom will fail to petition' (Zachary Macaulay to TBM, 3 May 1813: MS, Trinity).

[2] Lydia Babington, eldest daughter of Thomas Babington, married in 1809 the Rev. Joseph Rose, later Vicar of Rothley. The Macaulay family liked to imagine that it was descended from Olaus Magnus, King of Norway, whom TBM celebrated in his 'Olaus the Great, or the Conquest of Mona,' *c.* 1808–9. Several MS versions of this uncompleted poem are at Trinity.

[3] Cf. Ovid, *Metamorphoses*, IX, 666–797.

[4] This refers to an anecdote in Zachary Macaulay's letter of 3 May: 'When the Don Cossack was asked how many Frenchmen he had killed with his long spear during the last Campaign, he said 13 officers, but as for the *fry* he did not count them.'

the 1st time of going over I shall mark the passages which puzzle me, and then return to them again. But I shall have also to rub up my Mathematics, (by the bye I begun the 2nd Book of Euclid to day,) and to study whatever history may be appointed for the examination.

A great part of this work I shall do in the morning before breakfast, or in the afternoon in half-holidays. I cannot deny myself the pleasure of an evening walk, but I shall improve it as well as I can by repeating propositions of Euclid to myself. I assure you however that I shall not be able to avoid trembling, whether I know my subjects or not. I am however intimidated at nothing but Greek. Mathematics suit my taste, altho' before I came, I declaimed against them and asserted that when I went to college, it should not be to Cambridge. I am occupied with the hope of lecturing Mamma and Selina upon Mathematics, as I used to do upon Heraldry, and to change Or and Argent and Azure and Gules for squares and points and circles, and angles and triangles and rectangles and rhomboids and in a word: "All the pomp and circumstance of Euclid."[1]

I beg Henry's pardon most heartily for omitting to write him a letter. I enclose one for him, the 1st I believe that he has ever received. When I come home I shall, if my purse is sufficient, bring a couple of rabbits for Selina and Jane, and something for John, and Henry and Fanny and Hannah, and little pretty Margaret. Ask Hannah if she has forgot me. Give my love to Mamma and all at home. / I ever remain / My dear Papa
                                    Your affectionate Son
                                    Thomas. B. Macaulay.

TO SELINA MILLS MACAULAY, 17 MAY 1813

MS: Trinity College. *Address:* Mrs. Macaulay / Clapham.

                                    Little Shelford May 17th. 1813.
My dear Mamma
    Contrary to my expectations and those of all the boys, the subjects for the examination were not given out till Thursday evening. You may perhaps wish to know what they are. Les voici. Mathematics, Euclid from the beginning as far as we have done. Lyrics, The burning of Muscow. Since I have never done Latin Lyrics, I am to do an English Ode on it.[2] Hexa-

---

[1] Cf. *Othello*, III, iii, 354.

[2] A MS entitled 'The Northern War a Pindaric Ode,' at Trinity, may be the exercise referred to here. In a letter of August 1813, to Zachary Macaulay, Hannah More writes: 'Tom's "Moscow" is as good, and perhaps more faultless than any of his preceding verses' (Arthur Roberts, ed., *Letters of Hannah More to Zachary Macaulay*, 1860, p. 55).

meter Verse, "Toto divisos orbe Britannos" – that is the Britons separated from the whole world. For declamation the Question of the Crusades. In Latin, Horace's Epistles. In Greek, Part of the Anabasis, which is
an account of Cyrus's expedition against his Brother Artaxerxes. It was
written by Xenophon, who was a witness of the whole campaign. Finally
in History we are to study the Grecian, and the Persian as connected with
the Grecian.

I have written a declamation of five pages of great outsize paper, and a
copy of Latin Hexameters consisting of fifty lines. I shall to day if possible
do my English copy and fall to Greek, the only part of my examination
which frightens me, as I am tolerably perfect in Euclid. I should be very
much obliged to you for a Grecian History since I shall be unable to
borrow one, whilst all the boys have need of their own.

I got the Petits Romans last week, since Stainforths Packets did not
arrive till then. The time of the Holidays is drawing near very fast. Five
weeks and I shall be in a much happier state than I am now. I have, however, a horrid dread of the examination. I tremble at thinking of it. Either
Blundell or Stainforth will stand first. Stainforth will excel in Latin Verses,
and History. Blundell in Mathematics and declamation; and they are pretty
much upon a par in other branches of learning.

Stainforth is exceedingly kind to me. He looks over my verses and
points out all the faults in them to me. He always takes my part when the
boys plague me and though there are many older than he is, he has so much
authority in the school that I am completely safe under his protection;
Give my love to my Papa and to all at home. I ever remain, my dear
Mamma

Your affectionate son.

Thos. B. Macaulay

TO SELINA MILLS MACAULAY, [12 AUGUST 1813][1]

MS: Trinity College. *Address:* Mrs. Macaulay / 26 Birchin-Lane / London.

Shelford. Thursday

My dear Mamma.

I arrived here safe and sound, but as low-spirited as can well be imagined.[2] I cannot bear the thoughts of remaining so long from home. I do

---

[1] On 9 September 1813 TBM says that 'it is now four weeks, since I wrote my first letter to
you'; 12 August, a Thursday, thus seems certain.

[2] TBM apparently did not leave Shelford for the holidays until late June, but his letters for
that month are missing. He seems to have spent the time between his first and second terms

not know how to comfort myself, or what to do. There is nobody here to
pity me or to comfort me, and if I were to say I was sorry at being from
home, I should be called a baby. When I am with the rest I am obliged to
look pleasant, and to laugh at Wilberforce's jokes, when I can hardly hide
the tears in my eyes. So I have nothing to do but to sit and cry in my room,
and think of home and wish for the holidays. I am ten times more uneasy
than I was last half year. I did not mean to complain, but indeed I cannot
help it. Forgive my bad writing, for indeed, in the state in which I am it is
a great deal for me to write at all. Pray write as soon as possible. I ever
remain / my dear mamma

Your affectionate Son
T B Macaulay

P S My love to Papa[1] and all at home.

TO SELINA MILLS MACAULAY, 14 AUGUST 1813

MS: Trinity College. *Address:* Mrs. Macaulay / 26 Birchin-Lane / London. *Mostly published:*
Trevelyan, I, 46–7.

Little Shelford. August 14. / 1813.

My dear Mamma

I must confess that I have been a little dissapointed at not receiving a
letter from home to day. I hope, however, for one to morrow. My spirits
are far more depressed by leaving home than they were last half year.
Every thing brings home to my recollection. Every thing I read, or see, or
hear brings it to my mind. You told me I should be happy when I once
came here, but not an hour passes in which I do not shed tears at thinking
of home.

Every hope, however unlikely to be realized, affords me some small
consolation. The morning on which I went, you told me that possibly I
might come home before the holidays. If you can, confirm this hope.
Believe me when I assure you that there is nothing which I would not give
for one instant's sight of home. Tell me in your next, expressly, if you

---

entirely at Clapham; in August, 1813, Hannah More writes Zachary Macaulay that 'I did not
invite him this year out of pure consideration....I conceived his fond parents would be
glad to have him to themselves after this first separation' (Roberts, *Letters of Hannah More
to Zachary Macaulay*, pp. 55–6).
[1] Zachary Macaulay's reply to this letter suggests that TBM 'Pray to God...that he would
give you that calm fortitude and serenity of mind which it is our duty to cultivate under all
circumstances, and that he would enable you to give up cheerfully your own selfish pre-
ferences when these stand in the way of duty. And fix your eyes on that meek and patient
Lamb of God whose language and whose life exhibit one uniform and striking example of
self denial and resignation and holy and cheerful obedience' (15 August 1813: MS, Trinity).

can, whether or no there is any likelyhood of my coming home before the holidays.

If I could gain Papa's leave, I should select my birthday on the 25th of October as the time which I should wish to spend at that home which absence renders still dearer to me.

I think I see you sitting by Papa just after his dinner reading my letter, and turning to him, with an inquisitive glance, at the end of this paragraph. I think too that I see his expressive shake of the head at it. O may I be mistaken. You cannot conceive what an alteration a favourable answer would produce in me. If your approbation of my request depends upon my advancing in study, I will work like a cart-horse. If you should refuse it, you will deprive me of the most pleasing illusion which I ever experienced in my life.[1]

My love to Papa, Selina, Jane, John, Henry, Fanny, Hannah, and Margaret. Pray do not fail to write speedily. / I ever remain / My dear Mamma
Your dutiful and affectionate Son
T. B. Macaulay.

TO SELINA MILLS MACAULAY, 6 SEPTEMBER 1813

MS: Huntington Library. *Address:* Mrs. Macaulay / No. 26 Birchin-Lane / London.

Little Shelford September 6th. 1813.

My dear Mamma

I employ the time that remains before we go in to school at 7 o'clock in the morning, to write to you. I am surprized that you are alarmed at the thoughts of my having a fire Box, – I can easily prove to you that your apprehensions are groundless, and that, to speak methodically, for these three reasons

1. Imprimis. Mr. Preston was apprehensive himself when he saw Wilberforce's fire Box, and took it from him to examine it. But after looking at it, he found it harmless, and returned it.

2. You are mistaken in thinking that it is Phosphorius; the principal ingredient is vitriol, or to speak in loftier terms, it is a composition of sulphuric Acid, and Oximuriat of Pot-ash.

3. The Box and the Bottle are so constructed that it cannot burn any thing unless it be done purposely.[2]

---

[1] To this letter Zachary Macaulay replied: 'I am sorry you should have set your heart on anything so unattainable as a visit to Clapham before the regular holidays, because not only is such an intermission of school labours disapproved by Mr. Preston, but it is opposed to all my own views of what is right and proper' (17 August 1813: MS, Trinity).

[2] 'Your father has no apprehension about the fire box and you shall soon have it' (Selina Mills Macaulay to TBM, 15 September 1813: copy, Trinity).

Blundell has lent me Cowper's Homer's Illiad.[1] I prefer it to Pope's, considering it in the light of a translation of Homer. It is close, literal, and keeps all the idioms and phrases of the Original that can be rendered into English. Yet it is not on that account difficult to understand. It is, like every thing that Homer or that Cowper wrote, elegant and simple. Cowper was far more qualified for the work of translation than Pope because his taste was better suited to the work, whereas Pope did not wish to translate Homer, but designed to have translated Virgil in preference, had it not been translated by Dryden. Pope too was not well acquainted with Greek; he was forced to use a dictionary in translating it. While Cowper on the contrary was an excellent Greek Scholar.

I have written to Papa at Cheltenham; I am well and comfortable; and, absolutely [I][2] have nearly as much time to myself [as I][2] had at home; I cannot tell h[ow][2] it is; but I read ten times as much as I did at home; and walk nearly as much; and have time besides to sit and joke with the boys in the school-room. – My love to all at home.

I ever remain, My dear Mamma

Your affectionate Son.
T. B. Macaulay

TO SELINA MILLS MACAULAY, 9 SEPTEMBER 1813

MS: Trinity College. *Address:* Mrs. Macaulay / No. 26 Birchin- / Lane / London.

Little Shelford. September 9. 1813.

My dear Mamma

I hope you received my last letter, as I am rather uneasy at the silence which you have of late observed. Your correspondence is not quite so well kept up as it was last half year. You must consider that you have seven little creatures at home, besides Papa, to make you happy, and that I have nobody to supply the place of a mother or of a father here; I am in an unpleasant state at present, though I have the satisfaction of thinking, and I hope you will have satisfaction in hearing that on Monday morning next, a quarter of the time that is to separate us will be past. How time flies; it is now four weeks, since I wrote my first letter to you. And I am sure that I should feel now as bad as I did then unless it were that work in school and reading out of it keep me from being melancholy.

I first took up Cowper's works about a fortnight ago, intending merely to divert a spare half-hour with them on a holiday now and then. But

---

[1] *The Iliad and Odyssey... Translated into English Blank Verse*, 2 vols., 1791.
[2] Paper torn away with seal.

really they have chained me so that I fear I shall forget the more important business of reading history. Mitford[1] is lying on the shelf day after
day; and I fear will continue to do so until I have got through the two
volumes of Cowper's Poems. Blundell on Saturday night lent me his
translation of Homer; I have now read it over once; and have almost
devoured it again.

Kirke White lays it down as a rule never to write more than two letters
without receiving one in return.[2] Humbly hoping that you will *take an
hint*, I take my leave, with love to all the children – I ever remain / My
dear Mamma

Your affectionate Son
T B Macaulay

TO SELINA MILLS MACAULAY, 15 SEPTEMBER 1813

MS: Trinity College. *Address:* Mrs. Macaulay / No 26. Birchin- / Lane / London. *Partly
published:* Knutsford, *Zachary Macaulay*, pp. 308–9.

Little Shelford. September 15. 1813

My dear Mamma

I received your kind letter to day, but before I proceed to answer it, I
must observe that I wish you would direct to me as Mr., and not Master
Macaulay, since it subjects me to jokes which I could willingly dispense
with.

The last news of Vandamme's defeat[3] has contributed to raise our
spirits a good deal. Mr. Preston, (saving your presence,) is a very des-
pairing politician, and whenever he begins to talk of politics, I cannot help
thinking that he addresses us in the language of Kirke White

> "Come, let us sit, and weave a song
> "A melancholy song."[4]

To day Mr. Hodson came from Cambridge with the news. Mr. Preston
said, "Yes it seems to be favourable upon the whole." We all could not
help bursting out laughing, which I joined with all my heart. Mr. Preston

---

[1] William Mitford, *History of Greece*, 5 vols., 1785–1818. TBM devoted a review to Mitford
in *Knight's Quarterly Magazine*, III (November 1824), 285–304, and remarks on him in
'History,' *ER*, XLVII (May 1828), 360–1.

[2] Kirke White to his brother Neville, dated Michaelmas-day, 1800: 'never write three without
receiving one in return' (*Poetical Works and Remains of Henry Kirke White*, New York,
n.d., p. 63).

[3] The French general Vandamme was defeated and captured with his army at Kulm by the
Russians and Austrians, 20 August 1813.

[4] Misquoted from the first stanza of 'To the Herb Rosemary.'

continued, "My friends here are laughing," said he, "I have been croaking to them of late." Indeed he had been croaking, and foreboding nothing but

"Death, and defeat, and loss of fame."

Mr. Hodson said, "Take in the Morning Chronicle. It will croak to any tune you may devise."[1] So ended the dialogue, which to me seemed one of the most ludicrous I had ever heard.

What a happiness it is that I have a room to myself. I never enter it, and shut my monstrous oak door, and turn the huge iron bolt (for by the bye, my door is secured with a bar of iron an inch thick,) without exclaiming "I am King here." You may tell Alick Greig[2] that I do not envy him, his sleeping with sixteen in a room, or studying tongues and languages in the middle of such a crowd of boys. Mr. Preston is exceedingly kind to me. He has made me a present of Cecil's Biography,[3] very nicely bound. He read to us on Sunday night Mr. Hugh Pearson's funeral sermon,[4] and was very much pleased with it.

There is a story told of the celebrated French comedian Scarron, that he went to the court of Mary of Medici; and when she asked him what he came to solicit, he said "May I solicit the honour of being Valetudinarian to your Majesty." The queen laughed. Scarron took the laugh as a consent, and from that time absolutely subscribed himself, "Scarron, unworthy Valetudinarian to her Majesty."[5]

Give my love to Papa, who I suppose is now returned, and to all at home. / I ever remain / My dear Mamma

Your affectionate Son

T B Macaulay

[1] After James Perry took control of it in 1789 the *Morning Chronicle* 'was the most influential journal for thirty years' (*The History of the Times*, I, [1935], 33). 'Perry . . . was conspicuously independent – as journalistic independence went in those years' (*ibid.*, p. 215), but the *Chronicle* was Whig.

[2] Alexander Greig (1800?–55), one of TBM's Scotch cousins, the son of Zachary Macaulay's sister Catherine and the Rev. G. Greig. He was later in the East India Company's service.

[3] Josiah Pratt, *The Life, Character, and Remains of the Rev. Richard Cecil*, 1810. Cecil (1748–1810: *DNB*) was a leader of the Evangelical revival.

[4] Pearson (1776–1856: *DNB*), Curate of John Venn at Clapham, 1803–5, and one of the first Evangelicals to hold high ecclesiastical office, as Dean of Salisbury from 1823, had preached Venn's funeral sermon, 4 July 1813. Zachary Macaulay, writing to TBM from Oxford, 29 August 1813, says: 'I am here at Mr. Hugh Pearson's whose funeral sermon on Mr. Venn is just published. You may get a copy of it from Deighton's' (MS, Trinity). Presumably TBM had heard it delivered in Clapham church during his holidays. Years later, TBM recalled Pearson as 'a fawning Tartuffe' (Journal, XI, 116: 11 May 1857).

[5] Scarron made the request not of Marie de Médicis but of Anne of Austria, queen of Louis XIII. See Naomi Phelps, *The Queen's Invalid*, Baltimore, 1951, pp. 85–6.

TO SELINA AND JEAN MACAULAY, 25 OCTOBER 1813

MS: Huntington Library. *Address:* Mr. Macaulay / No 26 Birchin-Lane / London.

L[ittle] Shelford Octr. 25 1813

My dear Selina

I had always given you credit for good taste, and on this account I was a little, or rather not a little surprised to hear you pleading for a name like Frederic.[1] As if old England did not produce names for its inhabitants, you fly to Saxony and Prussia for names, which in themselves I do not think pretty. Yet do not think I am for Zachary or for Humphrey which I suppose papa intended as a burlesque upon Zachary. Is there no medium between the name of the Hero of a novel, and the waiter of an Inn? Name him Charles; or if you *will* give him a fine name, let it be a fine one indeed, such as Orlando, Hyacinthus, or Valentine.

My best respects to Mr. George.[2] Possibly if I can afford it, I may present him with a fiddle upon my return.

I ever remain etc.

My dear Jean

My sentiments about a name for little Master Anonymous Macaulay you have already heard. I am now going to write you a longer letter than I did last time according to your request, tho' I am afraid Selina will not be much pleased at my taking half of the sheet I intended for her to write to you. I shall be obliged to you, My dear Jean, for the History of Philip II of Spain[3] as soon as you can conveniently send it. This day I complete my thirteenth year. It is not kept, you may imagine, with any of "the Pomp and circumstance,"[4] with which it was at Clapham. I am in high hopes of capital fun on the fifth day of November. We have sent down for a great quantity of fireworks. We have got an immense pile of wood for a bonfire. And we are making all sorts of preparations.

I am much obliged to Mamma for her care of me with respect to the ale

[1] Charles Zachary Macaulay, ninth and last of Zachary Macaulay's children, was born at Clapham on 15 October and was baptized on 3 December. On 18 October Zachary Macaulay wrote to TBM that 'The House is strongly divided about a name for this nameless stranger. Mama says it shall be Zachary. I say – no – why should you afflict the boy with such a name? I prefer Humphrey to Zachary. Jean sides with Mama – but Selina goes to the West end of the Town for a name, and brings back Frederick; and carries with her all the other children except Margaret who says his name shall be "pretty Baby – sweet little Broder"' (MS, Trinity).
[2] A copy of this letter at Trinity, made by Fanny Macaulay, has a note identifying Mr. George as the dancing master.
[3] Probably Robert Watson, *The History of the Reign of Philip the Second*, 2 vols., 1777.
[4] *Othello*, III, iii, 354.

and nutmeg. How does Mamma go on? And Master anonymous? Give my love to Mamma, Papa, John, Henry, Fanny, Hannah, Meg.

Vale

Thos, B, Macaulay

TO SELINA MILLS MACAULAY, 4 NOVEMBER 1813

MS: Trinity College. *Address:* Mrs. Macaulay / No 26. Birchin- / Lane / London. *Partly published:* Knutsford, *Zachary Macaulay*, p. 309.

Little Shelford November / 4th 1813

My dear Mamma

I received your letter yesterday; and, to my great joy, found that you are so much recovered as to be able to renew your correspondence. I should have written before to day; and indeed I did write, and but that my epistle met with a misfortune, you would have received it to day, or to-morrow.

I should be obliged, if you, or the next member of the family who favours me with a letter, would inform me whether my uncle Colin is yet gone, or when he is going, or whether he prefers the pleasures of peace and tranquillity in Old England to fighting its battles, and earning the laurels of Victory in the vallies of the Pyrenees, or on the ramparts of Bayonne.[1] Time flies away so fast, that in six weeks I shall be packing up for my return and in less than a fortnight shall be commencing my examination studies. Our winter examination is much shorter and easier than our summer one.

There is just come here the son of Mr. Edwards of Lynn,[2] of whom I have often heard you and Papa speak. And also the son of the Revd: Mr. Hankinsson,[3] who has a rich living in Norfolk of fifteen hundred a year, and whose lands are only divided by a hedge from those of the invincible Margaret professor of divinity.[4] There has been a bible society established

---

[1] An undated letter from Hannah More in Knutsford, *Zachary Macaulay*, p. 284, says that Colin Macaulay 'has had a letter from Lord Wellington earnestly desiring him to join him in the Peninsula.' Wellington had entered France from Spain on 7 October 1813; the French army did not fall back on the citadel of Bayonne until 12 November.

[2] Edward Edwards (1766?–1849), Rector of St Edmund's, King's Lynn; an intimate friend of John Venn, he is said to have preached frequently at Clapham (Michael Hennell, *John Venn and the Clapham Sect*, 1958, pp. 130–1). His son, also Edward Edwards, B.A., Cambridge, 1820, died of tuberculosis, 1822.

[3] Robert Hankinson (1769–1863: *Boase*), Vicar of Walpole St Andrew, near Wisbech. His son, also Robert Hankinson (1798–1868: *Boase*), B.A., Cambridge, 1821, held livings in Norfolk, London, and Suffolk, and was Archdeacon of Norwich from 1857.

[4] Herbert Marsh (1757–1839: *DNB*), Lady Margaret's Professor of Divinity, Cambridge, from 1807; Bishop of Llandaff, 1816; Bishop of Peterborough, 1819–39. A rigid High Churchman, a long-time opponent of Simeon at Cambridge and a formidable controver-

under the very nose of this champion of the Anti-Biblical cause, who, I doubt not, thinks that he is upholding the cause of our venerable church, and may possibly [be] congratulating himself by applying to his own case the words of Milton

> "Amidst innumerable false, unmoved
> "His loyalty he kept, his love, his zeal."[1]

I am every day anticipating our fire-side pleasures in the Holidays.[2] I remember almost every little circumstance that took place in the summer. I have not forgot the Pears that John gave me the day before I came, nor Henry's eager desire to see the Blumbo, whom I hope he will again see before long.

My love to Papa, Selina, Jane, John, Henry, Fanny, Hannah, Margaret, Anonymous, – / I ever remain / My dear Mamma

Your affectionate Son
Thos B Macaulay

TO SELINA MILLS MACAULAY, 9 FEBRUARY 1814

MS: Trinity College. *Address:* Mrs. Macaulay / No 26 Birchin-Lane / London.

February 9. 1814.

My dear Mamma,

I received your letter yesterday while I was in the middle of a dull fit which I have thrice or four times a day.[3] To do justice to your Epistle it

sialist, Marsh had published a pamphlet in 1811 against the formation of an auxiliary Bible Society in Cambridge expressly because it 'sanctioned a union with dissenters and the circulation of the Bible unaccompanied with the liturgy' (*DNB*). A pamphlet war, particularly between Milner and Marsh, continued through 1813, but the Bible Society was established at the end of 1811: see D. A. Winstanley, *Early Victorian Cambridge*, Cambridge, 1940, pp. 18–25. TBM attended a meeting of the Cambridge Bible Society in 1813 (Journal, XI, 309: 11 May 1858).

[1] *Paradise Lost*, v, 898; 890.

[2] TBM returned to Clapham on 22 December (Zachary Macaulay to Kenneth Macaulay, 21 December 1813: MS, University of London).

[3] TBM had just returned to school after his Christmas holidays. On 24 January Zachary Macaulay wrote to Hannah More that 'Tom has given us much pleasure during his present sojourn with us. His passion for his Mamma and for the family circle is not at all diminished by absence. His very heart delights in home. We have had however a good deal to correct chiefly in manner since he has been with us – such as a loud and boisterous tone acquired among his school fellows. We have been labouring also to abate his self confidence, and his proneness unduly to estimate talent in others as compared with moral excellence. He has acquired too, partly I think from his associating so much with William Wilberforce, a tendency to laugh at whatever is capable of being made ridiculous in others – and therefore to caricature little faults and defects that he may laugh and make others laugh more heartily. He is however susceptible of monition, and the promptness of his compliance with every wish he hears expressed either by myself or his mother is very gratifying' (MS, Huntington).

completely dissipated my melancholy. – I am now recovered entirely from my cold, and the hoarseness does not trouble me any longer. Miss P[reston] desires me to mention that as I appear to be in good health she did not consider it necessary to put sleeves to my flannel-waistcoats.

An important domestic change has taken place here. The illustrious Miss Wa-a-afers, so universally admired for the amiable and unaffected simplicity of her manners, has given place to another of Mr. P:s' sisters, viz. the all-accomplished Miss Rebecca Preston.

By-the-bye, the Stainforth's are expected down at Shelford about the same time as you.[1] Do not, for the life of you come in a party, if you can help it. I want you to see my worthy preceptor not as he is when there are company at his house but in his true character which is that of a domestic man. I have read the Xtn: Observer's review of Norris twice over.[2] And I have both times felt my admiration for the talents of the writer increase; I cannot express how pleased I was with the severity of his sarcasms, and the modesty with which he defends his own character from the *demonstrations* of Mr. Norris. – I could not help saying to myself in Shakespeare's language as I read some of the assertions of that pillar of Orthodoxy. –

> "Call you this demonstrating your propositions? –
> "A plague upon such demonstrations?" –[3]

If ever Mr. Norris's zeal against the Bible Society should lead him to murder Lord Teignmouth,[4] which is not improbable, and he should be brought to trial, his friends may plead lunacy in his behalf in arrest of judgement, and produce this thick octavo as a proof. – I almost wish that this review had not been inserted in the Xtn: Observer, because I [think][5] that Mr. D[ealtry] ought to make it into a pamphlet, and publish it as an answer to the Curate of Hackney.

Sincerely wishing that the Said Curate may never be made a bishop, I

---

[1] Zachary Macaulay to TBM, 15 March, mentions plans for 'a tour to Shelford in the Summer' (MS, Trinity). It is still being discussed in May (Zachary Macaulay to TBM, 28 May: MS, Trinity).

[2] *Christian Observer*, XIII (January 1814), 37–60; a review of Henry Handley Norris, *A Practical Exposition of the Tendency and Proceedings of the British and Foreign Bible Society*, 1813, a High Church attack upon the Society. The reviewer was William Dealtry (1775–1847: *DNB*), Rector of Clapham in succession to John Venn. Norris (1771–1850: *DNB*), Perpetual Curate (later Rector) of St John's Chapel, Hackney, from 1809, made Hackney the High Church party equivalent of Clapham.

[3] Cf. *1 Henry IV*, II, iv, 165.

[4] John Shore (1751–1834: *DNB*), first Baron Teignmouth, Governor-General of India, 1793–8; resided at Clapham, 1801–8. He was the first president of the Bible Society, and is reported as saying that 'he would be content to be forgotten as Governor-General of India, if only he might be remembered as President of the Bible Society' (Howse, *Saints in Politics*, p. 113).   [5] Word obscured by seal.

take my leave of him and of you, with my love to Papa, the jilt and all the household; my best respects to Mr. Greaves, and to Mr. Dealtry. / I ever remain my dear Mamma

Your affectionate son

T B Macaulay

TO SELINA MILLS MACAULAY, 11 APRIL 1814

MS: Trinity College. *Address:* Mrs. Macaulay / No 26 Birchin-Lane / London. *Mostly published:* Trevelyan, 1, 49–50.

Shelford. Apr: 11. 1814.

My dear Mamma,

The news is glorious indeed. Peace! – Peace with a Bourbon, with a descendant of Henri Quâtre, with a Prince who is bound to us by all the ties of gratitude.[1] I have some hopes that it will be a lasting peace, that the troubles of the last twenty years may make kings and nations wiser.

I cannot conceive a greater punishment to Buonaparte than that which the allies have inflicted upon [him]. How can his ambitious mind support it? All his great projects and schemes which once made every throne in Europe tremble, are buried in the solitude of an Italian Isle. – How miraculously every thing has been conducted. We almost seem to hear the Almighty saying to the fallen tyrant. "For this cause have I raised thee up, that I might show in thee my power."[2]

As I am in very great haste with this letter, 1 shall have but little time to write. – I am sorry to hear that some nameless friend of Papa's denounced my voice as remarkably loud.[3] I have accordingly resolved to speak in a moderate key except on the undermentioned special occasions:

Imprimis. When I am speaking at the same time with three others.

2ndly. When I am praising the C[hristian] O[bserver].

3dly. When I am praising Mr. Preston or his sisters, I may be allowed to speak in my loudest voice, that they may hear me.

I saw to-day that greatest of Churchmen, that Pillar of orthodoxy, that inventor of theorems and Problems, that true friend to the Liturgy, that

---

[1] Zachary Macaulay wrote to TBM on 8 April that 'Bonaparte has thrown himself on the clemency of the Victors and...the Bourbons are proclaimed' (MS, Trinity). Napoleon abdicated on 6 April; on the same day the French Senate promulgated a royalist constitution. Louis XVIII had been in England since 1807.   [2] Exodus 9: 16.

[3] Zachary Macaulay wrote to TBM on 4 March that 'a friend' had 'received an impression that you had gained a high distinction among the young gentlemen at Shelford for the loudness and vehemence of your tones. Now My Dear Tom, you cannot doubt that this gives me pain' (MS, Trinity: Trevelyan, 1, 48). TBM's letter seems to be in reply to this, but the interval of more than a month is strange. TBM's letter is postmarked [1]3 April 1814 and is presumably correctly dated. Perhaps Zachary Macaulay misdated his.

mortal enemy to the Bible Society, – Herbert Marsh. DD. Professor of Divinity on Lady Margaret's foundation. I stood looking at him for about ten minutes, and invented an Hypothesis which I shall always continue to maintain that he is a very ill-favoured gentleman as far as outward appearance is concerned, that he has a nose like the beak of a Toucan, and that he has the most cross, sulky, aspect I almost ever beheld.

I am going this week to spend a day or two at Dean Milner's[1] where I hope, nothing unforeseen preventing, to see you in about two months longer.

Give my love to Papa and all the rest. / I ever remain my dear mamma,

Your affectionate Son,

T B Macaulay.

P.S. I have not had a letter from you for some time: Pray write soon.

TO SELINA MILLS, SELINA, AND JANE MACAULAY, [29 APRIL 1814][2]

MS: Trinity College. *Address:* Mrs. Macaulay / No 26 Birchin / Lane / London.

[Little Shelford]

My dear Mamma,

I mean by this single letter to pay off all that I owe to Selina, Jane, etc. and shall therefore split it into 3 parts, one for each of you. What would I have given to see the King of France enter London.[3] It was a day of triumph indeed, and crowned most gloriously the Events of the Year. What a scene for future Historians and Poets. It is a scene, however, I fear which we shall never see again.

I am much obliged to you for your kindness in offering me Lord Byron's Ode.[4] Stainforth made me a present of it Yesterday; – this is only one of the many instances of Kindness I have received from him; – I hardly ever saw such Kindness united with such Talents and Knowledge.

The Ode pleases me exceedingly. The passages that please me most are

> "If thou hadst died as honour dies,
> Some new Napoleon might arise,
> But who would climb the Solar Height
> To set in such a starless night."

[1] Zachary Macaulay to TBM, 22 April, refers to TBM's 'three days' at Milner's (MS, Trinity).
[2] Postmark of sending office dated 29 April.
[3] Louis XVIII, on his way to France, was officially received by the Prince Regent in London, 20 April.   [4] 'Ode to Napoleon Buonaparte' appeared anonymously on 16 April.

And again

> " The tumult and the Vanity,
> The rapture of the strife
> The EARTHQUAKE VOICE OF VICTORY
> To thee the breath of life."

What a grand metaphor is that "the Earthquake voice of Victory." The comparison between the late Emperor of the French, and Sylla I like. I cannot say I admire much that between him and Charles the Fifth. There is one couplet that strikes me

> "not till Thy fall could Mortal's guess
> ambition's less than littleness."[1]

To take leave of Lord Byron and Napoleon the ci-devant Emperor, I was much concerned to hear of the Battle of Toulouse, and yet I think it was a glorious ending of the Contest too. Lord Wellington's military talents seem to sink into nothing when compared with the Magnanimity and Forbearance which he displayed. He is indeed a Hero.[2]

After much talking and debating it has at length been all but decided that we shall go to Hayden.[3] This is not the least among the many and great advantages flowing from the peace.

We are now reading Clarkson's History of the Slave-Trade.[4] It interests me exceedingly. I am highly delighted with the character of Mr. Granville Sharpe.[5] Such noble boldness and zeal! Such self-devotion in the cause of liberty and justice! I think without depreciating the merits of Mr. Wilberforce, he holds a most exalted station among the Abolitionists. Think of a man at a time of life when the habits are formed, and when he was professionally engaged, spending all the time he could in studying the law that he might forward this great cause!

I hear that Mr. Wilberforce is deeply engaged at present in business re-

---

[1] The three passages quoted are from stanzas 11, 4, and 2.

[2] The battle of Toulouse was fought on 10 April 1814, Wellington not having received news of Napoleon's abdication. The battle was so fought as not to damage the city, and Wellington's men were received as deliverers.

[3] Not identified, though to judge from the conclusion of this letter, on the Isle of Wight. Preston was making preparations to leave Shelford. See 7 May 1814.

[4] Thomas Clarkson, *The History of the Rise, Progess, and Accomplishment of the Abolition of the African Slave-Trade by the British Parliament*, 2 vols., 1808. Clarkson (1760–1846: *DNB*) was the leader, outside of Parliament, of the agitation against the slave trade, as Wilberforce was within Parliament.

[5] Granville Sharp (1735–1813: *DNB*), scholar, philanthropist, and religious eccentric, had in 1772 secured the judgment in the Somerset case declaring slavery illegal in England after devoting two years of amateur and unpaid legal research to the question. He was a founder of the Abolition Committee, and inaugurated the Sierra Leone colony. Clarkson's account of him is in *History of the Abolition of the Slave-Trade*, I, 66–78.

specting the Slave-trade and I should be obliged to Papa to acquaint me with the nature of it.[1] / I ever remain, my dear Mamma,

Your affectionate Son
T B Macaulay

To Selina Macaulay. One of the High and Mighty Triumvirate of girls, member of the most Honourable Committee for circulating "the Bride of Abydos,"[2] Greeting. I am much obliged unto thee for thy Epistles, unto me sent, and by me received. I am about to tell unto thee a story which however strange it may appear unto thee, and though thou mayest think it a terry-diddle, is a very true fact.

Mr. Preston hath a gardener, and his name is Jennings. This man hath a sister. This sister hath a friend. This friend had a law-suit. She gained it. The sister of Jennings happening to be telling this story to a Lady whose servant she was, the Lady asked her straitly of her Kinsfolk, and learning that she had a brother named Jennings, said unto her "There is an Estate in Suffolk of six thousand a year named Acton place, that hath been in Chancery these 30 Years. The name of the late Proprietor was Jennings." The woman hereupon told her brother, and Jennings is now in a fair way of getting 6000 a year besides large property in the funds. The name of the Estate is Acton Hall. Jennings went to see it, and said that there were a Mort of Windows. Mr. Preston examined into it and thinks that Jennings hath hopes of getting the money.[3]

Farewell. / I ever remain my dear Selina

your affectionate Brother
T B M

Unto Jane Macaulay Greeting

My dear Jane,

I received your letter and made it out with out much difficulty. I think it contains a fine description of my Uncle Colin's taking you to Town. It lays things b[efore][4] one in so forcible a light. Allow me to paraphrase it.

---

[1] The Abolitionists were hoping to secure from the Allied powers assembled at Paris a general abolition of the slave trade. Zachary Macaulay was sent to Paris late in May as the party's agent, but without success: the Treaty of Paris secured the French slave trade for another five years. TBM's unpublished poem, 'The Vision,' [July] 1814, was written in reproach of the treaty (MS copy, Trinity).

[2] Published 29 November 1813.

[3] Preston's gardener did not get the money, if he ever applied. There were many claimants to the fortune of William Jennens, of Acton Place near Sudbury, West Suffolk, after his death in 1791. The house at the time TBM writes was described as inhabited only by 'an old man and woman' and as a 'deplorable spectacle of dilapidation' (John Britton, *et al., The Beauties of England and Wales*, XIV, [1813], 159).

[4] Obscured by seal.

"We had just sate down to lessons," to all that dull stuff [   ],[1] and geography, and stuff-a-nonsense, "when" O [sur][1]prize of surprizes, "a coach stopped at the door and in came Uncle Colin;" to crown all this "he took Selina etc. to town in a coach drawn by eight cream coloured horses"! This error amused me a little. You and the rest seemed to have intruded yourself into the Coach of the Regent. I found however that you had only made a little mistake in the Order and stops. I have appropriated so much room to Buonaparte, and Jennings that I have very little more left. You must let me say however that I am much pleased at going to the Isle of Wight. Give my love to Papa etc. / I ever remain / My dear Jane

Your affectionate Brother,

T B Macaulay

TO ZACHARY MACAULAY, 7 MAY 1814

MS: Trinity College. *Address:* Mr. Macaulay. / No 26 Birchin-Lane / London.

Shelford May 7. 1814. Saturday.

My dear Papa,

I did not receive your letter in which was enclosed Lord Byron's Ode for which I am exceedingly obliged to you, until some days after I had dispatched my *long letter*, as it had gone to Carmarthen instead of Cambridge.

The subjects for our Examination are not yet given out.[2] We are in daily expectation of them. I shall exactly follow the advice which you gave me with respect to my English Composition, and Exercises in general; – I shall take much pains with my Algebra, though it is the driest of dry studies. I do not include the Equations which really amuse me, and at the Holidays I hope I shall be able to find out any two unknown quantities, with sufficient Data. I must however allow that now and then they remind me of Misery Beresford's description of Algebra. "Says A to B "C". – Says C to D "E". – "No" says E "F." I demand who A was?"[3]

I am in high expectations of your promised visit. Miss Preston will I have no doubt bring out her best China tea-things, which have been collecting the dust ever since they came out of the maker's hands. I shall arrange my shelves to the best advantage, and perhaps borrow a few pictures to make the room gay. My bolt is really well-worth seeing; it is as strong as an Elephant and as thick as ever mortal man beheld.

---

[1] Obscured by seal.

[2] One of the subjects was the French Revolution; on 19 May Zachary Macaulay sent a collection of books and journals on that subject so that TBM might 'enter on hard fagging' (MS, Trinity).

[3] James Beresford, *The Miseries of Human Life*, II, [1807], 123. TBM's annotated copy of Beresford is in the library at Wallington Hall, Northumberland.

I congratulate my Uncle Colin upon the new honour heaped upon the Duke of Wellington. It was well done of the prince Regent not to change his name.[1]

Mr. Preston thinks of taking your hint about Dieppe. I hope however that we shall go to Hayden, for upon General Whale's[2] return, which is expected to take place very soon, Mr. Preston must change his quarters, and as there is no other convenient place to be had he must either go there or carry us about the country in a cart; – I should prefer the former. Possibly Mr. Preston might the latter.

I have been reading the Corsair[3] again. I am very curious to know whether Selina prefers it to the Bride of Abydos. I confess I prefer it even to Childe Harold. I hardly know of any Scene more grand that that when Conrad lies in the dungeon at Athens during the storm; when he drags himself to the grate and holds up his chains to attract the lightening.[4] What a picture! I know nothing like it in the bride of Abydos; – not even that sublime [   ][5] with which it opens "Know ye the land etc." – It is true that the Heroic Metre is not fitted for the song of the Pirate at the beginning, but the song notwithstanding is very fine. I think every Englishman might apply it to himself, rulers as we are of the sea,

> "Far as the winds can bear, the billows foam
> Survey *our* Empire and behold *our* home
> These are *our* realms; no limit to *our* sway
> *Our* flag the sceptre all who meet obey."[6]

Give my love to Mamma and the wee-things. / I ever remain, my dear Papa,

your affectionate son,

T B M

[1] Wellington was created Duke, 11 May.

[2] Preston's house at Shelford was the property of General Sir Charles Wale (1763–1845: *DNB*).

[3] Published in early February. On 28 February Zachary Macaulay wrote to TBM: 'I agree with you about the Corsair – the poetry is of the first stamp: but the characters are out of nature; and the moral is a blank' (MS, Trinity).

[4] Canto 3, stanza 7.

[5] Paper torn away with seal; one word of about five letters missing.

[6] Lines 3–6, evidently quoted from memory.

TO ZACHARY MACAULAY, 11 JULY 1814

MS: Mr Gordon N. Ray. *Address:* Z. Macaulay Esqr. (in Selina Mills Macaulay's hand).

[Brighton][1] July 11. 1814

My dear Papa,

We are arrived at Brighton and comfortably settled there, as I suppose Mamma's letter has before now informed you. We are as well off as we can be without your company. When are we to expect you here? Can you accompany my Aunt Babington[2] and Matthew?[3]

Yesterday we went to Lady Huntingdon's Chapel, and heard two very good sermons from one Mr. Muffin, a travelling Minister, I believe, who now officiates at Brighton.

We bathed to day for the first time; the baby,[4] I understand, put a very queer face upon the operation, and Fanny was actually petrified and overwhelmed by horror and amazement at finding herself precipitated from the tremendous height of the stairs of the machine (or, as Misery Beresford calls it) of the sea-hearse,[5] into the raging deep. The bathing women, I am informed, animated and encouraged them to take the dreadful leap, by blandishments of a very remarkable kind. When Henry made his appearance upon the stairs they saluted him thus " Come my darling, come my pretty prince, come my King, Come, *defence of his country.*"

I have not yet seen enough of this fashionable town to be able to give you any account of what is now going on in it. The Steine[6] is a rare medley; – Generals, and Drummers, and Deserters, and bathing-women, and Peeresses, and Quakers, and masters, and misses, and Sailors, are taking the air perpetually in its walks. I have heard that there are from twenty to thirty thousand persons at Brighton who are not stated inhabitants. I suppose we may expect his royal Highness the Prince Regent, as the Pavilion is now being repaired and done up.[7]

I was very sorry to hear of your tooth-ache. It is an additional reason

---

[1] 'Selina and her nine Children are at Brighton while our house at Clapham is painting and I have come in to Mr. Babington's house in town' (Zachary Macaulay to Kenneth Macaulay, 27 July: MS, University of London). In the years before Zachary Macaulay's financial troubles Brighton became almost a second home to his family. About 1820, after a succession of summers there, he took a house at 36 Bedford Square, Brighton, where (until 1823?) his wife and children spent a part of each year.

[2] See Introduction: Mrs Thomas Babington.

[3] Matthew Babington (1792–1836), third son of Thomas Babington, was a banker in Leicester.

[4] Charles: at the end of this letter TBM's mother has added a note in which she says 'dear Charles would have done exactly as a model, for a statue of surprize, when the [*word illegible*] bathing woman took him in her arms.'

[5] *The Miseries of Human Life,* II, 15, 'Dialogue the Fourteenth.'

[6] The square adjoining the Pavilion at Brighton.

[7] The Regent did not arrive in Brighton until 17 August.

however for coming to Brighton, and for taking the benefit of our fine sea-breezes, our ample beach, and our noble Cliffs.

I think I can venture to join with my own love the loves of Mamma, and all the youngsters who are at their favourite amusement of *shell*[*ing*][1] *pease*, which I dare not interrupt. / I ever remain, / my dear Papa,

Your affectionate Son,
Thos B Macaulay

TO ZACHARY MACAULAY, 13 JULY 1814

MS: Trinity College. *Address:* Mr. Z. Macaulay / Thomas Babington's Esqr. / No. 17 Downing Street / Westminster (in Selina Mills Macaulay's hand).

[Brighton] July 13 1814

My dear Papa

I never heard that the misfortune of being [   ][2] Son of a Minister, or of a Patron was the exact [   ][2] which debars a man from civil or Ecclesiastical [prefer][2]ment. I hope that the circumstance of being [   ][2] the Editor of the Christian Observer will [not i][2]mpede the admission of my works into it.[3]

I received your kind letter to day. I shall [take][2] my first lesson in writing on Friday, as no writing master is procurable till then. I shall certainly exert myself to the utmost, less, on account of the reward which you have been so kind as to promise me, than through a real desire of giving pleasure to you, and Mamma.[4] / I ever remain, / My dear Papa,

Your affectionate Son
T B Macaulay

TO HANNAH MORE, 27 JULY 1814

Text: Extracts in Sotheby's Catalogue, 4 April 1955, item 163, 3 pp. 4to: dated Brighton, 27 July 1814.

We are at present at this town, the Queen of watering-places, and the paradise of the idle. I think it the dullest, laziest, most indolent place I ever saw. Three fourths, at the very least, of the visitors here spend their time in

---

[1] Letter torn.

[2] Part of the right-hand edge of the letter is torn away, affecting a word or part of a word in six of the first seven lines of the MS; a tear on the left edge affects two words.

[3] See Appendix.

[4] TBM's 'execrable' handwriting was a particularly annoying fault to Zachary Macaulay (Trevelyan, I, 66). It is just possible that the lessons were a preparation for TBM's indexing of the *Christian Observer*.

conjugating, as Thiebault says, the verb s'ennuyer through all its moods and tenses[1]. . . .

Have you seen Scott's poem upon that subject [Pitt][2]. . . . It is a most beautiful little piece. It is very short and has not received the last polish, but it is uncommonly spirited and pathetic. I will present you with two stanzas. . . .

TO ZACHARY MACAULAY, 25 AUGUST 1814

MS: Trinity College. *Address:* Z Macaulay / No 26 Birchin-Lane / Cornhill / London.

Aspenden Hall[3] August 25. / 1814

My dear Papa,

I am a little better in spirits[4] and I shall be a great deal better if I receive from you a favourable answer to what I am going to communicate. Your friends here send you and Mamma hereby an invitation to Aspenden Hall, at any time you choose. From the words which Miss Preston used to me, she seemed to wish that it might take place about the beginning of October or even earlier. I told her that I had hopes of your visiting your friend Mr. William Smith,[5] and I said that I hoped you would visit us also at the same time. Surely you would not disoblige a Lady. And I hope that you will not refuse the invitation only because I happen to be here.

I received yesterday your letter and that of Miss Hannah More.[6] I send you back within this letter her very kind present of a 2£ note. It must be

---

[1] The anecdote, from Dieudonné Thiebault, *Mes Souvenirs de vingt ans de séjour à Berlin*, 1806, is quoted as the motto to Maria Edgeworth's *Ennui* (*Tales of Fashionable Life*), 1809, where TBM probably found it.

[2] 'Song, for the Anniversary Meeting of the Pitt Club of Scotland,' 1814. TBM's own 'Lines to the Memory of Pitt,' though dated 1813 in T. F. Ellis, ed., *Miscellaneous Writings of Lord Macaulay*, 1860, II, 378, were written in the summer of 1814 (Zachary Macaulay to Hannah More, 26 December 1814: MS, Huntington).

[3] Preston removed from Little Shelford to Aspenden (or Aspeden) Hall, near Buntingford, Hertfordshire, in the summer of 1814. The present Aspenden Hall is not the one TBM knew, which was demolished in 1850.

[4] Writing to Hannah More on 23 August Zachary Macaulay says that TBM left Clapham for school on the 20th: 'his first letters which have just reached us dwell only on the agonies of a four months seclusion from those he loves' (MS, Huntington).

[5] William Smith (1756–1835: *DNB*), Whig M.P. for Norwich 1802–6 and 1807–30. Smith was born and resided at Clapham, was an active associate of Wilberforce against the slave trade, and is therefore, although he was a Unitarian and opposed to the Tory politics of most of Wilberforce's friends, included in Sir James Stephen's canonical essay on 'The Clapham Sect.' His country residence, from 1812, was Parndon House, near Harlow, Essex.

[6] 19 August: she writes that 'I am in sad arrears to you for a book. You must have something by which to remember me now we are so long without meeting. Buy it with the enclosed' (MS, Trinity).

laid out upon a book, as she gave it for that purpose, though I could have
wished that there had been no restrictions. I am divided between three
books, and I leave it to your decision which I should have. The first is
Adolphus's continuation of Hume and Smollett.[1] This I cannot have unless there be an edition of it in the small duodecimo form, like the Hume
and Smollett which Uncle Babington[2] gave me, and bound in the same
manner, i.e. in calf. If there be such an edition, and you think that I ought
to have the book, I will send up a volume of my Hume that they may be
bound alike. The second book is Corneille's Dramatic works, which upon
the whole I should prefer to Adolphus. The third book I had rather have
than either of the other two, because some of the extracts from it which I
have read seem to me to be written in the purest style and with the most
pointed wit and humour. I mean Molière's Comedies. I never heard that
there was anything immoral or improper in the book; – I am sure there
was not in the extracts from it which I read. Not knowing, however,
whether it is quite proper for me to have it or not, I leave it entirely to you
to determine between the three books.

I expect a letter from Mamma shortly. The great coat about which she
was so anxious is found. When, or where, or how, I know not. I troubled
myself with nothing but the simple fact. I shall be very desolate when
Blundell is gone. At present I could manage without him; for I can sit and
read in my room. But in the winter when tha[t is][3] impossible on account
of the cold, I shall be forced to go and sit by the fire solus, or worse than
solus, with fellows who are like Tony Pasquin in Gifford's Baviad, "Within all brickdust, and without all brass."[4] This, you must remember, is
private and confidential.

Give my love to Mamma etc. / I ever remain My dear Papa

Your affectionate Son

T B Macaulay

Please to send down my Bland's Algebraical Problems.[5]

[1] John Adolphus, *History of England from the Accession of George III to the Conclusion of Peace in 1783*, 3 vols., 1802. A copy of the 1810 edition was in TBM's library: Sotheby's Catalogue, Macaulay Sale, 4 March 1863, item 184.
[2] See Introduction.
[3] Paper torn away with seal.
[4] William Gifford, *The Baviad*, 1794, verses in note to line 190.
[5] Miles Bland, *Algebraical Problems*, 1812.

TO SELINA MILLS MACAULAY, 26 OCTOBER 1814

MS: Trinity College. *Address:* Mrs. Macaulay / No 26. Birchin-Lane / London.

[Aspenden Hall] October 26th. 1814.

My dear Mamma,

I am both concerned and surprised that Papa should have found necessary to charge me with remissness in writing. I sent off a letter to you on Wednesday morning last, which would have reached you on Thursday. If it miscarried I most certainly am not to bear the blame.

Well then! – I am fourteen years old. The return of that memorable Æra brings with it many pleasant and many painful recollections. I cannot but smile when I remember my ninth birthday, upon which as I took a walk with you upon the Common I expressed my wonder, and actually doubted whether it could be really true that I was nine years old. The thoughts which struck me upon that reflection I cannot express better than in the Latin of my favourite Horace. Papa must construe it to you.

> "Immortalia ne speras monet annus et almum
>   Quae rapit hora diem.
> Frigora mitescunt Zephyris; – ver proterit æstas
>   Interitura simul
> Pomifer Autumnus fructus effuderit, et mox
>   Bruma recurrit iners."[1]

I like Smollett less and less the more I read of him. He has a ridiculous mixture of levity and anti-fanaticism whenever he mentions religion. He seems to use it and superstition as terms perfectly synonimous; – for instance in one of his Characters he says some such thing as this "He was ambitious, enterprising, and *religious.*"[2] He has a most furious invective against some misguided men who displeased him by carrying a bill in the house of Commons against "exercising the militia and volunteers on Sunday, which they gave the fanatical appellation of The Lord's day."[3] Things of this sort are more disgusting, (to me at least), than even the broad and shameless Scepticism of Hume, who in his history of the great Rebellion[4] puts religion at the head of the political engines which an able

---

[1] *Odes,* IV, vii, 7–12.

[2] There is no passage quite like this in Smollett, but perhaps TBM means the summary of the character of William III at the end of chapter 6, *History of England,* new edn, 1841, I, 383–4.

[3] *Ibid.,* ch. 26, III, 311.

[4] The first installment of Hume's *History of England,* published as *The History of Great Britain* [under the House of Stuart], 2 vols., Edinburgh, 1754–7. I find nothing explicit in Hume's *History* resembling the view here attributed to it.

governor should employ, and honestly avows, at least by fair inference, that that is its only use.

England has certainly been unfortunate in her Historians. Till the appearance of Hume's history it was her reproach that the best account of her Kingdom was written by a foreigner Rapin-de-Thoyras.[1] And now when one of her own children has produced a History equal to any of the Classical Models in elegance, and, except as far as regards religion, superior to them in authenticity, it is disgraced by the utter want of religious principle. This is a disadvantage, I think, not only as it tends to misrepresent those subjects in comparison of which history is unimportant, but as it takes away from the interest of the work. Livy and Herodotus believe [a]ll[2] the stories of their Jupiters and [Minerva]s[3]; – so that in reading their histori[es][2] we see that they enter into the spirit of the time, and yet can separate between what is true and what is false. Hume discards or omits every-thing about religion, except a very little which he distorts and misrepresents. I think that History should not only be pleasant and authentic, as Critics say, but that the Historian should not be entirely cold and incredulous upon the most important topic in every point of view that ever occupied the attention of man.

I did not perceive that I had filled 3 sides of a page with this stuff. To answer your interrogatories. I did not tell you how to send parcels when you asked last time, because when I wrote I expected to dine with Papa the next day; – The parcels are sent by the Cambridge coach which passes through Buntingford. There they are left, and transmitted to "the young gentlemen at the big Hall on the Hill."

Give my love to Papa, Kenneth,[4] Selina, Jane, etc. Thank them in my name for the "many happy returns" which I am sure they wish me. / I ever remain, My dear Mamma

Your affectionate Son

T B Macaulay

---

[1] Paul de Rapin Thoyras, *Histoire d'Angleterre*, 8 vols., The Hague, 1724.

[2] Paper torn away with seal.

[3] Part of initial 'M' and terminal 'va' remain in MS.

[4] The Sierra Leone Kenneth (see 30 September 1811). He arrived in England in September, probably for the inquiry into his conduct as Superintendent of Recaptured Slaves which led to his dismissal from the post for negligence in 1815. He returned to Sierra Leone in 1815 as agent for Macaulay and Babington.

TO SELINA MILLS MACAULAY, 14 NOVEMBER 1814

MS: Trinity College. *Address:* Mrs. Macaulay / No 26. Birchin-Lane / London.

Aspenden Novr. 14. 1814

My dear Mamma,

Before we enter upon anything else, I must beg to know the meaning of what Jane says, "Papa has got a bad pain in his Shin." Neither you, nor Selina, nor Papa himself in his letter which I received yesterday, make the least mention of it. Pray satisfy me about this.

As to my not having been sufficiently explicit and clear in my directions to the mode of directing parcels to me, ASPENDEN HALL is so well known that if you were to direct to it with nothing to guide the post-boy but Hertfordshire; ten to one I should receive it.

I have got the works of the most high mighty and puissant black-a-moor's Ambassadors and Secretaries of State,[1] for which I most heartily thank Papa; they have amused me much, and as I read them with a good-deal of care, have been of more use to me as to my French than any book which I have read for a long time. I really cannot find expressions strong enough for the ridiculous absurdity of the Scheme which the French have formed. The Ambigu, some Numbers of which Papa was so kind to send me, seems to be perfectly sensible of the madness of the undertaking.[2] After mentioning Limonade's[3] work, it adds, "Il paroît que ces Princes ne veulent guères se réduire à la condition des esclaves, ni soumettre leur flancs illustres aux coups du fouet."[4] –

I admire very much that paper of the Times which replies to the

---

[1] TBM means Henry Christophe, King Henry I of Haiti, and his ministers. On the conclusion of peace with the Allies, the French colonial interests were hopeful of reconquering Haiti, and some of the wilder proposals spoke of annihilating the population if necessary. Christophe's ministers published several proclamations and manifestoes in 1814, demanding recognition of their country's independence and vowing the readiness of the Haitians to fight. The abolitionists in London were active in publicizing these official statements, intended to make it clear that the French hope of regaining the lost colony was futile.

[2] *L'Ambigu, ou Variétés Littéraires et Politiques*, a journal published thrice monthly in London for French *émigrés*, edited by J. G. Peltier. In September and October 1814 it published a number of documents from both the French colonial party and the Haitians, taking a strong stand against the French plan of reconquest.

[3] Julien Prévost, comte de Limonade, Haitian minister of foreign affairs and secretary of state, the author of Christophe's public statements. 'Le nom du ministre Haytien fera peut-être sourire quelques personnes disposées à tourner tout en raillerie. Nous observons à cet égard que le quartier de Limonade d'où le ministre d'Hayti a reçu son nom, est un des plus riches et des plus fertiles de la plaine du Cap' (*L'Ambigu*, 20 September 1814, p. 669).

[4] No such remark follows any of the references to Limonade in *L'Ambigu*. The only passage at all resembling it is quoted from an article by M. Malte-Brun in *Le Spectateur*: 'Les empereurs, les princes, les géneraux noirs ne sont nullement disposées à déposer leurs brillants uniformes, et à livrer leur illustre personne au fouet d'un colon' (*L'Ambigu*, 30 October 1814, pp. 239–40).

animadversions of the French Papers upon the conflagration of the City of logwood Palaces.[1] It is I think humorous, convincing, and eloquent. Though I only know it through the Medium of L'Ambigu,[2] yet it seems to me, even in its translated condition, to be the best specimen of Newspaper-writing that I ever read.

I shall be very happy to see Kenneth, and so, I dare say, will William Wilberforce. But pray use all your interest with Papa to get him to visit me. Is there really some insurmountable obstacle? – Are the black Ambassadors still under his inspection?

I am very much obliged to you for offering to send me a pair of fleecy Hosiery. I shall, if you please, avail myself of the alternative, or rather, if it be not inconvenient, keep both pairs. Kenneth can b[ring][3] them, you know, even if he comes alone, but pray do your best with Papa. Give my love to him, to Kenneth, and to all the Children. Thank Selina and Jane, from me, for their letters. If it were not that our examination is upon the point of being given out I would answer them. I hope to do it when the 1st Hurry is over.

I ever remain, my dear Papa[4]

Your affectionate Son
T B Macaulay

TO HANNAH MORE, 16 JANUARY 1815

Text: Facsimile in Arthur Roberts, ed., *Letters of Hannah More to Zachary Macaulay*, 1860, opp. p. 68.

Clapham January 16th. 1815

My dear Madam,

My Mamma was on the point of writing to inform you that a supposed favourable alteration has taken place in Mr. Henry Thornton's[5] case. His physicians are still sanguine in their expectations, but his friends, who examine his disorder by the rules of common sense, and not by those of

---

[1] *The Times*, 6 October 1814, p. 3. The British burned Washington, D.C., 24–5 August.

[2] *L'Ambigu*, 10 October 1814, pp. 68–72, together with extracts from the *Journal des Débats*, 1 October 1814, and the *Journal de Paris*, to which *The Times* article is a reply.

[3] Obscured by seal.   [4] Thus in MS.

[5] Thornton (1760–1815: *DNB*) died of tuberculosis at Wilberforce's house in London on the day this letter was written. A banker and M.P. for Southwark, 1782–1815, Thornton was born and resided at Clapham, where his house at Battersea Rise was the meeting place of the Clapham Sect councils. He was the most active of the directors of the Sierra Leone company and the person upon whom Zachary Macaulay, when governor of the colony, most depended. Zachary Macaulay admired Thornton beyond even Wilberforce, and in the authoritative judgment of Leslie Stephen's life of Thornton in the *DNB*, he 'represented the best type of the classes from which was drawn the strength of the early evangelical movement.' There is a sympathetic account of Thornton in E. M. Forster's biography of Thornton's eldest daughter, *Marianne Thornton*, 1956.

medecine are very weak in their hopes. The warm bath has been pre-scribed, and it is the wish and prayer of all who know him that so excellent and valuable a Character may be preserved to the world.

You will believe, my dear Madam, that no one rejoices more than I do at your recovery from the effects of the fatal accident which threatened us.[1] Events like these prove to us the strength of our affection for our friends, and show the esteem in which great characters are held by the world.

We are eagerly expecting the promised essay,[2] which will indeed be a most important addition to the literary History of the year eighteen-hundred-and-fifteen, ample as that already is. Every eminent writer of poetry, good or bad, has been publishing within the last month, or is to publish shortly. Lord Byron's pen is at work over a poem as yet nameless.[3] Lucien Buonaparte has given the world his Charlemagne. Scott has pub-lished his "Lord of the Isles, in six Cantos," a beautiful and elegant poem, and Southey his "Roderic the last of the Goths." Wordsworth has printed "the Excursion" (a ponderous Quarto of five-hundred pages) "*being a portion of the intended Poem intitled the Recluse.*" What the length of this intended poem is to be, as the Grand Vizier said of the Turkish poet, "n'est connu qu'à Dieu et à M. Wordsworth." This forerunner however, is, to say no more, almost as long as it is dull; not but that there are many striking and beautiful passages interspersed; but who would wade through a poem

—————"Where perhaps one beauty shines
"In the dry desart of a thousand lines."[4]

To add to the list, my dear Madam, you will soon see a work of mine in print. Do not be frightened; it is only the Index to the XIIIth volume of the Christian Observer, which I have had the honour of composing. Index-making, though the lowest, is not the most useless round in the ladder of literature; and I pride myself upon being able to say that there are many readers of the Christian Observer who could do without Walter Scott's works, but not without those of, / My dear Madam,

Your affectionate friend,

Thomas. B. Macaulay.

P.S. Give my love to your sisters, if you please, and to my Aunt Thatcher,[5] if still with you. My mamma has just now received her letter.

---

[1] Late in 1814 Hannah More had narrowly escaped burning to death when her clothes caught fire.

[2] *An Essay on the Character and Practical Writings of St. Paul,* 2 vols., 1815.

[3] *Hebrew Melodies,* 1815.

[4] Cf. Pope, *Epistle I,* Book 2, 111.

[5] Mary Mills Thatcher (d. 1816), the widowed eldest sister of Selina Mills Macaulay.

TO SELINA MILLS MACAULAY, 31 JANUARY 1815

MS: Trinity College. *Address:* Mrs. Macaulay / 26 Birchin-Lane / Cornhill / London.

Aspeden-Hall / January 31. 1815.

My dear Mamma,

Here I am once more. Neither ill nor well, in that state of comfortless indifference which, with me, always follows separation from home. But, thanks to the inventor of letters, or to the inventor of postage! I can communicate to those whom I love best, what I think and wish and feel without any more restraint than if I were talking to them.

Do not believe what Waller and Theocritus write about their Corydons and Damons and Daphnises and Strephons dying of the pains of absence from the neat-handed Phillis or the charming Delia. The pains of that absence are most severe which parts a schoolboy from home.

Again do not give any credit to the supposed violence of the "maladie du pays" of the Swiss Mountaineer.[1] It was nothing – nothing at all to be compared to my "maladie du Clapham," any more than the Chicken-pox to the Small pox.

I am delighted, though I am sure I am not in a most delightful mood, at sundry changes which the school has witnessed since last half-year. Do not mention what I am going to say for the world, or as nurse would more poetically express it "for the Hindees of Gold." Wilson, a young Gentleman neither burthened with a superfluity of sense nor of good-nature, is gone. Not being blessed with the power of enduring insult or injury even from him though much my senior, I was the unhappy being on whom he vented all the acrimony and fury of his temper. And I was generally beaten or taunted by him ten times a day. Though I was much too wise and perhaps a little too *proud to let him perceive that I felt or heeded what he chose to do, yet I assure you my silence did not give consent. He is gone at last. And now I venture to tell you what while he was here I could not do. I thought that all my dislike of school was owing to the fear of meeting him. But alas!

> "How small, of all that school-boys' hearts endure
> The part that schoolfellows can cause or cure."[2]

Mr. Preston has promised us a prolongation of our Xtmas holidays for the future; Malden and Smith,[3] both new boys, (for we have now two

[1] See Boswell, *Life of Johnson,* 23 September 1777.
[2] Cf. Samuel Johnson, lines 429–30 added to Goldsmith's 'Traveller.'
[3] I cannot identify Smith. Henry Malden (1800–76: *DNB*) became Professor of Greek at the London University (later University College), 1831–76. Malden kept pace with TBM in academic competition from the time he entered Preston's school until 1824, when he was elected with TBM to a Trinity fellowship. He was one of the Cambridge group, with TBM,

Smiths) seem to me very amiable and intelligent. The school is beginning
to rise. I was afraid that [   ]¹ over. This half year has brought m[e
some] pleasant companions, to several of who[m I] talk upon politics or
literature w[ithout be-]ing laughed at or misunderstood. [To be] sure I
have had schoolfellows, [who confoun-]ded poetry and politics, because
they [both] began with p and had the same n[umber] of syllables.

I must beg you, my dearest Mam[ma, to] send me, instantly, without
a m[oment's de-]lay, the key of my box. I was i[n conster-]nation when I
missed it. And if it [please] you I should be obliged to you for Gibbon, as
I have now got an admirable set of shelves, for books. / I ever remain /
(with love to Papa, Kenneth, Cousin Bell,² and every body else)

your affectionate son
T B Macaulay.

* proud –
N B. I mean proper pride. – The second sort of pride.

O SELINA MILLS MACAULAY, 22 MARCH 1815

MS: Trinity College. *Address:* [Mrs. Mac]³aulay / [No. 26] Birchin / Lane / [Lo]ndon.

Aspeden Hall. March 22nd. / 1815.

My dear Mamma,

I really ought to beg pardon for being so late with my acknowledgements for your two last letters, but as, you know, ours is not a correspondence of ceremony, and as all my letters to Papa go to you strict observance of regularity is not necessary. I am very comfortable here. I say only
comfortable, for you know what are my opinions about happiness. Malden,

contributing to *Knight's Quarterly Magazine,* and he later wrote a little for the *ER.* Though
they were thrown closely together for nearly a decade of school and college, Malden and
TBM were never unreserved friends. By all accounts, Malden was shy, precise, and fastidious. On 24 May 1831 Margaret Macaulay reports that TBM 'talked of his old friend and
schoolfellow Mr. Malden. He said he was a very religious man, very scrupulous: "He had
scruples about writing in the *Edinburgh Review,* scruples about going into the Church,
scruples about everything but allowing me to pay his debts"' (*Recollections,* p. 220). TBM's
valedictory comment on Malden occurs in his Journal for 26 August 1852, after Malden had
paid a visit to him at Clifton: 'Esteem there is, and good will; and on my side a great sensibility to old recollections, and a great effusion of feeling. But he, though an excellent fellow,
is so dry and cold that he never uttered, as far as I know, a word indicative of tenderness in
his life. In old days I always had to make all the advances; and so it is still' (Trevelyan, 2nd
edn, II, 322).
¹ The right edge of the sheet is torn away, affecting one or two words at the end of each of
twelve of the next thirteen lines.
² A cousin of Zachary Macaulay; she died at his house in 1816.
³ Half of the second sheet is torn away, taking part of the address with it.

the young gentleman who called at our house, as, I suppose you remember, is a boy of uncommon abilities and application. We are already pretty intimate, and as he possesses very extensive knowledge of history and of modern poetry, his conversation is amusing to a high degree.

Having not much to say to you, and if I had much, not having time to say it in, for Mr. Preston works us so hard that we have not time to think, I shall just transcribe Lord Byron's piece upon his royal Highness the Prince Regent passing between the bodies of Charles I and Henry the Eighth.[1] Malden told it me.

> "Fam'd for their civil and domestic jars
> Here heartless Henry lies by headless Charles.
> Between them see another wretched thing;
> It lives; it moves – aye! every inch a King!
> Charles to his people, Henry to his wife,
> Behold the double monster start to life.
> Justice and truth have mixed their dust in vain,
> Each royal Vampire breathes on earth again.
> The deep recesses of the tomb disgorge
> Two such to make a Regent and a George."

I dare not hope to see you this half year. But Mr. Preston asked me the other day if we were to hope for Papa's company this half-year. I wish Papa would, if possible, I dare hardly hope it, come down on Easter Monday or Tuesday. I should then have several days for him. And if he could go down to Cambridge! – But I am afraid that I am dreaming.

Was there ever such a man as Buonaparte?[2] All my detestation of his crimes, all my horror at his conduct, is completely swallowed up in astonishment, awe, and admiration, at the more than human boldness of his present attempt. "May Heaven defend the right."

The supper bell is ringing; therefore, with love to Papa etc. I ever remain my dear Mamma

Your affectionate Son
T B Macaulay

---

[1] 'On a Royal Visit to the Vaults,' [1813]. There are two versions of these lines in E. H. Coleridge, ed., *Works of Byron: Poetry*, VII, [1904], 35–6. Neither version had been published by 1815, but the lines had been widely circulated. TBM's text is closer to the second version, not published until 1903, but differs from that in all but one line. The occasion of the verses was the opening, superintended by the Prince Regent, of the coffin of Charles I in the vault of Henry VIII, Windsor, 1 April 1813.

[2] Napoleon landed from Elba at Cannes, 1 March, and had entered Paris on 20 March to begin the Hundred Days.

TO ZACHARY MACAULAY, 10 APRIL 1815

MS: Trinity College. *Address:* Mr. Macaulay / No 26 Birchin-Lane / London.

April 10. 1815 / Aspeden Hall

My dear Papa,

As you desire me to write every week, I sit down for that purpose, though, like Socrates who only knew that he knew nothing, I can only say that I have nothing to say. I am pressed for time, having another Declamation in hand, and if I had not been burdened with this aditional load, news is so scarce in this quarter of our planet that I should only be able to say that I am well, that I give my love to mamma etc., and that I ever remain, / My dear Papa,

Your affectionate Son,
Thomas Babington Macaulay.

TO SELINA MILLS MACAULAY, 17 APRIL 1815

MS: Trinity College. *Address:* Mrs. Macaulay / No 26. Birchin-Lane / Cornhill / London.

Aspeden. April 17. 1815

Ma chère Maman,

J'espére que vous ne seriez pas fachée de recevoir une lettre dans cette langue si utile, dont je me sens un très grand avancé depuis quelques semaines, quoique, comme notre ami Angus Morrison a dit, M. Chastelain ne veut point que je me persuade que mon progrès a été le fruit d'une très-grande application.

J'ai lu cette brochure de mon Papa que M. Wilberforce m'a apportée. Que j'admire ce morceau-là. "Docteur Thorpe certainement connoît mieux que moi si son inimitié envers moi est occasionée par mon refus de lui prêter une somme de l'argent."[1] Que M. Thorpe brédouille ses mensonges. Magna est veritas et prævalĕbit.[2]

---

[1] Zachary Macaulay, 'A Letter to His Royal Highness the Duke of Gloucester,' 1815, p. 6: 'Whether, also, my refusal to comply with the earnest application of Dr. Thorpe for the loan of a sum of money, has had any influence on his feelings towards me, is, of course, best known to himself.'

Robert Thorpe, an Irish barrister, was appointed chief justice of Sierra Leone in 1808, though he resided there only from July 1811, to March 1813. In February 1815, he published 'A Letter to William Wilberforce,' accusing the Sierra Leone Company, the African Institution, Wilberforce, and, particularly, Zachary Macaulay, of seeking commercial gain and even the perpetuation of slavery behind the pretense of philanthropic concern for Sierra Leone. A pamphlet battle between Thorpe and his opponents, continuing through 1815, received wide publicity because it coincided with the efforts of the abolitionists to secure a

Avez-vous vu Guy Mannering,[1] l'œvre nouveau de l'auteur de Waverley. Nos papiers le "Times" et le "Courier"[2] l'ont annoncée. Il faut que vous l'aviez vu. Qu'en sentez-vous?

Avez-vous vu le Messiah de Klopstock.[3] Je vous serois infiniment obligé, si vous obligeriez vous-même par la lecture de ce livre si célebre, et peut-être justement. Rien n'est parfait; – Et certainément Klopstock ne l'est pas. Mais pour examiner ses sentimens, sa diction et sa figure, selon les regles d'Aristote, il est un grant poëte. Encore lisez-le, je vous prie.

J'avois oublié quand j'étais chez nous de faire remporter à M. Greaves sa Vie de Johnson par Boswell.[4] Je vous serez bien obligée de la rendre. Je lis à present les Georgiques de Virgile, et Tacitus, en Latin; en Grecque, Euripide et Thucydide. Rien n'est égal a Tacitus. Sa genie me paroît de ressembler beaucoup à celle de Lord-Byron. Euripide ne me plaît pas. Il peut etre un grand poëte moral; mais pour le comparer avec Shakespeare, c'est une sottise. Il est aussi inférieur a ce grand génie qu'il est superieur à Lord-Thurlow.[5] Sa dialogue est misérablement ennuyante; ses Chorus sont de Galimatias aussi obscur que pompeux.

Je n'ai rien, je crois, de vous dire de plus. Et j'intends cette lettre autant pour m'improuver moi-même que pour vous transmettre les nouvelles de ce lieu, si on peut appeller par ce nom les évènements d'une place qui est autant separée du monde que l'île de Robinson Crusoe. Donnez mon amour, (un François auroit dit, donnez-les assurances de ma très haute considération,) à Papa; –

Je reste toujour, Ma très chère maman,

Votre fils très affectionné,

T B Macaulay.

---

slave registration bill for the enforcement of the abolition act of 1807. Thorpe was dismissed from his judgeship in March 1815. The charges brought by Thorpe against Macaulay were repeatedly taken up by others after the campaign for the emancipation of the slaves began in 1823.

2 3 Esdras 4: 41; praevalet. (*From opposite page.*)

---

1 Published 24 February.

2 A Tory evening paper with a large circulation among clergymen.

3 Friedrich Gottlieb Klopstock, *Der Messias*, 1748–73.

4 In one of his education minutes written in India TBM says that he first read Boswell's *Johnson* when he was given a copy as a school prize book about this time: 'I never was better pleased than when at fourteen I was master of Boswell's Life of Johnson, which I had long been wishing to read. If my master had given me, instead of Boswell, a Critical Pronouncing Dictionary, or a Geographical Class book, I should have been much less gratified by my success' (Trevelyan, I, 411).

5 Edward Hovell-Thurlow (1781–1829: *DNB*), second Baron, whose poems were damned by Thomas Moore in the *ER* for September 1814, and burlesqued by Byron.

    In 1850, after dining with TBM, Lord Carlisle noted in his journal that 'the greatest marvel about him is the quantity of trash he remembers. He went off at score with Lord Thurlow's poetry' (Trevelyan, II, 194).

TO SELINA MILLS MACAULAY, 12 JUNE 1815

MS: Trinity College. *Address:* Mrs. Macaulay / No 26. Birchin-Lane / Cornhill / London.

[Aspenden Hall] June 12th. 1815

My dear Mamma,

Wednesday or Thursday next will begin the important contest. I wish it would come quick: for, as Lord Nelson used to say when he expected a battle shortly, "I do'nt like to have these things on my mind."[1]

There have arisen doubts about the Speaking. Miss Preston tells me her brother thinks that there will be none, Robert Hankinson, a very good Orator, having been forced to go home for illness, N.B. not the Cambridge Fever. I myself, happy in an almost complete indifference, can express an impartial opinion. I think that there will be no speaking. Unless I write again you may suppose that *there will be* Declamations, and come, according to your former intentions either on next Saturday or on the Monday following for the Speaking takes place, if it does take place at all, on Tuesday. I shall write again if any resolution be announced to the contrary.

I am so busy that I have no time to think. So that instead of thinking twice before I speak or write once, I am forced to write twice without thinking at all. If therefore I should not write twice as ill as usual it will be a true miracle. I dare not turn over the sheet, as I feel I should fill it if I did and I am in too much hurry to breathe. Love to Papa etc. Receive the concise Roman adieu. Vale. I turn over the sheet with all imaginable speed to tell you that at last it is determined that there is to be *no* speaking. I shall write again to tell you how I shall come back. / I ever remain / My dear Mamma

Your affectionate Son

T B Macaulay

TO C. HUDSON,[2] 22 AUGUST 1815

Text: Composite of copies at Trinity and in possession of Mrs Mary Moorman. *Address:* Mr. C. Hudson / Examiners Office / East India House / London. *Partly published:* Trevelyan, I, 55–6.

Aspeden Hall, Herts. August 22nd 1815

Dear Sir,

The correspondence which you have desired me to open will, I am sure, be productive of much satisfaction and profit to me, and in one sense to

---

[1] Southey, *Life of Nelson,* 1813, II, 235.

[2] A John C. Hudson is listed as a clerk in the office of the Examiner of Indian Correspondence, East India Company (*Royal Kalendar,* 1815). Perhaps, through Charles Grant (see next note), he had met TBM at Clapham. But the history of this correspondence, which TBM begins immediately upon his return to school, is evidently unknown even to Trevelyan.

you; for my letters without giving you much entertainment, will teach
you the art of deciphering hands, an art, as I understand, very requisite in
a Secretary of Mr. Grant.[1]

The Spectator observes, I believe in his first paper, that we can never
read an author with much zest unless we are acquainted with his situation.[2]
I feel the same in my epistolary correspondence; and supposing that in
this respect we may be alike, I will just tell you my condition. Imagine a
house in the middle of pretty large grounds, surrounded by palings. These
I never pass. You may therefore suppose that I resemble the Hermit of
Parnell:

> As yet by books and swains the world he knew,
> Nor knew if books and swains report it true.[3]

If you substitute newspapers and visitors for books and swains you may
form an idea of what I know of the present state of things. Write to me as
one who is ignorant of every event except political occurrences. These I
learn regularly: but if Lord Byron were to publish melodies or romances,
or Scott metrical tales without number, I should never see them, or perhaps hear of them, till Christmas. Retirement of this kind, though it pre-
cludes me from studying the works of the hour, is very favourable for the
employment of "holding high converse with the mighty dead."[4] And I
am sure that we gain more by being compelled to study, and to study
thoroughly, Pope, and Milton, and Shakespeare and Dryden, the giants of
British Poetry, the formers of the British Language, and the correctors of
British taste, than by 'preying upon the garbage,'[5] which daily pours
forth, in hot-pressed octavos, and splendid Quartos, from the London
Press.

I know not whether "peeping at the world through the loopholes of
retreat"[6] be the best way of forming us for engaging in its busy and active
scenes. I am sure it is not a way to my taste. Poets may talk of the beauties
of nature, the enjoyments of a country life, and rural innocence: but there
is another kind of life which, though unsung by bards, is yet to me infinitely superior to the dull uniformity of country life. London is the place
for me. Its smoky atmosphere and its muddy river charm me more than

---

[1] Another Clapham resident, Charles Grant (1746–1823: *DNB*), was a member of the Court
of Directors of the East India Company from 1794 and Chairman in 1805, 1809, and 1815.
His special concern, 'a cause emphatically Claphamic' (Stephen, 'The Clapham Sect,' *ER*,
LXXX, 343), was the campaign to introduce a Church establishment and Christian missions
into India. In 1805, the year in which he was first Chairman of the Court, Grant offered
Zachary Macaulay a place in the office of the Examiner of Indian Correspondence (where
James Mill later worked), but Macaulay refused on the grounds that too much of his time
would be claimed (Knutsford, *Zachary Macaulay*, p. 263).

[2] No. 1, first sentence (Addison).   [3] Cf. Thomas Parnell, 'The Hermit,' 22–4.

[4] James Thomson, *The Seasons*, 'Winter,' 431.

[5] *Hamlet*, I, v, 57.   [6] William Cowper, *The Task*, II, 88–9.

the pure air of Hertfordshire, and the crystal currents of the river Rib. Nothing is equal to the splendid varieties of London life, "the fine flow of London talk," and the dazzling brilliancy of London spectacles. Such are my sentiments, and, if ever I publish poetry, it shall not be pastoral. Nature is the last goddess to whom my devoirs shall be paid.

I must now conclude with begging you to tell William Babington that I shall speedily write to him. Remember me kindly to him and Samuel.[1]

Yours most faithfully

Thomas B Macaulay

TO SELINA MILLS MACAULAY, 23 AUGUST 1815

MS: Trinity College. *Address:* Mrs. Macaulay / 26 Birchin-Lane / London. *Mostly published:*
Trevelyan, I, 57–9.

Aspeden Hall. August 23d. 1815

My dear Mamma,

You perceive already in so large a sheet, and so small a hand the promise of a long, a very long, letter; larger, as I intend it, than all the letters which you send in an half-year together. I would likewise hint to you that a letter from home would be very acceptable to me; Papa's four or five lines only mocked me with the sight of his hand. I have again begun my life of sterile monotony, unvarying labour, the dull return of dull exercises in dull uniformity of tediousness. But do not think that I complain.

> "My mind to me a Kingdom is,
> Such perfect joy therein I find,
> As doth exceed all other bliss
> That God or nature hath assign'd."[2]

Assure yourself that I am philosopher enough to be happy, I meant to say not particularly unhappy in solitude; but man is an animal made for society. I was gifted with reason, not to speculate in Aspeden Park, but to interchange ideas with some person who can understand me. This is what I miss at Aspeden. There are several here who possess both taste and reading, who can criticize Lord Byron and Southey with much tact and "savoir du metier;" – But here it is not the fashion to think.

Hear what I have read since I came here. Hear and wonder! I have in the

---

[1] William Babington (1790–?) and Samuel Babington (1792–?), were the sons of Thomas Babington's brother William, Rector of Cossington, Leicestershire. Both were clerks in the London office of the East India Company.

[2] The version of Sir Edward Dyer's 'My Mind to Me a Kingdom Is' found in William Byrd, *Psalms, Sonnets and Songs of Sadness and Piety*, 1588.

first place, read Boccacio's Decameron, a tale of an hundred Cantos. If you remember, Boccacio was the first of the Italian, and indeed of the European writers who dispelled the darkness of the middle ages. If I remember right he wrote AD 1380, about a century, you see, before the invention of printing. He is a wonderful writer. Whether he tells in humorous and familiar strains the follies of the silly Calandrino, or the witty pranks of Buffalmacco and Bruno, or sings in loftier numbers

> "Dames, Knights, and arms, and love, the feats that spring
> "From courteous minds and generous faith," – [1]

or lashes with a noble severity and fearless independances the vices of the monks and the priestcraft of the established religion, he is always elegant, amusing, and, what pleases and surprises most in a writer of so unpolished an age, strikingly delicate and chastised.[2] I prefer him infinitely to Chaucer. If you wish for a good specimen of Boccacio, as soon as you have finished my letter, which will come, I suppose, at dinner time, send Jane up to the library for Dryden's poëms among the British Poets, and you will find among them several translations from Boccacio, particularly one entitled "Theodore and Honoria."

But, truly admirable as the bard of Florence is, I must not permit myself to give him more than his due share of my letter. I have likewise read Gil-Blas, with unbounded admiration of the abilities of La Sage. Malden and I have read Thalaba together, and are proceeding to the Curse of Kehama. Do not think however that I am neglecting more important studies than either Southey or Boccacio. I have read the greater part of The history of James the First,[3] and Mrs. Montague's Essay on Shakespeare,[4] and a great deal of Gibbon. I never devoured so many books in a fortnight. John Smith, Bob Hankinson, and I went over the Hebrew Melodies together; – I certainly think far better of them than we used to do at Clapham. That entitled "When coldness wraps this suff'ring clay," that beginning "My soul is dark," the "Destruction of Sennacherib," "Oh weep for those," "the Wild Gazelle," and some others whose names I cannot at present recal are among the happiest effort of Lord Byron's Genius. Papa may laugh, and indeed he did laugh me out of my taste at

---

[1] Ariosto, *Orlando Furioso*, I, i, 1–2; the translation is close to, but not identical with, that of John Hoole, 1773.

[2] As a writer in *Notes and Queries*, 14 October 1876, p. 305, observes of this passage, 'Of a truth, *puris omnia pura*; but it is hard to conceive how the story of the Nightingale, the relation of the manner in which a certain hermit and his female convert "put the devil in hell," or that particular "folly of the Silly Calandrino," where his friends persuade him that he is with child, can have seemed "strikingly delicate and chastized."'

[3] Perhaps Sir Walter Scott's edition of the *Secret History of the Court of King James the First*, 1811.

[4] Elizabeth Montagu, *An Essay on the Writings and Genius of Shakespear*, 1769.

Clapham, but I think that there is a great deal of beauty in the first melody "She walks in beauty," though indeed who it is that walks in beauty is not very exactly defined. My next letter shall contain a production of my muse entitled "an inscription for the column of Waterloo," which is to be shown to Mr. Preston to morrow[. Wha]¹t he may think of it I do not know. But I am [like]¹ my favourite Cicero about my own productions. It is all one to me what others think of them. I never like them a bit less for being disliked by the rest of mankind.

Mr. Preston has desired me to bring him up this evening two or three subjects for a Declamation. Those which I have selected are as follows. 1st, a Speech in the Character of Lord Conningsby impeaching the Earl of Oxford.² 2ndly, an Essay on the Utility of Standing armies. 3dly, an Essay on the policy of Great Britain with regard to continental possessions.

I conclude with sending my love to Papa, Selina, Jane, John, ("but he is not there," as Fingal pathetically says, when in ennumerating his sons who should accompany him to the chase he inadvertently mentions the dead Ryno),³ Henry, Fanny, Hannah, Margaret, and Charles.

Valete.

T B Macaulay.

TO C. HUDSON, 30 AUGUST 1815

Text: Composite of copies at Trinity and in possession of Mrs Mary Moorman. *Address:* C. Hudson Esq / Examiners Office / East India House / London.

Aspeden Hall, Herts. August 30th 1815

My dear Sir,

I must beg you to receive the following as an apology for a longer letter which an unexpected accession of business hinders me from writing. When I find time to answer your interesting letter you shall have a most bitter attack on your rich, and virtuous Anglo-Indians. I must check myself or I shall fill the sheet on this theme.

Yours most affectionately,

Thomas B. Macaulay

¹ Paper torn away with seal.
² On 14–15 October Zachary and Selina Macaulay visited Aspenden to hear TBM declaim in the role of 'Coningsby impeaching Harley, Earl of Oxford, for blasting Marlborough's laurels by the Peace of Utrecht' (Knutsford, *Zachary Macaulay*, pp. 325–6).
³ James Macpherson, 'Fingal,' Book 6, in *The Works of Ossian*, 3rd edn, 1 (1765), 119.

Inscription for the Column of Waterloo

Britons, attend, these trophied tow'rs proclaim
The field of blood and triumph, grief and fame,
When on the Belgian plains, to rise no more,
Napoleon's star of Conquest set in gore.
   In vain th'usurper led his myriads forth,
Red from the havoc of the vanquish'd north,
On ev'ry brow relentless vengeance sate,
Determin'd pride, and constancy of hate.
But false the tyrant's boast, and fruitless there,
The fire of rage, the madness of despair; –
The host of Britain pierc'd the vast array,
And swept their armies and their hopes away;
For more than mortal arms their wish supplied,
And Heav'n contended on the juster side.
O still let glory's just rewards repay
Th'unnumber'd Heroes of that well-fought day,
Nor be their praise forgot whose cold remains
Unhallow'd moulder on the Belgian plains,
Who in the face of danger dauntless stood,
And shed for Britain's cause their dearest blood,
Who liv'd to guard her, and who died to save,
The field their home, their deathbed, and their grave.
Tho' holy earth entombs not those who fell,
Tho' theirs no pompous train, no funeral knell,
Tho' o'er the simple mould that forms their grave
No sculptur'd marble vaunts, no banners wave,
Yet theirs Britannia's praise, affection's tear,
And glory show'rs her laurels on their bier.
   Thou too, the Muse's theme, thy country's pride,
Before whose sword, in fiercest danger tried,
Napoleon's vaunted legions roll'd away,
Like dewy mist before the blaze of day,
This column, emblem of thy well-earn'd fame,
To future ages shall record thy name.
As rearing to the clouds its stately form
It mocks the thunder and defies the storm,
Derides the tardy ravage of decay,
And stands unmov'd, while ages glide away,
So, Wellesley, shall thy fair renown defy
The waste of time, the blasts of Calumny; –

And when this pile to which thy deeds we trust
Shall sleep o'erthrown in nameless, noteless dust
Still unextinguish'd shall thy glory shine,
All earth its temple every heart its shrine.

This is the latest effort of my muse, and therefore ought in common reason to be the best. You asked for a specimen. I think, after this, it will be long before you ask again.

TO SELINA AND JANE MACAULAY, 23 OCTOBER 1815

MS: Trinity College. *Address:* Mr. Macaulay / No 26 Birchin Lane / Cornhill / London.

Octr. 23d. 1815. Aspeden Hall.

My dear Selina,

I am going to sit down to write you and Jane each a good long Epistle. I am glad to find that you and Georgiana[1] mean to "lie by", for some time, as you phrase it. After a stupendous exertion of genius repose is necessary. I shall not determine precisely how long you ought to forbear from entering the lists of Parnassus. – I would only repeat an admonition which I before gave you; – It is as ridiculous to think of composing P O Ë T R Y (I do not mean by poëtry tag rhymes) without having diligently studied the grand models, as it would be for Margaret to begin writing before she can read. – I would likewise again beg leave to remind you, though perhaps you may think my advice both harsh and useless, that there may be found better correctors for your first essays in poetry than a silly school-girl, without sense or imagination, who cuts out patterns for Sunday school-children, and admires Eumēnes more than any of the Captains of Alexander.[2] – Seriously, my dear Selina, I would wish to ask you what you learn from a connection with such a companion. – Listen and revere the words which follow; for it is Lord Bacon who speaks, the man who knew the human mind better than all others who ever lived. "No man" (or woman, I assure you, Selina) "no man ever attained to eminence in talents or virtue who was fond of the company of his inferiors in either."[3] – I do not consider it as a compliment to you or to any body to say that you are not inferior to Georgiana in talents, and as for virtue! – alas! alas!–

---

[1] Georgiana Stainforth (d. 1870), George's sister.
[2] See Plutarch's life of Eumenes.   [3] I cannot find such a passage in Bacon.

When I return at Xtmas I shall bring with me a little edition of Pope's Homer, which I shall positively insist on reading with you. You a poëtess! – and not know whether Troy was a man or a city! –

I made a few attempts to revive my Italian last week, but found it, I am sorry to say, utterly gone. I am resolved to attempt it seriously when I come home. Spanish may be deferred a few years. But I have fully resolved never to read Don Quixote except in the original.[1]

How goes on Rollin? – Who built Sicyon? Who were the four Sons of Tophet that peopled Greece? At what o'clock used Caesar to sup?[2] – These are Questions which I shall have to ask soon.

Farewell
T B M.

My dear Jane,

A thousand, or as our French master would say, a milliard of pardons for my neglect. Poor, unhappy, man that I am! Are all the ladies up in arms against Tom Macaulay? The two poetesses whom I satyrized are preparing to tear off my head like poor Orpheus's, if you ever heard of such a man, and to send it

"Down the swift Hebrus to the Lesbian shore."[3]

While my old ally, my sister Jane, falls on me with more fury than both together. Misericorde! misericorde! Pardon a poor unhappy fellow who swears never to offend so vilely again if you will but forgive him this once. You insist upon an apology. Accept it in an extempore effusion of verse, whose style I think approaches something to that of Selina's poetry.

"Now kneeling down upon one leg
I do your pardon humbly beg,
If you do not poor Tom forgive,
Poor Tom will surely cease to live.
Now my loud shrieks will strike your ear
"And now the screech-owl o'er the bier."

---

[1] Margaret Macaulay, *Recollections*, p. 209, in a passage perhaps wrongly dated 30 March 1831, reports TBM as saying that he lacks the courage to attempt Spanish. Later, in an undated passage perhaps from 1832, she writes that TBM is 'spending the vacation in studying Spanish' (p. 263). If TBM was just beginning the study of Spanish as late as 1832, he must have broken his vow never to read *Don Quixote* in the original, for he praises the novel in his 'Dryden,' *ER*, XLVII (January 1828), 6, saying that 'every school-boy thumbs to pieces the most wretched translations' of the book. He told Greville in 1841 that he had 'read Don Quixote in Spanish, five or six times' (*Memoirs*, ed. Strachey and Fulford, 1938, IV, 438).

[2] I assume that this is a joke. Rollin does not say who built Sicyon; the sons of Javan, not Tophet, are said to have peopled Greece; and as for Caesar, he 'passed whole nights in feasting with Cleopatra.' See Rollin, *Ancient History*, 18th edn, 1827, II, 159; VI, 389.

[3] Milton, 'Lycidas,' 63.

Better at Waterloo to fall
"Killed by the murd'rous Cannon ball; –"
Then in my grave to rest contented
And be with Monodies lamented,
Than like a lark to tumble down
Shot flying by my sister's frown; –"

This is I think the style of Selina's poetr[   ]¹
She disdains your corrections te[   ]
they are too good [   ]
impertinent, [   ]
upon her co[   ]
that I, Tom[   ]
of Aspeden [   ]
ted amo[   ]
which[   ]
in al[   ]
pro[   ]
re[   ]
m[   ]

TO C. HUDSON, 15 NOVEMBER 1815

Text: Composite of copies at Trinity and in possession of Mrs Mary Moorman. *Address:* C. Hudson Esq / Examiners Office / East India House / London.

Aspeden Hall, Herts. Novr. 15. 1815.

My dear Sir,

   May your company never have a worse advocate. I almost had changed my opinion in reading your letter and had begun to think that it was as virtuous and beneficent an institution as the world could boast. But I considered pretty attentively your defence of it; and I found in one part a slight flaw, which you must pardon me for grasping at. I am ready to allow you that the Eastern princes are as great wretches as the earth produces. But if we abhor cruelty and feel a disgust at arbitrary power in a country where to be born a prince is to be born a monster, what shall we say to the Heroes and Statesmen who have conquered and governed India in the name of Britain, the rapacious Clive, the imperious Hastings, the lavish Wellesley, the intriguing Minto, and the desperate Moira. For

¹ The sheet has been torn diagonally from the center right edge to the lower left corner, affecting at least thirteen lines.

desperate his Lordship certainly is, and sets the Empire of British India to hazard with as much nonchalance and I fear with as ill luck as he rattled the dice-box at Carlton House.[1] But let the company see to that. He has made peace, I was happy to see from your letter before the intelligence reached us by the newspapers. Oh that I were the Rajah of Nepaul! I would make the world ring with the desperation of my resistance to these forgers of chains for the nations of the East.

But to bid farewell to a company which I so much respect and admire; I suppose you have seen the third volume of Cowper's Poems.[2] Indeed it was out last Midsummer; but I had not time to read it. There is trash enough in that book to destroy any reputation for poetry less firmly established than Cowper's. All the neglect of Lord Thurlow[3] and the abuse of Miss Seward[4] have not done the poor poet so much harm as the ill-judged zeal of this friend! I believe I have closed the unhappy volume for the last time; – Homer may be allowed to nod occasionally. But for Cowper to snore through a whole volume! It is actually intolerable.

There are two or three Poets of the last century of established reputation whom nobody reads through. At least I myself could never wade through them. Akenside, I think, I would instance as one; Shenstone as another. I half tremble at putting down the great name of Thomson as a third. I do not know what you will think of my taste. But Akenside though frequently sublime, is in my idea far too metaphysical for poetry. Shenstone's verses are as smooth as cream, but they have not the nervous strength for which our language is calculated. And Thomson, poetical as he is, is not the poet for me. Men and manners, the camp, the court, the city, and the senate, are the subjects which interest and enchant my vulgar taste. Lovers blasted with lightening, a peasant buried in the snow, or the story of Boaz and Ruth done into blank verse with poetical names, do not please my fancy or excite my attention. Spring, Summer, Autumn and

---

[1] War had been declared on the Gurkhas of Nepal, 1 November 1814. A British victory in May 1815 had compelled the Nepalese to sue for peace, but it was not until March 1816 that a treaty was signed.

[2] *Poems, by William Cowper...Vol. III. Containing His Posthumous Poetry, and a Sketch of His Life by His Kinsman John Johnson*, 1815. Only vol. 3 of this edition was published.

[3] Edward Thurlow (1731–1806: *DNB*), first Baron Thurlow, 'neglected' Cowper in failing to offer him a place on being made Lord Chancellor in 1778 and in failing to acknowledge Cowper's present of his first volume of poems, 1782. Cowper's letters to William Unwin on these matters appeared in William Hayley, *Life of Cowper*, new edn, 1806, I, 149–50; II, 28–31.

[4] A characteristic example of Miss Seward's 'abuse' of Cowper, in the style that fascinated TBM by its badness (see Appendix IV in Trevelyan, 1908), is this: 'Cowper's Task, which the generous reader of poetic susceptibility at once censures and adores: O! that such a master of the metaphoric, the allusive, the scenic, and the pathetic graces, should so often lay them aside to whip the follies of the age with an iron-rod, sometimes mistaking good for evil propensities, as when he satirizes the amiable warmth of encomium upon the talents it reveres!' (*Letters of Anna Seward*, Edinburgh, 1811, I, 128–9.)

Winter, are good subjects for the sonnets of a young scribbler of rhymes. But four books! – I believe Thomson reckoned too much upon the power of his Muse if he imagined that four books of still scenery or of rural life could interest those who were accustomed to Shakespeare's pictures of the Heart, and Pope's gorgeous and enchanting prospects of the town. Candidly – did you ever read the Seasons twice through? Many seasons will pass, I fear, before I shall.

I was never more completely out of patience with the country than at present. I happened to stumble upon a piece of poetry by no less a person than Sam: Rogers, who to his shame ought to have known better. The wishes of this elegant poet bound themselves to a farm, a church-steeple, a flock, a crook, a blue apron for his Lucy etc. etc. etc. etc.[1] You may suppose the necessary concomitants to these insignia of the pastoral Muse.

I have just seen Scott's Waterloo.[2] I think of it very highly indeed. Added to the rapid and resistless fury of his description, there is a tender pensiveness thrown over it, which mellows the tints without weakening them. The simile of Napoleon to a winter current swolen by streams, falling back into a narrow brook when deprived of these auxiliaries is appropriate and noble.[3] The address to the stream of time which concludes the poem is very grand. –

Yours most affectionately

T. B. Macaulay.

TO ZACHARY AND SELINA MILLS MACAULAY, [4? MARCH 1816][4]

MS: Trinity College. *Address:* Mr. Macaulay / No 26 Birchin Lane / Cornhill / London.

Aspeden Hall.

My dear Papa⎫
    Mamma⎭

I am in daily expectation of the long promised parcel, and shall begin to think rather ill of your punctuality unless it is speedy. I am very well in every respect, and as busy as is necessary. I have read the whole of Simonde

---

[1] 'A Wish,' *Poems*, 1814.

[2] TBM recalled in his Journal for 11 May 1858 that, after attending a meeting of the Cambridge Bible Society in 1815 'I bought at Deighton's Scott's Waterloo, just published, and read it on a frosty journey back to Aspenden Hall' (Trevelyan, II, 429). The poem was published *c.* 21 October.

[3] Stanza 14.

[4] Postmark of the receiving post office dated 5 March 1816.

Sismondi on the Literature of the South of Europe,[1] on which I shall now proceed to criticize. –

It is in the first place a very amusing, and in the second a very instructive work; – the style is very agreable, and the taste which its criticisms display, very good. The morality is pure and unexceptionable. The author is liberal enough towards us poor Heretics out of the pale of the Roman church, to which of course he belongs, though once or twice I had almost set him down for a Heretic himself.[2]

One of the great benefits of reading is to find out how much we know, that is, in other words, how little we know. I have found out, in Sismondi, authors mentioned and quoted and criticized as men of the most transcendent genius whose names I hardly knew before. One of these is the Italian Poet, Vittorio Alfieri. I knew his name and no more. From Sismondi's account, he appears to be a poet of the highest class.[3] Another is Calderon de la Barca. And to conclude, I knew hardly any thing of Lope de Vega himself except that his countrymen thought him a great Genius, and that he thought himself so.

But what do you think[4] of "the Siege of Corinth," and of "Parisina."[5] The former, I think, has very feeble passages, but has also very great beauties. There is excessive affectation throughout it, and affectation of the most disagreable kind. Take as an instance, though it contains some powerful lines, the whole description of the dinner of the dogs upon the dead bodies.[6] But the Eleventh and the Last Stanza are unrivalled for beauty. – Parisina is certainly a piece of very great poetical merit. I think that it contains some of the finest passages which I ever read, passages which, like the gleam of the evening sun upon the axe which was to behead Hugo, "shine with a clear and ghastly glitter,"[7] and strike terror while they dazzle the reader. The last verse is very fine. It is Lord Byron's forte. The rooted despair of Azo is rendered more horrid by the calmness with which he bears his agony. – As to the morality of the poem, it is sub-

---

[1] J. C. L. Simonde de Sismondi, *De la Littérature du Midi de l'Europe*, 4 vols., Paris, 1813. Apart from his high reputation as an economist and historian, Sismondi may have been recommended to TBM as a favorite of Clapham. He was one of the group in Geneva, including Auguste de Staël and Etienne Dumont, who supported Wilberforce's anti-slave-trade agitation on the continent. Sismondi published pamphlets on the question in 1814 and 1815 and had some correspondence with Zachary Macaulay in connection with them. In 1819 he married a sister-in-law of Sir James Mackintosh, another of the abolitionists. TBM, meeting Sismondi in 1831, found him 'ugly' but sustaining 'his high character by his conversation' (Margaret Macaulay, *Recollections*, p. 220).

[2] Sismondi was a Protestant.

[3] In 'Criticisms on the Principal Italian Writers. No. 1. Dante,' *Knight's Quarterly Magazine*, II (January 1824), 211, TBM describes Alfieri as the restorer of Italian literature and calls *Filippo* and *Saul* 'the greatest poems...of the eighteenth century.'

[4] The MS reads 'you the think.'   [5] Published together on 7 February.

[6] 'Siege of Corinth,' stanza 16.   [7] 'Parisina,' line 425.

ject to some discussion. People must determine from their own feelings whether the penitence of Hugo, who c[erta]¹inly dies with much piety b[e suf]¹ficient to counteract the bad impression which the connection of great vices with dazzling qualities produces. Besides, upon second thoughts, Hugo seems to have been not over and above sorry for his guilt. He forgives his father. I do not see what he had to forgive him. This however I leave to the cognizance of the Christian Observer. And I remain, my dear Parents

Your affectionate Son
Thos. B Macaulay.

TO SELINA MILLS MACAULAY, 30 MARCH 1816

MS: Trinity College. *Address:* Mrs. Macaulay / No 26. Birchin-Lane / Cornhill / London.

Aspeden Hall. March 30. 1816.

My dear Mamma,

I am now most graciously devoting a half hour to write to such a very bad correspondent as you are. I believe, indeed I do not believe but am certain that it is about three weeks since I heard from home. Write when you have time; and till then you must be contented with receiving no more letters from me. For though it is a very great pleasure to me to write home, yet like all other pleasures it must be often denied to us in this world of contretemps.

As to Mr. Marryatt, I have thoroughly enjoyed the trimming he has received at the hands of Mr. Stephen.² Papa is a little too merciful,³ which however is no fault. Mr. Stephen has one most admirable note; that in which he pretends to prove that Mr. Marryat was not author of the Thoughts by showing how inconsistent that work is with his former

¹ Paper torn away with seal.
² James Stephen, 'A Defence of the Bill for the Registration of Slaves...Letter the First,' 1816, a reply to [Joseph Marryat], *Thoughts on the Abolition of the Slave Trade*, 1816, in which Marryat (1757–1824), chairman of the committee at Lloyd's, M.P. for Sandwich, and colonial agent for the islands of Grenada and Trinidad, repeated the charges against the African Institution, Wilberforce, and Zachary Macaulay made earlier by Robert Thorpe (see 17 April 1815).

James Stephen (1758–1832: *DNB*), a member of the Clapham Sect, Master in Chancery, and leading abolitionist. He was the most intransigent of Wilberforce's coadjutors and had just resigned his seat in Parliament because the government refused to support the Slave Registry Bill.
³ No reply to Marryat's first pamphlet by Zachary Macaulay is known. *The Christian Observer*, xv (March 1816), 189 [American edn] notices a pamphlet with the same title as Marryat's and calls it 'an Exposure of some of the numerous Mistatements and Misrepresentations Contained in a Pamphlet Commonly known by the name of Mr. Marryatt's Pamphlet.' It is possible that Zachary Macaulay wrote this 'Exposure.'

principles;[1] – Certainly it appears that his *thoughts* differ widely from his professions.

Glory to the House of Commons! Glory to the men who listened *for once* to the voice of the nation of which they are called the representatives![2] But glory above all to the ministers who loved their places so much better than their pledge that they stayed in after declaring that they would stand or fall with their darling child, the lovely, the enchanting, Property tax. Their partiality for their babe reminded me of Gay's admirable fable. – The nation and the Opposition were exclaiming.

> "What a squinting leer,
> "No doubt the fairy has been here."
> "The folks are blind" Vansittart cries
> "I see wit sparkle in his eyes."[3]

The Ministers seem to have forgotten the words "no longer" in their declaration that they would continue in place "no longer" than the property tax should exist. But this is no wonder seeing they forgot the same words in their bill about that very tax.[4] – Christiana in the Pilgrim's progress says at going up the hill of Difficulty, if I remember right, "This is a losing place. Here Christian lost his roll, and here we lose our bottle of cordials."[5] We may well say of the property tax, "This is a losing place. Here the ministry lost their honour, their temper, their supplies, and very nearly their places too." So much for the vilest of all taxes. And now, my dear Mother, with love to all to whom love is due,

Farewell

Signed   T B Macaulay

---

[1] 'Defence of the Bill,' pp. 21–24n.

[2] The government's proposal to continue the property – or income – tax for another two years had been defeated in the Commons, 18 March, following a flood of petitions against it got up by Brougham and Alexander Baring. The tax was opposed because it was regarded as a war tax that ought not to be continued after the peace, because of the general distress at the time, and because businessmen resented having to open their financial affairs to the tax officials.

[3] Cf. Fable 3, lines 19–22, in *Fables, First Series*. Nicholas Vansittart, as Chancellor of the Exchequer, was responsible for the bill in the Commons.

[4] 'The words with which the act had formerly closed "and no longer," which declared the tax should terminate with the war, had been omitted in the act of last year' (speech of Vansittart, 27 February 1816, *Hansard*, XXXII, 880).

[5] *Pilgrim's Progress*, Part 2: Mercy, not Christiana, is the speaker.

TO SELINA MILLS MACAULAY, [21? APRIL 1816][1]

MS: Trinity College. *Address:* Mrs. Macaulay / No 26 Birchin-Lane / Cornhill / London.

[Aspenden Hall]

My dear Mother,

I trust that the innumerable things which I have had to do of late, such as declamations etc. will excuse a silence which perhaps you may think too long. I would beg leave however to remind you that you are not the very best of Correspondents. I never reproach you with this, and I think I may claim equal indulgence, especially as this letter will not be worth the postage when it arrives.

You have heard of course of the abominable, unmanly, conduct of the Peer-poet to whom we once paid such admiration.[2] Once I may say for since his late actions I feel as little respect for his character as for that of Dr. Thorpe or Mr. Marryatt. Have you seen "Paul's letters to his Kinsfolk"?[3] They are Walter Scott's, and so of course good. I have not seen them yet, but hear them highly spoken of. –

And now, after long and anxious consideration I cannot find a word more to say. When you write to me and give me something to reply to, you may reckon upon a folio sheet. Henry Babington[4] is well, but a little too hard worked, in my opinion, which is partly his own, and partly (though unintentionally,) Mr. Preston's fault. I am one of those who think exercise of the body unnecessary, provided sufficient relaxation be allowed to the mind. But Henry has very little of either.

Give my Love to Papa etc. etc. / And believe me, My very dear Mother,

Your most affectionate progeny,

Thomas Babington Macaulay.

P.S. When Papa writes I should be obliged to him to favour me with his sentiments on the subject of debating Societies. We established one here with Mr. Preston's approbation some time ago. My uncle Babington I understand disliked the thing when he came here. Mr. Preston is in some hesitation about the pro and con, and asked me what I thought would be my Father's opinion. I said that I thought he would not disapprove of it. But I wish to hear his sentiments fully. Because if he likes the system, his

---

[1] Postmark of receiving post office dated 22 April 1816.
[2] Two poems provoked by the proceedings for separation from Lady Byron, 'Fare Thee Well' and 'A Sketch' – the one sentimental, the other savage – appeared in the *Champion*, 14 April, and were copied by other London papers in the week following. Byron had had the poems privately printed; who made them available for publication is not known.
[3] Published in early January.
[4] William Henry Babington (1803–67), fifth son of Thomas Babington, was in the East India Company's civil service, Madras Presidency, 1821–49.

opinion is omnipotent with our most virtuous and excellent Præceptor. And if not, I should resign the pleasure which the Society gives me without a single murmur; because to use an expression of Voltaire's *mutatis mutandis*, "Quand Monsieur Macaulay et Monsieur Babington pensent du même sur quelque sujet, il faut bien qu'ils eussent raison."

Farewell.

Will Papa be so good as to stop the weekly Paper which I get here. I find it now unnecessary as I have all the news without it by the Times, which we take in.

TO ZACHARY MACAULAY, 14 MAY 1816

MS: Trinity College. *Address:* Z Macaulay Esq. / No 26. Birchin-Lane / Cornhill / London.

Aspenden Hall. May. 14. 1816.

My dear Father,

I now proceed to inform you of the subjects of an examination of which, to use a favourite military phrase, I have already paralysed a great part. For Latin verses. Moses on Mount Pisgah.[1] Craniology: The monastery of Iona. An Heroic Epistle from Madame Bertrand[2] to some friend in France. – For English Verses, the Runic superstitions. If a book happens to lie about the house on that subject I should be very much obliged to you to send it me. If not it would be useless trouble to procure any, as I am pretty well acquainted with the outline at least of the Creed of the Scalds. We have also to draw up a Synopsis of the notes of Porson, Professor Monk, and Bloomfield, to Euripides' plays;[3] a very useful exercise, and approximating very nearly to my annual employment of index making. – As to the books in which we are to be examined, there is nothing either difficult or formidable in them, at least not to me. The Medea of Euripides, a pretty good play, not much worse than the worst of Racine's. Seriously, I think Euripides the vilest poet that ever put pen to

[1] MS Latin verses by TBM entitled 'Moses in monte Pisgâ' are at Trinity.
[2] The wife of the Napoleonic general, Henri Gratien, Count Bertrand; she and her three children accompanied Napoleon – against his will – in exile at St Helena. In the week before this letter Count Bertrand had been condemned to death in Paris for his part in the Hundred Days.
[3] Porson, *Euripides tragœdiae*, Leipzig, 1802; J. H. Monk edited *Hippolytus*, 1811, and *Alcestis*, 1816; C. J. Blomfield published a complete edition of Euripides in 1821 but nothing of Euripides earlier than this, so far as I can tell. Monk and Blomfield collaborated in editing Porson's *Adversaria*, 1812, which includes some notes on Euripides. All three were Trinity College men, and Preston may have had special access to the work of Monk and Blomfield.

paper. His three most famous plays are the Orestes, the Phœnissæ, and the Medea. There are ten good lines in the first, twenty in the second, and fifteen in the third. But I am digressing a little from the subject; we also read the 2nd Book of Thucydides (part of it rather), the Life of Agricola in Tacitus, and a few other trifling things not important enough to mention.

I was alarmed seriously at the account which the Times gave of the destruction of Sierra-Leone.[1] But I did not believe it? And why? Because an American related it. What is the cause that that people wherever they go, do nothing but mischief and inspire nothing but aversion and disgust? Of all the hideous reptiles which the new world produces, boa-constrictors, Alligators, snakes of all shapes and sizes, I think none so full of venom, so dangerous, and so detestable, as a full-grown United-States viper. I did not see at first the extreme aptness of the metaphor. Vipers are said to devour their parents. The Americans have attempted to do this. But if I were John Bull, as I have the honour of being one of his members, I would drub our graceless offspring into reverence, if not into love.

My admiration of Sismondi is extreme. I rank him among the best writers of the age. He joins the profound research of an Italian, and the liberal independance which is the characteristic of Britons, with the light, gay, and amusing, liveliness of the French. There is one most splendid passage which concludes his Chapter on Arabian literature. Not having the book here, I will attempt to give you the words in English as nearly as I can; indeed I ought to remember it, for I have sate for hours considering and revolving it.

"Perhaps in the course of some centuries, Europe itself, which is now the Empire of the arts and sciences, of Civilization and of greatness, which judges so well of the ages that are past, and calculates so wisely on the events that are to come, may lose those advantages which are now its boast, and the power which it exercises over the most remote regions of the habitable Globe. Her cities may sleep in the dust. Her temples may fall as the Capitol and the Pantheon have fallen already; and nothing may remain of this happy region of the world, but the memory of what it once was, of the Genius which inspired, and the wisdom which instructed it. Some other people may arise, perhaps in the mountains from which the Orinoco rolls, perhaps in the forests of New Holland, a people of other languages, other manners, other religions, which will restore the human race again, and moralize like us upon the past which when it reflects that we have existed, that we have known what they know, that we have, like

---

[1] *The Times*, 6 May, quoting the *Mercantile Advertiser*, reported the destruction of Sierra Leone by natives and the murder of most of the white inhabitants on the authority of a Captain Young, of the ship Charlotte. The report was corrected in *The Times*, 7 May, to state that a riot had occurred and that troops had been called out.

them, looked forward to an eternity of greatness, will pity the weak and unavailing efforts of man to obtain an immortality which fate has refused him; and will contemplate the names of a Newton, and a Tasso as instances of the fruitless struggle which genius maintains against the destiny which decrees that every thing human must perish."[1] This paraphrase is very free. The passage defies translation.

With this passage which will very well supply the pl[ace of][2] a letter and with love to My Mother etc. and many congratulations on Mrs. Thatcher's convalescence.[3]

Farewell.

T B Macaulay.

TO SELINA MILLS MACAULAY, 1 JUNE 1816

MS: Trinity College. *Address:* Mrs. Macaulay / No 26 Birchin-Lane / Cornhill / London.

Aspeden Juin 1er. 1816

Ma chère mère,

Je me persuade que vous vouliez bien me pardonner d'un silence qui m'a été aussi désagréable qu'à vous, quand je vous assure, que je n'ai fait aucune chose, il y a plus que quinze jours, que de rompre un cerveil que m'est pas tres bien organisé avec des livres Latines et Grec. Ces langues si célébres, quoique elles me charment beaucoup, et qu'elles ont, sans doute, des grandes beautés, n'excitent pas dans mon âme bas et chétif cette enthousiasme que quelques hommes sentent pour les reliques des "géans qui vécurent dans les siécles anciens." – Pourquoi les apprenons-nous de notre première enfance? Pourquoi dépensons-nous les plus belles années de notre vie, dans l'etude si pénible qui est nécessaire pour les entendre parfaitement ou même possiblement? Est-ce qu'elles contiennent des libres d'histoire, de poésie, de philosophie, plus estimables que ceux que notre patrie même a produits? Non, sans doute. Est-ce que nous voyons par-là le progrès du

---

[1] *La Littérature du Midi de l'Europe,* 1, 76–7. The original is worth giving: ' Qui sait si, dans quelques siècles, cette même Europe, où la règne des lettres et des sciences est aujourd'hui transporté, qui brille d'un si grand éclat, qui juge si bien les temps passé, qui compare si bien le règne successif des littératures et des mœurs antiques, ne sera pas déserte et sauvage comme les collines de la Mauritanie, les sables de l'Egypte, et les vallées de l'Anatolie? Qui sait si, dans un pays entièrement neuf, peut-être dans les hautes contrées d'où découle l'Orénoque et le fleuve des Amazones, peut-être dans cette enceinte jusqu'à ce jour impénétrable des montagnes de la Nouvelle-Hollande, il ne se formera pas des peuples avec d'autres mœurs, d'autres langues, d'autres pensées, d'autres religions, des peuples qui renouvelleront encore une fois la race humaine, qui étudieront comme nous les temps passés, et qui, voyant avec étonnement que nous avons existé, que nous avons su ce qu'ils sauront, que nous avons cru comme eux à la durée et à la gloire, plaindront nos impuissans efforts, et rappelleront les noms des Newton, des Racine, des Tasse, comme exemples de cette vaine lutte de l'homme pour atteindre une immortalité de renommée que la destinée lui refuse.'

[2] Paper torn away with seal.   [3] She died on 14 July.

Génie humain, et comment les premiers essais rudes et durs des tems semi-barbares, jusqu'à l'élégance accomplie de la civilization et du luxe? Ne voyons-nous pas le meme dans le progrès de la litterature Italienne, Françoise, Espagnole? – N'est il pas vrai, si l'on peut croire la parole du Chevalier Jones,[1] de Lord Teignmouth, de plusieurs autres hommes dont on ne peut douter ni le gout ni la probité, que les langues Arabes et Persannes contiennent des trésors aussi inestimables que ceux que tous les garcons et que tous les jeunes hommes à Oxford et à Cambridge, lisent sans cesse? Pourquoi dont se renforme-t'on· à l'étude des langues qui ne sont pas supérieures à tant d'autres ni par l'harmonie ni par l'utilité?

Ne croyez pas, quoique je parle ainsi, que je vais négligez une étude si necessaire et si agréable que celle des langues Classiques. Eschyle étoit Grec; et c'est assez pour m'exciter à apprendre la langue. De tous les poëtes que le monde a jamais produit, je le crois le plus sublime et le plus magnifique. "O woman woman, if you did but know the pleasure that we scholars feel, when we conster the crabbit words." Et vraiment il n'est guère possible de faire des mots plus durs et plus difficiles que ceux dont Eschyle se sert continuellement. Pourquoi a-t-on exclu les femmes de l'étude des langues, comme de la science des franc-maçons. – Peut-être on peut se promettre le rétour d'un âge d'or quand les jeunes demoiselles en-trenont dans nos universités, et deviendront "Senior Wranglers."

Je vous rémercie pour les libres sur les superstitions Runiques. Mais je crois que je n'en ferai guères d'usage. La poèsie ne peut pas m'employer à présent; ni le plaisir d'écrire à ceux que j'aime.

Vale; – et donnez mon amour à tous ceux qui m'aimez.

[no signature]

TO SELINA MILLS MACAULAY, 9 SEPTEMBER 1816

MS: Trinity College. *Address:* Mrs. Macaulay / No 26 Birchin-Lane / Cornhill / London.

Aspenden Hall. September. 9th. 1816.

My dear Mother,

I can make no apology for having written so little to you this half year, except the pressure of work, and the absolute necessity of spending all the time I could spare in exercise to recover my pristine vigour.[2] I am now, I

---

[1] Sir William Jones (1746–94: *DNB*), the greatest English scholar of Oriental languages in the eighteenth century. His *Memoirs* were published by TBM's Clapham neighbor, Lord Teignmouth, in 1804.

[2] TBM had apparently been ill in the summer of 1816. He was with his mother at Barley Wood in August, whence she wrote to Zachary Macaulay that 'I hope much from this weather which is here most delightful, for Tom' (24 August: MS, Huntington). Margaret Macaulay's statement that 'about sixteen [TBM] grew fat, after a fever' (*Recollections*, p. 207)

think, as well as ever, and preparing to carry on the campaign with the greatest vigour. – I am glad that Papa approves of the present plan of our debating Society. We discussed the other night a subject upon which there has been more misrepresentation and more prejudice than any which I can remember, the justice of the sentence of Mary Stewart, the Queen of Scotts. I cannot bear to hear this woman, who, but for a kind of romantic interest with which her beauty, her accomplishments, her passions, and her misfortunes have invested her, would have been ranked with Messalina, Agrippina, Cleopatra of Egypt, Catherine de Medicis, and Elizabeth of Russia, and all the other women whose names disgrace humanity, classed among the good and the great. Yet this is what Robertson[1] has done, and what Hume[2] has attempted to do.

The other day I happened to light upon a volume of Thomson's plays. I read two or three, and was astonished to see how miserably this great poet has failed in the dramatic art. "No man," says Dean Swift, "ever succeeded who mistook his own talents." Thomson, in my opinion most unfortunately mistook his when he clothed his foot in the tragic buskin.[3] Sophonisba is sad stuff. The murder of Agamemnon is a little better; – it is so noble, so truly tragical a subject, that neither Thomson nor Sotheby[4] have been able altogether to spoil it. – Tancred and Sigismunda is extremely mean. The moral is the best part of it. But there is not one interesting Character, nor one passage of true pathos. Coriolanus 1 did not read. I did not wish to see a subject which Shakespeare has treated with such a masterly hand spoilt by the daubing brush of a bad imitator.

To say the truth, the British Drama rests almost entirely on the merit of Shakespeare; at least as far as I have seen. I read some of Rowe's[5] most renowned plays at Miss Hannah More's, and saw little in them to admire except the pomp of the versification, which was perhaps rather a defect than a beauty. Home's Douglas[6] is dull, though it contains some beautiful strokes. I never read more than one play of Ben Johnson's, and I thought it deserved no commendation. *Cato*[7] is a Frenchified, stiff, uninteresting series of long conversations in blank verse; – I have heard Otway[8] praised, but I know nothing of him. – Miss Hannah More's tragedies have their beauties. Regulus is the most interesting, and Percy the best written.

---

may refer to this time. The dating of events in the *Recollections* before 1830 is, however, very approximate. See 8 December 1818. There is also a gap in TBM's letters from December 1816, to October 1817, which may perhaps be partly accounted for by an illness.

1 William Robertson, *The History of Scotland*, 1759.
2 See ch. 42 of Hume's *History of England*.
3 James Thomson's tragedies are *Sophonisba*, 1730; *Agamemnon*, 1738; *Tancred and Sigismunda*, 1745; and *Coriolanus*, 1749.   4 William Sotheby, *Orestes*, 1802.
5 Nicholas Rowe (1674–1718: *DNB*), writer of tragedies and editor of Shakespeare.
6 John Home, *Douglas*, 1756.
7 By Addison, 1713.   8 Thomas Otway (1652–85: *DNB*).

– I see little to admire in the Fatal Falsehood; – so little that I had rather Mrs. Cowley[1] had had the reputation of it than Miss Hannah More. Its tendency is not particularly good, and the suicide at the end is a piece of unnecessary violence and fury.

[no signature]

TO HANNAH MORE, 11 NOVEMBER 1816

MS: Trinity College. *Address:* Mrs. Hannah More / Barley-Wood / Wrington / nr Bristol.

Aspenden Hall Nov. 11th. 1816.

My dear Madam,

I have lately received your kind present of Books. Of one of them[2] I dare not speak because "praise," says some philosopher, "is only to be given by the greater to the less." Of Millar's Historical Essay[3] I cannot say much, because I have not thoroughly read it. The subject which he has undertaken to treat is one so vast, and so disjointed; it forms so immense a whole, and the subdivisions into which it is separated are so numerous, that I know not whether it be possible to effect so grand a design without either swelling the work by unnecessary particularity, or making it vague and uninteresting by a too general survey. When I have studied Millar more closely, I will make a report upon the manner in which he performs his difficult task. – He has not, I see, completed his plan. It will, I think, become more difficult, the more nearly he approaches to the present times. In ages of semi-barbarism, and it is through such that his course hath hitherto lain, great events are isolated. Reigns of twenty or thirty years roll away without one occurrence of sufficient importance to carry it down the stream of time. But in modern times every month has its events, – its debates, its laws, or its battles. –

Such at least used to be the case while I lived near London; – but in the retirement of the park of Aspenden, where I am as far remote from the bustle of London as if I were in the isle of St. Helena or on the summit of Apelachia, I know not what revolution may have taken place in the political or literary world; so that I am at present far more au fait of the history of

---

[1] Hannah Cowley (1743–1809: *DNB*), dramatist; at the second night of Hannah More's *The Fatal Falsehood*, 1779, Mrs Cowley shouted 'That's mine! That's mine!' and fainted away in her box.

[2] Perhaps Hannah More, *Poems*, 1816.

[3] John Millar, *An Historical View of the English Government from the Settlement of the Saxons in Britain to the Accession of the House of Stewart*, 1787. Millar died in 1801; editions adding to his work appeared posthumously, including one in 4 vols., 1812. One of the 'Scottish' school of philosophical historians, Millar's view of the process of historical development was an influence in TBM's own concept of progress in history.

the old than that of the modern world, and the Athenian expedition to Sicily is more rung in my ears than Lord Exmouth's bombardment of Algier.[1]

One fault of modern education, I think, is the far greater attention which is paid to the ancient than the modern classics. Old Eli Bates demands "if there is no smith in Israël, that we should go down to sharpen every man his coulter and his axe and his mattock, at the anvils of the Philistines."[2] Let the ancients have their due, and be allowed the honours which they deserve from the gratitude of nations to which they pointed out first the path of every art and science. Their poems are fine, their orations eloquent, their philosophy sometimes sublime, their languages the most perfect, and the most harmonious ever spoken. Yet our admiration of them is, I think, carried to a strange excess, when Latin and Greek are allowed to banish from our schools and our colleges the English, the French, and the Italian authors. To compare the ancients and moderns would be perhaps impossible. But I think it almost obvious that in one point the latter have the decided advantage, in depth and profundity of thought. And if their poetry have not equal simplicity and originality, its imagery is more beautiful and its finish more exquisite. On these grounds I think that the Writers of modern times ought to receive a greater share of attention than is commonly paid them; and that some time might advantageously be borrowed from what is now spent on the trash of Euripides and Aristophanes, to be applied to the study of Milton, Pope, Spenser, and Racine, Bacon, Johnson, and Bossuet. It is not without much timidity that I venture to impugn what the practise of Ages has sanctioned; – yet I think that it ought to be remembered that when classical studies first began to occupy the attention of the world, there were hardly any works in the modern tongues deserving of perusal; and all information was to be obtained through the medium of Greek or Latin. That is not at present the case; England can boast of a literature which, I think, need not shrink from a contest with those of Athens or of Rome; and which I think deserves to be as much attended too.

These remarks upon a subject on which it is almost impossible to determine, and on which I am desirous of information from some better judge have hardly left me room to give my love to Miss Patty and Miss Sally, and to assure you, my Dear Madam, that I am your most affectionate Friend.

Thomas B. Macaulay.

---

[1] 27 August 1816: Exmouth commanded an expedition sent to compel the abolition of Christian slavery in the Barbary states.
[2] Ely Bates, *Rural Philosophy*, 2nd edn, 1804, p. xv.

TO ZACHARY MACAULAY, 18 NOVEMBER 1816

MS: Trinity College. *Address:* Z Macaulay / No 26 Birchin-Lane / London.

Aspenden Hall. / November. 18. 1816.
My dear Father,

   The weather being in this part of our terrestrial Globe not a little severe, I cannot but be anxious to know how you have weathered the snow and the frost. I would also enquire whether the gloomy aspect of the clouds, and the drizzling darkness of our atmosphere has produced that corresponding dulness which is a great torment to invalids. To be sure, man was not made to be the slave of the elements or of the scenery, of the sun and the clouds. Our spirits ought not to rise and fall with Fahrenrheit's mercury, and the East wind has no right to blow dulness and ill-humour across the country. Yet, though, with Johnson, I despise the infirmity of our nature, which is in so great a degree the slave of the weather,[1] I cannot deny that I have often experienced the same uncomfortable dulness. – Were I indeed trying to form some new theory to account for the varieties of national character, I think I should be less disposed to refer it to the relative degrees of heat or cold, or even to the effects of political institutions than to the appearance of natural objects. Near the frozen circle, so often called the favourite domain of liberty, the Russian Emperors exert an authority as despotic as a Tamerlane or a Kouli Khan ever possessed. And the Haytians have written in blood the truth which speculatists have so long disputed, that men may have energy, courage, and love of liberty even within fifteen degrees from the equator. Political constitutions and laws have so little influence upon the habits of the lower classes, that it would be romantic to assign to them any share in the formation of national character. I should therefore, as I before said, be disposed to attribute the varieties observable in the dispositions of different nations to the aspect which nature wears amidst them. The Greenlander, whose eye wanders over wastes of ice and snow, and who sees hardly anything which gives the idea of comfort, has naturally a limited range of thoughts, and a narrow intellect. The Italian in countries

> "Ou la terre unit
> "Les fruits d'un eternel Automne
> "Aux fleurs d'un eternel printemps,"

is voluptuous, and idle; – the Chinese who sees nature altogether banished by rocks carved with heads, gilt trees, and japanned houses, banishes nature also from his habits, and becomes as affected – as a Chinese; – for

---

[1] See, e.g., Boswell, *Life of Johnson*, ed. Hill and Powell, I, 332.

no simile can add to this. The Englishman becomes hypochondriac, because, – but my paper is at an end. And therefore with affectionate love to Mamma, and earnest solicitations that either she or Selina would write soon to tell me how you are, I remain,

T B Macaulay.

– P.S. I have written to Miss H More.

TO SELINA MILLS MACAULAY, 9 DECEMBER 1816

MS: Trinity College. *Address:* Mrs. Macaulay / No 26 Birchin-Lane / Cornhill / London.

[Aspenden Hall] Monday. December. 9. 1816

My dear Mother,

I assure you that you need not be in the least degree anxious respecting me. I am as well as you could wish. I have not for nearly a week been troubled by my cold, which while it lasted was so slight that I hardly knew that I had one. If there is anything wrong about my health you shall yourself judge when I return, as I hope to do in a fortnight to dear Clapham.

I expected that your last letter would have been full of information respecting the factious disorders of Monday last.[1] Birchin lane must have been near the focus of Action, "if right the tale we hear." – The Lord Mayor is my Hero. He has shown himself a worthy successor of William Walworth who dashed out Wat Tyler's brains. Let me have some intelligence respecting these events. – At Aspenden they have thrown us all into confusion. And such is our loyal zeal that I would not advise Orator Hunt to venture within the precincts of the park. What to think of this man I hardly know. He is too mad for an impostor; – yet maniacs, it is said, are often cunning; – that is, I suppose, they propose to themselves some wild end, but are artful in the means which they employ to compass it. However this may be, Hunt approaches nearer to my idea of a Grecian or Roman demagogue, a Cleon or a Gracchus, than any gentleman of modern times. Of these his great prototypes the former was "pierced through the back with an ignoble wound."[2] The other had his brains dashed out with the legs of a table. Hunt however seems to me to be fated to a soaring

---

[1] A meeting addressed by Henry ('Orator') Hunt (1773–1835: *DNB*) at Spa Fields, 15 November, to petition the Regent concerning the popular distress, was followed by a second meeting at the same place on 2 December to consider the answer to the petition. Before Hunt had appeared to address this second meeting a part of the crowd left the place of meeting, looted a gunsmith's shop, and entered the Royal Exchange. They were met there by the mayor, Matthew Wood, and by police. The building was cleared and several of the rioters arrested. Hunt meanwhile was haranguing those who had remained at Spa Fields.

[2] Perhaps a reference to the account of Cleon's death in Thucydides, v, 10, but in whose phrase I do not know.

destiny. It has often been said that the leader of a mob enjoys but a dangerous elevation. – I accept the omen; and predict that the dangerous elevation of a gallows awaits this staple-hunter of Reform who rushes on to his object through hedges and ditches, not caring how much dirt he may splash through, or how many honest passengers he may trample down in his way.

He disclaims all idea of riot or insurrection. Is this any apology for his conduct. He rakes up the cinders of half extinguished Jacobinism; he attempts to light up again the flames of revolution; he touches every string which is likely to move the people to madness. He tells them that they are oppressed, trampled upon, starved, and insulted; – is it likely to quench the fires which speeches like these have kindled, to tell them, "you must be grave, and quiet; you must not bring disgrace upon your cause by rioting."[1] It is like pointing out to a man the advantages which would result to him from a murder, and give him a pistol [to] commit it, and then tell him, that it is very wrong to cut throats. And he reproaches the rioters for having been moved by his speeches to rise in arms; as if he should set fire to a house and say, "It is the fault of the wood. I laid a torch to it, but I did not mean it to take light." –

With love to my Father etc.

Farewell

T B M.

to Zachary Macaulay, [20? October 1817][2]

MS: Trinity College. *Address:* Z Macaulay Esq. / No 26 Birchin-Lane / Cornhill / London.

[Aspenden Hall]

My dear Father,

Mr. Preston returns to night to resume the delegated sceptre,[3] and to morrow Mr. Scholfield[4] leaves us. I like the deputy extremely upon the

---

[1] Hunt said in his speech of 2 December: 'He must however declare, that the worst way of supporting any cause was by acts of violence; that these afforded to their enemies the surest means of casting disgrace upon it, and enabled every man to say how bad must be a cause which is supported by men of this description' (*The Times*, 3 December).

[2] Postmark of receiving office is 2[?] OC 18[??]. This letter clearly precedes that of 24 October 1817 and is equally clearly the one referred to in Zachary Macaulay to Hannah More, 25 October: 'I inclose a letter I received from [TBM] a few days ago which you will see bears sufficient marks of juvenility. I have written him a long letter on the importance of attending to minutenesses, if he would do great things well; a rule applicable not merely to literature, but to morals and religion also. This is precisely the kind of discipline of which Tom stands especially in need' (MS, Huntington).

[3] 'Preston has been lately obliged to absent himself on account of his health for several weeks from Aspeden' (Zachary Macaulay to Hannah More, *ibid.*).

[4] James Scholefield (1789–1853: *DNB*), Fellow of Trinity, 1815–27 and Regius Professor of Greek, 1825–53. Scholefield was curate to Simeon in succession to Preston, and was de-

whole; He supplied the vacant chair admirably; but I think that he has
contracted too much of the University style of literature. There seems to
me to be the same difference between one of the accurate Cantabrigian
Scholars who compares readings and collates Editions, and gives to every
Greek particle its due honours and its definite significations, and an elegant scholar who tastes the beauties of the classics without condescending
to those minutiæ, which there is between a mixer of colours and an
amateur in painting, between a labourer who mends the roads on Malvern
or Richmond Hill, and the tourist who admires the picturesque beauty of
the scenery. The business of the one is to facilitate the enjoyment of the
other. But to make that the end which ought only to be the means, and to
consider the man who can give the best conjecture as to a corrupt passage
in a nonsensical chorus, which no body can ever understand, and which no
body would be wiser if he did, as a better scholar than him who can enjoy the
beauties of the classics without digging into the rubbish which sometimes
obscures and buries their meaning, is a truly deplorable perversion of
judgement. "Words" said the greatest linguist that ever lived, "are the
sons of earth; ideas are the daughters of heaven."[1] Words bear to fine
passages of writing, about the same relation which stones bear to the edifice
which they compose; – and I think that the man who should neglect the
magnificent architecture of St. Paul's in order to discuss the quality of its
Portland stone, is not more destitute of taste than he who descends from
the contemplation of the sublimity of Eschylus or the pathos of Euripides
to settle the force of every μεν and δε which occurs in their pages.

   I am indeed a little disposed to question that right of superiority which
classical literature has so long claimed over that of other nations. Systems
once believed impregnable, opinions once interwoven with the texture of
all science, have been disputed, contested and overthrown, and consigned
to oblivion; – Aristotle has fallen from the throne which he once shared
with the inspired writers, unless indeed he may be said to have looked
down upon them from a superior eminence of public estimation. The litterature of France has ceased to be the model of our belles-lettres; and
writers who, like Cowley and Ben Jonson, flattered themselves with the
hope of an immortality as durable as brilliant are hardly read or quoted.
Perhaps the time approaches when a more important revolution shall
break the fetters which have so long entangled the litterature of Europe; –
when some original thinker shall ask, why we spend the ten most impor-

votedly active in all the Evangelical enterprises of the University: 'he might almost be regarded as Simeon's successor' (F. W. B. Bullock, *History of Ridley Hall*, Cambridge, 1941,
I, 52). TBM's comment on Scholefield's scholarship may be contrasted to the statement in
the *DNB* that Scholefield 'held that Porson's followers attended too exclusively to verbal
criticism.'
[1] Johnson, Preface to the *Dictionary*; 'ideas' should be 'things.'

87

tant years of our life to enable ourselves to read odes and plays, about a tenth part as good as those in our mother tongue, or to understand histories of the quarrels of two little states like Athens and Lacedæmon, quarrels, about as important to the general system of the world as a lawsuit between two parishes. Àpropos of law-suits, – if anything on such a subject can be other than mal-àpropos, – so we must be content with our present abode – Amen.¹ We have other and more powerful consolations against greater calamities. Against this let us use the prescription of the Roman Epicurean; – worthy of a better sect than Horace's.

> "Nunc domus Umbreni sub nomine; nuper Ofelli
> Dictus erit nulli proprius, sed cedet in usum
> Nunc mihi, nunc alii. – Quocirca vivite fortes
> Fortia que adversis opponite pectora rebus"²

Loves to all. –

Farewell.

T B M.

TO ZACHARY MACAULAY, 24 OCTOBER 1817

MS: Trinity College. *Address:* Z Macaulay. Esq. / No 26 Birchin-Lane / Cornhill / London.

Aspenden Hall. Oct. 24. 1817

My dear Father,

You will hardly be surprized at my silence when I tell you that I am so busy that it is some weeks since I have spent half an hour in English reading; and that I have imposed upon my self the not very agreable labour of reading two Greek Tragedies every week. So that you see that my doubts as to the expediency of Classical literature are merely speculative. Indeed were it only that a certain degree of respectability is attached by common consent to proficiency in the languages of Greece and Rome, it would be the duty of every person who desired to qualify himself for extensive usefulness to devote a certain degree of attention to them. However I must be indulged in the privilege of exhaling upon paper a little of the spleen which I feel when my head aches over an unintelligible, defective, and mutilated chorus of Eschylus, or a stupid prologue of Euripides stuffed with genealogy and commonplace proverbs.

I confess I have been surprized at a phrase which I have often heard,

---

¹ 'The close of Tom's letter refers to a purchase of the house that was old John Thornton's, in which Henry etc. were born – which I had made – but was obliged to give up on account of a defective title' (Zachary Macaulay to Hannah More, 25 October: MS, Huntington). This was the house to which the elder Henry Thornton's grandfather had moved in 1735. 'The estate lay close to the present tube-station' (Forster, *Marianne Thornton*, p. 10).
² *Satires*, II, ii, 133–6.

and which is something akin to what you observed in your last letter. People often talk of the necessity of Latin to enable a person to grammaticize his English. The question naturally occurs, "How did the ancients learn to grammaticize their Latin and Greek, languages of which the inflections are so artful, and the collocation so difficult, – and that in ages and countries where the art of printing had not yet diffused litterature and intelligence, and placed the highest degrees of knowledge within the reach of all who have the power to purchase books." These writings which we are directed to study as models of accuracy, were composed without a model. And is there such a degeneracy in the mental constitution of mankind that in this most polished age, with all the masterpieces of our own language before us, we cannot attain to any degree of perfection or exactitude in style, without having recourse to the reliques of antiquity?

Nay, I would almost venture to say that part of the inaccuracy in the use of words which constitutes so great a defect in writing and speaking, that use of terms which do not precisely convey our meaning, is caused by this circumstance, that during our early years all our literary ideas are received through the medium of other languages, and that an undue degree of attention is paid to them; while the advancement of a student in English litterature and composition is entirely neglected. Is it natural that men who have hardly begun their acquaintance with their own language till they leave college, and many such there are, who look at it through the medium of classical prepossessions and tastes when at length they do pay any attention to it, should attain to a full knowledge of its force and meaning and be able to give every idea its full, perfect, and appropriate expression.

Of the positive merit of the classics much may be said. Time gives a mellowness to poetry as well as to painting. Posterity see or think they see in every Verse of an ancient poet some beauty of thought or expression. Meanings which the writer never imagined are discovered and admired. Scenes which would have been hissed off an English stage with the unanimous execrations of pit, boxes, and galleries, no sooner appear in a Greek clothing than all the terms of applause which a language affords are lavished on their meanest puerilities, and the brains of twenty editors are racked for language sufficiently strong to express the intensity of their admiration and delight. Like Patroclus in the armour of Achilles, or, to use a more homely illustration, like the ass in the lion's skin, they triumph not by their own merit but their clothing. – Hector terminated the delusion by killing Patroclus, and the ass betrayed himself by his voice. I have not the presumption to think that I can undeceive the world; but I am confident that I distinguish the bray of Euripides's ideas under their Greek disguise.

Perhaps at some distant period in the history of the world when the names of the sages and Heroes of Europe cast a faint and dubious beam through the intervening mists of tradition and ignorance, our literature may experience a similar canonization. The meanest puns of Shakespeare will be complimented with the Euges and Pulcherrimums of Editors yet unborn, and the White doe,[1] if the White doe should by some strange accident be rescued from destruction, (for indeed if the Orestes of Euripides enjoy immortality, nothing can be too bad to claim the same honours,) may be the model of those who shall write the yet unknown languages of those distant times. Something must then be deducted from the alleged merit of the classics on this ground. There is likewise another consideration to be taken into the account. When the Classics were first rescued from the shelves of Grecian monasteries, and ushered into the world by Aldus and Lascaris,[2] no other literature existed in Europe. All that we possessed was the few remaining reliques of antiquity. To these accordingly every student applied himself. Whatever place some of these applauded writers may hold in our estimation at present, it is no wonder that an ignorant yet curious generation should have been dazzled and confounded by their lustre. A farthing candle will almost blind with its light one whose eyes have been long accustomed to the darkness of a cellar. But shall its lustre be therefore considered as equal to the brightness of the sun? Our ancestors in the transports of their first admiration upon being admitted to the enjoyment of poetry and eloquence saw and admired and almost adored. Like the savages in the Pellew islands, who gazed upon the kettle and tongs of the ship which visited them with astonishment; and almost worshipped the bellows, though as the narrator confesses, that implement had a broken spout and a cracked side;[3] the scholars of the fifteenth century thought every fault of the classics beautiful, and every beauty divine. Their language was imitated by their successors; – every generation has tacitly acquiesced in the judgement of those who preceded it; and like the Parthians who in the height of their prosperity marched to war under a leathern apron for a banner, because under that standard their destitute ancestors had made their first incursions; the modern Europeans, while they have carried literature to a pitch far beyond what Cicero could have conceived, while they have produced poets, philosophers, and orators which may be well classed with the proudest names of antiquity, continue to act upon the same system which was introduced when all knowledge

---

[1] Wordsworth, *The White Doe of Rylstone*, 1815.

[2] Aldus Manutius (1449–1515) printer, and Constantin Lascaris (*c.* 1434–1501), grammarian.

[3] TBM may refer here to George Keate, *An Account of the Pelew Islands...from the Journals and Communications of Captain Henry Wilson*, 2nd edn, 1788, p. 63. The passage specifies a kettle, tongs, and bellows as objects exciting the interest of the natives but says nothing about the state of the bellows.

was necessarily conveyed through the medium of the dead languages. – Such are a few more of the ideas which I offer to your castigation. Give my love to my Mother and Sisters, and believe me your most affectionate Son.

T B M.

TO ZACHARY MACAULAY, [10? NOVEMBER 1817][1]

MS: Trinity College. *Address:* Z Macaulay Esq. / No 26 Birchin-Lane / Cornhill / London.

[Aspenden Hall]

My dear Father,

I am truly rejoiced to hear that your indisposition has abated, and I hope that before this time it has completely left you. My own health is not bad though not perfectly established; occasional attacks of cold and oppressions in my chest have a little unsettled it, and I am conscious of a susceptibility about my lungs which renders all my caution necessary. I hope to hold out till Christmas, when I shall surrender any superintendance into my mother's hands.

I fully coincide with your remarks on Classical literature, with which, to say the truth, Demosthenes, to whom I am at present pretty closely applying myself, has put me in a good humour. I remember that some years back, when I read parts of him, I thought him inferior to his great Roman Rival; my opinion has now changed; – although I cannot consider the superiority of the Athenian so decided as some of his admirers affect to do; and while I pronounce him the greater orator, I think Cicero beyond a doubt the greater genius. It is indeed in the suppression of luxuriance that Demosthenes's excellence consists, and in the unpruned exuberance of ideas that Cicero's fault, considered as an orator, lies. Whether the defect be not indicative of greater genius than the absence of it I dare not venture to say. I intend, in case I should not find myself too busy, to translate one of the master pieces of both orators; and compare them in our own language. Demosthenes would lose least by the translation. Eloquence which consists in the force and energy of ideas simply but nervously expressed, is the eloquence of all countries, of all ages, of all assemblies. At the bar, in the senate, from the pulpit, from the chair of the professor, from the hustings of palace yard, Demosthenes would have been heard with attention and delight. The eloquence of Cicero is not an equally hardy plant. It thrives and blossoms, and scatters its fragrance in its own soil; but has a sickly and exotic appearance in our tongue. Its great

---

[1] Postmark of receiving post office dated 11 November 1817.

excellence consisting in the beauty and art of the language which defies translation, while its copiousness renders it impossible to paraphrase, and the laws of translation forbid us to prune, will be a disadvantage to him. With all deductions however he will appear in any dress however mean, a giant in stature among the dwarfs of later ages.

Eloquence and history are the two branches of literature which, I think, we must yield to the ancients. That we have not rivalled them in the former no cause, I think, can be assigned except the negligence of our orators. That we have not far excelled them in the latter, considering the immense advances which moral philosophy has made, (and moral philosophy is closely connected with history,) is to me an anomaly. I can only account for it by supposing that our most admired historians, Hume and Gibbon, by rejecting that religion to which, I think, the superior advances which we have made in moral science must be wholly ascribed, descended from an elevation which would have given them the greatest advantage in an attempt to rival the ancients. My love to all.

Affectionately yours.

Thos. B Macaulay.

TO ZACHARY MACAULAY, 28 NOVEMBER 1817

MS: Trinity College. *Address:* Z Macaulay Esq / No 26 Birchin-Lane / Cornhill / London.

Aspenden November. 28. 1817

My dear Father,

I have received the mourning,[1] for which I am much obliged. It fits me as perfectly as William Huntington's miraculous suit of clothes.[2] – As I have nothing else to say, I mean to fill up the sheet with an exercise which I wrote a few days ago for Mr. Preston. It is on the idea of Horace's Car-

---

[1] The Prince Regent, 7 November, had directed a general mourning for the death of Princess Charlotte on the day before.

[2] William Huntington, S[inner] S[aved] (1745–1813: *DNB*), the untaught, independent preacher of Providence Chapel, London. In Huntington's autobiographical account the providential supply of a suit of clothes was a near-annual event, but TBM must mean the story that Huntington tells of the leather breeches sent in answer to his prayers: 'I tried them on, and they fitted as well as if I had been measured for them; at which I was amazed, having never been measured by any leather breeches maker in London' (*The Bank of Faith*, ed. Thomas Wright, 1913, p. 59). At a dinner at Holland House, 21 January 1841, Charles Greville says that he contributed to a discussion of the idea of myth by citing the story of Huntington's 'praying to God for a new pair of leather breeches and finding them under a hedge. . . . Now, I had just a general superficial recollection of this story in Huntington's "Life," but my farthing rushlight was instantly extinguished by the blaze of Macaulay's all-grasping and all-retaining memory, for he at once came in with the whole minute account of this transaction: how Huntington had prayed, what he had found, and where, and all he had said to the tailor by whom this miraculous nether garment was made' (Greville, *Memoirs*, IV, 350).

men Seculare; which is, you know, a series of blessings upon the Roman people, and wishes for their grandeur and prosperity during the coming century. My love to my Mother and Sisters –

Vale.
T B M.

> Wake not for me, ye choir of fabled maids,
> Melodious daughters of Aonia's shades.
> Let nobler Pow'rs celestial fire diffuse,
> And be the mighty theme itself the Muse.
> Let rapture tremble on each tuneful string.
> My country's fame, my country's fates, I sing.
>   Oh! Albion, could the minstrel's genius frame
> A tribute worthy thine immortal name,
> Thence should a lay arise of heav'nly birth,
> Whose deathless fame should gird the orb of earth;
> Should spread where'er my country rears her throne,
> Where'er her arts, where'er her arms are known;
> No wild-flow'r garland of neglected rhyme
> Cull'd but to vanish on the stream of time,
> But laurels which in deathless green array'd
> No storms should scatter and no suns should fade.
> Ev'n when, her warriors fall'n, her glories fled,
> Her chiefs, her sages, number'd with the dead,
> She sleeps where Rome and Athens slept before,
> And rules the waves, and awes the earth no more,
> Still should its leaves in lasting beauty bloom,
> And wreath their verdant honours round her tomb.
>   Then list, Britannia where thou sitt'st alone,
> Rocks pil'd on rocks thine everlasting throne.
> Thy hand displays the red-cross flag unfurl'd;
> Thine eagle glance o'erlooks the subject world,
> The earth which *thou* has sav'd, the peopl'd sea,
> Which rolls its billows, Queen of isles, for thee;
> Surveys thy warriors on whose helmed brows
> The wreath of Soignie's* oak for ever blows;
> Beholds thy countless fleets, the dread of Kings,
> Dart their red bolts, and spread their eagle wings.
> List, list, the minstrel's lay; to thee belong
> His lyre, his heart, the poet, and the song.
>   Thou first, fair Freedom, to whose high behest
> Kings bow the crown, and warrior's veil the crest,

---

* The wood of Soignie near the field of Waterloo. – [TBM's note.]

Whose vestal lamp, through many a troubl'd year
Of storms and darkness, cheer'd our path of fear,
Still on our children pour the holy ray
Which sooth'd the gloom of Sidney's parting day,
O'er Hamden's life its beams of glory pour'd
And hallow'd Milton's lyre, and Marlbro's sword.
Let dazzled nations bend before the blaze,
And distant tyrants tremble while they gaze.
And thou, oh sacred Truth, celestial guest,
On earth so long unknown, despis'd, opprest,
Here fix thine empire. From our sea girt shore
Unfurl thy cross, and bid the world adore.
Here raise the trophies which to earth shall tell
Thy deathless triumphs o'er the pow'rs of hell.
Let distant nations view thy reign complete,
And barbarous chieftains kiss thy sacred feet.
　　See, side by side, a godlike pair advance,
This wields the sceptre, *that* sustains the lance.
This musing moves with thoughtful step and slow,
And wreaths of olive crown his hoary brow.
His stately comrade strides with loftier tread,
And twines the laurel round his helmed head.
I know the peaceful vest, the beaming mail.
Hail rev'rend *Wisdom*, generous *Valour*, hail! –
Propitious, as in England's elder day,
Still rule our Empire with divided sway; –
Thou, warlike power, to earth's remotest bound
In martial thunder England's name resound.
The swarthy nations through whose wide domain
Hoangho's hundred torrents join the main,
The tribes, where summer holds eternal sway,
Which pant beneath the burning wheels of day,
The climes where heav'n matures with bounteous smiles
The virgin treasures of unrifled isles,
Which yet untrod, unknown in silence sleep
On the vast bosom of the western deep,
Shall crown with deathless fame thy glorious toils,
And swell thy triumphs with uncounted spoils.
　　And thou, with milder rule, imperial sage*
Curb by thy voice the storms of factious rage.
When Autumn's jocund call invites the swains,
Let golden plenty nod on all our plains.

* Wisdom [TBM's note].

While at thy feet benignant Commerce pours
From her full lap the spoils of distant shores,
The spicy sweets of India's dusky breast,
And all the blood-bought treasures of the west.
Mild Peace and Awful Law attend thy word,
And solemn Justice waves th'avenging sword.
Bright Virtue mounts thy throne and shares thy reign,
Art, Genius, Science swell thy glorious train.
There Music wakes the lyre's resounding tone,
And Sculpture moulds the animated stone.
Her fairer sister* soars on radiant wing,
Rifles the clouds of morn, the flow'rs of spring.
Through art, through nature, darts her piercing eyes,
And dips her brush in all the rain-bow's dyes.
See! o'er the lifeless mass her hand suffuse
The blended glories of celestial hues,
The lifeless mass, with genial motion rife,
With passion glows, and blushes into life.
There poesy, fair Sorceress of the soul,
With juice nectareous charms her mystic bowl,
Hymns her wild spells, and with resistless hand
Waves o'er th'ideal scene her painted wand.
There mingling with the blooming train is seen
A power of loftier port and stately mien,
Majestic Eloquence, whose lips diffuse
The soft mellifluence of ambros[ia]l[1] dews[.][2]
While spell-bound nations own his mental [sway?]
And awe-struck Senates listen and obey.
There Hist'ry's wand in phantom pom[p arrays?]
The dim procession of departed days,
Records the triumphs and the tears of states,
Recounts their past, predicts their future fates. –
    Nor ever had a prouder, dearer, name,
Fair herald! brighten'd on thy roll of fame
Than hers whom, snatch'd by too severe a doom,
The tears of nations follow to the tomb.[3] –
Oh! was it meet, when Love and Hope combin'd
The rose and myrtle for her brow had twin'd,

---

* Painting [TBM's note].

[1] Obliterated by crease in paper.
[2] Paper torn, affecting the end of this and two of the next three lines.
[3] Princess Charlotte, who died in childbirth.

When Fancy spread her visions of renown,
Fame's laurel wreath, and Empire's jewell'd crown – ?
No more, my lyre. Thy proud triumphant lay
In melancholy moaning dies away. –
Sad harp, no longer may the minstrel fling
The peal of joy or glory o'er thy string.
Unstrung, untun'd, in mournful silence wave
On the dark cypress which o'ershades her grave. –

TO ZACHARY MACAULAY, 18 APRIL 1818

MS: Trinity College. *Address:* Z. Macaulay Esq. / No 26. Birchin-Lane / Cornhill / London.

Aspenden Hall. Saturday / April. 18th. 1818.
My dear Father,
   I have lately been reading Cicero's Epistles; and should make a wonderfully good correspondent, if the perusal of them had improved my style of letter writing as much as it has diminished my esteem for their celebrated author. I had, I confess, always regarded the Prince of Oratory as a well meaning, honest, virtuous, patriot, whose judgement was too much biassed by personal friendship, or overawed by the dread of more powerful opponents, but who, though rendered inconsistent sometimes by timidity, and sometimes by favour, was yet in the main a sincere friend of truth and of his country. But the Epistles show him in a very different light; and I really do not think it too strong to say that he appears a cowardly, selfish, unprincipled, hypocrite; who loved or hated, supported or opposed as his interest or vanity prompted. Desirous to play a conspicuous part in the state, and qualified by his pre-eminent Genius to have shone its brightest ornament, with a judgement naturally powerful, and rendered so acute by experience that his contemporaries thought his voice prophetic, as we in similar times have considered that of Burke, he yet for the most miserable bribes sold every great or generous object. Melted by a compliment, and intimidated by a frown, he lived alternately the tool and the laughing-stock of the more intrepid ruffians among whom it was his lot to act. His professions and his conduct seem to have been so perpetually at variance, that at length falsehood became merely his diversion. The instances of shameless misrepresentation, gross inconsistency, and downright falsehood, with which the Epistles teem are innumerable. In one epistle he declares to a friend of the name of Appius his intention to break off a match between a young man of the name of Dolabella and his

own daughter Tullia because Dolabella had chosen to indict Appius of some misdemeanour. "Do you think," says this generous friend, "that I would contract any new connection with a wretch who seeks to reward my kindness by attacking the life and honour of my friend. I am rather disposed altogether to separate my self from him than to strengthen the bonds which connect us."[1] – Next comes a letter to another friend. And the immaculate Philosopher begins thus. "My daughter's marriage is on the point of being celebrated. Oh that you had seen my letter to Appius. You would have laughed to see how violently I protested my intention to break off the match. Thus we must dissemble if we would live in the world."[2]

But for the most striking specimen of Cicero's duplicity I think I may refer you to an Epistle to his friend Lentulus; Which is translated and given at length in a note to Hooke's Roman History.[3] You may easily find it, I think in the sixth volume. – It is a long and elaborate defence of all his own political inconsistencies. We have heard much of the change of principles of many of our great public men. But if an authentic and full account of all the delinquencies of this kind committed by all our states-men during this whole reign were compiled I do not think that it would display such a scene of unblushing, profligate, tergiversation as is con-tained in that single letter of the virtuous, the mild, the Philosophic Tully, the man who has been so often quoted as fixing the point to which heathen virtue might be carried. – I shall never cease to admire his talents, to think him the greatest prose writer that the world has produced. In oratory, in philosophic writing, and I think above all in criticism, (witness the Trea-tise De Oratore,) he transcends any writer that any country has seen. – Even those Epistles which exhibit his character in so black a light, have literary merit of the highest order. Nor do I look without complacency on his private character. He was apparently a very patient husband to an intolerably bad wife; a kind father to a very worthless son, an indefatigable benefactor to an ungrateful brother, a good tempered master to rascally servants. Yet with all this, I cannot but think his character most defective; And I think it perhaps mainly deserving of contemplation, in as much as it shows what baseness, profligacy and hypocrisy may coexist with the loftiest genius, the finest taste, the most extensive acquirements, the most just and elevated views of moral obligation and social duties. – So farewell to Cicero. My heart relents over him while I abuse him. – He was such a man, such a genius! –

In turning over the fragments of that Prince of Ancient poets, the Sub-

---

[1] *Epistulae ad Familiares*, III, xii: TBM's version is inexact.
[2] *Ibid.*, II, xv.
[3] Nathaniel Hooke, *The Roman History from the Building of Rome to the Ruin of the Common-wealth*, new edn, 1810, IX, 72–96: *Epistulae ad Familiares*, I, ix.

lime, the Incomparable Eschylus, I found among many uninteresting dispersed quotations which from the want of the context have nothing worthy of notice, a passage of the highest merit. It is extracted by one of the Christian fathers, Clemens Alexandrinus, from a tragedy, now lost, of the great father of the Drama.[1] It is well worthy of a Christian poet; and, though it loses in comparison with the parallel passages in the inspired poetry of the Hebrews, has, I think, scarcely a superior in human composition. It is on the nature of the Deity. I attempted a translation of it; and though it is impossible to transfuse into English the severe and awful sublimity of the original, I think that even in my version, though very paraphrastic, it can scarcely lose all its merit.

> "Hope not, vain mortal, in th'Almighty mind
> To trace the semblance of our feeble kind.
> Veil thy faint eyes. – Nor dare to face the rays
> Which robe th'Eternal in their quenchless blaze.
> Thou know'st him not. He, various yet the same,
> Controuls, pervades, inspires, Creation's frame;
> Roars in the dashing torrent's foamy wreathes,
> Low'rs in the cloud, and in the tempest breathes,
> Shouts in the thunder, whispers in the gale,
> Barbs the red bolt, and wings the steely hail.
> Hark, trembling at his voice through all her caves,
> The shudd'ring ocean swells in huger waves.
> The plains convuls'd in heaving billows rise,
> Storms sweep the forest, thunders rock the skies.
> Through all her empire nature owns the nod,
> And fades before the with'ring eye of God."

My love to my Mother and sisters. –

Farewell.

T B M –

---

[1] The fragment is no longer attributed to Aeschylus: see Augustus Nauck, *Tragicorum Graecorum Fragmenta*, Hildesheim, 1964: Aeschylus, fragment no. 464.

CAMBRIDGE, 1818–1824

1818 Early October?
Family leaves Clapham for Cadogan Place, London

– October 17
TBM leaves for Trinity College, Cambridge. Resides in Jesus Lane

1819 May
In first class, Trinity previous (i.e., freshman) examinations

– July 5
Recites prize poem, 'Pompeii,' in Senate House on occasion of royal visit to University

– Summer
In Clapham studying for scholarship exam with George Stainforth

1820 April
Wins Trinity Scholarship

– October
Wins Latin Declamation Prize

1821 February 12
Goes into rooms in college

– March 6
Wins Craven University Scholarship

– June 9
Wins Chancellor's English Verse Medal for 'Evening'

– July 11–late September
On reading party, Llanrwst, North Wales

1822 January 19
Takes B.A. without honors, having given up on mathematical examination

– January 25
Admitted student of Lincoln's Inn

- February 5
  First record of TBM's speaking at Cambridge Union; he remains an active speaker until 14 December 1824
- April–mid June
  In London and at Brighton with family
- June
  Returns to Cambridge
- July
  Engages to take two pupils

1823   May
  At Rothley Temple

- June
  First contribution to *Knight's Quarterly Magazine* published. Continues to contribute through November 1824
- Late July
  Leaves Rothley Temple for London
- August 16
  Returns to Cambridge
- October 1
  Sits, unsuccessfully, for Trinity Fellowship
- Late Fall
  Family moves to 50 Great Ormond Street, Bloomsbury

1824   June 25
  Speech to Anti-Slavery Society, Freemasons' Hall, London

- October 1
  Elected to Trinity Fellowship
- December
  Leaves Cambridge: does not again reside there

TO ZACHARY MACAULAY, 23 OCTOBER 1818

MS: Harvard University. *Address:* Z Macaulay Esq. / No 20 Cadogan place[1] / Chelsea / nr. London. *Mostly published:* Knutsford, *Zachary Macaulay*, pp. 342–3.

Cambridge.[2] Oct. 23. 1818

My dear father,

I would have written earlier had I had any thing to communicate, which however is not even now the case; so that all my information must be that I am alive, and well, and comfortable, that Cambridge is a strict exemplification of the old maxim, Magna urbs, magna solitudo,[3] and that I live among my small circle of friends as familiarly and as quietly as if we were in a desert island. I have resolved to have no second order of acquaintance, no deputy-friends who torment each other and themselves by ceremonies which only betray the coolness of their regard, and by a measured interchange of the dullest visits. I will be social and not gregarious.

George Stainforth makes a most excellent tutor,[4] and indeed his instructions and preparation for them occupy so much of my time that I have not an overplus to spare for more private studies. The mathematical lectures are merely like learning my horn-book again, and will be so during the whole of this year.

1 'In 1818 the family removed to London, and set up an establishment on a scale suited to their improved circumstances in Cadogan Place, which, in everything except proximity to Bond Street, was then hardly less rural than Clapham' (Trevelyan, 1, 125–6). Dickens describes Cadogan Place as 'the connecting link between the aristocratic pavement of Belgrave Square, and the barbarism of Chelsea. It is in Sloane Street, but not of it' (*Nicholas Nickleby*, ch. 21). The move was apparently made as late as October 1818: Zachary Macaulay's departure from Clapham thus coincided with TBM's going to Cambridge. All of the important remaining members of the Clapham Sect were now in London; to keep in touch with them was one of the reasons for the move.

2 TBM, accompanied by his father, by Henry Thornton, and by Thornton's guardian, Sir Robert Inglis, arrived in Cambridge on 17 October, where he was settled with Thornton in lodgings in Jesus Lane. Thornton (1800–81: *Boase*), the son of the Clapham leader Henry Thornton, had grown up from childhood with TBM but had not been at Preston's school. He became a successful banker and continued to reside in the Thornton house at Clapham until his death. On 18 October Zachary Macaulay wrote to his wife that 'yesterday was a busy day with us. We took possession of the lodgings at an early hour and found them excellent. Tom has a very good, comfortable, well furnished, parlour on the ground floor and a very nice bedroom on the next floor: on which floor Henry Thornton has his parlour and bed room together opening into one another. They drew lots for the occupancy and the lot thus determined the matter. . . . The lodgings are within two minutes walk of the gate of Trinity College. . . . We spoke to the tutor Mr. Browne who has promised to select from the thirty laundresses of Trinity one of exemplary virtue for our youths' (MS, Huntington).

3 From the anonymous Greek: see A. Meineke, *Fragmenta Comicorum Graecorum*, IV, 1841, 693, no. 361.

4 Stainforth had accepted the job of tutoring TBM only after at first refusing the offer: 'T. Macaulay would be a pupil of no ordinary attainments, and it would require much more time and exertion on my part to render him any effectual service in his studies, than I could afford to surrender with the prospect of a fellowship examination before me' (Stainforth to Richard Stainforth, 1 August 1818: MS, Huntington).

I could not trust myself to say and can hardly venture to write all I feel upon entering on this world of hazard and danger and competition and honour. The evils of Cambridge, from all that I have been able to learn, are evils which must be *sought*, and from such a depth of moral degradation I trust that the goodness of God, my own education, and the connections which I have formed will preserve me. Its honourable distinctions are it seems the hard earned, but the certain, fruit of exertion and perseverance. If I would not willingly fail of attaining to some share in them, I trust it is not from selfish motives. I am sure I never valued any human applause so much as your quiet approbation, nor desired any human rewards so much as your pleasure in my success. And I am far less desirous to return loaded with medals or distinguished on the tripos-paper, than to acquire here those accomplishments and that information which may qualify me to inherit your public objects; and to succeed to your benevolent enterprises. There is an anecdote in Roman History which always affected me much. Fabius who when he was a child had been carried on his father's knee on his triumphal entry into Rome, insisted that when he himself came home with similar honours his father should enter his chariot, and share the honours of his son. I never had a higher ambition than that we might, if it please God, triumph together over the enemies of humanity, and I will do my utmost to obtain those weapons of assault and that armour of defence which literature furnishes for such contests, in this seat of its dominion.

My dear Mother, I send you my most affectionate love. My dear Jane are your tears dry? I kiss you with my "mind's lips." –

Farewell.

T B M

TO ZACHARY MACAULAY, [3? November 1818][1]

MS: Trinity College. *Address:* Z Macaulay Esq. / No 20 Cadogan Place / Chelsea / nr. London.

Cambridge

My dear Father,

I have deferred writing for some little time, in order that I might tell you of my recovery from the effects of an accident, before I informed you of its occurrence. Last Monday as I was sitting at George Stainforth's, a knife dropped from the table with the point downwards, and fixed in my thigh. The wound was somewhat painful, and confined me for two days absolutely to my sofa. But I had little reason to murmur at the restraint; as

---

[1] Postmark of receiving office dated 4 November.

the knife, if it had perforated in any degree deeper, would necessarily have produced a highly dangerous wound of which, my Surgeon told me, a lock jaw would have been the slightest consequence. I am now perfectly well; and do not feel the slightest uneasiness. I have great reason to inscribe this interference of providence on the list of its other numerous mercies to me. God grant that my conduct here may shew a heart not ungrateful for his signal mercy at the opening of my Academical course. No situation can be more comfortable than mine is here. My rooms are good enough for a place where magnificence is no great object; – my conveniences for study excellent; and the labour of housekeeping no very difficult employment. Henry Thornton and I generally breakfast and drink tea together; and Malden is all but domesticated with us. Of Wilberforce I have seen as little as could be possibly expected; and with my Cousin[1] I have no other intercourse than a passing nod and smile. The reports which I hear of him do not of course come from any of his own associates, and seem rather to be the effects of an unfavourable opinion of him already formed than of any recent events which might justify a still wider separation from him. He is not, I have been told, by men of his year, very regular at lectures. But this, I understand, though perhaps a blameable neglect, is no proof of idleness; but is more generally found among those who do not wish the train of studies which they are vigorously pursuing to be interrupted by the vague and, (as I should pronounce them from my own experience,) generally useless dissertations which a lecturer can give. I cannot, you see, speak with precision on this subject, and you must consider the statement as dubious and the inference problematical alike. –

There is a new college regulation about Sunday evening chapel, dictated I am satisfied in my own mind by dislike to the Saints, which compels every person to attend there at the same time that Simeon's service opens, so that it is impossible to attend him more than once a day.[2] I heard a splendid discourse on Sunday in the university church, most strikingly

---

[1] John Heyrick Macaulay (1799–1840), eldest of the eight sons of Aulay Macaulay, Vicar of Rothley; B.A., Trinity, 1821. He was headmaster of Repton School, 1832–40. Zachary Macaulay reported to his wife that the tutors at Trinity 'think very ill' of John Macaulay (18 October 1818: MS, Huntington) and in a letter of 1 January 1821 speaks of John's 'idle and vicious course' (to Kenneth Macaulay: MS, University of London). At Repton he was remembered as '"of great natural abilities and conversational powers, of stupendous memory, and with a voice like a powerful organ...dreaded by the younger boys"' (Alec Macdonald, *A Short History of Repton*, 1929, p. 148).

[2] Simeon, after meeting years of official and undergraduate hostility to his ministry, was by now too well-established to be injured by this regulation. 'As for my Church, there is nothing new. Those who so greatly disturbed me are gone; and my Church is sweetly harmonious. As for the Gownsmen, never was anything like what they are at this day. I am forced to let them go up into the galleries, which I never suffered before; and notwithstanding that, multitudes of them are forced to stand in the aisles for want of a place to sit down' (Simeon to Thomas Thomason, 30 November 1818, in William Carus, *Memoirs of the Life of the Rev. Charles Simeon*, 3rd edn, 1848, p. 346).

delivered by Rennell,[1] son of the Dean of Winchester. But all that I have heard there besides is wretched indeed, half-political, half-polemical trash, against parliamentary reform and predestination, and Bible Societies. My love to Mamma and Jane with cordial thanks for her letter, which I would have answered but that your enquiries required previous satisfaction. By-the-bye, I wish you would instantly transmit the receipt for my Nasine Lotion.

Affectionately farewell.

T B M.

TO ZACHARY MACAULAY, 9 NOVEMBER 1818

MS: Trinity College. *Address:* Z Macaulay Esq. / No 20 Cadogan Place / Chelsea / nr. London. *Partly published:* Trevelyan, 1, 88–9.

Cambridge. Nov. 9. 1818.

My dear Father,

I am sorry that any uneasiness was occasioned to you and to my Mother by my silence, and I will take care not to fall into the same error. I am not surgeon enough to answer all your queries. But by Mr. Farish's[2] account the knife went very near a place called the pope's eye, the least injury to which occasions a lock-jaw. The wound is most perfectly healed, and for some days I have walked with perfect ease; – I was not able for a few days after the accident to do more than limp to and from hall and chapel.

Your letter which I read with the greatest pleasure on the subject of the Congress at Aix la Chapelle,[3] is perfectly safe from all persons who could make a bad use of it. The Emperor Alexander's plans as detailed in the conversation between him and Clarkson are almost superhuman;[4] and tower as much above the common hopes and aspirations of philanthropists as the statue which his Macedonian namesake proposed to hew out of

---

[1] Thomas Rennell (1787–1824: *DNB*), Vicar of Kensington, 1816–24. Rennell was a High Churchman and editor of the *British Critic*.

[2] Probably John Farish, a Cambridge doctor, brother of the prominent Evangelical William Farish, Jacksonian Professor of Natural Philosophy at Cambridge.

[3] The first of the Congresses instituted by the Treaty of Paris.

[4] The Emperor, after affirming his readiness to put an end to the slave trade, went on to tell Clarkson of his plan to secure international peace through meetings of the European sovereigns '"for the general objects of redressing wrongs, conciliating differences, checking tendencies to war, removing causes of discontent, and advising with each other as to the means of preserving the general tranquillity, promoting the general happiness, and diffusing knowledge, civilisation and the blessed light of religion throughout the world"' (Zachary Macaulay to Hannah More, 26 October 1818, Knutsford, *Zachary Macaulay*, p. 346). Clarkson's account of his interview was circulated at the time among friends. It has since been published by [P. H. Peckover], *Thomas Clarkson's Interview with the Emperor of Russia at Aix-la-Chapelle*, Wisbech, 1930.

Mount Athos excelled the most colossal works of meaner projectors. As Burke said of Henry the Fourth's famous wish that every peasant in France might have the chicken in his pot comfortably on a Sunday, we may say of these mighty plans, "The mere wish, the unfulfilled desire exceeded all that we hear of the splendid professions and exploits of princes." Yet my satisfaction in the success of that noble cause in which he seems to be exerting himself with so much zeal is scarcely so great as my regret for the man who would have traced every step of its progress with anxiety and hailed its success with the most ardent delight. Poor Sir Samuel[1] – Quando ullum invenient parem?[2] How long may a penal code at once too sanguinary and too lenient, half-written in blood like Draco's, and half indefined and loose as the common law of a tribe of savages, be the curse and disgrace of the country? How many years may elapse before a man who knows like him all that law can teach, and possesses at the same [time][3] like him, a liberality and a discernment of general rights which the technicalities of professional learning rather tend to blunt, shall again rise to ornament and reform our jurisprudence? For such a man, if he had fallen in the maturity of years and honours, and been borne from the bed of sickness to a grave by the [side][3] of his prototype Hale,[4] amidst the tears of [nobles?][3] and senators, even then, I think the public sorrow would have been extreme. But that the peaceful melancholy of the house of mourning should be changed for scenes of blood and terror and judicial inquest, that the last moments of an existence of high thoughts and great virtues should have past in the delirium of madness, agony and despair – I know of no tragedy which has drawn scenes so painful. In my feelings the scene at Claremont[5] this time last year was mere dust in the balance in comparison.

My affectionate love to my Mother and Jane my kind correspondent. I own and will atone for my ingratitude to her etc.

Farewell.

T B M

---

[1] Sir Samuel Romilly (1757–1818: *DNB*), the legal reformer; following the death of his wife on 29 October he committed suicide on 2 November by cutting his throat with a razor.
[2] Horace, *Odes*, I, xxiv, 8.
[3] Paper torn away with seal.
[4] Sir Matthew Hale (1609–76: *DNB*), Chief Justice under both Cromwell and Charles II, a model of 'stern integrity' ('Lord Nugent's Memorials of Hampden,' *ER*, LIV, 549).
[5] The death of Princess Charlotte, 6 November 1817.

TO HANNAH MORE, 11 NOVEMBER 1818

MS: Trinity College.

Cambridge. November. 11. 1818.

My dear Madam,

Your letter,[1] which from some confusion of persons existing between me and a namesake of mine at Cambridge did not reach me quite so soon as the date would have given me to expect, deserves my warmest thanks, especially when written under such circumstances. The only means which I possess of showing my gratitude towards such friends for their kind wishes, is to do my utmost to merit the regard which their kindness has bestowed by anticipation, and to attempt not wholly to dissapoint the hopes which their partiality may have led them to entertain. While I have any sense of gratitude I shall feel it to be due to them, and while I know my own true interest, I shall think it due to myself, not to lose by inactivity or indiscretion the esteem of characters whose friendship, like that of Sir Philip Sidney, would alone form praise sufficient for my epitaph. The wishes of my friends, and in particular, my dear Madam, your own, will I hope always be treasured, like the amulet of a savage warrior, nearest my heart, to animate me to exertion when relapsing into sloth, and to fortify me against temptation when on the brink of its perils. There is, indeed, an armour more impenetrable to the darts of temptation than earthly considerations can bestow, and a sword more powerful in the moral conflict than any with which affection or gratitude may arm the combatant. Yet these motives, if they spring from earth, tend to heaven; and while not less powerful than the turbid and ambitious principle of competition and restless vanity, are far more pure and exalted.

The influence of association at this seat of the muses is, as you suppose, strong. Yet, in itself, I am no great admirer of this monastic life: I love the cheerful blaze of a domestic hearth, the reciprocation of varied conversation and mixed company, too well to relish the state to which I am here necessarily doomed. "Mais courage," as the poor pretender said in forty-five when some untoward circumstances called his attention to the difficulty of the enterprise. "Mais courage; c'est le grand jeu après tout."[2] – I see and own the advantages of the place. But never, never, may I lose the acuteness with which I feel its disadvantages. Never may I mistake the means of improvement for the end, or forget that as the greatest linguist

---

[1] On 26 October Zachary Macaulay had urged Hannah More to write to TBM, saying that 'he will receive with filial reverence whatever you say to him' (Knutsford, *Zachary Macaulay*, p. 346). This letter in reply to Hannah More's must be the one that she sends on to TBM's parents, calling it 'Tom's incomparable letter' (November 1818, in Roberts, *Letters of Hannah More to Zachary Macaulay*, p. 124).

[2] Scott, *Waverley*, ch. 58, last sentence.

that ever lived said, "Words are the sons of earth, but things are the daughters of heaven."[1] This I look upon as the mere armoury of literature and of professional skill. The weapons which it furnishes for the contest of life are necessary to engage in it with distinction or utility. But though I would not neglect the acquisition and the practise of its weapons and its defences, I should still less desire to be loitering among the magazines while the battle is raging. To descend from metaphor, never may I be a mere man of words and particles and accents; one of those scavengers and road-menders of literature who clear the way for passengers who travel with more enlarged views to enjoy the prospect. I climb a fine hill, not to count the stones on its side, but to survey the expanse of wood and water from its summit. I study a language not to be the slave of its peculiarities, but the master of its beauties. Whenever I forget the purposes of education, and cease to look upon classical and mathematical acquirements as the means of something better and nobler, may I become that pitiable being an old fellow of a college, without domestic ties or liberal views or capacities of literary enjoyment, or sense of benevolent pleasures, and a living instance of the truth of Molière's excellent line

"Il n-y-a point si grands sots que les sots savans."[2]

But I hope better things of one whom you, my dear Madam, have permitted to entitle himself

Your affectionate Friend,
Thos. B. Macaulay.

Give my affectionate love to Miss Patty. Henry Thornton begs to be kindly remembered to you.

TO ZACHARY MACAULAY, 16 NOVEMBER 1818

MS: Harvard University. *Address:* To / Zachary Macaulay Esq. / No 20 Cadogan Place / Chelsea / Nr. London.

Cambridge Monday / 16 Nov. 1818

My dear Father,

You ask for the details of my days. These are not easily given. College which I had imagined the favourite abode of those powers of Method and Order the daughters of Mathesis and the Mighty Mother of the Dunciad,[3] is alas! the place where I find myself least able to apportion certain hours

---

[1] See [20? October 1817].

[2] *Les Femmes Savantes,* IV, iii, 1297–8: 'Et je vous garant / Qu'un sot savant est sot plus qu'un sot ignorant.'   [3] *Dunciad,* I, I.

to certain pursuits. Sometimes for a week together I never find it necessary to make the slightest preparation for lectures. At others I am employed for half-a-dozen hours in discovering the solution of some problem which is given out for the exercise of skill by our tutor. Sometimes George Stainforth finds me uninterrupted employment for a long course of time, and sometimes, while he is employed in collecting materials for me, I am left to my own devices.

I have not been idle, and I have not trifled. My veins have been like Maberley's strangers to the juice of the grape;[1] I do not go to wine parties. And yet I do not find that I have done what I should have expected. I cannot accuse myself of having read any thing but grave Latin and Greek. But there is something desultory about an unaccustomed mode of life which renders, as I am told, the first few weeks of a man's residence here less useful than those which follow. Business with people to whom I am not accustomed and in forms of which I know nothing, interrupts and delays me. If I rise at four the chapel breaks in upon my morning studies. If I sit down after dinner it interrupts me immediately again. I suppose I shall soon get to calculate upon these interruptions better, and be enabled to measure out my time more accurately.

I have long been doubting how far it would be expedient for me to return at Christmas. The scholarship[2] will not be contested till the last week of January, so that unless I paid you a visit before it, I shall not come home till Easter. I think, if you have no objection, of coming at the end of the term, about the 17th of December and staying over Christmas, and then returning to my preparations. I expect to do more in a day of the vacation when uninterrupted by lectures and chapel than in a week of the term. Francis[3] of whom you know something is here. He took a high degree, but I believe allowed by the Exa[min][4]ers themselves to be below his Mathematical merits. He has paid me very kind attention [and][4] offered his assistance to me in any diffic[ulties][4] that may arise in my mathematical studies. Stainforth is all attention and kindness. His system is most rational, and costs me as much labour as it ought, and himself, I believe, rather more. He is assisting Malden, in the most friendly manner, in his classical preparations. –

I enclose a translation which I wrote the other day of Vincent Bourne's

[1] Frederick Herbert Maberley (1781–1860: *DNB*), Curate of Bourn, Cambridgeshire. A violently eccentric Evangelical, Maberley published 'The Melancholy and Awful Death of Lawrence Dundas...with an Address...on the Evil Nature...of Drunkenness and Fornication,' 1818, on the case of a Trinity undergraduate who, in February 1818, died of exposure after falling in a ditch while drunk.

[2] The Davies university scholarship. See 29–30 January 1819.

[3] Clement Francis ([1792]–1829), B.A. (eighth wrangler) 1817; Fellow of Caius, 1820–9; a Cambridge friend of Henry Venn and a relative of Mme D'Arblay.

[4] Paper torn away with seal.

beautiful Latin Poem intended for an inscription on Milton's Statue in Westminster Abbey.[1] It is rather a paraphrase, and that a pretty free one, than a translation, so that if the original is not at hand, it may be judged by its own demerits. I am without apology towards my dear Jane. But though I am compelled to defer my tardy epistle by the necessity of answering her queries, she is never out of my head or my heart.

My affectionate Love to my mother, to her, and all at home.

Farewell

T B M

TO SELINA MACAULAY, 30 NOVEMBER 1818

MS: Trinity College. *Address:* To / Miss Selina Macaulay / No 20 Cadogan Place / Chelsea / Nr. London.

Cambridge Novemr. 30. 1818

My dear Selina,

Many thanks for your kind letter; I believe not much more correspondence will pass, before you will see me at Cadogan place. On the 16th of this month[2] our Commemoration feast takes place, and on the 17th, if Tutors, Deans, and Masters, are propitious, I expect to see you. I wish you could persuade my father to come down and partake our entertainment, and hear the declamation of Waddington[3] in our chapel. Then I could return together with him. If not I can come by the mail or one of the coaches. I wish that I may hear soon if he will find it possible to do this, as I understand Mr. Inglis[4] talks of it; – if not, I must take my place directly.

---

[1] 'In Miltonum,' *Poetical Works*, Oxford, 1826, pp. 40–1. A copy of TBM's version is at Trinity.

[2] TBM means December.

[3] Horace Waddington (1799–1867), B.A. and Fellow of Trinity, 1820; called to the bar, 1825; Recorder of Warwick and of Lichfield, 1838–48; Permanent Under-Secretary of State for the Home Department, 1848–66.

[4] Sir Robert Harry Inglis (1788–1855: *DNB*), second Baronet (succeeded 1820), was introduced to Clapham on the death of Henry Thornton in 1815, when he and his wife were made guardians of the Thornton children and came to live in the house at Battersea Rise. There is universal testimony that he was a remarkably mild and benevolent man; he was also an extremely rigid Tory, 'almost the only remaining specimen of the old High Tory and of the old-fashioned High Churchman' (Duke of Argyll, *Autobiography and Memoirs, 1823–1900*, 1906, I, 415). He represented Oxford in Parliament from 1829, having defeated Peel on the question of Catholic emancipation. In the House he opposed TBM on every important issue, including parliamentary reform, Jewish relief, repeal of the corn laws, and the Maynooth grant. Sir Frederick Pollock remembered two lines from some satirical verses by TBM on Inglis's victory over Peel at Oxford:

> 'Then called out all the doctors in the Divinity School,
> "Not this man, but Sir Robert" – now, Sir Robert was a fool'

(Grant Duff, *Notes from a Diary, 1873–1881*, 1898, I, 108). Despite this judgment, TBM remained on decent social terms with Inglis.

For you may conceive the competition for conveyance is likely to be hot when it is to be procured? – some hundreds of men are on their return homewards.

You form very ill grounded ideas of my opinion upon Milton's merits from my having paraphrased Vincent Bourne's eulogy of him. Milton was a poet whose powers, though great in degree, were not particularly high in order. He has, compared with Shakespeare, little knowledge of character or skill in delineation of passion, compared with Homer, little fire of description or power of pathos. All the advantages which the sacred literature of the Hebrews afforded him could not raise him above poets who exerted their abilities on the puerile fictions of a false mythology. Though as he himself says, his Muse took her flight from heights "above th'Aonian mount,"[1] yet she was passed in her career by others whose genius soared with mightier impulse, though from a lower stand. Take his description of hell. It is the finest part of his poem, far the finest. And compare it with the infernal regions of Homer. The hell of Milton is a scene of material suffering described with considerable power doubtless of imagination and language, but losing its horrors by being described at all. The very flames shed a light which takes from it the idea of horrible mystery. The shore of burning marl might torment corporeal forms, but seems absurd when used as an instrument of torture to spirits. But when he rises to higher beings, and attempts to delineate the power who dwells in the light which no man may approach, he sinks back from the refulgence, as Gray says, "blasted with excess of light."[2] Homer has made his infernal regions gloomy, silent, obscure, mysterious. The sun averts his face from their confines. No detail is given, but a single line conveys, to my mind, a degree of horrible energy to which all Milton's creations of terrror are far inferior. "Abodes dark and fearful, at whose name the very Gods tremble."[3] But I do not expect to make you a convert. Perhaps I carry my own prejudice too far. But I have lately been reading Homer in the original, and his effulgence casts a shade on every other creation of Human genius. –

Affectionately farewell.
T B M

I had forgot to say that Dean Milner wishes to procure some coffee, and he wants it to be of the very best order, Mocca if possible. Will Papa send him intelligence where and how?

[1] *Paradise Lost*, I, 15.
[2] 'The Progress of Poesy,' 101.   [3] *Iliad*, xx, 65.

TO THOMAS BABINGTON, 5 DECEMBER 1818

MS: Trinity College. *Address:* To / Thomas Babington Esq: / Rothely Temple / Leicester-shire.

Cambridge December 5th. 1818

My dear Uncle,

I fear you will have thought me strangely negligent of your kind and truly paternal letter. If you could have seen how often I have perused it, or discovered the feelings of gratitude and affection to yourself with which I read it, you would have thought otherwise. I have been silent, princi-pally, that I might be enabled to send you in reply something more than mere professions, and that before I assured you of my intentions to take your excellent advice, I might learn, in some measure, by experience how far it was in all points compatible with the forms of society established here. I am happy to be able to assure you that all that I heard at a distance from Cambridge, and that you, I doubt not, have likewise heard rumoured, of the immense amount of *gross* and *palpable* moral evil diffused through the body, and of the necessity of complying with, or at least the difficulty of evading invitations of the kind which you disapprove are chimeras. The universal aspect of things, as far as I have observed, is decent. The necessity of accepting wine-invitations, or of attending dinner-parties, is, I am fully convinced, a factitious necessity. I have universally declined invitations, and have never once known the refusal taken ill in the smallest degree. I fully agree with your objection to it on the ground of its being a waste of time. But instances of excess are extremely rare in any circle with which I have any connection even by the report of an acquaintance.

Those parts of your letter which relate to these and other direct acts and habits are most easily answered. Of the admonitions directed to less obvious subjects which your kind manual contained, I can only say that I feel their force, and that I hope I am not insensible to the motives which they urge. To the power of literary emulation few are insensible; of its danger, I am, I hope, aware. But I trust the time will never come when the mean operation of that selfish passion shall be more powerful in my breast, than the desire of qualifying myself for a life useful to my fellow creatures, and of giving pleasure to my numerous kind friends, – among the dearest of those friends, as long as I have gratitude or feeling, I am sure I shall never cease, my dear uncle, to number you.

Give my affectionate regards to my Aunt and my Cousins, and believe me ever, / My dear Uncle,

Your affectionate Nephew,
Thomas Babington M[acaulay][1]

[1] Paper torn away with seal.

TO ZACHARY MACAULAY, 8 DECEMBER 1818

MS: Trinity College. *Address:* Zachary Macaulay / No 20 Cadogan Place / Chelsea / nr.
London.

Cambridge December 8th. 1818

My dear Father,

I received yesterday your kind present without any means of ascer-
taining the donor; and to day your affectionate letter doubled and more
than doubled the value of the gift by announcing the giver. As such I shall
prize it, though as a momento I am sure I never shall need it. I want indeed
no remembrancer of my home. It is with me always; and I am sure I can
say with sincerity that the highest pleasures are those which are purely
domestic, and that of all others those are the most delightful which are
enjoyed in association with domestic feelings. Their fondness for home is
the first thing which schoolboys are taught to think it manly to shake off;
– but even now, in the possession of comparative freedom from restraint,
and without any of the minor motives which schoolboys feel, I have a
longing affection for the seat of all that I love which is the source, I may
truly say, of almost all my pains and pleasures. I hope in a very few days
to see you again. On Thursday week my place is secured; and on that day
Deo Volente, and Mr. Judgson[1] not refusing, I expect to dine at Cadogan
place. – That is if I am able, which I have not been for the last 3 days.
I have had indeed a strange want of appetite and dejection of spirits lately.
I have ate of late almost as little as in my fever at Aspenden.[2] Yet I feel no
weakness. I take exercise regularly, and am to all appearance, and as to
outward sensation perfectly well. Is this one of the freaks of our climate?
If so I am ashamed to be under its influence. I have always laughed at the
hypochondriac vassals of the weather-cock and the barometer, the minds
which are unnerved by an easterly wind, and the temper which is soured
by a rainy day. Even while I write I feel my disdain kindling, and I will not
be an apostate from my own principle. At all events I must do my utmost
to recover my powers of eating before Commemoration-day, or I shall
scandalize the whole college. I shall hope, at any rate, to recruit myself
completely at home.

Give my affectionate love to my dear Mother. She has been but a bad

[1] William George Judgson ([1780]–1825), Senior Dean, Trinity, 1816–21.
[2] Probably the illness referred to in TBM's letter of 25 March 1821. It seems to have occurred
in the spring of 1818, TBM's last term at Aspenden Hall; this would account for the absence
of letters from him between 18 April and 23 October. On 28 May 1818 Hannah More writes
from Barley Wood, where TBM was then staying, that he has been 'just snatched from the
jaws of death' (Roberts, *Letters of Hannah More to Zachary Macaulay*, p. 117). It is possible that TBM's illness when 'about sixteen,' mentioned in Margaret Macaulay's *Recollections*, was in fact the fever of 1818: see 9 September 1816.

Correspondent since I have been at Cambridge. Love to all the Girls, and Charles. Believe me ever / My dear Father

Your affectionate Son

T B M.

P.S. With my usual ingenuity and [   ]¹ I have [con]¹trived to omit the most impo[rtant   ]¹ of my letter, viz the Estimates and demands of Subsidy. I suppose it will be expedient to clear off Turner's² bill for the lodgings at the end of the term; and besides that he received a weekly pay for his services as Gyp, or is to receive one. I believe a College bill for Commons is generally sent in at the end of the term, and other demands from the college tradesmen are to be expected, all of which together my present funds will not satisfy.

TO ZACHARY MACAULAY, 31 DECEMBER 1818

MS: Trinity College. *Address:* Z Macaulay Esq. / No 16 George Street³ / Mansion House / London.

Cambridge. Thursday Dec. 31. 1818

My dear Father,

I had scarce arrived when I received Brown's⁴ bill. It is most grossly erroneous, surcharging in some points and not mentioning others. Yet the bill for lodging, the only one which was previously submitted to me, is accurate, so that he can scarce have confounded me with John Macaulay. There is a charge of five pounds for a shoe-maker's bill though I have employed no shoe-maker, and of 7 pounds for a tailor though I have not had one stitch put in for me. The total amount is however moderate being 53 pounds, a pretty fair sum for a third part of the year. I mean to speak to Brown, but I have not been able to get an audience. I think it best to wait

---

¹ Paper torn away with seal.
² TBM's landlord in Jesus Lane.
³ The new address of Zachary Macaulay's firm, though Macaulay apparently retained his Birchin Lane offices as well. George Street has been called Mansion House Place for the last century. It runs along the east side of the Mansion House.
⁴ John Brown (1775?–1850), Tutor of Trinity College, 1807–24; Vice-master, 1830–42. He was, according to Winstanley, *Early Victorian Cambridge*, p. 18, a 'zealous member' of the Evangelical party at Cambridge. Lord Teignmouth, as an instance of the power of habit among the Dons, states that Brown, who was an 'excellent private tutor,' had his life 'embittered' when Trinity changed the hour of dining in the hall (*Reminiscences*, I, 29). Perhaps TBM was thinking of Brown when he argued that the 'monastic' system of Cambridge inevitably produced 'impatience of petty privations' ('The London University,' *ER*, XLIII [February 1826], 324). Brown gave the mathematics lectures at Trinity, and was 'distinguished for the affability of his demeanour' ([J. M. F. Wright], *Alma Mater*, 1827, I, 127).

until I receive an answer from you; – I am almost clear that my cap, gown, and surplice were paid for at the time. If not the tailor's bill is accounted for. I wish to have your authority on the subject before I give Brown the trouble of an examination of the tailor, and a revisal of all the bills. This is the first effect of that most inconvenient system, (as I take it to be,) of paying bills by the hands of a person who cannot be assured of the accuracy of the demand.

I am perfectly well; all my indisposition has completely vanished; and I am immersed at once in various employments. This business of the bills vexes me, because I have no director in the case, since all my friends up here are freshmen like myself, and are as much puzzled as I am. Whether I receive a letter from you the day after to morrow or not I shall apply to Brown on that day. I think it possible that the use of the names Macaulay Senior and Macaulay Junior may be the cause of the mistake. I am senior on the boards[1] and junior in residence. The title of Senior certainly belongs to me, and I should be styled so in any College list or account. [   ][2] the servants of the College and the trades[men][2] know [my][2] Cousin to be the older resident th[ey][2] commonly call me Junior, and have entered my name as such in the buttery books.[3] So that it is possible that some articles from one name and some from the other may have been united. I shall settle the matter soon and then transmit the bill to you. It is to be paid to Brown's banker in London. – My affectionate love to my Mother, my Brothers and Sisters, and my Uncle.

Affectionately farewell

T B M

I could not write yesterday as I found that I was mistaken about the day of sending round the letters, and had to superscribe, subscribe, and distribute them late yesterday evening.[4]

---

[1] That is, entered for the college earlier; men were entered before coming into residence. TBM was entered on 26 April 1817 and came up in October 1818; John Macaulay was entered on 20 May 1817 and came up in October 1817 (information from Dr R. Robson, of Trinity).

[2] Paper torn away with seal.

[3] Among the undergraduates TBM was known as 'Beast' Macaulay to distinguish him from his cousin 'Bear' Macaulay ([Wright], *Alma Mater*, II, 218).

[4] Candidates for university scholarships had to announce their intention to compete in a Latin letter addressed to each of the Electors (information from Dr R. Robson).

TO ZACHARY MACAULAY, [22 JANUARY 1819]¹

MS: Trinity College. *Address:* Zachary Macaulay Esq / No 16 George Street / Mansion House / London.

[Cambridge]

My dear Father,

I have been shocked at receiving a letter from Tom Babington² inquiring for his 5th Volume of Mitford's History of Greece. When we left Clapham I laid it by itself in order to be returned and begged that particular directions might be given that it might not be packed with the other books. These however were not attended to, and it went with our other packages to Cadogan place. I did not stay there long enough to be present at the unpacking; but my last request at going was that as soon as it was found, it might be sent to Hampstead. If this is not done, I hope that a careful search will be made for it. It is a quarto book, and is in boards. It would I suppose be placed most likely among the books of that size in your room without being distinguished from the rest. I am impatient to hear the event of the search.

John Macaulay is at Rothely, and till he returns, an inspection into accounts cannot possibly take place. Brown with perfect tranquillity said that such things often happened, and that we must settle it among ourselves. To him it is certainly all the same how it is settled. But for my own part I feel extremely awkward about proceeding. Such things will not however again occur, as we have made provision for the distinction.

I send Pompeii³ herewith. Pray criticise it with the utmost severity and acumen. When I have received your advice and transmitted my corrections I shall be much obliged to Selina to transcribe it, as we are not allowed to show up our performances in our own hands. The transcription had better be made in the form, as nearly as possible, of the copy which I have sent though letter paper will be more respectful than foolscap. The

---

¹ Dated from reference to announcement of Cambridge honors, which was made on 23 January 1819.

² Thomas Gisborne Babington (1788–1871), eldest son of Thomas Babington, entered business partnership with Zachary Macaulay about 1810. When Macaulay retired from the daily management of the firm in 1823 to devote himself to the anti-slavery campaign, Babington took over the management; in three years his over-ambitious policies 'accomplished the ruin of himself and his uncle' (Knutsford, *Zachary Macaulay*, p. 398). His niece Eliza Rose Conybeare summarized him thus: 'My eldest uncle, so gentlemanly, so well informed, so very literary, and such a prig; his absurd sayings, his solemn flirtations, all noted in his diary, and hours of excited feeling referred to fifty years after with laughter-killing accuracy. His unhappy first marriage, and unwelcome, but comfortable, second marriage' ('Aunt Eliza's Story,' 1875: typescript memoir in possession of Mr B. Babington Smith).

³ TBM's successful entry for the Chancellor's English verse medal. The subject for the competition had been given out on 25 October and the entries were due by 26 March (*Cambridge University Calendar*, 1818, p. 46).

notes are I think redundant. Curtail all that you think superfluous. A writer is rarely a good judge of the clearness and force with which his own lines convey their idea to the minds of others.

A piece of paper must likewise be taken and folded up like a letter. My name at full length thus,

Thomas Babington Macaulay
of Trinity College

must be written within. No direction must be put outside, but the lines which stand as a motto to the poem must be written on it. It must be sealed, (not with the family arms.) The object of this is that the names of all except the successful competitor may be unknown; the papers being all destroyed unopened except that which is inscribed with the motto of the victorious poem.

Above all let nobody know of the existence of the poem excepting my Mother and Sisters. Success is highly improbable as Townsend,[1] I am informed, writes on the occasion. He has already gained one medal. However failure is here no disgrace, and therefore I venture.

Love to all at home.

Affectionately farewell
T B M.

Since I wrote the above a friend of mine who is going up to London after just taking his degree has charged himself with the poem. You will receive it therefore very soon.

King[2] of Queen's is senior wrangler, or at least not the slightest doubt is entertained that he will be proclaimed so to night. His superiority in the Examination was most splendid. Brougham[3] will scarcely be above the ninth or tenth wrangler. But to-morrow will show.

[1] Chauncey Hare Townshend (1798–1868: *DNB*), of Trinity Hall, won the Chancellor's English medal for 'Jerusalem,' 1817. Townshend, a collector, traveller, and dilettante, is perhaps best remembered now as the dedicatee of *Great Expectations*. As his literary executor Dickens faithfully published Townshend's *Religious Opinions*, 1869, but privately called them 'religious hiccoughs.'

[2] Joshua King (1798–1857), of Queens' College, senior wrangler, 1819; Fellow and Tutor of Queens', 1820; President of Queens', 1832–56. King succeeded Stainforth as TBM's tutor (see 12 March 1819). Henry Thornton remembered that 'in these years Macaulay evinced an interest in geometrical problems, and he and King would launch into interminable arguments, in which Macaulay asserted that such and such a thing must be, while King upheld its impossibility – Macaulay as usual tilting at windmills '(Alston, 'Recollections of Macaulay,' p. 61).

[3] William Brougham (1795–1886: *DNB*), brother of Henry, whom he succeeded as second Baron Brougham; B.A., Jesus College, 1819. His name does not appear among the wranglers.

TO SELINA MILLS MACAULAY, 29–30 JANUARY 1819

MS: Trinity College. *Address:* Mrs. Macaulay / No 16. George Street / Mansion House / London.

Cambridge January 29. 1819.

My dear Mother,

Our Examination[1] began on Tuesday and will probably last for a week longer at an average of six hours a day. The event which you seem to expect to learn soon, will probably not be known for the next month. The eight examiners have to read all the papers of fourteen or fifteen men who are examined and to compare them, before they come to a conclusion. I heartily wish it were over. Oliphant[2] is a clever man: but he will not get the Scholarship, unless I am much deceived. Platt[3] has twice his learning and three times his experience in similar contests. This last is a great thing. – Jan 30. I have just received my Father's letter. The time at which the Poems *must* be sent in is the 25th of March. I am waiting for your criticisms. I assent to the justice of one which my Father transmitted in his hasty letter, and will think on the line. No addition can, however, prudently be made. Three hundred lines is the quantity most approved, and all above this is considered as a drawback. I have done my utmost to bring it within this compass, and indeed left out many passages which I liked better perhaps than they deserved in order to effect the curtailment.

I will send my Father's great Coat with all expedition.

The result of the Senate-House Examination has made many miserable and many happy men. I witnessed King's triumph on Saturday, and was among those whose loud clapping on the occasion called forth the Vice-Chancellor's interference. I could not however help expressing my pleasure at seeing a young man, who has struggled by exertions of a very rare order to the most splendid superiority, (preserving at the same time a most respectable character,) congratulated by the Heads of the University on his success before a large assembly of gownsmen.[4]

It struck me that, as my Father mentioned to me in London his intention of getting a mathematical tutor for me, King would be the most desirable that could be imagined. I know he is willing to take pupils. His

1 For the university scholarship; presumably the men of TBM's year who competed did so only for the practice: see 12 March 1819.
2 Alfred Ollivant (1798–1882: *DNB*), Craven scholar, 1820; Chancellor's classical medal, 1821; B.A., 1821; Fellow of Trinity, 1823; Vice-Principal, St David's College, Lampeter, 1827–43; Regius Professor of Divinity, 1843–9; Bishop of Llandaff, 1849–82.
3 Thomas Pell Platt (1798–1852) won the Davies university scholarship, 1819. B.A. and Fellow of Trinity, 1820, he was 'librarian of the British and Foreign Bible Society some years' (*Boase*) and became a noted scholar of oriental languages.
4 King was sizar of Queens': 'Sizars are generally men of inferior fortune. They usually have their commons free, and receive various emoluments' (*Cambridge University Calendar*, 1818, p. 207).

mathematical attainments are not only, as you may judge, of the highest order, but of the latest standing, and have their freshest gloss upon them. This however I merely suggest as an accidental thought of my own. Dean Milner would be the person to apply to about him, as he is a Queen's man.

But my paper is full though my head is not empty of some things which I wished to say. However I can only add my thanks for your kind letter, my affectionate love to you and all at home, and my assurances that I ever remain my dear Mother

Your affectionate Son
T B M

TO ZACHARY MACAULAY, 5 FEBRUARY 1819

MS: Trinity College. *Address:* Zachary Macaulay Esq. / No 16 George Street / Mansion House / London. *Partly published:* Trevelyan, I, 89–91.

Cambridge Friday Feb. 5 1819
My dear Father,
Our contest, after a duration of nine days terminated yesterday at 3 o'clock. In a month its result will probably be known. Though I have been almost entirely debarred from exercise during its continuance I am in excellent health; and hope to be perfectly refreshed by a few days of idleness and amusement.

I have not of course had time to examine with attention all your criticisms on Pompeii. I certainly am much obliged to you for withdrawing so much time from other more important business to examine the effusions of a poetaster. Most of the remarks which I have examined are perfectly just. But I think that perhaps the use of the word barbarism[1] in the sense in which I have employed it may be defended. This word and its cognates in both the classical languages is used to express anything foreign. By English writers it is often employed strictly in the ancient sense to express anything not Greek or Roman. Thus Milton in a line not very different from mine

"Show'rs on her Kings *barbaric* pearl and gold"
Par Lost Book 2.

And Bowdler in the best poem he ever wrote has this line. I quote from memory but I think accurately

"And Persia flaming with *barbaric* gold."[2]

[1] The word does not appear in the printed text of the poem.

[2] 'And Thracia flaming with barbaric gold,' line 50 of 'A Fragment,' John Bowdler, Jun., *Select Pieces in Verse and Prose*, 1816, I, 66. Bowdler (1783–1815: *DNB*), nephew of the editor of Shakespeare, was an Evangelical who contributed to the *Christian Observer*; his early death cut off the high hopes that the Clapham Sect had in him.

Even Gibbon, and the more severe Mitford frequently admit the word into their prose, where at all events it is more objectionable than in poetry.

As to introducing the theatrical spectacles at noonday,[1] it is certainly in costume. Those of the Greeks were always celebrated in the morning; as also those of the Romans till the time of Nero. Tacitus mentions it as one of the disgraces of the reign of that monster that he changed the time of those exhibitions to the evening and thus rendered the theatre what it is in our country the centre of every thing that is vicious and disgusting.[2] We may however suppose that this custom of the capital had not extended to the provincial towns, or at least an anachronism of a few years is scarcely of much importance.

As to the more momentous charge, the want of a moral, I think it might be a sufficient defence that, if a subject is given which admits of none, though the man who writes on it may be blamed, yet his writing without a moral is scarcely censurable. But is it the real fact that no literary employment is estimable or laudable which does not lead to the inculcation of moral truth or the excitement of virtuous feeling? Do we not think with pleasure rather than disapprobation of a man who delights to amuse little children, to play with them, to tell them agreable stories, and to give them fruit and play things. We do not put him on a level with him who teaches them to read, or instructs them in the first rudiments of religion. Yet we feel an approbation of his conduct. On what principle do we feel it? He effects no moral purpose. He teaches them nothing important. He rouses no laudable passion. – Simply, I conceive, because he *communicates pleasure innocently*. This then I take as an axiom which experience and the common sense of mankind demonstrate, and on which, as on every thing else which reason obviously inculcates, Christianity likewise places the seal of her sanction, – that it is an employment in itself laudable *to communicate pleasure innocently*.

Books of amusement are to men what toys and sugar plums are to children. They are the employment of the moments of leisure, the relief of hours of languor, they afford a refined, an elegant, and often an elevated enjoyment. They tend to polish the mind, to improve the style, to give variety to conversation, and to lend a grace to more important accomplishments. He who can effect this has surely done something. Is no useful end served by that writer whose works, though perhaps inculcating no direct moral information, have soothed weeks of languor and sickness, have relieved the mind exhausted from the pressure of employment, by an amusement which delights without enervating, which relaxes the tension of the powers without rendering them unfit for future exercise. That men

---

[1] 'But see, the op'ning theatre invites / The fated myriads to its gay delights,' 'Pompeii,' lines 81–2.   [2] *Annals*, XIV, XX.

should be eternally happy is doubtless the great object of benevolence. That they should be happy on earth as far as they innocently may, is surely an object not to be despised. And in this point of view the poet whose trifle amuses the reader for a spare hour may claim to be considered as an inferior labourer in the same field of benevolence with the liberators of Africa, the explorers of our prisons, and the surgeons of our hospitals.

I have been so used to see opinions which I tenaciously held subverted by arguments which though pretty obvious had never occurred to me, that I should not be surprised to see these observations refuted; and I shall not be sorry if they are so. I feel personally little interest in the Question. If my life be a life of literature, it shall certainly be one of literature directed to moral ends. But I write thus because I think the restrictions which some excellent persons now impose on writers too severe. Do we not allow various callings to be exercised in society? Are all our artificers and our tradesmen employed in providing for the necessaries or even for the comforts of life? Our butchers and bakers are surely not reputed a more respectable class of the community than our Goldsmith's and jewellers. Then why should not some allowance be made to literary men. Is literature the only thing in which we are to be restricted from luxuries, and permitted to enjoy or manufacture nothing which does not come under the denomination of necessity. I can scarcely approve of this sumptuary law. 1 own I cannot see why the man who writes an amusing poem, the Lady of the Lake for instance, is not as well employed as the man who manufactures a pearl-broach. Which gives the more pleasure cannot be doubted. And certainly *I* cannot doubt which is of the more advantage to society. – "But the goldsmith lives upon his jewellery. He works for his subsistence." – And Southey has lived upon his poetry. So in a great measure has Scott. So has Campbell. So did Thomson, Pope, Johnson. – I cannot see why a useless book is worse than a useless necklace. And if it be an agreable book, I should not hesitate to pronounce it better.

At all events let us be consistent. I was amused in turning over an old volume of your kind present the Xtian Observer, to find a gentleman signed Excubitor, (one of my Antagonists in the Question of Novel-reading,)[1] after a very pious argument on the hostility of Novels to a religious frame of mind, proceeding to observe that he was shocked to hear a young Lady who had displayed extraordinary knowledge of modern and ephemeral literature, own herself ignorant of Dryden's fables![2] –

[1] See Appendix for TBM's contributions to the *Christian Observer*. 'Excubitor' published three articles 'On the Expediency of Novel-Reading' in the May, June, and July numbers of the *Christian Observer*, xvi (1817).

[2] *Christian Observer*, xvi (May 1817), 301: 'she had neglected to peruse, in passing, only Paradise Lost, Comus, Samson Agonistes, Dryden's Fables, Cato, the Castle of Indolence, and, if I remember right, the Night Thoughts.'

Consistency with a vengeance! – The reading of modern poetry and novels excites a worldly disposition and prevents ladies from reading Dryden's fables! – Excubitor who excludes Waverley from his library, who shudders at the sight of Roderick, who calls for salts at the name of Lord Byron, shocked at a Lady for not reading Dryden's fables!!! – This is only one out of ten thousand exemplifications of my meaning. There is a general disposition among the more literary part of the religious world to cry down the elegant literature of our own times, while they are not in the slightest degree shocked at atrocious profaneness or gross indelicacy when a hundred years have stamped them with the title of *Classical*. I pretend not to be right. But I am sure I am consistent. I say; "if you read Dryden you can have no reasonable objection to reading Scott." The strict antagonist of ephemeral reading exclaims, – "Not so. – Scott's poems are very pernicious. They call away the mind from spiritual religion and from Tancred and Sigismunda." "Do not expect perfection," says Hannah More, (herself, by the bye, not quite free from the fault which I censure) "but expect consistency." –

I intended to have added something upon the nature of the Ancient classic poets whom we are enjoined by all people to read, and to point out how much more exceptionable they frequently are than the very worst of the poets whose names excite the abhorrence of our modern critics. I plead for neither. I give no opinion. I merely demand a consistent sentence. I merely demand with Horace and Pope, that a hundred or a thousand years should not be considered as purifying the licentious or canonizing the impious writer. – If mankind continue the same, it is not improbable that a couple of centuries hence future Excubitors will with similar zeal exclaim against ladies who read the poems which will then come from the shops of future booksellers, to the neglect of Parisina, and Lalla Rookh, those noble monuments of *Classical* genius. But I have far exceeded all ordinary limits. If these hasty remarks fatigue you, impute it to my desire of justifying myself from a charge which I should be sorry to incur with justice. Love to all at home.

Affectionately farewell.
T B M.

TO SELINA MILLS MACAULAY, [24 FEBRUARY 1819][1]

MS: Trinity College. *Address:* Mrs. Macaulay / No 16 George Street / Mansion House / London. *Mostly published:* Trevelyan, I, 87–8.

Cambridge. Wednesday.

My dear Mother,

I enclose Brown's bill. The bill for the term amounts you will see to 41 pounds. The additional charge of 35 pounds is partly for the admission fees, and partly for the retention of my name on the boards. The 15 pounds charged as caution money are taken to ensure my proceeding to the Master of arts degree, and will be returned when that takes place. –

I shall send [   ][2] very soon. The Scholarship is not yet decided. I advise you not to give credit to reports however apparently authentic. Nothing certain can have transpired. I could have filled sheets had I wished to amuse you with the various fictions which have been flying about Cambridge.

King I am absolutely certain would take no more pupils on any account. And even if he would, he has numerous applicants with prior claims. He has already I believe six, who occupy him six hours in the day, and is likewise lecturer to the College. It would however be very easy to obtain an excellent tutor for Thornton. Lefevre[3] or Malkin[4] are men of first-rate mathematical abilities, and both of our college. I can scarcely bear to write on mathematics or mathematicians. Oh for words to express my abomination of that science, if a name sacred to the useful and embellishing arts may be applied to the perception and recollection of certain properties in numbers and figures. Oh that I had to learn astrology or dæmonology, or School divinity, oh that I were to pore over Thomas Aquinas and to adjust the relation of Entity with the two predicaments, so that I were

[1] Postmark illegible except for 25 and E. Wednesday was the 24th in February 1819.
[2] Word illegible: overscored by someone other than TBM.
[3] John George Shaw-Lefevre (1797–1879: *DNB*), of Trinity; a particularly distinguished senior wrangler, 1818, and Fellow, 1819. Called to the bar in 1825, Shaw-Lefevre, among other employments and at various times, was Colonial Under-Secretary, Poor Law Commissioner, Assistant Secretary to the Board of Trade, and Civil Service Commissioner. He was Clerk of the Parliaments, 1855–75, and Vice-Chancellor of the University of London, 1842–62. In a note to his *History of England*, III, [1855], 90, TBM calls him 'one of the most valued of my friends.'
[4] Benjamin Heath Malkin (1797–1837), of Trinity, third wrangler, 1818, and Fellow, 1819; called to the bar, 1823. Malkin and Thomas Flower Ellis (see Introduction) were in the same year at Trinity and afterwards shared rooms as law students in London (memoir of Ellis [by Louisa or Marian Ellis]: MS, Trinity). Malkin was one of the group of young Cambridge men, including Malden, Ellis, and George Long, who wrote for Brougham's Society for the Diffusion of Useful Knowledge. He went to the East as Recorder of Penang, 1832, and came into TBM's circle again as Judge of the Supreme Court, Calcutta, 1835.

exempted from this miserable study! Discipline of the mind! Say rather that it is starvation, confinement, torture, annihilation of the mind. But it must be. I feel myself becoming a personification of Algebra, a living Trigonometrical canon, a walking table of Logarithms. All my perceptions of elegance and beauty gone, or at least going. By the end of the term I shall be a complete scarecrow. My brain will be "as dry as the remainder biscuit after a voyage."[1] Oh to change Cam for Isis. But such is my destiny, and since it is so, be the pursuit contemptible, below contempt, or disgusting beyond abhorrence, I shall aim at no second place. But three years! I cannot endure the thought. I cannot bear to contemplate what I must bear to undergo. Farewell then Homer and Sophocles and Cicero.

> Farewell, happy fields,
> Where joy forever reigns, hail horrors hail,
> Infernal world. —[2]

How does it proceed? Milton's descriptions have been driven out of my head by such elegant expressions as the following

$$\text{Cos} \, x = 1 - \frac{x^2}{1 \cdot 2} + \frac{x^4}{1 \cdot 2 \cdot 3 \cdot 4} - \frac{x^6}{1 \cdot 2 \cdot 3 \cdot 4 \cdot 5 \cdot 6}.$$

or

$$\text{Tan.} \, \overline{a+b} = \frac{\text{Tan} \, a + \text{Tan} \, b}{1 - \text{Tan} \, a \cdot \text{Tan} \, b} \quad \text{etc. etc.} -$$

[My][3] Classics must be Woodhouse[4] and [ ][3] my amusements summing an infinite series, a[ ][3] I must – Oh miserable, miserable me! – Farewell, and tell Selina and Jane to be thankful that it is not a necessary part of *female* education to get a head ache daily without acquiring one practical truth or beautiful image in return. Again, and with affectionate love to my Father, farewell, wishes

Your most miserable and mathematical son

T B M

[1] *As You Like It*, II, vii, 39–40.
[2] *Paradise Lost*, I, 249–51.
[3] Paper torn away with seal.
[4] Robert Woodhouse (1773–1827: *DNB*), Fellow of Caius, succeeded Isaac Milner as Lucasian Professor of Mathematics, 1820. Woodhouse was the author of several texts of which TBM probably means the *Treatise on Plane and Spherical Trigonometry*, 1809.

TO SELINA MILLS MACAULAY, 4 MARCH 1819

MS: Trinity College. *Address:* Mrs. Macaulay / No 16 George's Street / Mansion House / London.

Cambridge. March. 4. 1819

My dear Mother,

In what a world do we live! – I had not had time to procure mourning for my poor uncle;[1] when an event, more shocking to me, because infinitely more unexpected, happened almost under my eyes. Poor Blundell is no more. On Thursday he was attacked by a violent inflammation in the chest. Bleeding, the usual remedy I believe in such cases, was ordere[d][2] by our physicians. But they shrunk from the respon[si][2]bility of prescribing a very large quantity, and the apo[the][2]cary who executed the operation went even below the[ir or][2]ders. His mother and brother, Dr. Blundell, came down on Sunday. The skill of the one, who bled him most profusely, relieved him for a time; and the affection of the other supported and consoled him during the remainder of his illness. Every attention of friendship was shown by numbers of his friends here. His room was perhaps too largely filled with his more intimate acquaintances. His stairs were sometimes crowded with inquirers, and even the Bishop of Bristol[3] sent repeated messages. It was however too soon apparent that nothing could save him. He expressed perfect resignation to the will of God, and penitence for his sins, of which he seemed to entertain a full and strong sense. He received the sacrament on Monday night from John Brown, whose kindness could not be surpassed. He even offered to sit up all night with Blundell. Of this however there was no need, as so many of his friends were present. He frequently named Preston; and once faintly said, "He was right all along; and we were wrong." – [He][2] was asked whether it would gratify him to see Preston a[gain].[2] He grasped at the offer with eagerness, [an][2]d George [Stain][2]forth set off at midnight in a postchaise for Wotton. [A][2]t 2 O'clock on Tuesday Preston arrived. But the Physicians were of opinion that an interview would agitate the patient to a dangerous degree; and, as Mrs. Preston[4] is not very well, he returned the same afternoon without seeing his poor pupil. Yesterday Blundell seemed much better, and at one time sanguine hopes were entertained. But towards evening he gradually grew worse; and after lying for a short time in a

---

[1] Aulay Macaulay (1758–1819: *DNB*), Vicar of Rothley and eldest brother of Zachary Macaulay, died on 24 February.   [2] Paper torn away with seal.

[3] William Lort Mansel (1753–1820: *DNB*), Master of Trinity since 1798, contrived to hold the Bishopric of Bristol together with his Mastership from 1808: 'Taking lightly his episcopal duties, he resided chiefly at his lodge' (Teignmouth, *Reminiscences*, I, 26).

[4] Preston had married Eliza Garratt of Clapham Common, 7 July 1818, at Holy Trinity, Clapham. Presumably TBM was among the wedding guests.

state of apparent torpor expired at half past eleven o'clock. Poor fellow!
the last time I saw him, just before his seizure, he was in the highest
spirits and health. I am a most sincere mourner for him. Whatever
might have been his other imperfections, towards me he was all kindness, ever since I was in that situation when kindness is most needed
but least found, a child among young men, a little boy accustomed
to home and crying for my papa and mamma and sisters, amon[g][1]
hardened, thorough bred schoolboys. Kindness in [such][1] circum[s][1]-
tances is not to be soon forgotten [   ][1] As yet I only relate
general particulars. [   ][1] to learn something more
fully as to the sta[te of his][1] mind. Scholefield was with him in his
last m[   ][1] and from him I dare say I shall be able to
procure information.

This is the second instance within a few weeks, at my own College, of
a young man cut off in the midst of early hopes and literary emulation.[2]
To us, at least, I hope these events may not speak in vain.

My love to My Father and Sisters.

Affectionately farewell
T B M.

P.S. I have got Pompeii written out here. I will write more fully about it
hereafter. – My observations on Mathematics, I understand, you take for
earnest, and my Father for jest. I cannot blame either of your opinions.
I was in earnest because I hate the study and in jest because I despise it.

TO ZACHARY MACAULAY, 12 MARCH 1819

MS: Trinity College. *Address:* Zachary Macaulay Esq / No 16 George St. / Mansion House /
London.

Cambridge. March. 12. 1819.

My dear Father,

Happy as I am to hear of your recovery, I am scarcely pleased that it is
communicated in such a manner that I cannot but apprehend that your
indisposition has been more severe than I was informed. I must really implore you to give me full and fair representations on all such occasions.
Otherwise that feeling of security as to the welfare of our absent friends
which Epistolary communication might bestow will be completely destroyed; every interval of silence will be suspicious and even favourable
assurances will scarcely obtain confidence.

[1] Paper torn away with seal.
[2] Richard Nethercoat Cooke died on 3 January 1819 at Trinity College, aged twenty-three.

I was too much occupied by poor Blundell's death to think of the result of the Scholarship when I last wrote. I had every reason to be satisfied. No list of names appeared officially. But Monk[1] who of course was a principal examiner told me that I had done myself very high credit particularly for my standing, and requested me to congratulate you in his name when I next wrote on my having passed an examination which must, he said, give me both experience in the tactics of the system and a character for scholarship in the university. I was certainly above every man of my year, except Coleridge,[2] a King's man, and consequently, as I suppose you know, an Etonian of great distinction, a nephew by the bye of the Poet. Monk gave me very earnest recommendations to addict myself particularly to Classics, and from the state of things in my own year I cannot but think that it would be the most prudent course; But more of this at Easter; – when I hope to see you all at Cadogan Place.

Apropos of Easter. It is during the Easter vacation that the examination for our College Scholarships takes place; and, had it been possible or proper to have been a competitor, I should not have scrupled to sacrifice the pleasure of a visit to my dear home for so great an advantage. But the fact is that in the first place it is more tha[n pro][3]bable that freshmen will not be pe[rmitted][3] to sit at all; as the Bishop has repeat[edly][3] threatened to refuse permission and last year actually did so. In the next place, the quantity of Mathematics required is considerable, much greater than I am master of:[4] – I intended to have added something about that study, but my hour for attending King is arrived; and I must make haste to fold up this letter. Affectionate love to all. Many thanks to my Mother and Selina for their letters. Where is my dear little correspondent Jenny's pen all this while? I am afraid she is angry with me for being so bad a correspondent; and indeed I have no defence to make but to throw myself on her goodness.

Vale.

T B M.

---

[1] James Henry Monk (1784–1856: *DNB*), Tutor of Trinity and Regius Professor of Greek. The only glimpse of TBM in the classroom is in his college contemporary Richard Perry's account of Monk's opening lecture in 1818: 'I have a distinct recollection of the kind, but somewhat pompous voice of the Professor, as he uttered his name, and of the short, ungainly figure of Macaulay, as he stood up, and began to read the opening chorus of the "Persæ"' (*Contributions to an Amateur Magazine*, 1857, p. 310). Monk became Bishop of Gloucester in 1830 and of Gloucester and Bristol, 1836. His *Life of Richard Bentley*, 1830, was one of TBM's favorite books, though TBM noted in his Journal for 16 September 1852 that he had, as an undergraduate, been 'ungrateful and impertinent to him' (Trevelyan, II, 321).

[2] Henry Nelson Coleridge (1798–1843: *DNB*), later Coleridge's son-in-law and the editor of Coleridge's *Table Talk*, 1835.

[3] Paper torn away with seal.

[4] In the event, TBM took the examination and was placed in the first class of the freshmen (*Cambridge University Calendar*, 1820).

TO ZACHARY MACAULAY, 17 JUNE 1819

MS: Harvard University.

Cambridge June 17. 1819

My dear Father,

Nothing, as you will believe, would be more delightful to me at any time than a visit to my home. But at the present moment absolute necessity interferes to prevent my returning. I have procured rooms in College for a time, and am now engaged in transferring my goods and chattels, and making arrangements for your reception.[1] I hope that your party will come down together with my Uncle Colin and Matthew,[2] or at least on the same day, as our arrangements are such that you must all proceed in one party. Matthew we shall be able to lodge at Turner's, and I have directed a bed to be put up for him in the sitting-room which was mine. Our common sitting room I propose to be a very elegant and handsome apartment at a small distance which I have taken. I have also taken the adjoining bed-room for my Uncle Colin, not, as you may suppose, for nothing. I have procured capital rooms, – a parlour and two bed-chambers for Augusta and her sister.[3] They will not be at liberty till Friday week. Pray make Tom understand this; or else if they come down the day before they may be compelled to lodge "*sub Jove frigido*."[4] I should not have engaged these rooms under this grievance, but that it is extremely difficult to obtain on any terms two bed-rooms without taking two sitting-rooms likewise.

I shall expect of course to hear when you intend to arrive. Remember not to direct any longer to Turner's but to Trinity College.

The Poem went to the Press to day. I am much obliged to you for the Report of the African Institution.[5]

Ever affectionately yours, with love etc. to My Mother and the Girls.

T B M.

---

[1] A family party of Macaulays and Babingtons was coming to Cambridge for the commencement exercises, which were also the occasion of a royal visit to Cambridge. On 5 July, the day before commencement, following the conferring of honorary degrees in the Senate House, TBM read his prize poem 'Pompeii' before the Duke of Gloucester, Chancellor of the university, the Duchess of Gloucester, Princess Sophia, and the academic assembly. 'After the Chancellor had conferred the degrees with his usual dignity, Mr. Thomas Babington Macaulay, of Trinity college, recited his English poem on *Pompeii*, which had gained the Chancellor's gold medal. The audience appeared much pleased by the interesting manner in which the youthful bard delivered his admirable lines, (from which we have given some extracts in our Poets' Corner.) When he had concluded his recitation, he was conducted to the Chancellor, who presented him with the medal, and passed some gratifying compliment upon his poem' (Cambridge *Chronicle*, 9 July 1819).

[2] Babington: see 11 July 1814.

[3] Augusta Noel (1796?–1833), fourth daughter of Sir Gerard Noel Noel, married Thomas Gisborne Babington in 1814. I do not know which of her sisters is meant: there were six daughters among the eighteen children of Sir Gerard.   [4] Horace, *Odes*, I, i, 25.

[5] The African Institution, largely an Evangelical body, was formed in 1807 in anticipation of

TO ZACHARY MACAULAY, 21 JUNE 1819

MS: Trinity College. *Address:* Zachary Macaulay Esq. / No 16 George Street / Mansion House / London.

Cambridge June 21. 1819.

My dear Father,

My business here is at an end. I compounded for the rest of the poem by sacrificing forty or fifty lines,[1] which, entre nous, were the best in it. I felt at the extraction as if a pound of flesh had been cut from my side, nearest my heart; and I shall never look on Smythe[2] again without thinking of the knife and balance of Shylock.

It is high time that you should make up your minds as to the accommodation which you will want. My hands are of course tied till I learn the result of Gorham's[3] application to Mandell.[4] Tell Tom Babington that I am doing my utmost to secure the lodgings which he wants. If you are at liberty for the meditated excursion to Oxford, I can go thither by the Cambridge coach which travels every other day. – Supposing that I go on Thursday I shall have the whole of the Wednesday to settle matters for your reception at Cambridge, provided you write to-morrow.[5] I can go to any inn at Oxford where you may appoint to meet me. –

Affectionate love to My Mother and Sisters.

Accept the assurances of my high consideration.

T B Macaulay.

the death of the Sierra Leone Company by the Company's directors to promote trade and education in Africa. It was the only organized means for anti-slavery activity in the long interval between the abolition of the slave trade in 1807 and the opening of the campaign for the emancipation of the slaves in 1823. Zachary Macaulay was its unpaid secretary from its founding until 1812.

[1] 'Pompeii' contains 280 lines. Many lines have been deleted from the MS version of the poem at Trinity, and do not appear in the printed text, but there is no evidence to tell at what stage they were rejected.

[2] William Smyth (1765–1849: *DNB*), who as Professor of Modern History was *ex officio* one of the examiners for the Chancellor's English medal. Smyth was famous for his musical parties at Cambridge, had published verse himself, and was something of a literary *précieux*. 'Even when in the busy metropolis, at the height of the season, when a welcome guest at Holland or at Lansdowne House, a Whig of the old school, the Professor retained his academical costume of short breeches, cotton stockings, and shoes' (Teignmouth, *Reminiscences*, I, 66).

[3] George Cornelius Gorham (1787–1857: *DNB*), Fellow of Queens', 1810–27, and Curate of Clapham, 1818–27; afterwards notorious through the 'Gorham Case,' concerning the authority of the state in matters of Church doctrine.

[4] William Mandell (d. 1843), Fellow and Tutor of Queens' and a 'notable figure among the Cambridge Evangelicals' (Venn, *Alumni Cantabrigienses*). See also 13 January 1821.

[5] TBM is writing on a Monday.

TO ZACHARY MACAULAY, 29 JUNE 1819

MS: Harvard University. *Address:* To / Zachary Macaulay Esq. / No 16. George Street / Mansion House / London.

Cambridge June 29. 1819

My dear Father,

I am now settled in Trinity College, in Malden's rooms. The Poem is being finally struck off; for, as the errors of the Press were such as could be corrected in five minutes, I thought it worse than useless to trouble you with the revisal.

On Friday I shall expect to see you all. Turner's had better, I think, be the place of rendezvous, though it will not be the head-Quarters.

Tom Babington's note was good for nothing. A member of the senate is required to attend in propria persona, and put his signature and seal upon the tickets. I found out Mandell however, who has been so kind as to procure them all.

Every thing is monstrously dear. Rooms are going for 30 Guineas a week. Sleeping-holes for Servants are at half-a-guinea a night. We shall not be quite so ill off however.

Though this grand season is approaching, all is still dullness and stupidity. Not a soul to be seen in a gown. It will be a different scene however this time week.

My love to all at home.

Affectionately Farewell
T B M

P.S. I think it would not be amiss if you were to engage horses at all the stages pretty soon. The crowd of travellers will be immense.

TO THOMAS BABINGTON, 23 AUGUST 1819

MS: Trinity College. *Address:* Thomas Babington Esq / Rothely Temple / nr. Leicester.

Clapham.[1] Augt. 23. 1819

My dear Uncle,

I have just found by a letter from Jane[2] that you had sent a letter for me to Cambridge, which I have not received. I shall write for it immediately,

---

[1] Following his performance at Cambridge, TBM visited Hannah More at Barley Wood and then went to Clapham where he read with George Stainforth in preparation for the Craven scholarship examination (Zachary Macaulay to Hannah More, 31 August 1819: MS, Huntington).

[2] Probably Jean Babington (1798?–1839), called Jane, second daughter of Thomas Babington, but possibly TBM's sister Jean.

but I would not delay, as my father is on the point of departure, to thank you for a letter, which, coming from you, must be all that is kind and affectionate. The sight of the enjoyment of others gives you so sincere a pleasure, that I believe I cannot better acknowledge your kindness to me than by saying that the days which I passed at Rothely Temple were among the happiest of my life. I shall probably long look back upon them with regret amidst the contests and agitations of a life, not destined I fear to be past in the enjoyment of that polished simplicity and rural elegance, which Rothely Temple taught me first to love and admire. – I believe my faults do not lie on the side of a disposition to compliment where I do not approve, or to profess sentiments which I do not feel. But I shall scarcely regret the coldness of my style towards those to whom I am indifferent, if it renders those whom I love more certain, that, when I speak with affection, I speak with sincerity.

I have seen Charles.[1] – We met, oddly enough, on the top of the Clapham Coach coming from London. It was late; and we sate together some time without the slightest idea of our vicinity. At last, while I was amusing myself with the dexterity which the incognito displayed in exercising the coachman's whip on every body who went by, he said something to our fellow passenger, which struck me as a well known tone. I looked at him pretty intently before I ventured to jog him. Round he turned and stared at me with a face of as much terror as if I had been a ghost; and I believe, if I had immediately descended from the box, and sacrificed my place to the joke he would have noted down the time, and expected to hear of my decease at Cambridge the very same hour and minute with my preternatural appearance to him. I shall see him again to day, and I shall do my very utmost to influence his style of reading, for the better. I should be sorry to see his fine temper spoiled and his keen sensibilities perverted by a habit which, I think, is dangerous almost in proportion to the natural excellencies of the character. I owe besides some reparation to the severe Muses of History and Philosophy for certain derelictions of my own, of the same kind, at an age when such an error is quite as pernicious and much less pardonable; and I feel all the ardour of an enfranchised slave to liberate from bondage the partners of my chains; – and I am sure I owe to all who are connected with you, all that affection and gratitude can perform. Remember me in the kindest manner to my Aunt and Cousins and believe me ever, My dear Uncle,

Your most affectionate Nephew
Thos. B Macaulay

[1] Charles Roos Babington (1806–26), youngest son of Thomas Babington, who entered the Charterhouse in September 1819.

TO ZACHARY MACAULAY, [14 SEPTEMBER 1819][1]

MS: Trinity College. *Address:* Zachary Macaulay Esq. / Post Office / Edinburgh.[2]

[London]

My dear Father,

The pen which Swift employed to take an inventory of the goods and chattels at his curacy might find admirable employment in describing the furniture of the room where I am sitting viz. the drawing room at Cadogan place. Whatever German critics may determine about the site of Paradise, I am inclined to think that Chaos was in our house, and that it was on the table at which I am writing that "the Anarch old"[3] was found by Milton's Hero sitting in state. Sofa's and chairs and tables and rings in such quantities as Hannibal never gleaned from the field of Cannæ, where, if I recollect, he measured them by the bushel, and strings and brass rods and tables, and a piano-forte, seeming to speak of harmony in the midst of discord. In the midst of this confusion worse confounded[4] I sit with one leg in the fender and one on a heap of carpets to give you an account of my movements and intentions.

George Stainforth set off for Cambridge on Saturday to sit for the Trinity fellowships. I intend to follow him the day after to-morrow and to resume my studies with all the energy in my power. A longer stay would be inexpedient, as study is impossible in a house so confused as this is at present. Possibly when mathematics have produced their full effect on my mind, I may like the Syracusan Geometrician[5] be able to solve problems in the din of an assault, and turn my compasses with a firm hand while the sword is over my head. I should have been most desirous to have seen you again before I commenced a course of study which will scarcely admit of interruption till the beginning of next long vacation. I hope however to be able to spend a few days at home about the close of January. At Easter the thing would be quite impossible.

I could say much more. Indeed the events of yesterday, Hunt's procession etc.[6] and my part therein as a spectator, and the more pr[ominen]t[7]

---

[1] Postmark of sending office. The reference to Hunt's procession 'yesterday' confirms the date.

[2] Zachary Macaulay and his family except TBM were absent from London in August, visiting Rothley Temple and touring in that area. At the end of the month Zachary Macaulay went on to Scotland on business.

[3] *Paradise Lost*, II, 988.   [4] *Ibid.*, II, 996.   [5] Archimedes.

[6] 'Orator' Hunt, whose arrest at the meeting of 16 August 1819 at St Peter's Field, Manchester, set off the Peterloo massacre, had been committed for trial on conspiracy on 27 August but had been admitted to bail the next day. On 13 September he entered London in a procession that, on its way through the City, is said to have attracted a crowd of 200,000.

[7] Paper torn away with seal; here and in the following bracketed passages missing parts are supplied from a copy in Fanny Macaulay's hand (Trinity).

part of my hackney-coachman w[ho stopped][1] while he was driving me to h[arangue][1] the multitude from the box, might fur[nish][1] out matter for an Epistle which you could reprint in the Edinburgh Papers under the title of "Extract of a letter received from a Gentleman in London." – But a Carpenter and a bell-hanger who are assisting in our repairs are at this moment deafening me with the noises proper to their professions. I must accordingly confine myself to necessary information. We are all as well as people can be, all whose senses are undergoing simultaneous mortification, – who are deafened by hammers and choked by dust and, – but your imagination must supply the rest. For my paper will not contain it. All send their most affectionate love and I ever remain your most affectionate Son.

T B M.

P.S. Intelligence just arrived from Barley Wood. Patty More is severely, indeed alarmingly ill.[2]

TO ZACHARY MACAULAY, [SEPTEMBER 1819]

MS: Trinity College. *Address:* Zachary Macaulay Esq / No 16. George Street / Mansion House / London. *Partly published:* Trevelyan, 1, 93–5.

[Cambridge]
My dear Father,
   My mother's letter, which has just arrived, has given me much concern. The letter which has, I am most sorry to learn, given you and her uneasiness, was written rapidly and thoughtlessly enough, but can scarcely, I think, as far as I remember its tenour, justify some of the extraordinary inferences which it has occasioned. I can only assure you most solemnly that I am not initiated into any democratical societies here, that I know no people who make politics a common or frequent topic of conversation, except one man who is a determined Tory. It is true that this Manchester business[3] has roused some indignation here, as at other places, and drawn philippics against the Powers that be from lips which I never heard opened before but to speak on University contests or University scandal. For myself I have long made it a rule never to talk on politics except in the most general manner; and I believe that my most intimate associates have no idea of my opinions on the general questions of party. I can scarcely be censured, I think, for imparting them to you; – which however I should

[1] Paper torn away with seal; here and in the following bracketed passages missing parts are supplied from a copy in Fanny Macaulay's hand (Trinity).
[2] Martha More died on 14 September.   [3] Peterloo.

scarcely have thought of doing, (so much is my mind occupied with other concerns,) had not your letter invited me to state my sentiments on the Manchester Business. Political questions must necessarily occupy some portion of every man's thoughts. There is scarcely a man in the country above the lowest classes who has not a chance and an expectation of being, at some period of his life, a wheel, more or less important, in the political machine. And, though it may be to be regretted that boys will form crude opinions on such subjects, it will scarcely be easy to prevent any person of reflection however young, who is engaged in studying the history and the politics of other nations from forming certain notions on such subjects and applying them to his own. All that can be expected is, I think, that he should do what I do, refrain from expressing them, from the knowledge that he may learn many facts and hear many arguments which will alter their whole character; and carefully keep from doing or saying any thing which he may repent, when time and experience have sobered his judgement. This has really been my course, and, if I have laid my crude ideas before you, (and it has been before you alone,) it has been by no means so much that you might approve as that you might correct them.

I hope that this explanation will remove some of your uneasiness. As to my opinions I have no particular desire to vindicate them. They are merely speculative, and therefore cannot partake of the nature of moral culpability. They are early formed, and I am not solicitous that you should think them superior to those of most people at eighteen. I will however say this in their defence. Whatever the affectionate alarm of my dear mother may lead her to apprehend, I am not one of the "sons of Anarchy and confusion,"[1] with whom she classes me. My opinions, good or bad, were learnt not from Hunt and Waithman,[2] but from Cicero, from Tacitus, and from Milton. They are the opinions which have produced the greatest men that ever ornamented the world and redeemed human nature from the degradation of ages of superstition and slavery. I may be wrong as to the facts; – but if they be what I have seen them stated, I can never repent speaking of them with indignation. When I cease to feel the injuries of others, warmly detest wanton cruelty, and to feel my soul [rise][3] against oppression, I shall think myself unworthy to be your son, and to share, as I hope one day to do, the palm of the benevolent conquerors of West-Indian tyranny and inhumanity.

[1] The phrase 'anarchy and confusion' occurs in Bacon, *Advancement of Learning* (*Works*, ed. Spedding, 1870 edn, v, 70), where Bacon speaks of Pompey's design to 'cast the state into an absolute anarchy and confusion.'

[2] Robert Waithman (1764–1833: *DNB*), a wealthy London merchant active in liberal reform politics during the years when it required courage to be so. He was Alderman, 1818, Sheriff, 1820, and Lord Mayor of London, 1823, and was elected M.P. for the City in 1818.

[3] Paper torn away with seal.

I could say a great deal more. Above all I might, I think, ask, with some reason, why a few democratical sentences in a letter, a private letter, of a collegian of eighteen, should be thought so alarming an indication of character, when Brougham[1] and other people, who at an age which ought to have sobered them, talk with much more violence, are not thought particularly ill of? – But I have so little room left that I abstain and will only add thus much. Were my opinions as decisive as they are fluctuating, and were the elevation of a Cromwell or the renown of a Hampden the certain reward of my standing forth in the democratical cause, I would rather have my lips sealed on the subject, than give my mother and you one hour of uneasiness. There are not so many people in the world who love me, that I can afford to pain them for any object of ambition which it contains. If this assurance be not sufficiently strong, clothe it in what language you please, and believe me to express myself in those words which you think the strongest and most solemn. Affectionate love to my Mother and sisters.

Farewell

T B M.

TO ZACHARY MACAULAY, [22][2] OCTOBER 1819

MS: Trinity College. *Address:* Zachary Macaulay Esq / No 16 George Street / Mansion House / London.

[Cambridge] Friday. Oct. 1819

My dear Father,

Two declamations, a Latin and an English one, which I have on my hands together, must be my excuse for not having written before.[3] I speak the former to morrow; the latter on Wednesday week. – Your last letter is so full of queries that my present Epistle will I fear scarce hold answers to all of them. So I will begin with them directly.

[1] Henry Brougham (1778–1868: *DNB*), afterwards first Baron Brougham and Vaux, lawyer, Edinburgh Reviewer, Whig M.P., abolitionist, political, educational, and legal reformer, Lord Chancellor. Brougham had long been identified with liberal policies, but his response to Peterloo was uncertain and he had made no public statement on the matter by the time of this letter. Brougham and Zachary Macaulay, who had worked together in the cause of abolition since 1804, were close friends despite great differences in temperament and politics. Brougham remained a helpful and loyal friend to Zachary Macaulay and his family, but the relations between him and TBM were quickly strained and soon thoroughly hostile once TBM was out in the world. Brougham could not stand rivalry, and TBM could not stand Brougham's affectation of superiority.

[2] Postmarked 23 October 1819. Friday was the 22nd.

[3] 'In the Second Year each man has to compose two Declamations, one in Latin, and the other in English, upon some historical subject generally; but, occasionally, in the other branches of polite literature. This he has to deliver a fortnight afterwards in the chapel, immediately after Evening Prayers, before the Dean, Head-Lecturer, and all such others as happen to be present, and against an opponent right opposite' ([Wright], *Alma Mater*, 1, 199).

Imprimis as to Kenneth's coming to Cambridge, pray send him at the Commemoration,[1] and not at the Bible Society. He may hear better oratory under any barn or from any tub than we are regaled with here. Seriously, our meetings are much below par. He may attend better near London every week; but there is but one Commemoration Day in the year.

My gallant steed is much honoured by the appellation of White Surrey. When did the girls become such readers of Shakespeare as to think of the name. For I suppose they must take it from his hero, Richard, I think, who says

"Saddle White Surrey for the field to morrow."[2]

Or are they obliged for the thought to some body else. The tea still holds out and so do my finances. The speculation has answered admirably. It is excellent tea indeed.

King is not yet arrived. I intend to commence most energetically with him. –

Lawson's[3] scholarship was vacated two years ago and gained by Horace Waddington whom you heard recite at the Commencement. More than one Scholarship is never vacated in a year. If the holder dies, the salary goes to his legal heir until the proper time arrives for the vacancy. This is a recent regulation, intended to ensure a certain succession of Scholarships.[4]

I have no idea, though I do not talk here upon the subject, of contesting the next Scholarship.[5] I have no chance of gaining it; and my long neglect of mathematics is only to be repaired by vigorous and undivided exertion for several months. I revolved the subject long and maturely. I hope you will think that I have decided wisely. I have resolved to devote myself principally to mathematics; and though the time has past when I might have thought of the highest honours to obtain a creditable place on the Tripos. I have unfortunately been languid in studying them, and sacrificed them to more agreable pursuits. The forfeit must and shall be paid without repining. I will at least purchase one claim on my own respect, by not permitting regret to make me idle and remiss, or sitting down in despondency because I might have been on higher ground.

---

[1] 16 December. Kenneth Macaulay of Sierra Leone was on one of his visits to England.

[2] *Richard III*, v, iii, 64.

[3] Marmaduke Lawson (1793–1823), the first holder of the Pitt scholarship, 1814–17.

[4] By the new regulations one university scholarship was to be vacant each year, the examinations being held in the last week of January (*Cambridge University Calendar*, 1819, pp. 352–3).

[5] But he did. See 25 January [1820].

But our dinner time is approaching. I can only add my affectionate love to my mother and sisters, and bid you most affectionately farewell.

T B M

P.S. I called on the dean;[1] but did *not* receive the 11/6; though I asked very attentively both about the patient and the machine. The very Reverend seemed to think that the pleasure of doing good was a sufficient recompense. However he has lent me a Demosthenes which I shall keep as a hostage.

T B M

TO ZACHARY MACAULAY, 3 NOVEMBER 1819

MS: Trinity College. *Address:* Zachary Macaulay Esq / No 16 George Street / Mansion House / London.

Cambridge Nov. 3. 1819.

My dear Father,

One of my declamations is spoken; – the other will be spoken to night, and I am pausing to take breath, not from the trouble of composing, but from that of pruning and correcting, which I hate beyond all names of abomination. I do not think the composition improved by it after all. However you shall judge at my next return.

As to the University Scholarship, my sole reasons for not desiring to contest it are these. I am sure that I shall not get it, morally certain. – That would not weigh much with me; since the exercise is useful. – But I am sure that, if I read mathematics as I fully mean to do, if I read them so as to secure a place in the first Class of this year,[2] (where the Examination is wholly mathematical,) I shall not do as well at the Trial for the Scholarship as I did last year. I think it most prudent to retire with the credit which I obtained, which was indeed more than my general knowledge intitled me to, and for which I was partly indebted to the favourable turn of the examination. The pecuniary profit is nothing, 20 pounds[3] I believe, very irregularly paid.

Be assured that [it] is not my intention, anything herein contained notwithstanding, to abandon Classical studies. On the contrary, I propose to myself a richer enjoyment of them than I have ever known. While they

---

[1] Milner. Perhaps he owed Zachary Macaulay for the coffee mentioned in 30 November 1818.

[2] TBM's name does not appear in the Trinity first class list for 1820. One wonders if King had to pay the penalty mentioned in this letter? TBM was, however, elected to a Trinity scholarship following the annual examination.

[3] The Craven university scholarships were then worth £25; in the next year they were raised to £50.

were a principal employment, it was necessary to read them with an immense farrago of critical stupidity and dulness, which served only to blunt my perceptions of their beauties of sentiment and expression. Now that I mean to trust to mathematics for University Success, I shall read the Classics as a real pleasure; proceeding regularly at the rate of two or three hours a day, for some years to come, through their most celebrated works; – and I hope thus to make myself, if not a medallist, something much better, a man who has got a few *ideas* from the writers of Antiquity, though he may not know much of the critical peculiarities of *words*.

King came up a few days ago. To night, as I said, my declamation is spoken, and I am left at liberty. To morrow my new scheme of study commences. I hope to receive your approbation of it. It is a subject on which I am much better able to judge than John Brown, who does not know in the slightest degree the state of my studies or the amount of my stock of learning. Stainforth, I firmly believe, would agree with me. I have often heard him say that a good mathematician who is a decent scholar, plays the surest game at Trinity.

King has bound himself in a penalty of 500£ to put me into the first Class next June. So that you see my gains even if I fail in my new plan will be greater than if I succeeded in gaining the Craven's Scholarship.

But I must go and learn my declamation. – I enclose a paper which has been for a week the talk of all Cambridge, and for whose results many are looking with impatient eagerness.[1] I have had a peep behind the scenes, and think that it will be successful and [de]²serv[ed]²ly so.

Ever affectionately yours.

T B M.

Let me hear when my Mother and Sisters are gone to Barley Wood. – Love to them and all at home. Many thanks to Jane for her letter. –

TO ZACHARY MACAULAY, 24 NOVEMBER 1819

MS: Trinity College. *Address:* Zachary Macaulay Esq. / No 16 George Street / Mansion House / London.

Cambridge Nov. 24. 1819.

My dear Father,

I received very great pleasure from your last letter, and I trust I shall do my utmost to follow its directions and to merit its kindness. We are in

---

[1] A syndicate appointed in 1818 to consider the institution of a classical tripos reported sometime before 1820; TBM may refer to that report, which never reached the University Senate for action (see Winstanley, *Early Victorian Cambridge*, p. 66).   [2] Letter torn.

great bustle here. A living of very great value, I believe 1500 a year, has fallen into the gift of the University, owing, I understand, to the circumstance of the patron being a Roman Catholic. The incumbent is to be nominated by the votes of the Masters of Arts, and the Canvass is, you may conceive, pretty vigorous. Clarke[1] the Traveller is among the candidates. Trinity supports Professor Monk, St. John's a mathematical lump of stupidity of the name of Bland,[2] Pembroke French,[3] the tutor of that college, who was second wrangler in Dicey's[4] year, and should have been first. Among these candidates Lee[5] has been persuaded to offer himself, – a most foolish measure, which has drawn down great odium on the heads of the Religious party from their own warmest supporters, at least among the undergraduates. Monk has my best wishes. Probably you could contrive to send him up a few voters. Poor man! with all his oddities he has deserved well of the University, (almost a tenth part of what he thinks he has,) and he has been engaged to a lady for years in expectation of some such provision.[6]

But I must not forget in sending this University intelligence, as I did in my last letter, to mention my own necessities. My tea-canister and purse are exhausted together, and for a fortnight I have been living without money, and drinking a decoction of chopped hay. It quite escaped my memory in my last. Perhaps you will think that this state of my finances inspired the production which I have enclosed.[7] I believe not. But to put you at ease as to the lines themselves, they were not composed in any hours which should have been devoted to other purposes, but were all made in bed, one night when I was not particularly inclined to sleep. The

---

[1] Edward Clarke (1769–1822: *DNB*), Professor of Mineralogy, published *Travels in Various Countries of Europe, Asia and Africa*, 6 vols., 1810–23.

[2] Miles Bland (1786–1867: *DNB*), Tutor of St John's, 1809–23; Rector of Lilley, Hertfordshire, 1823–67; author of several popular mathematical texts.

[3] William French (1789–1849: *DNB*), second wrangler in 1811, became Master of Jesus College, 1820.

[4] Thomas Edward Dicey (1789–1858), B.A., Trinity, 1811. Proprietor of the *Northampton Mercury*, Dicey was connected with the Clapham Sect through his marriage in 1814 to Anne Mary, the younger daughter of James Stephen. In that year he accompanied Zachary Macaulay to Paris on his embassy from the abolitionists to the allied powers (Knutsford, *Zachary Macaulay*, p. 313).

[5] Samuel Lee (1783–1852: *DNB*), a one-time carpenter's apprentice whose genius for languages led to his being sent by the Church Missionary Society to Queens' College, 1814, where he was Milner's protégé. B.A., 1818, he was allowed by special dispensation to proceed M.A. in 1819 in order to become in that year Professor of Arabic. His gift for Oriental languages was turned to Evangelical account by translations of the Bible and liturgy.

[6] Monk married Jane Hughes in 1823. None of the candidates named seems to have been successful, but I do not know what living TBM has in mind.

[7] Perhaps 'Lines in Imitation of Lord Byron,' which begins 'Weep not for me. – Thou cans't not know / How souls like mine confront their fate' and continues in that vein for forty-four lines (copy in Hannah Macaulay's hand, dated 1819: Trinity).

situation and the time must be the excuse both for their existence and their defects. I suppose my mother and sisters are still at Barley wood. Affectionate love to all at home. I shall soon write to Jane.

Ever most affectionately yours

T B M

TO ZACHARY MACAULAY, 5 JANUARY 1820

MS: Trinity College. *Address:* Z Macaulay Esq. / No 16 George Street / Mansion House / London. *Partly published:* Trevelyan, I, 95–7.

Cambridge Jany. 5th. 1820.

My dear Father,

Nothing that gives you disquietude can give me amusement. Otherwise I should have been excessively diverted by the dialogue which you have reported with so much vivacity. The accusation, the predictions, the elegant agnomen for which I am indebted to this incognito, (whom I shall designate, as algebraists do their unknown quantities by the letter (x)) are so gloriously absurd, so *utterly* and *absolutely false*, that I cannot help suspecting that the gentleman must be Marryatt[1] of Trinity Hall, the son of your M P friend. He is at least endowed with some of the talents which distinguish the author of " Thoughts," and "more thoughts," and "more thoughts still."[2]

I went in some amazement to Malden, Romilly,[3] and Barlow.[4] Their acquaintance comprehends, I will venture to say, almost every man worth knowing in the University in every field of study. They had never heard the appellation or the slightest allusion to any such propensity in me, from any man. Their intimacy with me would of course prevent any person from speaking to them on the subject in an insulting manner. For it is not usual here, whatever (x) may do, for a gentleman who does not wish to be kicked down stairs to reply to a man who mentions another as his particular friend, "Do you mean the blackguard or the novel-reader?" But the habit of novel reading is too frequently indulged to excess to be con-

---

[1] Samuel Marryat (1800–25), the third son of Joseph Marryat and brother of the novelist, Frederick.

[2] See 30 March 1816. Marryat's *Thoughts on the Abolition of the Slave Trade* were in fact followed by *More Thoughts*, 1816, and *More Thoughts Still*, 1818.

[3] John Romilly (1802–74: *DNB*), B.A., Trinity, 1823. The second son of Sir Samuel Romilly, he had a distinguished legal career. Appointed Master of the Rolls, 1851, he was created Baron Romilly in 1866.

[4] John Barlow (1798–1869), B.A., Trinity, 1820, was minister of the Duke Street Chapel, St James's, and one of the Chaplains to the Queen, 1854–69. Secretary to the Royal Institution, 1842–62, Barlow, according to Sir Frederick Pollock, 'rescued it from a position of serious financial difficulty' and 'induced many friends and acquaintances to become members' (*Personal Remembrances*, 1887, I, 242–3). TBM joined the Royal Institution in 1842.

sidered as a subject of reproach; and I am fully convinced that had the charge prevailed to any extent it must have reached the ears of one of those whom I interrogated. At all events I have the consolation of not being thought a novel-reader by the three or four who are entitled to judge on the subject, and whether their opinion be of equal value with that of this John-a-Nokes against whom I have to plead I leave you to decide.

It is absurd to suppose that I should have acquired this name, had my voracity been even extreme, considering how many scores of under-graduates might dispute the title with me. I cannot conceive how I should have gained it even if I had deserved it. The charge of having deserved it I shall not condescend to deny, until you tell me that you give it credit.

But stronger evidence, it seems, is behind. This gentleman was in com-pany with me. Alas! that I should never have found out how accurate an observer was measuring my sentiments, numbering the novels which I criticised, and speculating on the probability of my being plucked. "I was familiar with all the novels whose names he had ever heard." – If so frightful an accusation did not stun me at once, I might perhaps hint at the possibility that this was to be attributed almost as much to the narrowness of his reading on this subject as to the extent of mine. If my conjectures as to the gentleman are right, every man who has studied Milton is familiar with a book which *he* has never read, and probably never heard of. – Yet to accuse the poor man on that account of being immoderately addicted to poetry would be scarcely just. A man may be familiar with all the novels whose names are known to some people without being much of a novel reader. Probably the conversation turned on some popular works of that nature; and I joined in discussing the merits of Miss Edgeworth or of the Scotch novels, or very likely of some tragedy of Shakespeare's or poem of Lord Byron's, or tale of Dryden's, whose title he had heard and fancied it that of a novel. I have heard of such things, and seen such men, – mere mathematical blocks, whom the Tripos serves for a graduated scale of intellect, who plod on their eight hours a day to the honours of the Senate House, who leave the groves which witnessed the musings of Milton of Bacon and of Gray, without one liberal idea or elegant image, and carry with them into the world minds contracted by unmingled attention to one part of science, and memories stored only with technicalities. How often have I seen such men go forth into society for people to stare at them, and ask each other how it comes that beings so stupid in conversation, so un-informed on every subject of history, of letters, and of taste, could gain such distinctions at Cambridge. It is in such circles, which, I am happy to say, I hardly know but by report, that knowledge of modern literature is called novel-reading – a commodious name, invented by ignorance, and applied by envy, in the same manner as men without learning call a

scholar a pedant, and men without principle call a Christian a methodist.
To me the attacks of such men are valuable as compliments. The man
whose friend tells him that he is known to be extensively acquainted with
elegant literature may suspect that he is flattering him. He may feel real
satisfaction when some Johnian, who plods on day after day at the pace of a
tortoise, and with the insensibility of one, sneers at him for a novel reader.

I will attempt to make up my mind as well as possible to the fate with
which this gentleman menaces me. "I am to lose ground," it seems. "My
friends told him so." My friends *did not* tell him so. They could not tell
him so. Calumny is not *every body's* trade. No person could estimate my
progress or declension but Malden and Stainforth. Malden did not tell him
so. Stainforth could not – for he thinks the direct contrary. –

As to the main question, I shall leave that for time to answer. I cannot
afford to sacrifice a day every week in defence and explanation as to my
habits of reading. Next June will come, and then – "Nous verrons."

I saw John and his mother to day. They think of setting out on Monday.

My Uncle[1] wished to procure a book for Baptist Noel.[2] I cannot of
course learn exactly what he would like. A Newton was what I thought of;
but he has one. I think a Cicero would do. He sent to borrow mine the
other day; – and a good Edition is at once a handsome and an appropriate
part of the library of every scholar.

My most affectionate love to My Mother and all at home.

In about three weeks I shall come into college, I hope finally. Barlow is
going to leave Cambridge, after taking his degree, for a few months, and
very kindly insisted on my occupying them till his return, by which time
I shall probably have procured a Scholarship[3] and become entitled to a
set of my own.

---

[1] Thomas Babington.

[2] Noel (1799–1873: *DNB*), in the first class of Trinity freshmen with TBM, 1819, M.A., 1821,
was the youngest son of Sir Gerard Noel Noel and the brother of Thomas Gisborne Babington's wife Augusta. He began his clerical career as curate to John Babington at Cossington,
Leicestershire; from 1827 to 1848 he was minister at St John's Chapel, Bedford Row,
London, where the Macaulay family regularly attended during their residence at Great Ormond Street. Noel was a much-admired Evangelical preacher when, in 1849, he left the
Church of England in protest against the judgment in the Gorham case and joined the Bap-
tists. Henry Thornton remembered that 'Macaulay, knowing how exemplary [Noel's] life
had been, always wondered how he had spent his time, seeing that vice had had no part of it.
"He is a most ignorant fellow," he said. "He once asked me who Erasmus was"' (Alston,
'Recollections of Macaulay,' p. 60). Selina Macaulay reports that when Noel preached at
Rothley Temple 'even Tom praised his sermon' (Diary, 5 June 1826); 'even' seems the key
word.

[3] TBM became a scholar of Trinity in April 1820 (Zachary Macaulay to Hannah More, 17 May
1820: Knutsford, *Zachary Macaulay*, p. 354). Although he was being given the use of Barlow's rooms, he does not seem to have obtained rooms of his own in college until the next
year: see 12 February 1821. Trinity was very crowded; in 1820, 'of the three hundred and
fifty-four Fellows, Bachelors, and undergraduates in commons, only about one hundred
resided in college' (Winstanley, *Early Victorian Cambridge*, p. 58).

I think I have said all that I have to say. I hope so at least. For my paper approaches its ter[mi]¹nation. You allude to my having said, that [I]¹spent two days with Malden in reading novels. It is but fair to remember that it was at the end of a *vacation* spent in hard work, and of a trying examination of ten days. I value, most deeply value, that sollicitude which arises from your affection for me – but let it not debar me from justice and candour. / Believe me ever, my dear Father,

Your most affectionate Son

T B M.

TO ZACHARY MACAULAY, 25 JANUARY [1820]

MS: Trinity College.

Cambridge. Jan. 25. 1819

My dear Father,

I sit down to devote one of the intervals of our examination² to answering your letter. The contest commenced on Monday and will end perhaps next Tuesday. I hope then to be able to spend a few days at home. Of this I am not at all certain, as it is very difficult to obtain leave of absence just as lectures are commencing. I hope however that, as I am rather a favourite, it will not be refused. I should like to bring Malden with me for a few days. He wishes to leave Cambridge for a short time, and has no place to go to. He has, I fear, injured his health by unremitting exertion, and it is of serious consequence to him, and, of course, to me, that he should be able to recruit it. I remember you and my Mother expressed a wish to see him at Cadogan Place; and as my Uncle is gone, I suppose you cannot be in want of room.

I enclose a copy of the Tripos. It is a glorious triumph for Trinity:³ and it gave me very sincere pleasure to witness the success and honours of my friend Coddington,⁴ whose amiable character and elegant manners, much more than even his superior talents, have made him the most popular man in Cambridge. I have no heart to write about poor Barlow's⁵ place.

---

¹ Paper torn away with seal.   ² For the university scholarship.
³ Of the eighteen wranglers, eight were from Trinity, as were both Chancellor's medallists and both Smith's prizemen.
⁴ Henry Coddington (1799?–1845: *DNB*); senior wrangler and Fellow of Trinity, 1820; Tutor, 1822–33; Vicar of Ware, 1832–45. 'Senior Wrangler at an unusually early age, and a successful competitor for the classical honours of his University, he yet found time to master most of the continental languages, to become an excellent performer on various musical instruments, to be a learned botanist and exquisite draughtsman, and to introduce those improvements into the microscope which bear his name' (*Gentleman's Magazine*, 1845, Part II, 90).
⁵ Barlow was fourth among the junior optimes.

Illness, unfavourable circumstances, and, it is suspected, some misfortune in the giving up of his papers, threw him into a place which his examiners themselves owned was very much below his known merits. He bore his dissapointment like a true hero, but felt it very deeply, and has gone to repair his exhausted health and injured nerves in Devonshire. He has, in his usual friendly manner, left me his rooms, which are very convenient, and in which I hope soon to be settled. My reflections on the event were simply these. Here is a man of talents and great industry who after working six or seven hours a day to my certain knowledge at this science for 3 years, and gaining repeatedly high honours from his proficiency in it, is all on a sudden by mere accident dropped down below men whom he has always beaten, men without either application or ability. It is then very unwise for a man to set his heart on success in a field where rewards are so ill apportioned to merit. I shall be glad to acquire a sound knowledge of the principles of the science, because they are useful in every point of view. But I will never be agitated by the prospect of the Senate-house, or form any very earnest wishes of success *there.* My affectionate love to my mother and all at home.

T B M.

TO ZACHARY MACAULAY, [23? FEBRUARY 1820][1]

MS: Trinity College. *Address:* Zachary Macaulay Esq. / No 16 George Street / Mansion House / London.

[Cambridge]

My dear Father,

I have intentionally delayed writing till I could send you news of the result of our late examination. To do it in the clearest manner, I transcribe the following paper which was suspended this morning at Deighton's by the Vice-Chancellor.

"Craven's Scholar. 1820
"Alfred Ollivant. Trinity

"The following Gentlemen, (*arranged in alphabetical order,*) are judged by the Examiners to have distinguished themselves

Arnold.   Trinity
Barnes.   Trinity
Coleridge.   Kings

[1] Postmarked 24 February by receiving office.

143

Long.	Trinity
Macaulay.	Trinity
Malden.	Trinity
Malkin.	Trinity
Marriott.	Trinity
Okes.	Kings
Talbot.	Trinity

You cannot but remark how highly honourable this list is to our college.

Monk met me as he was going to put up this catalogue. He shewed it me; and told me that though he could not congratulate me on having gained the Scholarship, yet I had not[1] myself very great credit. – Malden, I understand, has done remarkably well. –

I hope to see you for a few days, (a *very few* days I may say) at Easter. But you must tell my affectionate little Jane not to set her heart so much on it as her letter indicates, since it is very doubtful whether it may be expedient. My Mathematics are very backward, and my chance of the first Class of this year, as the examination is almost wholly mathematical, is very doubtful.

As to the bill – I believe the tailor is in the right. Last term includes a great time, – a large part of the vacation, from the Commencement to Christmas, and his bill takes in all my apparel from the black silk waistcoat and coat in which I recited before the daughters and nieces of Royalty, to the yellow waistcoats which dazzled the ladies so much during my last visit. –

I had almost forgot to mention that I am destitute of money, as I have paid Turner on leaving his rooms for all my debt during my late residence, which amounted to upwards of five pounds. –

I have seen the Controversy of Africanus and Investigator.[2] I had conjectured the person of the former champion through his closed visor. – But I am compelled to break off. One word more. How is John Macaulay? I am perpetually interrogat[ed about][3] him by Monk and Brown, and kn[ow no][3] more when he will return than I do whether the Queen will be

[1] Thus in MS.
[2] A long letter to *The Times*, 4 January 1820, signed 'Investigator,' after cataloguing the horrors of Sierra Leone – disease, filth, thievery, even cannibalism – concluded that the country was no fit place for the seat of a government. 'Investigator' was answered by 'Africanus' – evidently Zachary Macaulay – on 11 and 12 January. The argument ran on through January and February, 'Investigator' publishing further letters on 19 and 20 January and 16 February. He was overwhelmed, however, by the indefatigable energy of 'Africanus,' who replied in letters of 3, 5, 8, 9, 10, 14, and 29 February and with whom remained the last word.
[3] Paper torn away with seal.

divorced,[1] a point which puzzles all our Cambridge politicians and none more than your affectionate Son

T B M.

Loves in abundance. Kenneth is out of the reach of thanks by this time, or I should load him with them for his present. He has sent me a seal which belonged to his poor Brother.[2] But I must absolutely stop.

TO ZACHARY MACAULAY, [19?][3] AUGUST 1820

MS: Mrs Humphry Trevelyan. *Address:* Zachary Macaulay Esq / No 16 George Street / Mansion House / London *Partly published: Christian Observer,* XIX (September 1820), 587–8.

Trin: Coll: Saturday August 20. / 1820

My dear Father,

I feel most painfully solicitous about poor dear Stainforth.[4] I hope you will let me learn every change of every kind that takes place. Is he near you? By all the reports that I hear his case is considered as absolutely hopeless; but I cannot cease to hope where I desire so fervently.

Continued and regular reading which I have been practising with great success of late keeps my mind from dwelling on this painful subject. I have been deep in Plato, Aristotle, and Theocritus ever since I left home, and admiring more and more every day the powers of that mighty language which is incomparably the best vehicle both for reasoning and for imagery that mankind have ever discovered, and which is richer both in abstract philosophical terms and poetical expressions than the English, French, and Latin tongues put together.

I have been particularly charmed with Theocritus, and have several times thought of translating or imitating some of his Idyllia. It has often

---

[1] The Regent became George IV on the death of his father, 29 January 1820. The question of his relation to Queen Caroline, from whom he had been separated in 1796 and who had been living amid scandalous rumors on the continent since 1814, became matter of speculation when an order in council of 12 February announced a new form of prayer in the litany of the Church, omitting any specific mention of the Queen. George IV wished to obtain a divorce immediately, but was for the moment restrained by his ministers.

[2] George Macaulay, who succeeded his brother Kenneth as Superintendent of Recaptured Slaves at Sierra Leone and died there in 1816.

[3] TBM dates the letter Saturday, August 20, but August 20 was a Sunday in 1820. The letter is postmarked 21 August.

[4] A letter from Stainforth's mother, Maria Baring Stainforth, to Henry Venn, [1 August 1820], says that she has given up hope: 'the fever and expectoration increase.' But she means to bring her son into town to be close to the doctors and has asked Zachary Macaulay to find a house near Cadogan Place (MS: Church Missionary Society). Stainforth died in Cadogan Place, 31 August.

struck me that Palestine is the land of pastoral poetry. In that delightful country, flowing with milk and honey, abounding in rich landscape and fertile plains, and enjoying an almost radical degree of liberty before there were any Kings, while "every man did that which was right in his own eyes,"[1] many of the visions of Arcadian beauty and freedom were probably realized. A few evenings ago, it occurred to me that the custom which existed among the young ladies of Israel, of going every year to the mountains to bewail the sacrifice of Jephthah's daughter, (who, whatever the commentators may say, it seems to me, we must in common sense understand to have been really sacrificed,) would be a good subject for a Hebrew Eclogue. I send you the fruits of two or three hours labour on the subject.[2] I mention the time partly that you may not suppose that my days are spent in writing verses, and partly as an excuse for the imperfections of the piece. As Jephthah was a Gileadite, I have supposed Gilead to be the scene of the celebrat[ion,][3] and I have, as you will see, followed Warburton[4] in supposing, what, in truth, I feel much inclined to believe, that the Jews had no very fixed ideas on the subject of a future state, [but][3] were left to believe it like Plato or to deny with Epicurus, according to the strength of their intellects, or the state of their moral feelings. But to descend, I hope Mr. Foyard[5] has been paid for my Equestrian studies. – By the [bye][3] I wish you would mention to Mr. Inglis if you see him, that the rooms which Henry Thornton inhabited have been seized, his right to them having expired, and learn what he wishes to be done about securing others. – Give my love to all at home, and believe me ever, my dear father, most affectionately yours

T B M

---

[1] Judges 17: 6.

[2] These were published, with a paraphrase of parts of TBM's letter for introduction, as 'The Lamentation of the Virgins of Israel for the Daughter of Jephthah: A Hebrew Eclogue,' *Christian Observer*, XIX (September 1820), 587–9.

[3] Paper torn away with seal.

[4] William Warburton argues in *The Divine Legation of Moses*, 1738–41, that, since the Mosaic dispensation has no doctrine of future rewards and punishments, it must be of divine origin, for such a doctrine being humanly necessary its omission is therefore a sign of 'extraordinary providence.' See *The Divine Legation*, Book 1, section 1.

[5] Not identified; the name is not quite clear in the MS. TBM evidently rode during this year at Cambridge (see [22] October 1819), but he remained a pedestrian: 'He seldom crossed a saddle, and never willingly' (Trevelyan, I, 119).

TO ZACHARY MACAULAY, [27? OCTOBER 1820][1]

MS: Huntington Library. *Address:* Zachary Macaulay Esq: / No 16 George Street / Mansion-House / London.

[Cambridge]

My dear Father,

I have only this morning learnt that a packet which I sent to Mr. Inglis at his inn to deliver to you arrived too late by the awkwardness of my Gyp. You have however received intelligence of my having gained the first Latin Declamation prize.[2] I am to speak in Latin in a few weeks a panegyric on some eminent man educated at our College. I have selected my favourite Dryden for the theme of my eulogium. –

The regulation which you mention on the subject of the English Declamations[3] did not I think exclude mine from a prize. It has been occasionally broken through, and in fact in the present instance, our Dean selected seven declamations of which mine was one as so equal in merit that none could claim priority. He referred the choice to another fellow, who gave the preference to the three which have obtained the prizes. The Dean himself told me that mine had been highly approved.[4] –

I am curious to learn whether Selina has returned from Leicestershire; and how all are going on at home. I am well and comfortable here; and in expectation of getting into excellent rooms in college by Xtmas. Love to my dear Mother and my sisters. I suppose the boys are still at school. How is my little Jenny and "the sparkling cross on her white breast?"[5] She will understand the question.

Ever affectionately yours
Thomas Babington Macaulay.

[1] Postmarked 28 October by receiving office.
[2] An annual college prize of £4: 'The successful student delivers on the 6th of December (the day after the audit) a panegyric upon some illustrious character' (*Cambridge University Calendar*, 1820, p. 272).
[3] Another annual competition, 'for the three best English Declamations, upon subjects relating to the History of England' (*Cambridge University Calendar*, 1820, p. 272), won in 1820 by John William Hamilton, Henry Malden, and Francis White.
[4] 'Trinity men find it difficult to understand how it was that he missed getting one of the three silver goblets given for the best English Declamations of the year. . . . His own version of the affair was that the Senior Dean, a relative of the victorious candidate, sent for him and said: "Mr. Macaulay, as you have not got the first cup, I do not suppose that you will care for either of the others"' (Trevelyan, I, 81).
[5] Pope, 'The Rape of the Lock,' II, 7.

TO ZACHARY MACAULAY, [13? NOVEMBER 1820][1]

MS: Mrs Humphry Trevelyan. *Address:* Zachary Macaulay Esq. / No 16 George Street / Mansion House / London. *Mostly published:* Trevelyan, I, 99–100.

[Cambridge]

My dear Father,

All here is ecstasy.[2] – "Thank God, the Country is saved!" were my first words when I caught a glimpse of the papers of Friday night. "Thank God, the country is saved," is written in every face and echoed by every voice. Even the symptoms of popular violence, three days ago so terrific, are now displayed with good humour and received with cheerfulness. Instead of curses on the Lords, on every post and every wall is written, "All is as it should be" – "Justice done at last." – and similar mottoes expressive of the sudden turn of public feeling. How the case may stand in London I do not know, but here the public danger, like all dangers which depend merely on human opinions and feelings, has disappeared from our sight almost in the twinkling of an eye.

I hope that the result of these changes may be the secure reestablishment of our commerce which I suppose political apprehensions must have contributed to depress. I hope at least that there is no danger of any misfortune to ourselves of the kind at which you seem to hint.[3] Be assured however, my dear father, that be our circumstances what they may, I feel

---

[1] Postmark; this date is consistent with the reference to 'three days ago' as a time of threatened violence; probably Friday, 10 November, is meant.

[2] The Bill of Pains and Penalties – in effect, proceedings for divorce on grounds of adultery – introduced against Queen Caroline on 5 July 1820, after her return to England, passed its second reading in the Lords on 6 November but was abandoned on Friday, 10 November, the date assigned for its third reading. The whole shabby affair, a contest of parties rather than an honest inquiry, created violent popular feeling, especially against George IV. Just what TBM thought about the question of the Queen's innocence is not entirely clear. Trevelyan, I, 98, prints two stanzas of an 'Ode' by TBM welcoming the Queen on her return to England; the piece is so effusive as to require ironic reading (a copy by Hannah Macaulay and marked by her 'very good' is at Trinity). The remarks in 21 November 1820 show TBM thoroughly sceptical about the Queen's virtue, and one witness says that TBM was 'very strong in his denunciations of Queen Caroline and her advisors' (Perry, *Contributions to an Amateur Magazine*, p. 311). Yet Henry Thornton remembered TBM as obdurate in favor of the Queen (Alston, 'Recollections of Macaulay,' p. 60), and TBM later wrote to Lord Mahon that he thought 'the late Queen was abominably used' (31 December 1836).

[3] The first reference in TBM's letters to the troubles of his father's firm, Macaulay and Babington. They cannot have been very severe at this point, and probably had nothing to do with the over-ambitious policy that later ruined the firm. Trevelyan, I, 126, says that the letters between TBM and his father in 1819 contain indications of possible financial trouble, but I have found none in the letters surviving from that year. Though TBM took pupils in 1822 after receiving his B.A. in order to help with the expenses of his continued residence at Cambridge, the fact that Zachary Macaulay was prepared to resign the active direction of his business to his partner in 1823 in order to devote his full time to the anti-slavery campaign does not suggest that the firm was in special difficulties. The crisis did not occur until 1826, and the partnership was not dissolved until 1828.

firmly prepared to encounter the worst with fortitude, and to do my utmost to retrieve it by exertion. The best inheritance you have already secured to me, an unblemished name and a good education. And for the rest, whatever calamities befal us, I would not, to speak without affectation, exchange adversity consoled, as with us it must ever be, by mutual affection and domestic happiness, for anything which can be possessed by those who are destitute of the kindness of parents and sisters like mine.

But I think, on referring to your letter, that I insist too much upon the signification of a few words. I hope so; and I trust that everything will go well. How did Thorpe's plea[1] turn out. The papers are so full of the Queen's business, that the affairs of the Courts of Law are never reported there, or occupy a very small space. The business of the Court of Chancery is particularly neglected, 1 suppose because the Chancellor[2] does not attend.

But it is chapel time, and I must conclude. I suppose my Mother is still at Barley-wood.

Ever most affectionately yours
T B M

TO ZACHARY MACAULAY, 21 NOVEMBER 1820

MS: Trinity College. *Address:* Zachary Macaulay Esq. | No 16 George Street | Mansion House | London. *Extract published:* Trevelyan, I, 81.

Cambridge Nov. 21. 1820

My dear Father,

It was certainly my intention to pass a few days at the beginning of our Christmas Vacation at home. Should it interfere with any plan of yours I would cheerfully give my project up. But my present intention is to come home on the seventeenth of December next, and stay over Xtmas day.

---

[1] In December, 1818, Zachary Macaulay brought suit for £1,000 damages for libel in the Court of King's Bench against Robert Thorpe (see 17 April 1815); in his pamphlet, 'A View of the Present Increase of the Slave Trade, and the Cause of that Increase,' published in January 1818, Thorpe had renewed the charges of his earlier attacks, the substance of which was that behind the pretense of anti-slavery zeal Macaulay was in fact promoting the slave trade for his own profit. To counter Macaulay's action, Thorpe filed a bill in Chancery praying for a discovery of facts and a commission to examine witnesses abroad. To this Macaulay's lawyers demurred. The case was argued before the Vice-Chancellor on 2 and 19 November 1820; on 19 December the Vice-Chancellor gave judgment, ruling against the petition for a discovery of facts but in favor of the commission. On this development, Zachary Macaulay presumably abandoned his original action. See *The Times*, 20 December 1820, and Henry Maddock, *Reports of Cases Argued...in the Court of the Vice Chancellor*, v (1822), 218–31.

[2] Lord Eldon. But the case was heard by Sir John Leach, the Vice-Chancellor. The delays of the Court of Chancery under Eldon were proverbial.

Nothing can be more absurd than the reports of the London papers about our Cambridge tumults.[1] The disturbance had nothing whatever to do with political feeling, but was merely an ebullition of insolence in the lower orders of the town and of high spirits and frolic among the gownsmen. Many men who look upon the Queen as an injured Saint, and the Milan Commission[2] as an assembly more atrocious than the Council of Pandemonium, were concerned in the attack on the townspeople. Romilly for instance, a friend of mine who has inherited his father's politics as well as his warmth of heart and energy of character, after haranguing me for an hour in support of the Queens innocence, got his gown torn and his head broken in attacking her champions.[3] The disturbance was greater than I ever saw before in Cambridge, though both parties have overstated the number of the combatants. There might be four hundred gownsmen at the scene of the main battle, but certainly not more. I did not display so much heroism as you exhibited in Cadogan place. Indeed if my windows had been broken, I could neither have slept in my rooms that night nor sate in them next day. There was not, however, I believe, much danger; at least the injury done fell far short of the public apprehensions. –

I am very much amused with the disguise in which poor Pompeii has been arrayed.[4] I hardly knew it again, and therefore, as the dissimilarity from the original is so great, it can hardly be accounted vain to say that I think the specimens read very well for French poetry. By the bye Wordsworth,[5] our present Vice Chancellor, has given "*Evening*"[6] as the subject for the next Chancellor's Medal.

---

[1] On 13 November, following the abandonment of the Bill of Pains and Penalties against Queen Caroline, there had been town and gown riots in Cambridge when the town illuminated and the colleges refused to. 'The disturbances which occurred were confined to the Market-Hill and its vicinity, and were in some instances occasioned by parties of the undergraduates coming in contact which the populace, the former of whom were as vociferous in their expressions of attachment to the King, as the latter were to the Queen' (*Cambridge Chronicle*, 17 November 1820).

[2] The commission set up by the Prince Regent in 1817 to inquire into the conduct of Caroline.

[3] J. M. F. Wright says that in the 'memorable battle of Pease Hill' on this occasion nobody was killed, but that 'with poor R——y [Romilly?], of Trinity, and a few others, "it was too near to be pleasant"' (*Alma Mater*, 1, 73–4).

[4] 'Pompeïa. Poëme, par Thomas Babington Macaulay. (Traduit de l'anglais),' *Bibliothèque universelle...de Genève*, nouvelle série ('Littérature'), xv (September 1820), 98–105. This rendering of TBM's couplets into prose begins thus: 'Salut, belle Italie! terre jadis chérie de la liberté: contrée féconde en poëtes et en guerriers, célebre par la lyre et les armes; toi qui prodigues les richesses du pampre et des bosquets odorans, patrie des arts, terre du génie et des amours, salut!'

[5] Christopher Wordsworth (1774–1846: *DNB*), brother of the poet, was appointed Master of Trinity on the death of Mansel in June 1820, and was elected Vice-Chancellor for the academic year 1820–1. He was an unpopular master, remembered for his strict discipline. His High Church orthodoxy put him in conflict with Evangelicals as well as with the more liberal sort at Cambridge. He told one of the tutors, who 'wished to employ a Fellow of

But I must conclude, for my Latin Speech[1] is proceeding but slowly, and must be ready at all events in a fortnight. How in the world I blundered upon the first Latin Declamation prize has been to me an inscrutable mystery. I never wrote any but the vilest Latin at Preston's and never practised composition a single hour since I have been at Cambridge. I have ordered a very elegant edition of Johnson's works for my prize.

Adieu. I am tremendously fagged. For this is the carnival season, I know not why, at Cambridge, when more parties of different kinds are given than in all the rest of the year, and the consequence is that I am forced to steal time for dissipation from my hours of exercise. Mandell has a grand assemblage this evening when I am invited and it would be the height of impropriety to refuse. I am glad to say that I preserve my reading hours inviolate. But the consequence is that you will see me looking very much like a ghost when I come back, unless circumstances alter.

Farewell.
T B M.

TO ZACHARY MACAULAY, 13 JANUARY 1821

MS: Trinity College.

Saturday. January 13. 1821

My dear Father,

I enclose a bill or rather two bills of Brown's. The arrears are for my residence in the long Vacation. He did not send in that bill till very late, and it was therefore not paid till Xtmas when he makes up his accounts. It is, I suppose, paid by this time.

The principal part of the Bookseller's charge is occasioned by the prize[2] which Trinity college professes to give, when in fact the successful candidate pays for every thing but the lettering and gilding.

The deduction at the bottom is from the milliner's bill, about which John Brown had made some absurd mistakes, which at last I have been able to rectify. I am in daily expectation of getting into rooms in College, which will very much diminish the expenses of residence.

high attainments, combined with evangelical piety, that "he would have no Simeonite lecturers"' (Claude Smith Bird, *Sketches from the Life of the Rev. Charles Smith Bird*, 1864, p. 56). On the other side, he earned a bad name for his conduct in Thirlwall's case: see 15 December 1834.
6 The prize was won by TBM: see 10 July 1821. (*From opposite page.*)

---

1 See [27?] October 1820.
2 This probably is the set of Johnson that TBM ordered as his Latin declamation prize: see 21 November 1820.

I was much shocked to see Mrs. Cunningham's[1] death announced in the papers. What were the particulars?

Queen's College is in a most extraordinary situation.[2] If you should be called by any business to Lincoln's inn on Tuesday you will hear the cause pleaded. King has gone up to London about it. Little doubt is entertained that the Master will lose his seat, and it is pretty well agreed that Monk will succeed him. If he should it will be a splendid event for the Classical Scholars who are dissapointed of fellowships at Trinity.

Give my love to my Mother and to all at home.

Farewell
T B M.

P S I forgot to mention that the Chandler's bill is not for candles alone but for the glasses and decanters with which I was compelled to fit myself over at the beginning of the October term, and that the 5£ for Cash were paid to the Vintner, who sells no wine without ready money, and who was employed at a time when all my stock was lent to Malden.

TO ZACHARY MACAULAY, 12 FEBRUARY 1821

MS: Huntington Library. *Address:* Zachary Macaulay Esq. / No 16 George Street / Mansion House / London.

Trinity College Feby. 12. 1821

My dear Father,

Our examination is over, after having lasted upwards of a week, during which time I had no time for writing or indeed for any thing else. To day I get into college rooms,[3] and am now in that melancholy state in which a person is who has stripped his former rooms of all his property, and not yet furnished his new habitation. I am bargaining for chests of drawers, bolsters, chairs, bits of drugget, hearth rugs and fire-irons, and piquing myself on the penetration which I display in so unwonted an employment.

[1] The wife of J. W. Cunningham, Vicar of Harrow and formerly Curate at Clapham, died of pleurisy on 9 January, aged forty-one, leaving nine children.

[2] On the death of Milner in 1820 Henry Godfrey (1781–1832), Fellow of Queens', had been elected President. In petitions laid before the Court of Chancery William Mandell, who had been defeated by Godfrey in the election for the presidency, and King charged that Godfrey had illegally voted for himself and that he had not properly gone through the forms of admission to his office. The Chancellor decided in favor of Godfrey, 27 March. See J. H. Gray, *The Queens' College*, 1899, pp. 269–71. Gray explains, somewhat obscurely, that Mandell's defeat in the election was owing to 'the unhappy mental aberration of which he was afterwards the victim' (p. 271).

[3] TBM first lived at Trinity 'in the centre rooms of Bishop's Hostel' (Trevelyan, 1, 72), but whether on the first or ground floor is not known.

In the mean time I hope that my new mattress will be as dry as can well be expected, and that I shall not be eaten up by the rats who are not unfrequently tenants of these venerable haunts of Mathesis and the Muses, as well as of St James's and Westminster-Hall.

Our examination passed off, on the whole, as well as I had any right to expect. The decision will be known in three weeks, I suppose, at farthest. I do not allow myself to be sanguine. Nor, be the result what it may, do I intend to be miserable.

Indeed, I have been witnessing scenes of real distress, enough to strengthen me against such fictitious and fanciful calamities as those of literary failure. My poor friend Barlow, since I wrote to you last, has been deprived of his father,[1] by a sudden attack. This blow, always overwhelming, was rendered more painful by its stunning suddenness, and by the circumstances of the family. For a clergyman's family, however, (it is surely a disgraceful thing that Society should be so constituted that this should seem a natural expression,) they are pretty well provided for. They have however to endure many of the inconveniences to which circumstances almost inevitably subject the families of the clergy. A mother, (an amiable and elegant woman I understand,) and six or seven children, some young, compelled, almost in the first moment of grief, to leave their home, to look out for another, to be surrounded with attorneys and appraisers, and tortured with the impertinence of all that stupid and hard hearted part of mankind who are utterly insensible to the sanctity of the tomb or of the house of mourning! – Poor Barlow has gone through his part of the duty well, and has just returned to Cambridge, after three weeks absence, in consequence of the express request of his dying father. He is thin and pale but composed and seems likely soon to recover his health and spirits.

But I must break off to attend on [an][2] upholsterer, or I shall run some chance [of][2] sleeping to night without blankets or of being forced to bivouaque in Neville's Court.

My affectionate love to my Mother and Sisters. I pant for Easter.

Farewell
T B Macaulay

[1] Thomas William Barlow, Vicar of Halberton, Devon, died on 17 January.
[2] Paper torn away with seal.

TO ZACHARY MACAULAY, 6 MARCH 1821

MS: Mrs Humphry Trevelyan. *Address:* Zachary Macaulay Esq. / No 16 George Street Mansion House / London.

Trinity College. Cambridge / March 6th. 1821.

My dear Father,

I have just been elected an University Scholar. Malden, and a man of the name of Long, (likewise of Trinity College,) have been elected with me.[1] This honour is far beyond my expectations and more than satisfies all my hopes of University distinction. – I steal the first moments during which I can escape from congratulation and friendly applause, to communicate my success to those for whose sakes alone success is dear to me. –

I am happy to say that a stipend of 50£ a year accompanies this honour, which will, I hope, in some degree relieve you from the expenses of my residence here.

I must however draw to a close, or I shall lose the post. Give my affectionate love to my Mother and Sisters. I am sorry that I shall not see my poor dear Jenny at Easter. I must positively have her up from Brighton or take a trip down to see her.

Farewell,
T B Macaulay

TO SELINA MILLS MACAULAY, 25 MARCH 1821

MS: Mrs Humphry Trevelyan. *Address:* Mrs. Macaulay / No 20 Lower Cadogan / place / Chelsea / London. *Mostly published:* Trevelyan, 1, 100–1.

Trinity College. Cambridge. / March 25th. 1821.

My dear Mother,

I intreat you to entertain no apprehensions about my health. My fever, cough, and sorethroat have all disappeared for the last four days. But I have been tormented by a pain in my back which kept me from sleeping

---

[1] TBM, Malden, and George Long were rated equal by the examiners for the Craven university scholarships. What they won were the three 'new' Craven scholarships added, by decree of the Court of Chancery in 1819, to the existing two scholarships, and for which twenty-five candidates competed. TBM wrote years later that when he won the scholarship 'I was as proud of it as a peacock of his tail' (Journal, XI, 222: 2 December 1857). George Long (1800–79: *DNB*) was Professor of Ancient Languages, University of Virginia, 1824–8, and the first Professor of Greek at the London University, 1828–31. Long did much editorial work for the Society for the Diffusion of Useful Knowledge, particularly as editor of the *Penny Cyclopaedia*, 1833–46, and produced a number of school texts, histories, editions, and translations over a wide range of classical and legal subjects. He was Classical Lecturer at Brighton College, 1849–71.

two night together, and depressed my spirits in consequence during the day. Yesterday I took the warm bath which has almost entirely dislodged this troublesome visitant; and I have no doubt that to morrow I shall be as well as I ever was in my life.

Many thanks for your intelligence about poor dear John, which has much exhilarated me. I am glad too to learn that you are spared much of the trouble of nursing. Yet I do not know whether it is not rather a pre-rogative than a trouble. I am sure that it is well worth while being sick to be nursed by a mother. Half of what is ardent and persevering in her affection is only developed then. There is nothing which I remember with such pleasure as the time when you nursed me at Aspenden.[1] The other night when I lay on my sofa very hypochondriac and sick with physic, I was thinking over that time. How sick, and sleepless, and weak I was lying in bed, when I was told that you were come! How well I remember with what an ecstacy of joy I saw that face approaching me, in the middle of people that did not care if I died that night, except for the trouble of burying me. It was a feverish and restless night with me, full of odd thoughts and unconnected images, but I see before me now as distinctly as any thing that ever was offered to me, that smile which of itself seemed to give health and strength. The sound of your voice, the touch of your hand are present to me now, and will be, I trust in God, to my last hour. The very thought of these things invigorated me the other day. And I almost blessed the sickness and low-spirits which brought before me associated images of a tenderness and an affection, which however im-perfectly repaid are deeply remembered. Such scenes and such recollec-tions are most dear to me. They are the bright half of human nature and human destiny. All objects of ambition, all rewards of talent sink into nothing in my mind compared with that affection which is independant of good or adverse circumstances, excepting that it is never so ardent, so delicate, or so tender as in the hour of languour and distress. – But I must stop. I am not often sentimental, and I had no intention of pouring out on paper what I am much more used to think than to express. Give my love to my Father and Sisters. Farewell my dear Mother.

T B M

[1] Probably the spring of 1818. See 8 December 1818.

TO SELINA MILLS MACAULAY, 10 JULY 1821

MS: Trinity College. *Address:* Mrs. Macaulay / No 20 Cadogan Place / Chelsea.

Shrewsbury¹ July 10. 1821

My dear Mother,

Here we are, after many wonderful adventures and escapes, after being locked into the gardens of Baliol college at Oxford, after nearly breaking our necks on the precipices of the Wye, and being almost poisoned in a bottle of execrable perry by mine host of the Talbot inn, in this most ancient and celebrated city.

To morrow we are to be at Llanrwst. Oh my dear mother, how I long to be with you all at Cadogan place! – I had rather see my Jenny again, or argue with Selina for half an hour about the long Parliament,² than contemplate all the wonders that art has done for Stowe, or nature for Piercefield.³

Have you got the copies of 'Evening'⁴ that I ordered to be sent to you from Cambridge? –

I have been rigidly observing your commands, and keeping Hal from eating fat. He pleads hard for ham, but I am inexorable. Admire me. For well you may. Was there ever such a son and such a brother?

Hannah More is worse than I ever saw her, yet much better than I expected to see her; at all events she is still as kind, as cheerful, as lively, and as fascinating as ever.

How is my Jenny. I was frightened by what I heard about her. Give my

¹ TBM left Cambridge on 2 July in company with his father and his brothers Henry and John for a tour first to Bristol to see Hannah More and then to Llanrwst, Denbighshire, where TBM was to join a reading party during the long vacation under C. S. Bird (see 31 August 1821) in preparation for the B.A. examination in the coming January. TBM had presumably recited his prize poem, 'Evening,' at the Cambridge commencement, though I can find no record that he did so. Their route from 2–5 July took them through Bedford, Newport Pagnell, Stowe, and Oxford. By the 7th they were to be in Bristol (Zachary Macaulay to Selina Mills Macaulay, 5 July: MS, Huntington). In the same letter Zachary Macaulay describes some of TBM's annoying mishaps: 'On Wednesday morning we set off from Bedford at ½ past 6. When we had gone half a mile Tom discovered he had left his watch behind him and had to go back for it. . . . In the [next] morning we were to have been off at ½ past 6 – but Tom had lost the key of his bag and before he could shave or dress it was necessary to have a blacksmith to break open his lock, so that we lost half an hour by his carelessness.'

² According to Hannah Trevelyan's Memoir of TBM, p. 29, TBM's conversion to Whig principles at Cambridge 'was a great grief to his Mother and eldest sister.'

³ Stowe House, Bucks., and Piercefield Park, Mons.

⁴ The poem with which TBM won his second Chancellor's medal: 'Evening. A Poem which obtained the Chancellor's Medal at the Cambridge Commencement, July 1821. By Thomas Babington Macaulay, Scholar of Trinity College' [Cambridge, 1821].

affectionate love to Selina and [   ]¹ and all the other girls. Is my [   ]¹
gone back to school[?]

Farewell my dear Mot[her.]¹
T B M

My Father is in excellent health and spirits as far as I can judge.

TO SELINA MILLS MACAULAY, [20?]² JULY 1821

MS: Trinity College. *Address:* Mrs. Macaulay / No 16 George Street / Mansion House London. *Partly published:* Trevelyan, I, 102–3.

Llanrwst³ July – 1821

My dear Mother,

You see I know not how to date my letter. My Calendar in this se-
questered spot is as irregular as Robinson Crusoe's after he had missed
one day in his calculation. What news can I be expected to send from this
wilderness to you who must have been enjoying the full splendour of the
Coronation,⁴ – in report at least. – But I – I have not seen a newspaper
for a week. Somebody told me yesterday that Lord Harrowby had resigned, and had been succeeded by Lord Sidmouth.⁵ Have mercy on me
who am

"Far in a wild, remote from public view"⁶

and if any very great event should happen, a war, for instance, or a revolution, let me know of it.

I have no intelligence to send you in return, unless a battle between a
drunken attorney and an impudent publican which took place here yesterday may deserve the appellation. You may perhaps be more interested to
hear that I sprained my foot, and am just recovering from the effects of the
accident by means of Opodeldoc⁷ which I bought at the tinker's. For all
trades and professions here lie in a most delightful confusion. The druggist

---

¹ Paper torn away with seal.
² Postmark of receiving office dated 23 July. From the evidence of TBM's other, dated letters
from Llanrwst, delivery to London took three or four days.
³ Twelve miles south of Conway, on the river Conway, Llanrwst boasted an old church, a
bridge attributed to Inigo Jones, and nine fairs each year.
⁴ 19 July. The reading party at Llanrwst had a holiday on the occasion, and 'provided dinner
for the children of all the Sunday schools, – above two hundred and thirty in number, – to
be served up in the Town Hall or Market-house, and likewise a dinner at the inn for all the
teachers and all the singers at the church' (C. S. Bird, *Sketches from the Life of Charles Smith
Bird*, p. 72).
⁵ Lord Harrowby remained President of the Council until 1827 and Lord Sidmouth Home
Secretary until 1822. Lord Harrowby, independently of the government to which he belonged, had supported parliamentary reform and Catholic relief earlier in 1821.
⁶ Thomas Parnell, 'The Hermit,' line 1.   ⁷ A soap liniment.

sells hats, the shoemaker is the sole bookseller; if that dignity may be allowed him on the strength of the three Welsh Bibles and the Guide to Caernarvon which adorn his window; – ink is sold by the Apothecary only; the grocer sells ropes; (a commodity which, I fear, I shall require before my residence here is over,) and tooth-brushes. A clothes'-brush is a luxury yet unknown to Llanrwst. When I asked for one, they brought me a stupendous old blacking brush which had been worn to the stumps on all the shoes and boots of, I suppose, half a dozen generations, and asked if that would do! –

Still I am contented, though I grumble. The people are harmless and quiet, and though ignorant, far from stupid. My old Woman is the best creature alive, if she were not so afraid of my catching cold. And as to books, for want of any other English literature, I intend to learn Paradise lost by heart at odd moments.

But I must conclude. Write to me often, my dear Mother; and all of you at home. Or you may have to answer for my drowning my self, like Gray's bard, in "old Conway's foaming flood,"[1] which is most conveniently near for so poetical an exit.

My love to my Father and all at home.

Ever most affectionately yours.

T B M

TO ZACHARY MACAULAY, 9 AUGUST 1821

MS: Trinity College. *Address:* Zachary Macaulay Esq. / No 16 George Street / Mansion House / London.

Llanrwst Denbighshire. August 9. / 1821

My dear Father,

I have received the letter and am much obliged to you both for the money and the directions. I thought that I had given an account in a former letter of the nature of the sprain. It was in the ancle. I am going for a few hours to Bangor to execute your directions. It gives me no pain in general, but is uneasy and weak when I get up in the morning, and the slightest false step brings on a renewal of the pain for some time. At Bangor, I doubt not, I shall get all necessary assistance.

A report has just reached me of the Queen's death;[2] – left, it is said, by one of the coaches that passed Bettws last night. A similar report was afloat last week but turned out false; This however comes with circumstance, and though the last bulletin which I have seen, that in the Courier of Monday, was favourable, her state appeared precarious. What an event,

---

[1] 'The Bard,' line 16.   [2] Queen Caroline died on 7 August.

if it be true! His Majesty, I presume, must return.[1] He has left Plas-something or other, the Marquis of Anglesea's seat, for Ireland. But he cannot in decency spend in pageantry and revels the interval between the death and burial of his wife. Her vices and their enmity would only make the event more shocking to a well regulated mind. It remains to be seen whether his be so. The ceremonies of the Coronation have not raised my opinion of his sense.[2] As a pageant, it seems, nothing could be more perfect, and the King's taste is said to have contributed to the elegance of the dresses and decorations. Such is the language of all the courtly writers on the subject. – High praise to a sovereign of sixty years of age that he is a good upholsterer and man-milliner! I am not, in truth, a great enthusiast about the Coronation, perhaps from envy. It is a magnificent but I think an unmeaning, and, I am sure, an expensive ceremony. Its principal value is that it preserves some of our ancient national garbs, rites, and usages. But that 100000 pounds should be squandered,[3] that the courts of law should be pulled down[4] to make room for a pageant of a few hours, and all this boyish folly committed by a man for whom the archbishop may very likely be required in a few months to perform the burial service within those very walls – this strikes me as most frivolous and contemptible and m[akes][5] me think that our country is suffering u[n][5]der the woe denounced against those whose ruler is a child.[6] –

Many thanks to Jenny for her letter. Poor dear girl! I am still anxious to hear more about her health.

I want very much to write to Henry; but I suppose he will be at School now. If so my letter will be stopped by Mr. Elwell,[7] who is in that, as in

---

[1] George IV left London on 31 July for a visit to Ireland, the first of an English sovereign in time of peace since Richard II. Travelling by sea from Portsmouth, he was at Holyhead on 4 August, from which he visited Plas Newydd, the Marquess of Anglesey's seat. The Queen's death did not prevent George from carrying out his tour; he reached Dublin on 12 August, remained in retirement until after the Queen's funeral, and made his public entry into the city on 17 August.

[2] The coronation of George IV, notable both for antiquarian fidelity and lavish expense, followed the precedents for the coronation of James II.

[3] Greville puts the cost of the coronation at £240,000 (*Memoirs*, II, 183). Greville, as Clerk to the Privy Council, had the means of knowing.

[4] The coronation banquet was held in Westminster Hall – the last one given there.

[5] Obscured by stain from seal.   [6] Ecclesiastes 10: 16.

[7] The school kept by Richard Elwell in Queen Street, Hammersmith, was a favorite among the Evangelicals. John, Henry, and Charles Macaulay were sent there, as were children from the Venn, Thornton, Elliott, and Pearson families. Gathorne Hardy, first Earl of Cranbrook, was there until 1825 and remembered it with loathing: 'What a place of narrowness, bigotry, hypocrisy, and meanness! spying on the part of the masters, deceit justified on the part of the boys – forced "voluntary" contributions to Bible and Missionary Societies.... Letters from home, and to home, opened and read' (A. E. Gathorne-Hardy, *Gathorne Hardy, First Earl of Cranbrook*, 1910, I, 14). Charles Macaulay spoke of the school as 'our loathsome dungeon' (to Henry Macaulay, [7 February 1825]: MS, University of London). Sometime late in the 1820s Elwell succeeded to the school at Clapham Common where TBM had been the pupil of Greaves.

every thing else that I can learn about him, the most absurd and illiberal of school-masters. Tell him that that is my reason for not writing to him; – he is immensely solicitous that my letter should be kept extremely secret.

My love to Hannah and Madge.[1] I am delighted with their pretty letters. I hope to hear from my mother. My affectionate love to her and everybody else.

T B M.

TO SELINA MILLS MACAULAY, 30 AUGUST 1821

MS: Trinity College. *Address:* Mrs. Macaulay / No 16 George Street / Mansion House / London.

Llanrwst Denbighshire August 30. 1821

My dear Mother

All my complaints have long been over, – and without medecine. On that point indeed I become more and more a Molierist. I run indeed little danger of dying " de deux medecins et trois apothécaires,"[2] in this quarter of the world; since no professor of the murderous art authorized or otherwise, lives within some miles, to my knowledge, except an old methodist who sells gin, wafers, packthread, and Epsom salts, and on the strength of an old purple jar which stands in his window, dignifies himself with the title of chemist and druggist. – I have sate a quarter of an hour meditating for something more to say. But in vain. – Where nothing happens what can be narrated? Where no new books arrive what can be criticized? – I have therefore nothing more to send than my love to my father and sisters. I am very glad that John is so comfortably settled; and that Jenny is well again. Why does not Selina write to me. She has not sent me one letter since I came here.

T B M.

TO ZACHARY MACAULAY, 31 AUGUST 1821

MS: Trinity College. *Address:* Zachary Macaulay Esq. / No 16 George Street / Mansion House / London. *Partly published:* Trevelyan, I, 103–4.

Llanrwst August 31 1821

My dear Father,

I have just received your letter and cannot but feel concerned at the tone of it. I do not understand how I can be said to have written only two letters

---

[1] Margaret Macaulay.
[2] Molière, *L'Amour Médecin*, II, i, 9–10: 'Elle est morte de quatre médecins et de deux apothicaires.'

within the last five weeks, since *not one week* has elapsed during that time in which I have not sent a letter to Cadogan place. Nor do I think it quite fair to attack me for filling my letters with remarks on the King's Irish expedition. It has been the great event of this part of the world. I was at Bangor when he sailed. His bows and the Marquis of Anglesea's fête were the universal subjects of conversation; and some remarks on the business were as natural from me as accounts of the Coronation from you in London. In truth I have little else to say. I see nothing that connects me with the world except the newspapers. I get up, breakfast, read, play at quoits, and go to bed. This is the history of my life. It will do for every day of the last fortnight. –

As to the King, I spoke of the business not at all as a political but as a moral question, as a point of correct feeling and of private decency. If Lord Roseberry[1] were to issue tickets for a gala ball immediately after receiving intelligence of the sudden death of his divorced wife I should have said the same. I pretend to no great insight into party politics, but the question whether it is proper for any man to mingle in festivities while his wife's body lies unburied is one, I confess, which I thought myself competent to decide. But I am not anxious about the fate of my remarks which I have quite forgot, and which I dare say, were very foolish. To me it is of little importance whether the King's conduct were right or wrong; but it is of great importance that those whom I love should not think me a precipitate, silly, shallow, sciolist in politics, and suppose that every frivolous word that falls from my pen is a dogma which I mean to advance as indisputable; – and all this only because I write to them without reserve, – only because I love them well enough to trust them with every silly or inconsistent idea which suggests itself to me. In fact I believe that I am not more precipitate or presumptuous than other people, but only more open. You cannot be more fully convinced that I am how contracted my means are of forming a judgement on public affairs. If I chose to weigh every word that I uttered or wrote to you, and, whenever I alluded to politics, were to labour and qualify all my expressions as if I were drawing up a state paper, my letters might be a great deal wiser, but would not be such letters as I should wish to receive from those whom I loved. Perfect love, we are told, casteth out fear.[2] And I could not perfectly love any one to whom I durst not exhibit all that interior mechanism of my mind, which cautious people conceal, and exhibit only its result. To whom else would I display all my crude notions, defective information, and

---

[1] Lord Rosebery (1783–1868: *DNB*) had divorced his wife in 1815 for *crim. con.* with Sir Henry Mildmay and obtained £15,000 damages. The case was doubly sensational because Lady Rosebery was Sir Henry's deceased wife's sister. Rosebery had received an honorary degree from Cambridge at the ceremonies at which TBM had read 'Pompeii.'
[2] 1 John 4: 18.

inconsistent or half formed opinions? If I say, as I know I do, a thousand wild and inaccurate things, and employ exaggerated expressions about persons or events in writing to you or to my mother, it is not, I believe, that I want power to systematize my ideas or to measure my expressions, but because I have no objection to letting you see my mind in dishabille. – I have a court-dress for days of ceremony and people of ceremony, nevertheless. But I would not willingly be frightened into wearing it with you; and I hope you do not wish me to do so. For my own part at least I always love those best who show so much confidence in my regard and candour as to trust me with their foibles; and I do not like a person less for venturing to talk a few flippancies or a little nonsense to [me.][1] In a man of any sense it is a sure proof [of][1] kindness and esteem.

I have not exhausted much more than half of the money which you sent me. But I have not as yet paid the weekly rent of my lodgings. My weekly expenses, (exclusive of the lodgings,) are, upon an average, about 12 shillings for bread, butter, etc.; 3 or four shillings for washing, about 15 shillings for dinners. There are of course occasional additional expenses for postage, parcels, and other miscellaneous articles and services.

I am not at all able to pronounce upon the success of my mathematical reading. If I can get up accurately all that I am likely to read I shall do well enough. Bird[2] seems quite satisfied. But I shall be better able to report progress a fortnight hence.

My affectionate love to my Mother and every body else. As Henry is come home I shall soon write to him.

T B M

TO ZACHARY MACAULAY, 8 SEPTEMBER 1821

MS: Trinity College. *Address:* Zachary Macaulay Esq. / No 16 George Street / Mansion House / London.

Llanrwst Denbighshire. / September 8 1821

My dear Father,

Three weeks more will bring the time of my return. I hope I have profited by my absence. But time must show. I have passed the last week with scarcely any society but that of Newton and Homer, the Prince of Philo-

---

[1] Paper torn away with seal.

[2] A young Evangelical Fellow of Trinity, Charles Smith Bird (1795–1862: *DNB*) was third wrangler and Smith's prizeman, 1820. He held various curacies while, for twenty years, continuing to take pupils. In 1843 he became Vicar of Gainsborough, and in 1859, Chancellor of Lincoln Cathedral. Bird published some devotional poetry and a number of polemical works against Romanism. The event of this reading party that he remembered best in his autobiography was TBM's refusal to take part in a Bible Society meeting at Llanrwst (C. S. Bird, *Sketches from the Life of Charles Smith Bird*, p. 71).

sophers and the Prince of Poets. – The former I am not philosopher enough to appreciate as he deserves, by the universal testimony of all who understand him. – But my admiration of Homer increases with every persual. – How strange a thing is literary immortality. – What a magnificent preeminence! What could Buonaparte do more than force the often reluctant service of a few thousand hands for ten or twelve years. – What a superior rank is to be assigned to the man who through six and twenty centuries has influenced the feelings, interested the sympathies, governed and fixed the standard of taste of vast and enlightened empires. And what an incalculable debt do we owe to that little speck of land, Greece. – The principles of taste, the finest models of composition, the doctrines and the glorious examples to which we owe political freedom, the arts, the sciences, architecture, sculpture, every thing that is great and splendid in literature and politics, must be considered as ultimately derived from that little peninsula. I hope from the bottom of my soul that they will be able to beat off the Turks, and that without the pernicious aid of the Arch-Tartuffe of Russia.[1] From England I suppose, they have nothing to hope. – We have in general made it our policy to uphold Turkey, reasoning I suppose as some of the ancient naturalists did about the spleen. They could find no possible use for such a part in the body, and maintained accordingly that it was put in, as we cram brown paper into portmanteaus, to keep the contents close packed, and prevent them from dancing about. Turkey, I suppose, has been patronized as a kind of spleen in the body politic of Europe.

So William Babington and George Stephen are plunging into politics,[2] – and pretty decidedly too. I cannot blame them much. The conduct of the rabble, of the jury, and of Sheriff Waithman,[3] sometimes turns me for

---

[1] The revolt against Turkish rule that eventually became the Greek War of Independence had begun in March 1821. Russia did not intervene until 1827, and then in company with Great Britain and France.

[2] It seems unlikely that this is the William Babington of 22 August 1815, but I know of no other. George Stephen (1794–1879: *DNB*), fourth son of James Stephen, was a solicitor who later took an important part in the abolition of slavery as founder of the Anti-Slavery Agency Committee. His *Anti-Slavery Recollections*, 1854, is an interesting account of the abolitionists at work. Stephen was called to the bar in 1849, practised for a while in Liverpool, but emigrated in 1855 to Australia; he died at Melbourne.

[3] Robert Waithman (see [September 1819]), now Sheriff of London, had recently been prominent in the tumults produced by the funeral of Queen Caroline. Two men had been killed in a scuffle between the Guards and the mob at the funeral procession of Caroline on 14 August; the funeral procession of these two men on 26 August led to a riot at Knightsbridge barracks when the Guards and the marchers clashed. Waithman, regarded as the popular leader, was caught up in the riot and in some danger. On 11 September the Common Council passed a vote of thanks to him for his conduct on the occasion. The coroner's juries at the inquests on the bodies of the two men killed returned verdicts of manslaughter against the first regiment of Life Guards in one case, and of wilful murder against a Lifeguardsman unknown in the other.

a few hours into a Tory. I now and then fear that I shall be a perfect jure-divino man if the[se]¹ things go on. – Of all the *ocracies*, blackguardocracy is surely the worst. If the liberties of the country are to be taken away, I hope we shall at least have the privilege of being choked, like the Duke of Clarence, in Malmsey wine, not drowned in a filthy kennel. – But I am summoned to attend Bird, and must hasten to a conclusion. Love to all at home. The weather here is delicious.

T B M.

to Zachary Macaulay, 12 September 1821

MS: Huntington Library.

Llanrwst Denbighshire September 12. 1821

My dear Father,

I have just received your kind letter. Be assured that I never looked upon any of your remarks but as proving the most sincere affection and concern for my welfare. I quite acquiesce in the justice of your observations.

My present intention is to set off for London about next Monday fortnight. Bird departs for Liverpool towards the close of the preceding week. I hope that my mother will be back by that time.²

As to money matters I imagine that the 15£ which you have sent me together with what remains of the former sum will very nearly clear all my debts at Llanrwst up to the day of my departure. The lodgings will come to about nine pounds, the dinners to perhaps seven or eight pounds more. Bird's fee is 30 guineas; – I must also make a present to the old woman who waits on me, and to whom I feel really much obliged for her attention to my health and comfort. I shall be able to speak more accurately on these points in my next letter.

But I must stop, in order to discharge my debts to Jane and Henry. Pray let nobody open Henry's letter but himself.³ He has requested this very earnestly.

T B M.

¹ Paper torn away with seal.
² Selina Mills Macaulay paid an annual visit to Hannah More in the late summer or autumn.
³ 'I was amused to hear today from Fanny how mysterious you are about the letters you receive. She says you make Tom write Private and nod your head very knowingly as you are reading his letters. I think there is no real secret between you but as you are very curious yourself you love to excite the curiosity of others' (Mary Babington to Henry Macaulay, 30 June 1823: copy, Mrs Lancelot Errington).

TO HENRY MACAULAY, 12 SEPTEMBER 1821

MS: University of Texas. *Address:* Mr Henry Macaulay / To be opened by himself.

Llanrwst Denbighshire. September 12 / 1821
My dear Hal,

You complain that I have neglected your letter I understand; – but not with much justice. I wrote an answer to you some weeks ago. But it occurred to me that you were at Mr. Elwell's, and that your good master takes upon himself to inspect all the correspondence of his pupils. Therefore, as you wished our letters to be a great secret, I did not send what I had written. But as I find that you can receive my letter on a Saturday at home, I venture now to answer your questions.

Many of them indeed I scarcely know how to answer. I know very little of the details of the system of education at Oxford. There are certainly some colleges both there and at Cambridge where an idle man runs a chance of a fellowship; but I trust that this will be no inducement to any brother of mine.

If you fully intend to go into the church, which after all is a point respecting which, at your age there is not the least reason to decide, you must of course pass through one of the Universities. Cambridge, I think, would then clearly suit you best. You complain that you are backward for your age. I think that you underrate your progress. But if you are deficient in classical knowledge it affords a strong argument for your preferring Cambridge, since there a man may attain the highest honours of the Senate house, and at most of the Colleges, be certain of a fellowship, without the slightest knowledge of the ancient languages. Not that I mean to encourage you to neglect those pursuits. They are ornamental and honourable in all ranks of life. They give elegance to the taste and accuracy to the style; the very exercise of the acquisition tends to invigorate the mind. In a clergyman above all, if you are to be a clergyman, they are of immense importance. Without them he cannot judge for himself as to the meaning of the sacred writings which it is his office to explain, and he is likewise debarred from many of [the][1] most valuable theological works both of ancient and modern times.

Therefore, my dear Boy, let me intreat you to prosecute your classical studies actively. If, as is not altogether impossible, I should spend some months after taking my degree at home, I should have great pleasure in assisting you. You would soon find how all the difficulties of those languages vanish, before perseverance and accuracy. We shall soon be better able to discuss this point. Till we meet each other, my dear Hal, farewell.

                                                                T B M.

[1] Letter torn.

TO SELINA MILLS MACAULAY, 17 SEPTEMBER 1821

MS: Trinity College. *Address:* Mrs. Macaulay / at Mrs. More's / Barley Wood / near Bristol.

Llanrwst. Denbighshire. September 17. 1821

My dear Mother,

I hope to be at home in about a fortnight, and I shall be bitterly dissapointed if I do not find you there. I look forward to my return with great pleasure. Yet I shall not leave Llanrwst without regret.[1] It must be owned that it is a very dull place, that the uniformity of its events is diversified only by drunken battles, exhibitions of Jumpers, and fairs which keep every man who values his existence a prisoner to his rooms. At this moment one of these elegant scenes is going on. The streets are choked with pigs and calves, horses and horse-dealers, singing men and singing women, drunkards fighting, children screaming, cows lowing, and every now and then poking their heads in at my window to examine the furniture of my apartment. So much for the blessings of my Arcadia. Yet I shall, as I said, regret it, though I do not know why. I love every thing old and even when I have been accustomed to a place for three months only, I cannot part from it for ever without some concern. However, as our friend Preston said of his marriage, I will endeavour to be resigned to the prospect of returning to you all; – and I hope that you will receive so high a compliment with as much satisfaction as his mistress did.

You had better keep the 5 £ till we meet. Assure Mrs. Hannah More that I can never receive any mark of her kindness but with gratitude and pride. I envy you her society, and I am delighted to see that you think her still in the full vigour of her mind. I have certainly never seen an intellect so remarkably superior to the ordinary laws of decay, so much vivacity at such an age, or so much cheerfulness in such trying circumstances. How invalids support existence I scarcely can conceive. I would sooner, I think, be broken on the wheel at once than condemned to a darkened room and a feverish bed for months; perhaps for years. I have sometimes thought, hypochondriacally I dare say, that this might perhaps be my own case. With unclouded intellects and unconquerable spirits like those of your hostess any thing would be endurable. But if the mind were to share, as usually it does, the decay of the body, I would say with the old Count Roussillon in Shakespear

---

[1] 'When the party left Llanrwst, the inhabitants gave them quite an ovation. Bells were ringing, and flags flying, and at dinner an address was presented, signed by various classes, thanking Mr Bird and his pupils for their general conduct, and benevolent public spirit shewn on several occasions' (C. S. Bird, *Sketches from the Life of Charles Smith Bird*, p. 73). The address is printed in Trevelyan, I, 101–2.

"Let me not live,
After my flame lacks oil, to be the scoff
Of meaner spirits." —[1]

Apropos of invalids, I am quite uneasy about my little Jenny. I had a letter from her last week overflowing, as usual, with affection for me, and with gratitude and tenderness for [you][2] on account of your attention to her; but in all that she writes there is something so plaintive and depressed that it almost breaks my heart. But of this we shall be able to talk the week after next.

Give my love to Hannah More the lesser[3] and (if she will accept a sincere though very worthless present,) to her greater namesake. – Ever believe me, dear Mother, affectionately yours.

T B M.

TO SELINA MILLS MACAULAY, [25? NOVEMBER 1821][4]

MS: Trinity College. *Address:* Mrs. Macaulay / No 16 George Street / Mansion House / London. *Mostly published:* Trevelyan, I, 105–6.

[Cambridge]

My dear Mother,

I possess some of the irritability of a Poet, and it has been a good deal awakened by your criticisms. I could not have imagined that it would be necessary for me to have said that the execrable trash entitled Tears of Sensibility[5] was merely a burlesque on the style of the magazine verses of the day. I could not suppose that you could have suspected me of *seriously* composing such a farrago of false metaphor and unmeaning epithet. It was meant solely for a caricature on the style of the poetasters of newspapers and journals; and (though I say it who should not say it,) has excited more attention and received more praise at Cambridge than it deserved. If you have it, read it over again, and do me the justice to believe that such a compound of jargon, nonsense, false images, and exaggerated sentiment is not the product of my serious labours. I sent it to the Morning Post, because that paper is the ordinary receptacle of trash of the description which I intended to ridicule,[6] and its admission therefore pointed the jest.

---

[1] *All's Well that Ends Well*, I, ii, 59–61: 'to be the snuff / Of younger spirits.'
[2] Paper torn away with seal.   [3] TBM's sister.
[4] Postmark of receiving office dated 26 November.
[5] 'Tears of Sensibility' appeared anonymously in the 'Original Poetry' section of the *Morning Post*, 16 November, and is dated 'Barnwell, Cambridgeshire, Nov. 14, 1821.' Seven of its ten stanzas are reprinted in Trevelyan, I, 105.
[6] So worthless are the literary dissertations in *Don Quixote*, TBM says, that 'in our time they would scarcely obtain admittance into the literary department of the Morning Post' ('John Dryden,' *ER*, XLVII [January 1828], 6).

I see however that for the future I must mark more distinctly when I intend to be ironical.

There is, I hope, no ground for believing that the fever has broken out here.

Give my love to my father and sisters. / Ever, my dearest Mother,

Your affectionate Son,

T B M

TO ZACHARY MACAULAY, 2 JANUARY 1822

MS: Trinity College. *Address:* Zachary Macaulay Esq / No 16 George Street / Mansion House / London.

Trinity College Cambridge January 2. 1822.

My dear Father,

After a long silence I borrow a few minutes from necessary employment and exercise to thank you for the kind letters which I have lately received. I could have wished to have spent the late Christmas by that happy fire side which has always been the centre of my hopes and affections.[1] It is a beautiful coincidence that the day on which we commemorate the origin of our religion is likewise a day inseparably connected by the associations of childhood with those domestic feelings and enjoyments which that religion has created or purified. Every peaceful Christmas hearth in England, which is protected by just laws, blessed by mutual affection, and cheered by temperate hospitality is a monument more glorious than that of Trajan or Napoleon to the beneficial influence of Christianity on the morals and the happiness of nations and families. But for the great event which that festival commemorates, how scanty and how sullied a portion of domestic virtue and enjoyment would now exist among mankind. How degraded would still be the condition of that sex whose influence has made hostility gentle and vice decorous, and, like the branch thrown by the Hebrew Lawgiver into the bitter waters of Marah,[2] has converted the wormwood of society into sweetness and its poison into nutriment. Christmas is the festival not only of our religion, but of civilization, of morals, of toleration, of domestic happiness, of social courtesy. These circumstances have always appeared to me beautifully to elucidate the song of the Angels "Glory to God in the Highest, and on earth peace, good will towards men."[3]

---

[1] TBM was at Cambridge 'labouring hard to avoid the discredit of not having Mathematics enough to fit him to sit for the classical medal. . . .It has been a great mortification to him to be absent from us at this season the first time we were ever apart at Christmas; but still it was his own voluntary choice' (Zachary Macaulay to Hannah More, 27 December 1821: MS, Huntington).

[2] Exodus 15: 23–4.   [3] Luke 2: 14.

I shall take my degree on Saturday fortnight[1] and probably return on the Monday. The fees required on the occasion are between 10 and 11 pounds. I have sent up a draught to London on the Craven fund which will, I hope, be accepted in time to discharge this sum. But the Banker here who manages the business for me tells me that he is not quite certain whether I shall receive it sufficiently early. If not, I will write up to you for a supply.

I should like to hear something more about the articles in the Edinburgh and Quarterly Reviews on the Foreign Slave Trade.[2] You are, I suppose, at least acquainted with their secret history. I do not recollect that the Quarterly has ever taken so decided a tone before.

I hope to be able to defray in a measure at least the expenses of my residence here after Christmas. I have already one application for tuition and I believe I shall have others.

I direct to the City, on the supposition that you have returned from Brighton.

Give my love to my dear Mother and all the family. I am a debtor for many kind letters, and, I fear, what is worse than a debtor, a bankrupt.

Farewell.

T B M.

---

[1] 19 January. The event was a disaster. TBM attempted the examination for honors, but 'finding after two days struggle that he would be distanced by his competitors he withdrew from the conflict.... He is labouring at present poor fellow under all the agitation of remorse to think how well he might have done had he had self denial enough to sacrifice his more miscellaneous reading to Mathematics' (Zachary Macaulay to Hannah More, 23 January 1822: MS, Huntington). The repercussions of TBM's fall were heard throughout Clapham. Emelia Venn wrote to her brother John: 'Tom Macaulay alas! poor Tom! goes into the gulph and is numbered among the οἱ [*polloi*, i.e., the mere pass-men]. He has been idle, I suppose.... A sore trial this will be to his Father and all his family – and he may one day bitterly regret the having lost this opportunity of gratifying and delighting his Parents' (23 January 1822: MS, Church Missionary Society). Marianne Thornton, writing to Hannah More on 21 January, reported that TBM 'did not know mathematics enough to enable him to sit for the medal. Tho' his is not a mathematical head, they say this little may be gained by almost any body who will read with attention, and I am therefore doubly sorry, not on his own account only, but on that of his sire, who has been so wise and so wary in his management of his "son of genius." Perhaps it may be of use to Tom in showing that there is no royal way to Honours' (Forster, *Marianne Thornton*, p. 79). When TBM returned to his family after the examination, Hannah Macaulay writes, 'I can recall my mother telling him that he had better go at once to his father, and get it over, and I can see him as he left the room on that errand' (Trevelyan, I, 83). The matter was not made better by the fact that the other Clapham B.A., Henry Thornton, achieved high distinction as fourth wrangler.

[2] 'Foreign Slave Trade,' *ER*, XXXVI (October 1821), 34–52, was by Brougham; 'Fernando Po – State of the Slave Trade,' *Quarterly Review*, XXVI (October 1821), 51–82, was by (Sir) John Barrow.

TO SELINA MILLS MACAULAY, 16 FEBRUARY 1822

MS: Trinity College. *Address:* Mrs. Macaulay / No 36 Bedford Square / West Cliff / Brighton /
Sussex.

Trinity College Cambridge / February 16. 1822

My dear Mother,

George Babington[1] has been here for about twenty four hours, and, I
think, saw as much of our public buildings as was possible in that time.
Dr. Hewett[2] the Downing Professor of domestic medicine introduced
him to the Fitzwilliam Museum and the University library, the only sights
in the University which require any other introduction than that of a
shilling. He seemed very much pleased with his visit.

I am most comfortably and not expensively settled, and shall not think
of changing again while I remain in Cambridge.[3] My Books are in good
order, and I have begun to put every thing in its place and do every thing
at its proper time with many other very excellent habits which will astonish
you when I come back next.

I have also fallen on a vigorous plan of retrenchment, which might
satisfy Mr. Joseph Hume[4] himself, and will I hope cover the expences of
buying the furniture of my new rooms. I have found that books may with
a little management be got out of the College libraries, and that my Bookseller's bill may be materially reduced without denying myself any work
that is necessary for study.

Retrenchment will indeed be pretty necessary; for I can hear nothing of
my expected pupil, who, I believe, has not returned to Cambridge; and

[1] George Gisborne Babington (1794–1856), fourth son of Thomas Babington; M.R.C.S.,
1816; F.R.C.S., 1843; one of the surgeons to St George's Hospital. In 1817 he married
Sarah Anne, the daughter of the Evangelical John Pearson, surgeon, of Golden Square;
George, too, lived and practised in Golden Square. He was the Babington cousin that TBM
liked best, though they quarrelled after TBM went to India and the close relation between
them was never restored. In the decade before that the two young men were much together
and on terms of 'closest intimacy' (Trevelyan, I, 120). His niece Eliza Rose Conybeare
described him as 'a distinguished surgeon, and the truest Christian, spending hours daily in
unpaid service in the lowest courts of London.... By natural disposition so sceptical, so
inquiring, always ready for an argument...a great friend of John Newman's, though taking
very different views from him'; she adds that he made a 'mess' of money matters ('Aunt
Eliza's Story': typescript memoir in possession of Mr B. Babington Smith).

[2] Cornwallis Hewett (1787?–1841), Downing Professor of Medicine, 1814–41.

[3] Presumably TBM had just moved to the set of rooms which is still identified as his at
Trinity: E1, Great Court. Having taken his B.A., TBM was now eligible to compete for a
Trinity fellowship; candidates could sit the examination in each of the first three Septembers
following the B.A., but it was unusual to attempt it on the first occasion. Trevelyan, I, 82,
states that 'Macaulay was not chosen a fellow until his third trial,' but there is no evidence
in his letters of 1822 that he took the examination in that year.

[4] Joseph Hume (1777–1855: *DNB*), Radical M.P. from 1818 until his death, was noted
especially for his policy of financial 'retrenchment' and for his speaking in the Commons
'longer and oftener and probably worse than any other private member' (*DNB*).

this is an unfavourable time for getting others, as almost all provided themselves at October with instructors for the year. I had an offer, (keep this a profound secret from every body but my father) of very handsome terms for writing political articles in a newspaper.[1] You may suppose that I excused myself, perhaps with too much brusquerie.

Have you read Milman's Martyr of Antioch?[2] It is, in my opinion, much superior to the Fall of Jerusalem.[3] This will not, I think, be the general decision. The heroine is charming. But it is rather remarkable that while all the Pagan hymns introduced are full of poetry and elegance, the Christian hymns on the contrary are poor both in thought and language. This is not Milman's fault. Poetry is too sensual an art for the higher parts of Christianity. The gorgeous mythology of Greece, the beautiful profiles, the majestic forms, the magnificent drapery with which sculpture pourtrayed her deities, the fanciful loveliness of their rites, the Corinthian Colonnades of temples surrounded by groves, the altars crowned with flowers, the dances, and the music, the victim covered with garlands, the censer steaming with incense, are far more suited to the genius of poetry than the worship of a being

"that doth prefer
Before all temples th'upright heart and pure."[4]

It is remarkable that in Catholic times the human mind took the same course, and finding it difficult to shape to itself an object of love and adoration in a mysterious and invisible being, embodied all the attributes of female loveliness in the Virgin, called on the painters and poets of a reviving age to adorn her with all that the glowing imagination of Italy could bestow, and then fell down to adore the being that it had created, just as in former ages it would have adored a Venus or an Apollo.

I have just received your letter. I do not quite understand why my correspondence is considered as remiss. You request a letter every fortnight. I hope to send one oftener. But I have only been a fortnight from home, and I have written once already. I sent the certificate to my father because, after examining the Court Calendar and enquiring of all my friends here who belong to Lincoln's Inn, I could not find out how the Steward spells his name.[5]

Love to my father and all at home.

                                                                                        T B M

[1] Nothing more is known of this offer.
[2] Henry Hart Milman, *The Martyr of Antioch: A Dramatic Poem*, 1822.
[3] *The Fall of Jerusalem: A Dramatic Poem*, 1820.
[4] *Paradise Lost*, I, 17–18.
[5] His name was Thomas Lane. TBM was admitted to Lincoln's Inn on 25 January 1822, six days after taking his B.A., and was called to the bar on 9 February 1826. Before the reforms of the middle of the century, to be called to the bar a student with an Oxford or Cambridge degree had only to 'eat his dinners' – i.e., to eat in the hall of his Inn of Court a few times

TO ZACHARY MACAULAY, 28 FEBRUARY 1822

MS: Harvard University. *Address:* Zachary Macaulay Esq. / No 16 George Street / Mansion House / London.

Trinity College Cambridge Feby. 28. 1822.

My dear father,

I cannot plead guilty to unnecessary delay, since I wrote on the subject of my pupil as soon as I had received the answer from Barlow's brother[1] which led me to despair of seeing him here. I imagine that I shall not now procure any pupils till October. In the mean time I am perfectly at your disposal.

My own plan is to return to Brighton at Easter, to remain at home till Commencement which happens in July, and then to return and spend the Long Vacation at Cambridge. All persons are subject to many interruptions of study while Cambridge is full, and none more than Bachelors. Every body thinks their time at his disposal. At Brighton I could read during the term-time, and then return to the solitude of our empty groves and cloisters during the summer, when no interruptions exist, and when a man must read or hang himself.

I am getting on at present pretty rapidly with Herodotus and Locke. I told my scheme of study to Monk, who approved it highly and advised me to act upon it. You have seen in the newspapers, I suppose, that he has

in each of the four annual terms for a total of twelve terms. This was called 'keeping terms.' Various patterns of attendance in each term were permitted, but none required more than a few days. See Thomas Lane, *The Student's Guide Through Lincoln's Inn*, 4th edn, 1823. Information about TBM's legal studies is very meager. There are some scattered references to them in the family letters of 1822–4 but no very definite information; e.g., Zachary Macaulay writes on 24 March 1824 that 'Tom is making himself expert at conveyancing and will be proceeding by and by to acquire the necessary skill in the art of special pleading. He seems on the whole to take to the law' (to Hannah More: MS, Huntington). The only other evidence of TBM's efforts to prepare himself for what was, nominally at least, to be his profession, is given by the anonymous writer, identified merely as a 'literary and legal friend,' in [Eliza Rennie], *Traits of Character*, II, 15–16. This writer says that TBM 'placed himself under the tuition of the late Mr. Duval, his fellow-pupils being the eldest son of the celebrated Wilberforce, and Mr. now Sir W. F. Channell. The shrewd special pleader characterized the trio thus: – "Young Wilberforce is volatile and utterly unstable – he will do nothing. Channell has sense and steady perseverance – he, sir, will rise, and, if life be spared him, may make a very useful puisné judge or baron of the Exchequer. As for Tom Macaulay, he has splendid talents and great application; but then he rather loves to pore over the State Trials than master Tidd or Christy's books of practice. No man knows more about the Ship Money, or the Seven Bishops's cases, and he would figure doubtless on a parliamentary impeachment question; but Tom Macaulay, sir, will hold few briefs at *Nisi Prius*."' Lewis Duval (1774–1844) was the 'acknowledged head' (*DNB*) of English conveyancers; Sir William Fry Channell (1804–73), who was called to the bar in the year after TBM, was made a Baron of the Exchequer in 1857. The notice of him in the *DNB* says that he studied under the special pleader Colmer but does not mention Duval.

[1] Philip Barlow (1804–58), matriculated at Peterhouse, 1821; B.A., 1825.

been made Dean of Peterborough.[1] He has lately published a very temperate and well-written pamphlet on the system of University education, under the name of Philo Grantus.[2] It is the manifesto of a large and increasing party which, in our College in particular, gains vigour every day.

I think that this is Selina's Birthday.[3] I wish the dear girl many, very many happy returns. I wish I were at home to thank her and Jenny for their letters.

My mother wishes for a fuller view of my plans than I can at present give. When I come home, I will tell her all the conflicting views and motives which actuate me in my present reflections on the choice of a profession.[4] They would appear inconsistent if not unintelligible on paper. In the mean time as so much has been done and paid with a view to the bar, I should wish to keep my terms as quickly as possible.

Give my affectionate love to my Mother and all at home.

T B M.

PS. I should like to hear something about the late Spanish regulations relative to the Slave Trade.[5] Spain it seems has allowed the independance of her American possessions. If so, is not the prohibition of the trade by Spain nugatory? Will not the trade be left in the hands of states which have immense temptation and unlimited means to continue it, states too, over which the influence of the European powers, and the sentiments of the European public will have but little controul?

[1] Monk was officially appointed Dean of Peterborough on 7 March.

[2] 'A Letter to the Right Reverend John, Lord Bishop of Bristol,' 1822; at the end of the text, dated 1 February 1822. It was written in support of the movement to establish a classical tripos in addition to the existing, exclusively mathematical examination. Trinity was particularly active in this campaign, and through the efforts of Monk, Wordsworth, and others a classical tripos was established in very restricted form in 1822 and first given in 1824.

[3] Her birthday was 27 February.

[4] TBM may have been flirting with the idea of entering the Church. Zachary Macaulay writes to Selina Macaulay on 2 April that 'I rejoice in what you say of Tom's feelings on the subject of the Ministry. I should indeed be most thankful were his views to point that way – but that is in the hands of a higher influence. God make him, if not an able minister of the New Testament, yet a faithful servant of his' (MS, Huntington).

[5] In August 1821 Spain, which with Portugal was the last European country to keep up the slave trade, declared itself ready to enforce the treaty against the trade; in January 1822 'an article for repressing the trade was...introduced into the criminal code of Spain' (*Annual Register*, 1822, p. 518).

TO SELINA MILLS MACAULAY, [15][1] MARCH 1822

MS: Trinity College. Address: Mrs. Macaulay / No 36 Bedford Square / Brighton / Sussex.

Trinity College Cambridge. Friday. March 16. 1822

My dear Mother,

I am just recovering from a kind of influenza which has been prevailing here and which has infested me for two or three days, keeping me stupid and uncomfortable without conferring the privilege which more important maladies bestow, of being disagreable to every body about me. I almost doubt whether all the sufferings of an invalid are not overpaid by the dignity of parading his misery and extorting the sympathy of all his neighbours. The gout or the liver complaint is a cheap price to pay for the pleasures of licensed fretfulness and egotism.

You may expect to see me about the first of April. Mind, I do not mean to play you an April fool trick by keeping you all in anxious expectation of my arrival, and then breaking my engagement. If my father continues to approve of my plans, I hope to remain with you till the beginning of July.[2]

I do not know whether you have heard of the death of Dr. Clarke[3] the famous traveller, and professor of Mineralogy in our University. It has excited much interest here. He was a man of extraordinary enthusiasm and activity of mind, a great lover of science, and a very amiable member of society. He has left a young wife and a large family. –

That impudent dog De Vitry[4] is here, teaching, and begging and stealing. He has returned on a sudden after a considerable absence. In the name of justice and humanity, I adjure you let me have your consent to bring him up before the Mayor and provide him with lodgings in the County gaol. At all events get his wife and children passed to him. He hanged himself, if I remember right. – The law will probably save him the trouble of repeating the operation. I cannot express the indignation I feel when I see a man who has left his wife and infant children to starve walking about as the instructor of men who would kick him down stairs if they knew his character. Whenever you write mention particularly whether my Father is at Brighton or London.

[1] Friday was the 15th; the letter bears a London postmark dated the 16th.
[2] TBM apparently returned to Cambridge in the middle of June: see 4 January 1823.
[3] Clarke died on 9 March.
[4] Not identified. A letter from Selina Mills Macaulay to Zachary Macaulay, 24 September 1821, cautions him against 'taking [Madame Christophe] as de Vitry said under your patronage' (MS, Huntington). De Vitry thus may be linked with the widow of Henry Christophe, who, after her husband's suicide in 1820, fled to England, where she was provided for by the abolitionists. See Knutsford, Zachary Macaulay, pp. 367–8.

Why is poor Sir Benjamin[1] turned out of favour? Have you learnt anything from your friend the Court Chaplain?[2] I suppose that you are in the very centre of the Scandal of the Royal circle; – though by the bye I believe that the King has left Brighton.[3]

My love to my Father and the girls. They are very kind to me as Correspondents. / Ever, my dearest Mother,

Affectionately yours

T B M.

PS. Harford[4] and his wife are here.

TO ZACHARY MACAULAY, 26 JULY 1822

MS: Harvard University. *Address:* Zachary Macaulay Esq. / No 16 George Street / Mansion House / London. *Extract published:* Trevelyan, I, 106.

Cambridge July 26. 1822

My dear Father,

The fever and all the apprehensions to which it had given rise have completely disappeared. I have been in the meantime pestered with a succession of small complaints, – a cold one day, a rheumatism the next, a headache, and a most inveterate boil on my hand, which rendered three days of poulticing and confinement necessary. All however have departed, and I am now perfectly well, and, as good boys say in their letters from school, I hope you are well too.

I have been engaged to take two pupils[5] for nine months of the next year. They are brothers whose father resides at Cambridge; – I am to give them an hour a day, each; and to receive a hundred guineas. – It gives me great pleasure to be able even in this degree to relieve you from the burden of my expences here. I begin my tutorial labours to morrow. – My pupils are young and are not yet entered, but I hear excellent accounts of their proficiency, and I intend to do my utmost for them.

[1] Sir Benjamin Bloomfield (1768–1848: *DNB*) had just been dismissed as the King's private secretary (*The Times*, 13 March 1822).

[2] Hugh Pearson (see 15 September 1813) was Chaplain to the Court at Brighton, where the Royal Chapel had been opened and consecrated in January 1822.

[3] The King remained in Brighton until 27 March.

[4] John Scandrett Harford (1787–1866: *DNB*), the son of a wealthy Bristol Quaker, came under the influence of Hannah More, joined the Church, and to make up the deficiencies of a Quaker education spent several terms at Christ's College, Cambridge. He was active in abolitionist and Evangelical enterprises and is said to have been the model for Hannah More's Christian young man, Coelebs. Harford used his wealth in Italian travel, in forming a collection of paintings at his residence, Blaise Castle, near Bristol, and in helping to found St David's College, Lampeter. His wife was the daughter of Richard Hart Davis, M.P. for Bristol. [5] See 2 August 1822.

We had the Baron de Staël[1] here. Henry Venn entertained him at dinner. Elliott[2] gave him a breakfast the next morning, and he then departed, having given only a very cursory survey to our buildings, and received only a very imperfect account of our system. He was introduced to several distinguished men; and all of them whose opinions I heard agreed in expressing their admiration of his sense and information. The character which his mother, I understand, was in the habit of giving him, was "Très semblable à son père, mais pas si bête."

I am much obliged to Jane for her letter. I will write to her soon. In the mean time all news from home will be most acceptable. Love to all. I hope my mother has escaped from the consequences of her late duties as a nurse.

Farewell

T B M

P.S. When am I to expect the Babingtons? Or are their intentions changed? – Assure them that the fever is completely gone.

TO ZACHARY MACAULAY, 2 AUGUST 1822

MS: Trinity College. *Address:* Zachary Macaulay Esq. / George Street / Mansion House / London. *Extract published:* Trevelyan, 1, 107.

Trinity College Cambridge. August 2. 1822

My dear Father,

I am much obliged to you for the letter and its enclosure which I have just received. I am in perfect health, and I trust that notwithstanding the present mutable weather, which resembles April more than August, care and exercise will keep me so. –

---

[1] Baron Auguste de Staël (1790–1827), Madame de Staël's son, was one of the influential friends of the Claphamites on the continent and was especially concerned in the causes of abolition and of the Bible Society. He was in England with his brother-in-law, the Duc de Broglie, where they were entertained by Wilberforce and his circle. Lord Teignmouth, meeting de Staël at this time, observed that he seemed 'a pious, sensible, and much-inquiring man, but apparently out of spirits' (*Reminiscences*, 1, 311). De Staël published *Lettres sur l'Angleterre*, Paris, 1825.

[2] Edward Bishop Elliott (1793–1875: *DNB*), Fellow of Trinity, 1817–24; Vicar of Tuxford, Notts., 1824–40. In 1853 he became Perpetual Curate of St Mark's Church, Brighton, opened by his brother Henry. The Elliotts, of Grove House, Clapham, were a notable Evangelical family. The mother was John Venn's sister; both Edward and his brother Henry became well known clergymen; and their sister Charlotte was a popular writer of hymns and devotional poems. Thomas Babington, writing to his daughter Jean, 30 December 1822, says 'I judge well of both the Elliotts as to stirling worth and piety' (MS, Huntington); TBM, on the contrary, detested the Elliott piety: see 14 October 1846. Edward Elliott's special study was biblical prophecy, interpreted according to evangelical Protestantism; he published *Horae Apocalypticae*, 3 vols., 1844.

My pupils are named Stoddart.[1] Their father was, I believe, one of the unfortunate persons who were detained by Buonaparte in France, at the beginning of the last war. He passed several years in confinement at Fontainebleau, where both of his sons were born. One of them is fifteen, the other thirteen years of age. They are both sensible, but the younger is much superior in acuteness and industry to his brother; – notwithstanding the difference of their ages, he is much better acquainted with both the Latin and Greek languages, and I do not despair of seeing him obtain the highest classical distinctions of the University.

I do not dislike the employment. Whether that I am more patient than I had imagined, or that I have not yet had time to grow tired of my new vocation. I find, also, what at first sight may appear paradoxical, that I read much more in consequence, and that the regularity of habits necessarily produced by a periodical employment which cannot be procrastinated fully compensates for the loss of the time which is consumed in tuition.

I engaged to take my pupils for nine months of the next year. The three months of vacation I was to take at such times as it suited myself – I stipulated for this in order to enable me to keep my terms in London. I believe the next term occurs in November. If so, I shall delay my visit till that time, more especially as I suppose that my mother will then have returned from Barley Wood.

When you write next, give me an account of the late proceedings at the India House.[2] From the short abstract in the papers, I should suppose that they must have been satisfactory.

My love to all at home.

T B M.

[1] John Lawrence Stoddart, the son of Lawrence, of Fontainebleau, was admitted to Downing College, 21 January 1823, aged seventeen, and matriculated at Michaelmas 1823. The younger brother appears neither in Venn, *Alumni Cantabrigienses*, nor in Foster, *Alumni Oxonienses*. Probably it was he who fell ill: see 15 March 1823.

[2] At a special general court of proprietors of the East India Company, 26 July, called to consider the bill then before Parliament to continue the duties on East Indian sugar, Zachary Macaulay moved for a committee to inquire into the subject. From the report in *The Times*, 27 July, it does not appear that the motion came to a vote; a resolution to bring the meeting to a close, 'lest subjects might be again touched upon which were better left alone,' was carried unanimously. The duties on East Indian sugar, imposed in order to protect West Indian production, were opposed by the abolitionists as a bounty on slavery.

TO [THOMAS?] TAYLER,[1] 29 SEPTEMBER 1822

MS: Osborn Collection, Yale University.

Trin Coll. Cambridge / Septr. 29. 1822

My dear Tayler,

Your books are returned to the Library. No others can be procured for the next week. As soon as I can, I will send you those which you want.

I received a letter from you some months ago about a certain hood. As Malden had carried it away with him, (for what earthly purpose I cannot conceive,) to his hermitage in Surrey, I left it to him to take all proper measures.

I understand from Lady Harwood[2] that we are to see you here before long. Come, – and come quickly, or you will lose half the advantages of coming. – The actors will have left Cambridge, and Derwent Coleridge's[3] hair will have grown again. Do not let slip an opportunity which may never return of seeing him in a wig. – He fights battles with me about Wordsworth every day. –

Remember me kindly to Townsend,[4] if he is still with you. – Present my humblest homage to Mrs. Tayler, if you can prevail on her to receive that of a cruel wretch who rejoices in the deaths of bad poets.[5]

Ever, my dear Tayler,

Affectionately yours
Thomas Babington Macaulay

TO ZACHARY MACAULAY, 5 OCTOBER 1822

MS: Trinity College. *Address:* Zachary Macaulay Esq. / No 16 George Street / Mansion house / London.

Trinity College Cambridge. October 5th. 1822

My dear Father,

George's success gives me great pleasure.[6] I am impatient to learn the nature and advantages of his new situation. Congratulate him warmly in

---

[1] TBM's correspondent is probably the Thomas Tayler (1794?–1867?) who graduated from Trinity in 1820 and in 1821 married the daughter of the late Master of Trinity, William Lort Mansel. Tayler held various curacies from 1821.

[2] The widow of Sir Busick Harwood (1745?–1814: *DNB*), Downing Professor of Medicine.

[3] Derwent Coleridge (1800–83: *DNB*), the poet's second son, was at St John's and was one of TBM's circle of Cambridge friends. He spent most of his life as a schoolmaster, first in Cornwall, and, from 1841, as the first Principal of St Mark's College, Chelsea. He was Rector of Hanwell, 1864–80.   [4] Probably Chauncy Hare Townshend.

[5] Perhaps a reference to Shelley, who died on 8 July, and whose *Hellas* was published earlier in this year.

[6] Evidently George Babington is meant, but I cannot explain the reference.

my name. Jane and Selina seem to be excellent Canvassers. – I shall depend on their support whenever I stand for the city of Westminster, and John, I hope, will find them influential supporters, when he aspires to be Alderman of Farringdon-without.[1]

Elections have been taking place in our quarter as well as in yours. Two bachelors of our College, whose names you probably never heard, Barron[2] and Goode,[3] have been chosen fellows. – Ollivant's failure has excited surprise. He will now come into competition with us. Of his success next year there is no doubt.

How are your projects affected by the recent ministerial changes?[4] Is Canning likely to do more or less than his predecessor in relation to the slave trade? Do you expect any thing from the Congress at Verona?[5] It is more to be wished than hoped, I fear, that those who assemble to rivet the chains of one quarter of the globe should relax those of another. The Cause of the abolition cannot gain so much by their direct support as it must lose by the indirect results of their policy. They must, I presume, be desirous to give to the Ultra-Royalists of France a predominance over the Liberaux: And the Ultra-Royalist is, I believe, the same with the Colonial faction. – The only strong enemies of the slave trade in France, as far as I am aware, are the partisans of Constant[6] and Foy.[7] If their politics are to be proscribed by the Holy Alliance, no speculative declaration on the guilt of the trade can prevent its being continued under the connivance of an administration which seems composed of the lowest and foulest dregs of the slavish nobility of the old regime. I am impatient for what, I fear, can alone terminate this and innumerable other abuses, an explosion in France, which may at once overthrow a family on which prosperity and adversity, empire and exile, have in vain been tried, – and whom the tremendous past has not instructed to read the most palpable signs of the more tremendous future.

[1] At this time it was expected that John Macaulay would succeed his father in the firm of Macaulay and Babington. On 10 January 1823 Zachary Macaulay writes that John 'has come into my Counting house' (to Kenneth Macaulay: MS, University of London).

[2] Arthur Barron (1798?–1856: *Boase*), B.A., 1820; called to the bar, 1826, and practised as a conveyancer.

[3] Francis Goode (1797?–1842: *DNB*), B.A., 1820; went to India for the Church Missionary Society; he later held lectureships in London and Clapham.

[4] Castlereagh committed suicide on 12 August; Canning succeeded him as Foreign Secretary.

[5] The last of the Congresses held under the Treaty of Paris met at Verona, 20 October–14 December. Its main object was to secure allied agreement to the intervention of France against the liberal government of Spain, but Wellington, the English representative, refused to support the measure.

[6] Benjamin Constant (1767–1830), the author, then head of the liberal opposition in the Chamber of Deputies.

[7] Maximilian Sébastien Foy (1775–1825), general under Napoleon and liberal politician under the Restoration.

O'Meara's book[1] has made me Buonapartiste. I speak comparatively, with reference to my former opinion of the man. He was wicked, no doubt. So are all conquerors, and almost all kings. – But I do not think that mankind has reason to execrate his memory. Nor do I think that his errors deserve to be insulted as they are by thousands who, in his situation, would have been far less great, and far more guilty. – There is hardly a celebrated Prince who has not deceived, – massacred, – oppressed. – But who has ever obtained such splendid triumphs, destroyed such immense and ancient abuses, given, in the midst of [   ][2] and confusion, so admirable a [system][2] of jurispr[u][2]dence to his people, conciliated the [   ][2]ment of so many nations, retained [the][2] admiration of his followers so completely, even after his fall, and been regretted so deeply even by conquered and enslaved states? – I think that, when prejudices have subsided, he will be ranked with the great mixed Characters of ancient and modern times, Alexander, Cæsar, Peter, Cromwell, Elizabeth. It would be unjust to his memory to compare him to Frederic the great so long the good brother and ally of our Kings, the theme of our Poets, and the ornament of our sign-posts. He happened to be our ally, Buonaparte was our enemy. And this, I believe, alone occasioned the difference in their reputations. But I must stop. By the bye the stock of wine which I brought hither with me is exhausted, and my acquaintance are beginning to re-assemble; so that unless I am to poison them with certain beverages at which a stronger stomach than Mr. Accum's[3] would revolt, I must beg a supply from home. I assure you that your Port and Madeira are held in high esteem by my Connoisseur acquaintances. I shall write to my Mother at Barley Wood. Love to all at home.

Ever affectionately yours

T B M

---

[1] *Napoleon in Exile; or a Voice from St. Helena*, 2 vols., 1822. Barry O'Meara (1787–1836: *DNB*), a naval surgeon, accompanied Napoleon to St Helena as his medical attendant. O'Meara quarrelled with the governor of St Helena, Sir Hudson Lowe, and was dismissed in 1818. The book, as TBM says, is *Buonapartiste*, and its popular reception was split on party lines. TBM's copy of the book, 5th edn, 1822, is in the library at Wallington.

[2] Paper torn away with seal.

[3] Friedrich Christian Accum (1769–1838: *DNB*), German chemist, published several works while in England, among them *A Treatise on Adulterations of Food, and Culinary Poisons*, 1820.

TO SELINA MILLS MACAULAY, 26 OCTOBER 1822

MS: Trinity College. *Address:* Mrs. Macaulay / at Mrs. More's / Barley Wood / Wrington / Somersetshire.

Trinity College Cambridge. Octr. 26. 1822

My dear Mother,

I have been of late a shamefully negligent correspondent; but my avocations must be my excuse. This is the beginning of the Cambridge year. The gownsmen are assembling by hundreds after a separation of five months. The ceremonies of meeting, recognitions, inquiries, answers, and all the duties of friendship or courtesy occupy a considerable portion of the day.

The University is at present, as you probably know, agitated from another cause. One of our representatives died last week;[1] and the vacant seat, which is considered as a very high distinction, is an object of competition to several men of rank and talents. Lord Hervey and Charles Shore are canvassing warmly. The Solicitor General has announced himself as a candidate. Goulburn, Robert Grant, and Scarlet, the celebrated barrister, are expected to follow his example.[2] – Robert Grant is the only candidate whose success would give me pleasure. There are boroughs enough for venal lawyers like Copley, or silly sons of peers like Hervey. But an University should send up to parliament a man qualified to represent the literature of the Country, to do honour to its established system of education and to exhibit in his public conduct, the elegance, the manliness, and the liberality which our academical institutions are intended to produce. Shore has not, I believe, any title except a respectable character and a gentlemanly address, to a seat which was an object of ambition to Pitt and Lord Lansdowne. – But I do not mean to fill my letter with academic politics.

Our tutor Browne yesterday offered me another pupil. I declined, partly because I thought three hours a day too much to transfer from my own studies to those of others; and partly because I should in that case have been unable, with justice to my pupil, to keep my terms in London. –

[1] John Henry Smyth, M.P. for Cambridge since 1812, died on 20 October.
[2] There were, all told, eight candidates for the seat: Lord Frederick Hervey, eldest son of the Earl of Bristol and just made M.A. of Trinity; TBM's former Clapham neighbor and schoolfellow, Charles John Shore, afterwards second Baron Teignmouth; the Solicitor-General, John Singleton Copley, later Lord Lyndhurst; Robert Grant, son of another Clapham neighbor, the elder Charles Grant; James Scarlett, later Lord Abinger; William John Bankes; Charles Manners-Sutton, Speaker of the House and later Lord Canterbury; and Spencer Perceval, M.A., Trinity, 1816, the son of the prime minister who was assassinated in 1812. Henry Goulburn did not enter. By the time of the poll only three candidates remained: the high Tory Bankes, the liberal Tory Hervey, and the Whig Scarlett, who finished, on 28 November, in that order. See Teignmouth, *Reminiscences*, I, 300–3; and Charles Henry Cooper, *Annals of Cambridge*, Cambridge, IV, 1852, 539. Bankes, the college contemporary and friend of Byron, sat for Cambridge until 1826.

Browne thought me in the right. – He says that one of our Bachelors who lost a fellowship this year, failed solely from having employed too much of his time in tuition.

On Thursday week, at farthest, I expect to be at home. I am delighted with what you tell me of Henry.[1] I hope that he will succeed completely. His talents are very good. Confidence in his own powers is what he wants, – a deficiency very rare at his age, and much more amiable though much more pernicious than the opposite error.

Remember me in the kindest manner to your hostess. When I recall the indulgence which she showed to my childhood and the friendship with which she honoured my youth, I sometimes feel affected beyond what I should find it easy to express. Things even the most trifling or ludicrous, the pies, the pease, the ducks, the bad verses which I wrote when a boy, acquire a solemnity from distance, time, and regret. The thatch, the trellice with its roses, the temple, the hermitage; – but here comes my dear friend Henry Thornton. I have not seen him for months, and shall not see him again for several more. So I must stop abruptly. Farewell my dearest Mother.

T B M

TO ZACHARY MACAULAY, 4 JANUARY 1823

MS: Trinity College. *Address:* Zachary Macaulay Esq/No 16 George Street/Mansion House/London.

Trinity College Cambridge / January 4. 1823

My dear Father,

I enclose John Brown's bill for the late term. The former bill for the long vacation had not been paid at the time when this was made out and has therefore been added as arrears. The whole bill at present includes the expenses of Residence since the middle of last June.

Cambridge is empty. Only the Questionists and the Candidates for university Scholarships remain up. A sad contrast from the domestic Christmas of my former years. Perhaps it is not the less adapted to keep Christmas associations and domestic recollections in the mind. The Jew who looked from the waters of Babylon towards Jerusalem, while he uttered his prayer, had probably a stronger feeling of patriotic affection for his country than those who prayed within the walls of the city. And I believe the hollies in the chapel and the plumb-pudding in the hall of our College made me think more fondly of old times and of home than I might have done at Cadogan place.

[1] Henry Macaulay entered the Charterhouse as a day boy in 1822.

There are certain spirit-stirring words which act with the force of enchantment on the minds of men. Every nation has some. In Venice the words *St. Mark* have, I am told, an effect beyond any of the proud historical names in the annals of the republic; and, after having for centuries excited the pride, can now hardly be uttered without calling forth the tears of her patriots. In England – Christmas is perhaps the most expressive word. It speaks volumes; Large fires and good dinners, smiling schoolboys, cheerful servants, hospitality without ostentation, warmth and comfort in the coldest season of a cold country, charity and liberality which even poor laws cannot check, religion which wears even to the eyes of its enemies, a smile of domestic happiness – these are a part of the delightful things which it brings with it. It is the characteristic festival of the only religion which ever made mankind happier or more humane than it found them. We should be too happy if all the year were a Christmas. –

But these are rather reflections for you who are enjoying the season at home than to me who, though surrounded with comforts, and enjoying that great blessing, the society of friends whom I have made for myself, am debarred from the still dearer society of those from whom my greatest happiness has always risen. Remember me on Twelfth night.

What news from Verona? I mean on the subject of the slave trade. I should suppose that Montmorenci's retirement and C[hateau]¹briand's elevation portended success.² [Le]¹ Genie du Christianisme is shallow enough to be sure. And the man hates Shakespeare. But he has some romance if not some principle. And there is something so picturesque in the idea of free blacks dancing among bananas and palms, that it cannot but strike the imagination of the author of Atala.

À propos, I open a debate at the Union on the British Colonial system in a few weeks.³ We shall have a large audience, perhaps a hundred, com-

---

¹ Paper torn away with seal.
² The Duc de Montmorency (1760–1826), minister for foreign affairs, resigned on 25 December 1822 when the government hesitated to intervene in Spain. François René, Vicomte de Chateaubriand (1768–1848), succeeded as minister for foreign affairs. The references that follow are to Chateaubriand's *Le Génie du Christianisme*, 1802; 'Shakspere, ou Shakspeare,' 1801; and *Atala, ou les Amours de Deux Sauvages dans le Désert*, 1801.
³ On 4 February TBM spoke in the negative on the question 'Has the system pursued by Great Britain with respect to her colonies (up to the year 1800) been beneficial to the nation?'; there were fifty-eight negative and two affirmative votes (*Laws and Transactions of the Union Society...to January 1830*, Cambridge, 1830, p. 25). Debates at the Union had been suppressed by the university authorities in 1817. It continued as a mere reading club until 1821, when debating was resumed with the proviso that no political matter after 1800 could be discussed. TBM was secretary of the Union in the Easter term, 1820, and treasurer in the Lent term, 1823. In the time between taking his degree and winning a Trinity fellowship, speaking at the Union, where he divided the leadership with Winthrop Mackworth Praed (see 20 June 1823) and the brilliant Charles Austin (see Trevelyan, I, 75–6), seems to have been TBM's favorite activity. The *Laws and Transactions of the Union Society* records seventeen speeches by him between February 1822 and December 1824. 'At the Union...

posed partly of future senators and planters. I am studying Mill[1] for the œconomical part of the Question and am preparing no small quantity of declamation and invective. If you could in a letter give me a few popular arguments on the misery and inexpediency of the slave-system it might perhaps strengthen the detestation which *here* at least, thank God, is felt against it. Loves etc.

T B M.

TO HENRY MACAULAY, 4 JANUARY 1823

MS: University of Texas.

Trin Coll Cambridge Jan 4 / 1823

Dear Hal,

I sit down with a detestable pen to employ exactly three minutes in writing to you. I know nothing of your difficulties or advantages and therefore can give you no advice about your arrangements for the Olaïde.[2] All I have time to say is that I like your scheme, that I swear allegiance to you as editor, and that whenever you write for an article you shall have it.

T B M.

You ask about some books. All that I have of them are in requisition for my brats.

---

he was for a long time the chief speaker,' Margaret Macaulay writes; 'his power there was supreme, and he sometimes now accuses himself of having used it tyrannically' (*Recollections*, p. 238). Reports of several of TBM's speeches are given in [Robert A. Willmott], *Conversations at Cambridge*, 1836, pp. 130–44, and in Trevelyan, 1, 80.

[1] James Mill, 'The Article Colony, Reprinted from the Supplement to the Encyclopaedia Britannica,' [1820?]. In 1825 Mill boasted that his reprinted articles were 'the text-books of the young men of the Union at Cambridge' (Alexander Bain, *James Mill*, 1882, p. 292).

[2] *The Olaides*, a magazine of his family's productions and of family traditions compiled by Henry, was named in allusion to the family's chosen ancestor, Olaus Magnus (see 8 May 1813). A quarto MS notebook of 149 pages, entitled 'Olaides. No. 1.' and inscribed 'To my dearest Mary / from her affectionate and grateful cousin, / Henry William Macaulay. – / Omnia vincit amor' is in the possession of Mrs Lancelot Errington. It contains various essays, letters, and poems either unsigned or initialled; none of the items seems attributable to TBM.

TO ZACHARY MACAULAY, 15 MARCH 1823

MS: Trinity College. *Address:* Zachary Macaulay Esq / No 16 George Street / Mansion House / London.

Trinity College Cambridge 15 March. 1823.

My dear Father,

I am not at all skilled in medical science, and therefore I hope that my alarms are groundless. Yet I cannot but feel very anxious about this nascent malady. I am sure that something more is required than leeches and blisters. After the unremitting exertions of so many years, several of which have been passed in tropical climates, you must require much more indulgence and repose, much more easy exercise and mental relaxation than you allow yourself. I hope therefore that your medical attendants will recommend a considerable change of hours and of occupations. Above all my dearest father, I hope most earnestly that you will not incur any risk by exertions for children who already owe to you more than they ever can repay, and whom no worldly advantages would console for the pain of witnessing your declining health and spirits.

I have read Brougham's letter[1] with great interest. I feel highly gratified by his kindness, and not the less so because I am aware that I can owe it only to his regard for you. If you write to him thank him in the warmest manner, on my part.

As to the question whether it would be desirable for me immediately to commence my legal studies, – it is one which I have carefully considered and am disposed to pronounce in the affirmative. The chance of my obtaining a fellowship next October is very small, or rather none at all. There is at present only one vacancy, and there are at least three candidates, if not more, who would have a decided superiority over me, Ollivant, – Long, and Malden.[2] I might probably succeed in the following year. But I doubt whether the chance be worth the loss of eighteen months of legal

---

[1] In a letter to Zachary Macaulay dated Newcastle, 10 March 1823, Brougham, writing 'in consequence of some conversation I have just had with Lord Grey, who has spoken of your son (at Cambridge) in terms of the greatest praise,' offered his advice as to how TBM ought to prepare himself for distinction as an orator. Brougham recommended, first and needlessly, 'talking much,' and second, the study of Demosthenes and Dante. The second part of this advice evidently had some effect, for TBM writes in his essay on Dante, *Knight's Quarterly Magazine*, II (January 1824), 222, that 'I have heard the most eloquent statesman of the age remark that, next to Demosthenes, Dante is the writer who ought to be most attentively studied by every man who desires to attain oratorical eminence.' Soon after TBM's death Brougham's letter was published in *The Times*, 18 January 1860. There is reason to think that it had been published also near the time when it was written, but I have not found any such printing. Greville, writing in 1836 of the early relation between Brougham and TBM, says that Brougham 'put himself forward as the monitor and director of the education of Macaulay, and I remember hearing of a letter he wrote to the Father on the subject, which made a great noise at the time' (*Memoirs*, III, 280).

[2] Ollivant and Long both won fellowships in this year.

study, – more particularly since the value of our fellowships has fallen, I understand, to about one third of what it was six years ago.[1]

Under all these circumstances I feel at present disposed, if you approve of the plan, to act according to Brougham's suggestion, and to commence the study of the law directly.[2] My pupils are the only tie which I have at Cambridge. One of them is unwell, and probably will not again attend me. I think, therefore, that their father would willingly agree to cancel the remainder of an engagement under which he pays for the tuition of one son, what he calculated on paying for both.

Should you approve of this scheme and should the father of my pupils be found practicable, I shall not return to Cambridge after Easter. My residence there has been pleasant, and never more so than of late. But I think that other pursuits would at present lead me more speedily to that honourable independance and distinction, which next to the affection of my friends, is the favourite object of my earthly wishes.

Give my affectionate love to my Mother. I am distressed about her indisposition. But the weather will, I hope, soon change for the better and disperse all maladies. Love to Jane and thanks for her letter. Love to all.

T B M

TO HENRY MACAULAY, [20 APRIL 1823][3]

MS: University of Texas.

Trin Coll. Cambridge

My dear Hal,

I have but little to send you. I find on examination that I have but very few of my own compositions here, and all the time which I can spare for writing, I am forced to employ in publications[4] more lucrative to the authors than the Olaides is likely to prove.

I send you the fragments of the poem which I wrote on Waterloo.[5]

---

[1] See 1 October 1824.
[2] Brougham's letter had advised that 'professional eminence can only be attained by entering betimes into the lowest drudgery, the most repulsive labors of the profession; even a year in an attorney's office, as the law is now practised, I should not hold too severe a task, or too high a price to pay, for the benefit it must surely lead to; but at all events the life of a special pleader, I am quite convinced, is the thing before being called to the bar.' TBM did leave Cambridge to apply himself to the law, but when the one fellowship suddenly became five, 'he immediately returned to Cambridge to put himself in training' (Zachary Macaulay to Hannah More, 8 September 1823: MS, Huntington).
[3] Endorsed 'Cambridge April 20.'   [4] *Knight's Quarterly Magazine:* see [7? June 1823].
[5] TBM's unsuccessful entry for the Chancellor's English medal in 1820. Zachary Macaulay wrote to Hannah More, 19 June 1820, that one of the examiners told TBM that his poem would have won the prize had it been more detailed about the fighting (Knutsford, *Zachary Macaulay*, p. 355). The winner was George Erving Scott, of Trinity Hall, who had actually fought at Waterloo. Two MS copies of TBM's poem are at Trinity.

Any thing in my mother's or sisters' possession you may insert. But remember to mark the dates, and put in nothing of which the date is not
affixed.

Prosperity to you, my dear boy, in this and every other undertaking.
Go on to cultivate your intellect and your kind affections as you have
done; and, as long as we both live, be assured that you will always have
the sincerest love of your brother TBM.

TO ZACHARY MACAULAY, [7? JUNE 1823][1]

MS: Harvard University. *Address:* Zachary Macaulay Esq / No 16 George Street / Mansion
House / London. *Extracts published:* Trevelyan, I, 114–15.

[Rothley Temple][2]

My dear Father,

I have seen the two last letters which you have sent to my mother. They
have given me deep pain; – but pain without remorse. I am conscious of
no misconduct – and whatever uneasiness I may feel arises solely from
sympathy for your distress.[3]

You seem to imagine that the book is edited or principally written by
friends of mine. I thought that you had been aware that the work is conducted in London, – that my friends and myself are merely contributors,
and form a very small proportion of the contributors. I believe that
not one third part of the volume is written by persons whom I ever

[1] Postmark of receiving office dated 9 June.

[2] TBM's birthplace, the seat of his uncle Thomas Babington. A few miles north of Leicester,
near Rothley, it was once a preceptory of the Knights Templar and is now a hotel. Zachary
Macaulay sent his whole family to Rothley Temple this summer while he remained in
London to find a new house. When they returned it was not to Cadogan Place but to Great
Ormond Street: see 31 December 1823.

[3] After the first number of *Knight's Quarterly Magazine* (note 1, p. 188) appeared, Zachary
Macaulay wrote to his wife that 'the more I look into this magazine in which Tom cuts so
conspicuous a figure the more am I dissatisfied with it, and the more pained am I at the
associations which Tom has formed. It is a loose, low, coarse and almost blackguard work
in *some* of its parts. In others, where there is less of coarseness there is still a strain of volup-
tuousness and even licentiousness which is quite intolerable and which almost rivals Little's
poems. There is one poem of Tom's own which would find its place very well as far as the
sentiments go in that vile repository. I am quite shocked and pained that a son of mine
should have linked himself with such associates and should countenance and even compose
such mischievous effusions. This matter presses heavily on my mind at present; but I wish
to consider it more calmly. Something however must be done and that speedily. – I did not
want this at present to add to my cares – but I desire to receive it as a part of my merited
chastisement at the hand of God.

'I do think that the general complexion of the work in a moral point of view is most discreditable to Tom and his friends' (7 June 1823: MS, Trinity).

saw.[1] I have not yet seen the work. To the very few papers which I saw I am sure that no moral objection could exist, – with the exception of one in which I earnestly recommended alteration. The manners of almost all of my acquaintances who have contributed to it are so utterly alien from coarseness, and their morals from libertinism, that I feel assured that no objection of that nature can exist to their works. As to my own contributions I can only say that the Roman Story[2] was read to my mother before it was published and would have been read to you if you had happened to be at home. Not one syllable of censure was uttered.

The Essay on the Royal Society of Literature[3] was read to you. I made the alterations which I conceived that you desired, and submitted them afterwards to my mother. As to the poem which you parallel with Little's,[4] I am utterly unable to conceive what poem you mean.

If any thing vulgar or licentious have been written by myself, I am willing to bear the consequences. If any thing of that cast have been written by my friends, I allow that a certain degree of blame attaches to me for having chosen them at least indiscreetly. If however a bookseller of whom we knew nothing have coupled improper productions with ours in a work over which we had no controul, I cannot plead guilty to any thing

[1] *Knight's Quarterly Magazine*, which first appeared in June 1823, and ran for six numbers only, was founded on the initiative of Winthrop Mackworth Praed (see 20 June 1823), who had as a schoolboy already worked with the Windsor publisher and bookseller Charles Knight in getting out the *Etonian*, 1820–1, a magazine edited by Praed and published by Knight. Knight (1791–1873: *DNB*), an earnest, energetic man, devoted to the cause of popular education, was later the publisher to the Society for the Diffusion of Useful Knowledge and edited several large popular histories. Chapters 9–10 of his *Passages of a Working Life*, 3 vols., 1864–5, give an account of the career of *Knight's Quarterly*. What TBM says here of his relation and that of his friends to the magazine is misleading. Of the thirty-eight items, large and small, in the first number of *Knight's*, twenty-six were by TBM and his Cambridge friends and acquaintances: Praed, John Moultrie, William Sidney Walker, Henry Nelson Coleridge, Derwent Coleridge, Henry Malden, and, as he then was, Edward Bulwer. For Moultrie, see 20 June 1823. Walker (1795–1846: *DNB*), the oldest of the group, was then a Fellow of Trinity; he, Praed, Moultrie, and Henry Coleridge had all been associated earlier on the *Etonian*. Of the remaining items, eight were by Knight himself, and though he may not have been a friend, TBM had certainly seen him (Knight, *Passages of a Working Life*, 1, 295). One contribution was from Knight's friend, the barrister Matthew Davenport Hill (1792–1872: *DNB*); two were from the poet and miscellaneous writer Allan Cunningham (1784–1842: *DNB*), and one from an unidentified Mr Taylor. All of the contributions were either anonymous or, more often, signed with the initials of a pseudonym given in the table of contents. TBM's pseudonym was 'Tristram Merton.' For these attributions, see Knight, *Passages of a Working Life*, 1, 280–334, and G. J. Gray, *Notes and Queries*, 1 October 1881, pp. 261–3.

[2] 'Fragments of a Roman Tale,' *Knight's Quarterly Magazine*, 1 (June 1823), 33–44.

[3] 'On the Royal Society of Literature,' *Knight's Quarterly Magazine*, 1 (June 1823), 111–17.

[4] Some of Thomas Moore's 'warmer' poems appeared under the title of *The Poetical Works of the Late Thomas Little*, 1801. TBM's two poems in the first number of *Knight's* are 'Oh Rosamond,' and 'By Thy Love, Fair Girl of France,' pp. 219–20. His remaining contribution to this first number, 'On West Indian Slavery,' pp. 85–94, escaped censure for obvious reasons.

more than misfortune – a misfortune in which some of the most rigidly moral and religious men of my acquaintance have participated in the present instance.

Can it be supposed that I could have thought of introducing an immoral book into our family? Could it be conceived, on any principle of worldly prudence, that I should have invited your attention and that of my mother to a work in which I could expect that any thing exceptionable would find a place? – This would have been gratuitously to insult your feelings, and to throw away your regard. The more charitable interpretation would be that I had no cause to expect that any such articles would be admitted, and that I had not voluntarily transgressed in my own contributions.

I am pleading at random for a book which I never saw. I am defending the works of people most of whose names I never heard. I am therefore writing under great disadvantages. I write also in great haste. I am unable even to read over what I have written. I have only to say that I await your arrival with great anxiety; unmingled, however, with shame, remorse, or fear. / Ever my dear Father

affectionately yours
T B M

TO CHARLES KNIGHT, 20 JUNE 1823

MS: Mr F. R. Cowell. *Address:* Mr. Charles Knight / No 7 Pall-Mall East / London. *Published:* Charles Knight, *Passages of a Working Life*, 1 (1864), 304–5.

Rothley Temple Leicestershire June 20. 1823

My dear Sir,

As I fear that it will be impossible for me to contribute to your Magazine for the future, I think it due to you and to myself to acquaint you, without reserve, of the circumstances which have influenced me.

You are probably aware that there are among my family connections several persons of rigidly religious sentiments. My father, in particular, is, I believe, generally known to entertain, in their utmost extent, what are denominated evangelical opinions. Several articles in our first number, one or two of my own in particular, appeared to give him great uneasiness. I need not say that I do not in the slightest degree partake his scruples. Nor have I at all dissembled the complete discrepancy which exists between his opinions and mine. At the same time, gratitude, duty, and prudence, alike compel me to respect prejudices which I do not in the slightest degree share. And, for the present, I must desist from taking any part in the Quarterly Magazine.[1]

[1] Zachary Macaulay soon dropped his objections, and TBM resumed his contributions to *Knight's* with the January 1824 number.

The sacrifice gives me considerable pain. The Magazine formed a connecting tie between me and some very dear friends from whom I am now separated, probably for a very long time; – and I should feel still more concerned if I could imagine that any inconvenience could result from my [compulsory]¹ conduct.

I shall probably be in London in about a month. 1 will then explain my motives to you more fully. In the mean time, I can only say that all that has passed between us increases my regrets for the termination of our connection, and my wishes that it may be renewed under more favourable circumstances.

Let me beg that you will communicate what I have said to nobody excepting Coleridge, Moultrie,² Praed³ or Malden; and to them under the injunction of secrecy. / Believe me, my dear Sir,

Yours Sincerely

T B Macaulay

TO ZACHARY MACAULAY, [17 AUGUST 1823]⁴

MS: Harvard University. *Address:* Z Macaulay Esq / No 16 George Street / Mansion House / London.

Cambridge Sunday

My dear Father,

I arrived here late last night. Things stand thus. Five fellowships are vacant. There is, I find, very little hope of another.

---

¹ Overscored in MS.

² John Moultrie (1799–1874: *DNB*), B.A., Trinity, 1823; Rector of Rugby, 1825–74. Moultrie endeared himself to the Macaulay family by writing, on the death of Margaret Macaulay, whom he had never met, verses entitled 'To Margaret in Heaven.' He published also a sonnet 'To Thomas Babington Macaulay' in *Poems*, 1837. His *The Dream of Life*, 1843, contains sketches of TBM and of their contemporaries at Cambridge. See Moultrie's *Poems*, new edn, 2 vols., 1876, with a memoir by Derwent Coleridge.

³ Winthrop Mackworth Praed (1802–39: *DNB*), B.A. Trinity, 1825. The brilliant schoolboy who founded the *Etonian*, Praed shared the leadership of the Cambridge Union with TBM, where their opposition could remain good-tempered, and presided over the *Knight's Quarterly* group. After leaving Cambridge TBM kept in touch with Praed: they were both members of John Stuart Mill's London Debating Society in 1826 ('List of Members,' 1826, in British Museum); there is record of letters that have not survived from TBM to Praed in 1827 and 1830; on 17 March 1828 Selina Macaulay notes in her diary that TBM has just left 'to pass two days with Mr. Praed.' Crabb Robinson tells an anecdote about TBM, Praed, and Charles Austin at Cambridge discussing what political characters they should choose to take when they enter Parliament (Edith J. Morley, ed., *Henry Crabb Robinson on Books and Their Writers*, 1938, I, 393), but the event proved to be no joke. Praed, who had become a thorough Tory, is said to have been offered a seat in Parliament expressly to oppose TBM but had refused such terms. Nevertheless, after Praed entered the House of Commons late in 1830 the friendship between him and TBM, which had probably at best been brittle, soon broke under the strain of party animosity.

⁴ Postmarked 18 August 1823. Sunday was the 17th.

The year below mine will, I believe, be permitted to sit. This is not certain. It has not been formally announced. But those who are in the secrets of our government, Scholfield for instance, consider this as beyond a doubt. Now this takes away certainly one fellowship – probably more. Airy,[1] the Senior Wrangler of that year, is one of the first men whom Cambridge has produced; and has been called by the somewhat hyperbolical name of the Second Newton. It is likewise extremely probable that other men of that year will surpass me. Ollivant has every possible claim to a fellowship. Malden, Long and Marryatt[2] must at the least equal me at present in Classical Knowledge. In mathematics competition is out of the question. There are also several other very formidable competitors.

I therefore do not hesitate to say that I have, in common probability, no chance of success.

Still it may happen that more fellowships may be vacant, – that the year below us may not receive the expected permission, – or that the examination may take a turn peculiarly favourable to me.

I feel, upon the whole, rather inclined to take the chance.[3] A month will pass away usefully and pleasantly in reading Cicero, Juvenal, and Locke: and will be terminated, at the worst, by a failure in which there will be neither dissapointment nor discredit.

I leave it however to you to decide[. I][4] have endeavoured to state the case a[s][4] fairly as possible.

Love to my Mother.

Yours affectionately
T B M.

[1] George Biddell Airy (1801–92: *DNB*), won his fellowship with TBM in 1824; as Astronomer Royal, 1835–81, one of the most distinguished scientists of the time, of great public authority: 'he was consulted about the launch of the Great Eastern, the laying of the Atlantic cable, Babbage's calculating machine, the chimes of Westminster clock, and the smoky chimneys of Westminster Palace' (*DNB*).

[2] William Henry Marriott (1800?–?); he won the Latin declamation prize in 1820 with TBM (see [27? October 1820]) and ranked just after TBM, Malden, and Long in the Craven scholarship examinations, 1821.

[3] He did: 'We were all very sorry for Tom's failure but I believe no one thought he could possibly obtain the Fellowship' (Mary Babington to Henry Macaulay, 20 October 1823: copy, Mrs Lancelot Errington).

[4] Paper torn away with seal.

TO ZACHARY MACAULAY, 31 DECEMBER 1823

MS: Trinity College. *Address:* A Monsieur / Monsieur Macaulay / Chez M. F. Faber[1] / à
Paris.

No 50 Great-Ormond Street[2] London / December 31st. 1823

My dear Father,

I received your letters on the evening of the twenty-ninth, and I employed myself yesterday in collecting the suffrages of those whom, as I
thought, you would have wished to consult. Their unanimous opinion is
against the publication of the letter.[3] And mine agrees with it.

When I read the letter the first thing that struck me was that it was not
sufficiently strong and indignant. To those who are acquainted with your
character and your principles the mild and temperate tone which you have
adopted will appear perfectly to harmonize with that character and those
principles. But the great majority of mankind, accustomed to resent with
the utmost bitterness an imputation on their own characters, will attribute
to timidity or even to guilt the forbearance and courtesy with which you
have treated the calumniators. I should hardly have ventured to state to
you what you may perhaps think an intemperate and juvenile view of the

---

[1] Faber is identified in Zachary Macaulay's letter to his wife, 30 May 1814, as 'a great merchant who lives at the foot of Montmartre' (Knutsford, *Zachary Macaulay*, p. 315). Macaulay had gone to Paris in the middle of December to seek official support against the slave
trade.

[2] On 26 September 1823 Zachary Macaulay wrote to Hannah More that 'our future domicile
is now fixed. It is in Great Ormond Street. . . . We expect to be fairly set down in it for life
in less than a month' (Knutsford, *Zachary Macaulay*, p. 392). The move from Cadogan
Place to Great Ormond Street was made, Trevelyan says, 'under the pressure of pecuniary
circumstances' (1, 126). The house stood on that corner of Great Ormond Street and Powis
Place which is now occupied by a wing of the Royal London Homoeopathic Hospital.
TBM regularly lived with his family from 1824 until 1830, the first time he had done so since
leaving for school in 1813; in consequence the house in Great Ormond Street was the place
where for him 'the dearest associations gathered' (Trevelyan, 1, 129). There is a pleasant
account of the family's life there in Hannah Trevelyan's Memoir (Trevelyan, 1, 127–9).

[3] In response to the government's effort to secure improvement in the condition of the slaves,
and to the Demerara insurrection which followed (see note 1, p. 194), the West Indian
slave owners made many angry attacks on the abolitionists. *The Times*, 18 December,
printed part of the resolutions made by the residents of the parish of Port Royal, Jamaica,
including their protest 'against the injustice of pronouncing us guilty of the foulest crime
on the evidence of men like ZACHARIAH M'CAULEY, whose crimes, whose oppression to
the slaves under his charge as overseer, compelled him to self-banishment from this colony,
to seek affluence by calumniating those who abhorred his iniquity.' To this *The Times*
added: 'We have quoted the preceding passage, in order to attract the attention, and receive
the proper explanation of the person charged – a person with an ominous name, certainly,
but who yet may be a very good man. ZACHARIAH M'CAULEY! We are sure he was a very
good tempered boy, if he did not throw stones at his godfathers and godmother whenever
he saw them.' Macaulay wrote a reply to the editor of *The Times* from Paris, 26 December
(Knutsford, *Zachary Macaulay*, p. 415), and sent it to his friends in England for consideration. It does not appear in *The Times*.

case, had it not been that James Stephen[1] seems to see this in a still stronger light than I do. "No man" said he "but a religious man would have treated a slanderer with such gentleness, and no man but a religious man will assign a creditable motive for it."

Another, and, I think, a still stronger objection is this. The letter is too extended for a denial, and not sufficiently so for a defence. It is so long and circumstantial that people will expect it to contain a complete refutation, and this they will not find. It is merely assertion put in several various forms. No witnesses are adduced. To an attack which rests only on assertion, denial is a satisfactory reply; and it is only invalidated by partial and qualified proofs. Witnesses it is impossible to produce. The Counsel retained against John Bull[2] have resolved that the libel of June,[3] the same in

[1] (Sir) James Stephen (1789–1859: *DNB*), third son of the elder James Stephen, perhaps the most loyal of the second generation of the Clapham Sect to the inherited standards: he married the daughter of John Venn, devoted himself to anti-slavery work, and wrote the best-known sketch of his father's generation in 'The Clapham Sect' – a phrase that Stephen apparently invented, though Stephen himself thought that it was Sydney Smith's (Howse, *Saints in Politics*, Appendix). At the time of this letter Stephen was a barrister in private practice; he became counsel to the Colonial Office and Board of Trade in 1825 and from 1834 he was permanent Under-Secretary of State for the Colonies, in which office, according to his son Leslie's life of him in the *DNB*, he was so influential that he was nicknamed 'King Stephen' and 'Mr. Oversecretary Stephen.' Made a K.C.B. on retiring, 1847; succeeded William Smyth as Regius Professor of Modern History, Cambridge, in 1849. John Stuart Mill wrote that 'Stephen is reputed a saint: I do not know in what sense he is one, though I know that he carried the observance of the Sabbath to the extent of puritanism. But if all the English evangelicals were like him, I think I should attend their Exeter Hall meetings myself, and subscribe to their societies' (Francis E. Mineka, ed., *The Earlier Letters of John Stuart Mill, 1812–1848*, Toronto, 1963, I, 86).

[2] The *John Bull*, a weekly paper both Tory and pro-slavery, edited by the novelist Theodore Hook, had repeatedly attacked Zachary Macaulay for his anti-slavery work in 1823, notably in articles of 15 June, 26 October, and 9 November. The burden of all these was the same, and evidently relied heavily on Robert Thorpe's earlier allegations: Macaulay, it was asserted, had for years made use of the African Institution solely as a means of promoting his business. 'Well, and what harm is there in this? We answer, none upon earth...he was quite right to conceal, and misrepresent, and deny, and assert, in the way of business, because, more or less, every man of business does the same – but Saints do not – sanctified, holy persons, carefully eschew all such proceedings' (*John Bull*, 9 November 1823). Zachary Macaulay's solicitors served notice on the *John Bull* late in November that Macaulay was about to take action against the paper; on 24 January 1824 he brought suit for £10,000 damages for libel in the Court of King's Bench against Edward Shackell, Thomas Arrowsmith, and William Shackell, the printers and publishers of the *John Bull*. The proceedings of the defense closely followed those earlier used by Robert Thorpe (see [13 November 1820]). Before the case could be heard, Edward Shackell, the principal defendant, whose plea was that the libels were true, obtained from the Chancellor's Court commissions to examine witnesses in the West Indies and Sierra Leone and an injunction against further proceedings against him until the commissions had completed their inquiries. The case was fully reported in *The Times* during 1824 and in the *Law Journal*, 1825, III, 27–42. For other details of the case, see 4 August 1824 and 29 March 1827.

[3] The *John Bull*, 15 June 1823, printed an extract from the *Jamaica Almanacks*, 1817–20, describing Zachary Macaulay when an overseer in Jamaica, as 'remarkable for his cruelty and severity to the slaves who were unfortunately placed under his power.' The *John Bull* adds: 'was he not dismissed by his master (now alive) as overseer, in consequence of the

substance with the Port-Royal resolutions, shall be included in the Declaration. This being the case a detailed vindication, in which names and dates should be fully given, would only enable the enemy to overlook our hand.

Mr. Stephen is against any publication at all. But I place little value on his opinion. Of his friendship and sincerity it is impossible to speak too highly. But, as it appears to me, the same irritability of temper which has so often made him rash, now makes him unreasonably timid. He complains that there is a run of ill-luck against us. The attacks in the Times, the Demerara insurrection,[1] the execution of Smith,[2] of which, I fear, no doubt can be entertained, and other minor occurrences have agitated him to such a degree that, as he himself said to me, he cannot open a paper without trembling. Of the power of the Times over public opinion he seems to entertain a very exaggerated idea, and is disposed to worship it from the same feeling which leads savages to sacrifice to the Devil.

Mr. Wilberforce is decidedly against the publication of this letter, but does not seem to agree with Mr. Stephen as to the impolicy of *any* answer. James Stephen, Henry Stephen,[3] and myself think that something should be said, but that it would not be prudent to send your lett[er][4] to the Times without such alterations as we do no[t][4] think ourselves authorized to make.

I enclose a letter which I have drawn up, in order clearly to show my

slaves under his care dying in numbers beyond the mortality on other estates, and from mismanagement of his master's affairs?' The charge has this much support from Zachary Macaulay's account, written in 1797, of his life in Jamaica: finding that cruelty to the slaves was expected of him, he says that 'I resolved to get rid of my squeamishness as soon as I could, as a thing which was very inconvenient. And in this I had a success beyond my expectations' (Knutsford, *Zachary Macaulay*, p. 7).

[1] A three days' insurrection of the slaves broke out in Demerara on 18 August. It came just after the government had recommended new and more humane regulations to the West Indian colonies, the first result of the efforts of the Anti-Slavery Society's activity (see 26 May 1824), and thus seemed to vindicate the prophecy of the slave owners, that any movement toward emancipation would create insurrection. See *Annual Register*, 1823, pp. 244–50.

[2] John Smith (1790–1824: *DNB*), an English missionary, was sentenced to death by a military court in Demerara, 24 November 1823, for inciting the slaves to revolt. He died of tuberculosis in his prison, 6 February 1824, while confirmation of his sentence was being awaited from England. The injustice of Smith's treatment provided the abolitionists with a case that more than offset the damage done to their cause by the Demerara revolt; Brougham made a brilliantly successful speech on Smith in Parliament on 1 June 1825, a landmark in the progress towards emancipation.

[3] Henry Stephen (1787–1864: *DNB*), second son of the elder James Stephen; a barrister, in 1823 living with his widowed father in London; made serjeant-at-law, 1828, and, in 1842, a commissioner of bankruptcy at Bristol, where he spent the rest of his life. 'A nervous and retiring temper prevented him from achieving any great professional success, but he was one of the most distinguished writers of his time upon legal subjects' (Leslie Stephen, *The Life of Sir James Fitzjames Stephen*, 1895, p. 26).

[4] Paper torn away with seal.

own opinion as to what ought to be done. I stated its contents in conversation to James and Henry Stephen, and they both seemed satisfied with it.

The Quarterly Review came out yesterday; – it contains a long article on Slavery,[1] – in the true spirit of the Work, professed moderation, and real partiality of the grossest kind. I must do it the justice to say that it is personally extremely courteous, and that its mention of you and your writings is not unhandsome. This will do good as far as it goes; and tend to undeceive some of the high-church party who may have given credit to John Bull.

Yours affectionately

T B M

TO THE EDITOR OF *THE TIMES*, [31 DECEMBER 1823][2]

MS: Trinity College.

To the Editor of the Times

Sir,

Had the calumnies which have appeared against me been confined to the resolutions of the Slave-Holders of Port-Royal, I should have returned no answer. From a contest with the invectives of defeated and desperate avarice I could expect no advantages. The honour of such a victory would but poorly compensate for the infamy of such a combat. I should have felt assured that the public would despise these malignant and unsupported calumnies, and would consider them as springing from the same spirit which has produced the outrages of Barbadoes[3] and the judicial murders of Demerara.

Inserted, however, in your Journal these charges acquire a different character. And to you I will say, what I would never had condescended to say to the flagitious men whose practice it is to defend by falsehood a system of oppression. I assert then that the whole accusation is false, malicious, and unfounded from the beginning to the end.

Assertion is a sufficient answer to assertion. It is in my power, however, to add the most convincing proofs; and, if I at present abstain from doing this, it is only because, within a few months, they will be submitted to a British jury.

[1] [David Low], 'Condition of the Negroes in Our Colonies,' *Quarterly Review*, xxix (July 1823), 475–508. The July number of the *Quarterly* did not appear until December 1823 (Hill and Helen Shine, *The Quarterly Review under Gifford*, Chapel Hill, 1949, p. 85). Zachary Macaulay's anonymous pamphlet on 'Negro Slavery,' 1823, is commended for the 'ability with which it is composed' (p. 480).

[2] This is enclosed with the letter preceding. It does not appear in *The Times*.

[3] The mob in Bridgetown, Barbados, demolished the meeting house of a Methodist missionary named Shrewsbury on 18 October 1823 for his having reported to England that the population of Barbados was depraved (*The Times*, 11, 12 December 1823).

As you have stated that your only object in quoting the resolutions of Port-Royal was to give me an opportunity of denial or explanation, I trust that you will give as wide and conspicuous a circulation to the reply as you have done to the slander.

TO HENRY MACAULAY, 26 MAY 1824

MS: University of Texas. *Address:* H. W. Macaulay (in another hand).

Great Ormond Street / May 26th. 1824

My dear Hal,

I am waiting here for my dinner with nothing to do. Says Meg, "Now do just spend these two minutes in writing to Hal. He will be so delighted to hear from you." "You simpleton," said I, "what have I to tell him? I never can write without something to say." Says our revered parent – my mother I mean, "Say anything. He will be glad to hear from you." So my vanity was flattered. And I was ashamed moreover of not having written you a line for so long a time. And as members of parliament are always very complaisant to the people just on the eve of an election, I was inclined to give you a letter just before you came home – lest I should be exposed to your reproaches. "So," said I, "bring the pen and ink." In it came. Down I sate. And here you have the fruits. Never imagine, my dear Hal, that, because I do not write to you as often as the young ladies who have nothing to do, and who, moreover, have no objection to write when they have nothing to say, I have forgotten you. None of them, you may depend upon it, is more anxious to see you. We are all delighted to learn that you are so useful to the old Quaker.[1] Stick by that, my boy. If you

---

[1] Henry Macaulay had been sent to Liverpool in April 1824, to work in the counting house of the Quaker merchant and philanthropist James Cropper (1783–1840: *DNB*), partner in the firm of Cropper, Benson and Company, who had since 1816 been one of the most enthusiastic and effective of the abolitionist leaders. Cropper may, indeed, claim to be the founder of the movement in England to abolish slavery itself, as distinguished from the efforts to put an end to the slave trade. The Liverpool Society for Promoting the Abolition of Slavery that he established in 1822 was the first such society. Cropper's example led to Zachary Macaulay's founding in 1823 of the London Society for the Mitigation and Gradual Abolition of Slavery throughout the British Dominions, better known as the Anti-Slavery Society, through which the emancipation movement became national. TBM's name appears on the first list of the Anti-Slavery Society's committee, and he addressed the first annual meeting of the Society in the month after this letter (see 7 October 1824); it is not likely, though, that he had much to do with the committee's work. The names of several other sons of the first generation of abolitionists – Thomas Gisborne Babington, William Wilberforce, Jr, Henry Thornton, Henry Venn – were also on the list, presumably for ornamental rather than practical purposes. The continuing work of the Society was carried on by Zachary Macaulay beyond all others.

are inclined to turn Quaker yourself, I am sure, I have no objection. The drab will become you. And you have already the demure look – the sharp eye to the main-chance, and the coolness – aye, Hal, and, if I remember right, the obstinacy too, necessary for supporting the character. The whine of the meeting thou hast not yet acquired. But what of that? The Spirit can impart gifts even more miraculous. And even if thou shouldst never become a public friend, thou mayest still be a conspicuous member of the body.

However, Quaker or not, whether in drab or in blue, with a dandy hat or a broad-brim, come home to us, Hal, as fast as thou canst. – How indeed canst thou reconcile it to thy conscience to be from London at the Season of the yearly meeting,[1] when the friends are gathered together like many waters, and the godly ones like the sands of the sea? Behold thy sisters, that is to say Margaret and Hannah and Fanny, went unto their worship meeting, and were moved to laugh, as though they had been full of new wine. Come then thou and admonish the sinful damsels and delight the eyes of

Thy brother after the flesh
T B M

TO ZACHARY MACAULAY, 4 AUGUST 1824

MS: Harvard University. *Address:* Zachary Macaulay Esq. / No 16 George Street / Mansion House / London.

Rothley Temple. August 4. 1824

My dear Father,

Thanks for your kind letter. I had read Sumner's book[2] before; and I have looked over some parts of it again. It is, I think, a better work than Paley's.[3] Though I by no means agree in all his positions, I should have had no objection to review it if I had time.[4] But at present I am employed without intermission from seven in the morning till three in the afternoon on most days; and even my lighter reading is almost wholly such as bears

---

[1] The annual meetings, held in May, of the many religious societies were the climax of the Evangelical year. At this time they were held in Freemasons' Hall, Great Queen Street. They were transferred to Exeter Hall after it opened in 1831.

[2] John Bird Sumner, *The Evidence of Christianity, Derived from Its Nature and Reception*, 1824. Sumner became Archbishop of Canterbury, 1848.

[3] William Paley, *A View of the Evidences of Christianity*, 1784. Such theological knowledge as Cambridge required of its undergraduates was furnished by this book.

[4] Presumably reviewing for the *Christian Observer* is meant. Zachary Macaulay had turned over the editorship of the magazine to the Reverend S. C. Wilks in 1816, but he still had a voice in its affairs. Sumner's book was favorably reviewed in the *Christian Observer*, XXIV (October 1824), 640–55.

some reference to the subjects of our examination – metaphysics, classical antiquities, and history.[1]

I have no news for you. Mr. Pearson[2] is here – in good humour and good spirits. Selina is not, I think, much better for the change of air.[3]

I need not say with what feelings we have read the legal proceedings in your case,[4] or with what anxiety we all wait to learn your final determination. I wish that you could find time to leave London for a few weeks, and to vist Mr. Evans[5] at Allestree. You would find it a delightful place. And I need not say that you would have an excellent host. I was delighted with him. His cordiality was rendered more remarkable by its contrast with the manner of his wife – who is at the very freezing point of the moral thermometer. Cold water seems warm after a raspberry ice. And Mr. Evans gains in the same manner: – though indeed he is too honest and amiable a man to need a foil.

---

[1] 'Tom is reading to Selina and me Mitford's Greece so you may think of us sometimes between two and five, he sitting reading aloud in the midst of my garden, in all parts of which I can hear him, whilst I am employed with my flowers, and Selina at work in the arbour. The maps are consulted on all proper occasions, and his observations answer the purpose of a historical lecture' (Jean Babington to Thomas Gisborne Babington, 24–5 July 1824: MS, Huntington).

[2] John Pearson (1758–1826: *DNB*), F.R.S., M.R.C.S., the father-in-law of George Babington. He was in effect surgeon in ordinary to the Evangelicals of London and was closely connected with their affairs, being one of the original committee of the Church Missionary Society and assisting in the founding of the *Christian Observer*. James Stephen names him among the members of the Clapham Sect, though Pearson lived in London, calling him 'a Surgeon who died immensely rich and lived to teach Theology as well as Surgery' (to Macvey Napier, 5 February 1844: MS, British Museum).

[3] Selina was subject to migraine headaches and eventually became chronically invalid.

[4] Shackell, of the *John Bull* (see 31 December 1823, to Zachary Macaulay), had filed a bill in the Vice-Chancellor's Court petitioning that Zachary Macaulay should be required to make a 'full discovery' of the matters alleged in the *John Bull*, that 'one or more commissions might issue for the examination of witnesses residing on the west coast of Africa, or in the West Indies, or other parts beyond the seas, as to the several matters aforesaid,' and that in the meantime Macaulay be restrained by court injunction from proceeding with his suit in the King's Bench. To this Macaulay's lawyers put in a demurrer, which the Vice-Chancellor allowed, 30 June. But on 18 July the Lord Chancellor (Eldon) overruled the demurrer, and on 19 July granted an injunction staying the trial in the King's Bench. See the report in the *Law Journal*, 1825, III, 27–42. Notices of the proceedings appear in *The Times*, 19 and 20 July 1824. Rather than submit to the inquiries of the commissions, Zachary Macaulay appealed to the House of Lords: see 29 March 1827 and the correspondence in Knutsford, *Zachary Macaulay*, pp. 424–5.

[5] William Evans (1778–1856: *Boase*), of Allestree Hall, near Derby, the owner of the Darley cotton mills, was Whig M.P. for East Retford, 1818–26, and for Leicester, 1830–4. He was linked to the Evangelicals through his marriage to the daughter of the clergyman and minor poet, Thomas Gisborne, himself the husband of Thomas Babington's sister. Evans served as secretary of the African Institution, 1825–6, and is said to have made a large loan to the firm of Macaulay and Babington during the crisis of its affairs (Knutsford, *Zachary Macaulay*, p. 403). TBM refers to Evans in his Reform Bill speech of 20 September 1831 as 'a most respectable and excellent friend of mine' (*Hansard*, 3rd Series, VII, 301).

But I must conclude. Affectionate love to all the world. Tell my mother that I found my things; though I cannot much applaud her device of wrapping them up in paper with Selina's name upon them. As she never told me of it, I put the parcel apart for Selina – who, of course, having no occasion for the contents, never asked for them. –

Farewell

T B M.

TO SELINA MILLS MACAULAY, [23 AUGUST 1824]

MS: Trinity College. *Address:* Mrs. Macaulay / No 50 Great Ormond Street / London. *Frank:* Leicester August twenty three 1824 / R H Inglis.

[Rothley Temple]

My dear Mother,

I return the Bill. It is correct. We have good news from Cambridge. Another fellowship is vacated by Kindersley's[1] marriage.

As to Henry's expedition, I suppose that you are acquainted with some circumstances respecting it which have not reached us: for neither my uncle nor my aunt, nor Selina nor myself had suspected, judging from Matthew's[2] account, that it would afford you anything but pleasure. We inferred from Matthew's expressions that he had obtained Mr. Cropper's full consent. And if that were the case, I must confess myself at a loss to conceive where the impropriety of his conduct lies. When a boy is sent by his parents to such a distance from home perpetual reference is impossible. In cases which give time for correspondence he clearly ought to wait for their opinion. But in those which require an immediate decision he is, I think, to judge for himself with the advice of those under whose super-intendance his parents may have placed him. – Delay would in many cases, as in this, be equivalent to a decision. Therefore if, as I before said, Henry obtained Mr. Cropper's consent, I own that I cannot blame him. If not, he certainly deserves very severe censure. – I have no doubt that you will act rightly – and, were it otherwise, I have no right to offer my advice. Yet, since both Selina and myself, who, I am sure, have not been inclined to judge poor Henry's freaks too favourably, never entertained a suspicion that you would be displeased with him for judging for himself in such circumstances, I hope that you will give some weight to opinions which have at least sinceri[ty and][3] anxious affection to all parties to recom[men]d[3] them. If I have said more than I ought, I can only excuse myself upon the plea of great solicitude. Our family is separating into

---

[1] (Sir) Richard Torin Kindersley (1792–1879: *DNB*), Fellow of Trinity, 1815–24; a barrister, he became a Vice-Chancellor, 1851.

[2] Matthew Babington, of Leicester: see 11 July 1814.

[3] Paper torn away with seal.

different walks of life – it is being dispersed to different places. Separation must involve independance. The restraints which boys experience at home are compensated by the exercise of the domestic affections and the enjoyment of domestic comforts. But if those who are excluded from the blessings of the family circle are still to feel its restraints and hear only its reproofs – I tremble for the consequences. I have seen hundreds of families made miserable by these means. Again and again my dear Mother, if I have written too freely I beg your pardon. Love to my father and all at home particularly poor dear Meg.

T B M.

TO ZACHARY MACAULAY, 1 OCTOBER 1824

MS: Trinity College. *Address:* Zachary Macaulay Esq / No 16 George Street / Mansion House / London. *Mostly published:* Trevelyan, 1, 107.

Trinity College Cambridge Oct 1. / 1824

My dear Father,

I was elected fellow this morning,[1] shall be sworn in to morrow, and hope to leave Cambridge on Tuesday for Rothley Temple. The examiners speak highly of the manner in which I acquitted myself, and I have reason to believe that I stood first of the Candidates.

I need not say how much I am delighted by my success, and how much I enjoy the thought of the pleasure which it will afford to you, my mother, and our other friends. Till I become a master of arts next July the pecuniary emolument which I shall derive will not be great. For seven years from that time it will make me almost an independant man.[2]

Malden is elected. You will take little interest in the rest of our Cambridge successes and disappointments.

I shall want a few pounds more than I am now possessed of for the purpose of discharging my Cambridge Bills, and travelling to the Temple and back again. We get no dividend till December.

---

[1] 'At the beginning of October I went to Cambridge with Mr. Hill. We arrived on a day of jubilation, for Mr. Macaulay and Mr. Malden had each gained a Trinity fellowship. There was a happy dinner in Mr. Malden's rooms' (Knight, *Passages of a Working Life*, 1, 334). The examination was held 22–4 September, and the new fellows were admitted on 2 October (George Biddle Airy, *Autobiography*, Cambridge, 1896, p. 61).

[2] The revenues of the college designated for the payment of the master and fellows were counted in 'original dividends' – i.e., sums of £1,000 – which were divided according to a fixed scale and which varied in number from year to year. The master and fellows divided thirty-two original dividends in 1817 but only ten in 1823: thus a senior fellow received £800 in 1817 but only £250 in 1823. TBM as a B.A. was entitled to only £5 in each original dividend; upon proceeding M.A. his share would jump to £12. 10, and would increase as he acquired seniority. In the years 1825 through 1831 the value of TBM's fellowship varied from £175 to £225, averaging £209 (information from Dr R. Robson, of Trinity College).

Kindest love to my Mother and everybody at home. I forgot Hal's direction; but of course somebody will write to him. Remember me kindly to George.[1] I owe this in some degree to his exhortations. / Ever, my dear Father,

Yours most affectionately
T B M.

TO ZACHARY MACAULAY, 3 OCTOBER 1824

MS: Huntington Library. *Address:* Zachary Macaulay Esq / No 16 George Street / Mansion House / London.

Trinity College Cambridge Oct. 3. 1824

My dear Father,

I have received your letter. The £25 will be more than sufficient for all my purposes and for our travelling expenses.

I think of remaining at Rothley for a week, or perhaps a day or two longer. My uncle and aunt are kindly, and, I am sure, sincerely urgent. I feel such an interval to be absolutely necessary to my health and comfort. The last three weeks have been, till within a very few days, a continued series of petty indispositions, mortifying accidents, tormenting anxieties, sleepless nights, and days of nervous depression. With a feverish body and a harassed mind, I have been compelled to go through an examination which required great mental and great corporeal exertion. Success, distinction, and the kindness of my friends here have restored my cheerfulness. Calomel, flannel, and fine weather have dispelled my maladies. But I am still weak; and pant, like a slave in a mine, for liberty, rest, and fresh air.

It is my intention to leave Cambridge early on the Tuesday[2] morning. It will therefore be useless to address any more letters to me here.

My kindest love to my Mother and all at home. / Ever, my dear Father,

Yours most affectionately
T B M.

TO ZACHARY MACAULAY, 7 OCTOBER 1824

MS: Trinity College. *Address:* Zachary Macaulay Esq / No 16 George Street / Mansion House / London. *Partly published:* Trevelyan, I, 116.

Rothley Temple. Octr. 7. 1824.

My dear Father,

Selina and I intend, nothing unforseen preventing, to be in London on Tuesday next.

---

[1] Babington.   [2] TBM is writing on a Sunday.

As to the speech,[1] I suppose that the defects of it escaped my notice in revising it. I knew that this might easily happen. And it was on that account that I wished to see it again in the proof-sheets. There are some omissions of relatives which are extremely inelegant. It is however of little consequence. I am sorry to find that I wrote so petulant a letter on the subject.

As to Knight's magazine, I really do not think that, considering the circumstances under which it is conducted, it can be much censured. Every magazine must contain a considerable quantity of mere ballast, dead weight, – of no value but as it occupies space. Other works fill up their due measure of paper with births and deaths, promotions of clergymen and prices of stock. These we do not insert; and therefore some nonsense, and now and then something worse than nonsense, has crept in from absolute want of materials. In the next place we have no Editor; I mean no literary man to whose judgement the whole is submitted: and Knight, though for his situation, a very intelligent and well informed man, has, naturally enough, little of delicacy or discrimination. Yet, in spite of all these unfavourable circumstances, I think that the general tone and spirit of the work will stand a comparison, in a moral point of view, with any periodical publication not professedly religious. I will venture to say that nothing has appeared in it, at least since the first number, from the pen of any of my friends which can offend the most fastidious. There is a tale about Henri Quatre[2] to which I suppose your nameless correspondent alluded, which certainly it would have been wiser to omit – though I cannot conceive why it should be locked up, at least in any library which contains the works of Milton and Spenser. It was not written by any acquaintance of mine.

Knight is absolutely in our hands, and most desirous to gratify us all,

---

[1] TBM's speech delivered at Freemasons' Hall, 25 June 1824, at the first general meeting of the Anti-Slavery Society, was printed in the Society's first *Report*, 1824, pp. 70–9, where it is noted that on concluding '*the speaker sat down amidst loud cheering, which lasted several minutes*' (p. 79). The occasion, TBM's first genuinely public appearance, had been an overwhelming success. There are accounts of it in Trevelyan, I, 110–12; Trevelyan, 1908, Appendix 1; and Knutsford, *Zachary Macaulay*, pp. 420–2; 426. It was printed the next day in the *Morning Chronicle*, 26 June 1824, p. 2, as by 'Mr. J. Macauley.' Lord Teignmouth says that he met TBM on the day of the speech 'at his father's table, round which were assembled the élite of the abolitionists, and was surprised by his rising during dinner from his seat, and, as he perambulated the room, looking and gesticulating like one inspired' (Teignmouth, *Reminiscences*, II, 215n.). The speech was praised by Brougham in the *ER*, XLI (October 1824), 226, and criticized by John Miller and John Taylor Coleridge in the *Quarterly Review*, XXXII (October 1825), 510–13, while congratulatory letters poured in on Zachary Macaulay. The speech was reprinted in various periodicals in 1824, and as late as 24 September 1831 in the Leeds *Mercury* to demonstrate TBM's soundness on the question of abolition.
[2] 'The First Love of Henri Quatre,' *Knight's Quarterly Magazine*, II (April 1824), 326–34. Attributed to Francis Barry Boyle St Leger (1799–1829: *DNB*), the Irish novelist (*Notes and Queries*, 1 October 1881, p. 262). The story is of a peasant girl's seduction and suicide.

and me in particular. We hope to get Malden to devote a little time to re-vi[sing][1] the work, and if he will do so, I have no doubt that nothing which the most severe judgment would condemn will ever obtain admittance. When I see you in London I will mention to you a piece of secret history[2] which will shew you how important our connection with this work may possibly become.

Love to my mother and all at home. / Ever, my dear Father,

Yours affectionately

T B M

[1] Paper torn away with seal.

[2] Trevelyan, I, 116, understands this to mean that TBM has been asked to contribute to the *Edinburgh Review*. TBM's work in *Knight's Quarterly* had certainly attracted notice. In May 1824 William Maginn advised William Blackwood to try to secure TBM for the Tory *Blackwood's*, calling him 'the young man who writes the very clever things signed T.M. or Tristram Merton in Knight's Quarterly. He appears to me to be the very cleverest young man at all dabbling in periodicals' (*Notes and Queries*, June 1955, p. 265). But the details of the negotiation that led to TBM's first appearance in the *ER* are obscure and likely to remain so, especially since the correspondence between TBM and the editor, Francis Jeffrey, does not seem to have survived. Brougham, who was working closely with Zachary Macaulay in the anti-slavery campaign and whose influence on the *ER* was unrivalled, might well have been the intermediary. He was certainly informed about TBM's first article and contributed an article supplementing it to the number of the *ER* in which it appeared. Frederick Arnold, *The Public Life of Lord Macaulay*, 1862, p. 46, and [John Camden Hotten], *Macaulay, the Historian, Statesman, and Essayist*, 1860, p. 23, suggest that TBM's speech of 25 June 1824 decided Jeffrey to approach him, but there is no evidence for this. Given TBM's prominence at the Cambridge Union, his contributions to *Knight's*, his speech in June, his father's intimacy with Brougham, and Jeffrey's interest in securing new contributors, it is easy to imagine any number of reasons and means for an invitation from the *ER* to TBM. But if by the phrase 'secret history' in this letter TBM means a negotiation with the *ER*, then his articles in *Knight's* were the immediate cause. This seems to be confirmed by Hannah Trevelyan, who says that 'when [*Knight's Quarterly*] came to an end Jeffrey, who was always on the look out for fresh hands, asked him to write for the E.R.' (Memoir of TBM). What is certain is that TBM's first article in the *ER* was 'The West Indies,' *ER*, XLI (January 1825), 464–88, and not, despite the tradition established by Trevelyan, I, 117, the essay on Milton in the August 1825 number of the *ER*. The whole question of TBM's first article in the *ER* is thoroughly reviewed by Jane Millgate, 'Father and Son: Macaulay's *Edinburgh* Debut,' *Review of English Studies*, N.S., 31 (May 1970), 159–67.

IN LONDON AND ON CIRCUIT
1825–1829

1825 January
First article in *Edinburgh Review*: 'West Indian Slavery.' Studying law in London

– August
'Milton,' *ER*

1826 February
'The London University,' *ER*

– February 9
Called to the bar

– March 8
Joins Northern Circuit at Lancaster

– May 23–June 25
In Leicester as counsel to William Evans in contested election

– July 8–August 21
On circuit

– October 17–27
Attends West Riding Quarter Sessions

1827 March
'Machiavelli' and 'Social and Industrial Capacities of Negroes,' *ER*

– March 10–April 12
On circuit

– April 23–27
Attends West Riding Quarter Sessions

– June
'The Present Administration,' *ER*

– July 9–September 15
At West Riding Quarter Sessions and on Northern Circuit. Receives first brief

- [October 16–26]
  Perhaps attends West Riding Quarter Sessions

1828 January
  'Dryden,' *ER*

- January 15–23
  Attends West Riding Quarter Sessions

- January 18
  Appointed a Commissioner of Bankrupts by Lord Lyndhurst

- April 8–[13]
  Visits Francis Jeffrey at Craigcrook

- April 14–18
  Attends West Riding Quarter Sessions

- May
  'History,' *ER*

- July 15–August 30
  At West Riding Quarter Sessions and on Northern Circuit

- September
  'Hallam's *Constitutional History*,' *ER*

- October 14–22
  Attends West Riding Quarter Sessions

1829 January 13–22
  Attends West Riding Quarter Sessions

- March
  'Mill's *Essay on Government*,' *ER*

- March 7–April 4
  On circuit

- June
  'Bentham's Defence of Mill,' *ER*

- August 1–September 14
  On circuit

- October 14
  Finishes 'Utilitarian Theory of Government' (*ER*, October)

Late 1829–early 1830
  Takes chambers in Gray's Inn: leaves Great Ormond Street

TO HENRY MACAULAY, 12 DECEMBER 1825

MS: University of Texas. *Address:* Henry Macaulay Esq / Liverpool.

50 Great Ormond St. / Decr. 12th. 1825

My dear Henry,

I send you the best maps which I have been able to procure upon the conditions which you imposed. For 3 guineas I could have procured Arrowsmith's Atlas[1] – a very excellent set – indeed the best extant. I think however that those which I send you are very respectable. They do not quite take in the changes of modern times. But that is perhaps no disadvantage, if you wish to study the history of Europe previous to the French Revolution.

Apropos of the French Revolution, – a mercantile revolution – a perfect reign of Terror is going on around us.[2] The country bankers, it is said I do not know with what truth, have deluged the country with their paper – and this deluge, like other deluges, is beginning to *break the banks* – a decent pun that! But seriously all is confusion and dismay in the city and has been so for a week or more. But I suppose you know as much or more of these things than we. Heaven send that James[3] may be safe – and that David[4] may have as little reason for apprehension as when the King's Ship bombarded his steamboat the other day!

Jane is very poorly. A second blister has just been applied to her. The rest of us are well. At this present writing the sun is darkened – nothing is to be seen but an orange-coloured fog. Candles are lighted in every house – and the ladies look frightful – as hideous as the women in Rubens's pictures – nothing red but their noses and their eyes. This gloom in the heaven on the first day of so important a week se[ems][5] to me to portend terrible events [to][5] the commercial world. What says Horatio?

> In what particular thought to work I know not
> But in the gross and scope of my opinion
> This bodes some strange eruption to the state.[6]

I hope that you will be pleased with your maps. Love and adieu.

T B M

---

[1] Aaron Arrowsmith, *A New General Atlas*, 1817. In an undated letter, Hannah More says that she sent Henry a pound note when she heard that 'he was at a loss for an atlas, which he feared he should never be rich enough to buy' (Roberts, *Letters of Hannah More to Zachary Macaulay*, p. 196).

[2] The *Annual Register*, 1825, pp. 123–4, names seventy-three London and country banks that failed or suspended payments in the panic of December 1825. The unsuccessful efforts of TBM's friend Henry Thornton to keep the family bank afloat during this crisis are described in E. M. Forster, *Marianne Thornton*, ch. 3.   [3] James Cropper.

[4] David Hodgson, of the family of Liverpool merchants, a partner in Cropper, Benson and Company. He was mayor of Liverpool in 1845.

[5] Paper torn away with seal.   [6] *Hamlet*, I, i, 67–9.

TO ZACHARY MACAULAY, 30 MARCH 1826

MS: Trinity College. *Address:* Zachary Macaulay Esq / 16 George Street / Mansion House / London. *Extract published:* Trevelyan, I, 141.

York.[1] March 30. 1826

My dear Father,

I do not wonder that you should have been angry at what, unexplained, must have seemed to be unpardonable negligence. The fact is that I never received your letter of last week till yesterday morning. It had been in the hands of Brougham's Clerk; so that I had a better reason than I was aware of at the time for what I said on that subject in my last letter.

I have received your letters and the money for which many thanks. I think of setting off for Pontefract[2] on Monday. I have been very comfortable here, bating a vile cold and sore throat which in common with all the rest of the circuit I have been troubled with since the late change of weather. I am expelling it with flannel and hartshorn.

The writ of right[3] did not come on. The record was withdrawn. Copley[4] came down, pocketed three hundred guineas, danced at the Assize ball and went off again the next morning.

I am much obliged to Fanny and Hannah for their letters and I wish that I had anything half so pleasant to send home in return. In default of

---

[1] Following his call to the bar in February, TBM joined the Northern Circuit at Lancaster on 8 March 1826, according to Sir Frank Mackinnon, who was able to see the circuit records (*On Circuit*, Cambridge, 1939, p. 168), and not at Leeds, as stated in Trevelyan, I, 108. The assize towns of the Northern Circuit were York, Durham, Newcastle, Carlisle, Appleby, and Lancaster. TBM, on this first venture and afterwards, did not go the full circuit but confined himself to the Lancaster and York assizes, and to the quarter sessions of the borough of Leeds and of the West Riding of Yorkshire, which were held in succession at Wetherby, Wakefield, Doncaster, Pontefract, Skipton, Bradford, Rotherham, Knaresborough, Leeds, and Sheffield. The spring assizes in 1826 were at Lancaster, 7–8 March; York, 18 March– 4 April.

[2] For the Easter quarter sessions of the West Riding of Yorkshire, held at Pontefract, Monday, 3 April–Thursday, 6 April.

[3] 'A procedure for the recovery of real property after not more than sixty years' adverse possession; the highest writ in the law, sometimes called the writ of right proper' (*Wharton's Law Lexicon*, 14th edn, 1938). Such cases had to be tried by a Grand Assize of sixteen jurymen, four of whom were required to be knights. The writ of right was abolished by the Real Property Limitation Act, 1833. The case in question was that of *Angell* v. *Angell*, which came on at the York summer assizes, 1826; it is reported at length in *The Times*, 19 and 20 July 1826. Sir Frederick Pollock, who as a boy was taken on circuit by his father (see 2 April 1826) that summer, remembered 'the great case of *Angell* v. *Angell*, almost the last Writ of Right which was tried before the abolition of Real Actions, and sixteen jurymen went into the box, four of them as "knights girt with swords".... Copley came down special from London on one side, and was opposed to Scarlett on the other' (*Personal Remembrances*, I, 20–1).

[4] Sir John Singleton Copley (1772–1863: *DNB*), afterwards first Baron Lyndhurst, son of the American painter, was then Attorney-General. He became Lord Chancellor and was raised to the peerage in the next year.

anything better I will eke out my paper with some lines which I made in bed last night – An inscription for a picture of Voltaire.

> If thou would'st view one more than man and less,
> Made up of mean and great, of foul and fair,
> Stop here; – and weep and laugh, and curse and bless,
> And spurn and worship; for thou seest Voltaire;
>
> Teacher of truth, and lies, and good, and crime,
> Martyr, and knave, and moralist, and rake,
> Most weak, most wise, most abject, most sublime,
> The guardian Angel, the seducing Snake.
>
> From all that God revealed, – that jugglers feigned, –
> That crippled reason, – that restrained from sin, –
> His venturous wit a fettered race unchained,
> And left them slaves to nothing – but a grin.
>
> That flashing eye blasted the conqueror's spear,
> The monarch's sceptre, and the Jesuit's beads;
> And every wrinkle in that haggard sneer
> Hath been the grave of Dynasties and Creeds.
>
> In very wantonness of childish mirth
> He puffed Bastilles and thrones and shrines [away]¹
> Insulted Heaven, and liberated earth; –
> Was it for good or evil? – Who shall sa[y?]¹

Kindest love to my Mother and sisters – to John too, if, as I suppose, he be at present with you.

Ever most affectionately Yours
T B M.

TO ZACHARY MACAULAY, 2 APRIL 1826

MS: Trinity College. *Address:* Zachary Macaulay Esq / 16 George Street / Mansion House / London. *Partly published:* Trevelyan, I, 140–1.

York April 2nd. 1826

My dear Father,

I am sorry that I have been unable to avail myself of the letters of introduction which you forwarded to me. Since I received them I have been confined to the house with a cold; and now that I am pretty well re-

---

¹ Paper torn away with seal.

covered, I must take my departure for Pontefract. But if it had been otherwise I could not have presented these recommendations. Letters of this
sort may be of great service to a barrister. But the barrister himself must
not be the bearer of them. On this subject the rule is most strict – at least
on this circuit. The huggery of the Bar, like the Simony of the Church,
must be altogether carried on by the intervention of third persons. We
are sensible of our dependance on the attorneys, and proportioned to that
sense of dependance is our affectation of superiority. Even to take a meal
with an Attorney is a high misdemeanour. One of the most eminent men
among us, Frederic Pollock,[1] brought himself into a serious scrape by
doing so. But to carry a letter of introduction, to wait in the outer-room
while it is being read, to be then ushered into the presence, to receive
courtesies which can only be considered as the condescensions of a patron,
to return courtesies which are little else than the blessings of a beggar,
would be an infinitely more terrible violation of our professional code. If
Mr. Pearson[2] had written, for instance to Mr. Thorpe,[3] without sending
his letter to me, Mr. Thorpe might, if he had been inclined to pay any
attention to the recommendation, have looked at the bar-list which lies
open to public inspection, and which, of course, he must perpetually have
to consult. He would there have seen where I lodged, and might have sent
me briefs, if such had been his good pleasure. This would have been the
regular and decorous course. As it is, every barrister to whom I have applied for advice, has most earnestly exhorted me on no account whatever
to present the letters myself – I should perhaps add that my advisers have
been persons who cannot by any possibility feel jealous of me.

It is not indeed of much consequence, since, as I have said, my cold has
prevented me from stirring abroad, and to morrow I leave York. But the
intimation may be useful in case you should have it in your power to
make interest among the attorneys of the West Riding.

One W[ord][4] more. Do not mention w[hat][4] I have said about Pollock.
These are awkward stories; and, in some sense, circuit secrets. He has
been very kind and civil to me, and the error is now of old date. I should
be sorry therefore if any hint of it should get abroad by my means. Love
to my Mother and Sisters.

Ever yours most affectionately

T B M.

---

[1] Jonathan Frederick Pollock (1783–1870: *DNB*), one of the leaders of the Northern Circuit.
He was Attorney-General in Peel's first and second administrations; appointed Chief Baron
of the Exchequer, 1844; created baronet, 1866.
[2] John Pearson, the surgeon, was a native of York.
[3] Anthony Thorpe, attorney, of York (*Law List*, 1825).
[4] Paper torn away with seal.

TO ZACHARY MACAULAY, 31 MAY 1826

MS: Trinity College. *Address:* Z. Macaulay Esqr / 16 George Street / Mansion House (in Selina Mills Macaulay's hand).

Bell Inn Leicester.[1] May 31. 1826

My dear Father,

We want a copy of the last Catholic Bill, that of 1825. We cannot obtain it in Leicester. But there must surely be copies in the Parliamentary Debates. If I recollect right it was printed at length by the Morning Chronicle during the discussions. If you can find it either in the file of Chronicles at a Coffee-House or in any Collection, be so kind as to let William Baines[2] have it to copy and send it us.

Sir Charles or his friends from him solemnly deny the charge of slaveholding. We are going on as well as possible, but rather impatient for the poll. The mob are with us so completely that we fear lest they should give us too energetic a support, and break the heads of our opponents. Their windows are already broken.

Mr. Evans tells me to thank you for the trouble which you have taken.[3] Love to my Mother and sisters. I am going out to Rothley this evening.

Ever yours affectionately
T B M.

[1] TBM was in Leicester serving as counsel to the election committee of William Evans. In the general election of this year the two seats for Leicester were contested by Evans, Whig M.P. for East Retford, by the Tory Sir Charles Hastings, and by the Canningite Robert Otway-Cave. The issue was Catholic emancipation, and though Evans, who supported it, was favored to win, the election went against him through the actions of the city corporation in creating new freemen and through unfair arrangements at the poll. The polling began on 13 June; the next day there was a riot; and on 23 June Evans at last conceded the election. A young cousin of TBM's remembered that TBM, during the contest, produced 'unwearied amusing invective of the other party.... His one sided Whiggish invective against the Tories and the anecdotes he would pour out against them are among my earliest recollections of his talk. I know I grew up, I think chiefly from Macaulay influence, with a profound conviction that the head and heart of a Tory were both alike beneath contempt, that their eyes had been blinded that they should not see' (Eliza Conybeare, Recollections of TBM: MS, Trinity. Mrs Conybeare, born Eliza Rose, was the daughter of Lydia Babington Rose and grew up at Rothley vicarage). Two of TBM's election handbills have been preserved: 'Fragment of an Ancient Romance' printed in W. T. Lowndes, *The Bibliographer's Manual of English Literature*, ed. Henry G. Bohn, Part 6, 1861, pp. 1433**–1433***, and in Robert Read, Jr, *Modern Leicester*, 1881, pp. 244–6; and 'A New Song,' a copy of which is at Trinity. The contest was expensive: William Gardiner says that 'the upright William Evans, Esq., told me that his committee had spent him twenty-two thousand pounds; which sum was found insufficient to send him to Parliament' (*Music and Friends*, III [1853], 13–14). A special study has been made of this election by R. W. Greaves, 'Roman Catholic Relief and the Leicester Election of 1826,' *Transactions of the Royal Historical Society*, 4th Series, XXII (1940), 199–223.

[2] Zachary Macaulay's clerk?

[3] While TBM was busy in Leicester, Zachary Macaulay was speaking in favor of Evans at meetings of the Leicester freemen resident in London (Knutsford, *Zachary Macaulay*, p. 436).

TO SELINA MILLS MACAULAY, 1 JUNE 1826

MS: Huntington Library. *Address:* Mrs. Macaulay / 50 Great Ormond Street / London. *Frank:* Leicester June One 1826 / W: Evans. *Mostly published:* Knutsford, *Zachary Macaulay*, p. 436.

Bell Inn Leicester June 1. 1826

My dear Mother,

You cannot do better than pay William[1] out of the money in your hands. It will last for three weeks. One week indeed is already due. I want no money here. Indeed I live at free quarter.

We have a short breathing-time at present. But the public feeling is very excitable; and it is scarcely to be expected that it will evaporate in words. If Evans should fail, and Sir Charles venture to be chaired, I would not answer for his life.

Pares[2] has been extremely civil and kind to me: he has offered, in case it should be possible for me to visit Cambridge and give my vote there either before or after the poll here, to take me with him.[3]

If De Stael really wishes to see public feeling in its highest state of excitement, and that not on mere party grounds, but on great principles, he cannot do better than come to Leicester.[4] No town in the Country except the Capital, has so many voters. Manchester, Leeds, Sheffield, and Birmingham are unrepresented. At Bristol, Liverpool, and Nottingham, the only remaining towns in England which are more populous than Leicester, the right of suffrage is comparatively very confined. At Leicester there are very nearly 50,000 inhabitants and, I hear, about 6,000 voters. If the Baron would come hither, and proceed hence to Westmoreland, where the election would probably be later, he would see both a town and a county contest in the highest perfection.

We confidently expect to be at the head of the poll.

Ever yours affectionately

T B M

Love to my father and all at home.

[1] Perhaps TBM's clerk.
[2] Thomas Pares (1790–1866: *Boase*), of Kirby Frith Hall, Leicestershire. He succeeded Thomas Babington as M.P. for Leicester in 1818 but did not stand in 1826.
[3] The contest for the University of Cambridge, where again the issue was Catholic emancipation, was between four varieties of Tory: Henry Goulburn, Sir John Singleton Copley, and the incumbents, Lord Palmerston and William Bankes. Palmerston retained his seat, but Copley defeated Bankes. Since the poll opened on 13 June in both Leicester and Cambridge but closed in Cambridge on 16 June and remained open in Leicester until 23 June it is unlikely that TBM voted at Cambridge.
[4] De Staël (see 26 July 1822) intended to add an account of town and county elections to his *Lettres sur L'Angleterre* but lived to write only a fragment on the subject, without specifying the elections he had observed. See *Lettres sur L'Angleterre*, nouvelle édition, Paris, 1829, pp. 315–27.

TO ZACHARY MACAULAY, 21 JULY 1826

MS: Trinity College. *Address:* Z. Macaulay Esqre / N 16 George Street / Mansion House / London. *Frank:* York July twenty one 1826 / John Wood.[1] *Partly published:* Trevelyan, I, 141–2.

York[2] July 21. 1826

My dear Father,

I have received your letter and its inclosure. Many thanks for both. I shall soon, I hope by what I hear from the Temple, repay you.

I shall be at Skipton by nine on Monday Night, at Bradford on Wednesday evening, at Leeds on the following Monday morning by eleven. I am not quite certain when I shall reach Rotherham.[3] But you shall know in time. There will be an interval of three or four days between the close of the Sessions for the West Riding and the Commencement of the Assizes at Lancaster. Perhaps I may go to Manchester, which lies almost in the way, and see George Phillipps.[4]

Àpropos of visits, the other day as I was changing my neckcloth which my wig had disfigured, my good land lady knocked at the door of my bed room, and told me that Mr. Smith wished to see me and was in my room below. Of all names by which men are called there is none which conveys a less determinate idea to the mind than that of Smith. Was he on the circuit? For I do not know half the names of my companions. Was he a special messenger from London? Was he a York attorney coming to be preyed upon, or a beggar coming to prey upon me; a barber to solicit the dressing of my wig, or a collector for the Jews' Society?[5] Down I went, and to my utter amazement beheld the Smith of Smiths, Sidney Smith, alias Peter Plymley.[6] I had forgotten his very existence till I discerned the

---

1 Wood (1790–1856: *Boase*), was a barrister on the Northern Circuit, a Yorkshire magistrate, Recorder of York, and Whig M.P. for Preston, 1826–32. He was, successively, Chairman of the Board of Stamps and Taxes, of the Boards of Revenue, and of the Board of Inland Revenue, 1833–56.

2 The York summer assizes opened on 8 July and closed on 20 July.

3 The quarter sessions of the West Riding began officially on 14 July at Wakefield, but on account of the conflict of schedule with the York assizes, were adjourned to Skipton, Tuesday, 25 July; Bradford, Thursday, 27 July; Rotherham, Wednesday, 2 August. The sessions at Rotherham closed on 3 August. TBM then attended the assizes at Lancaster, which opened on 8 August and closed 21 August. He thus had the interval between 3 and 8 August free from attendance at court.

4 George Philips (1766–1847), created baronet, 1828, was the son of a Manchester cotton merchant and lived at this time at Sedgley House, Manchester. He was Whig M.P. from 1812 to 1825 for, successively, Ilchester, Wooton Bassett, and Warwickshire. Sydney Smith called Philips 'the happiest man, and the worst rider, I ever knew' (Nowell C. Smith, ed. *Letters of Sydney Smith*, Oxford, 1953, II, 681). TBM had already been entertained by Philips at his London house (note 6, below).

5 The London Society for Promoting Christianity Amongst the Jews, founded in 1809, was one of the multitude of religious societies patronized by the Evangelicals.

6 Sydney Smith (1771–1845: *DNB*), clergyman, Edinburgh Reviewer, wit, had been living in Yorkshire since 1809 and at the house he built at Foston since 1814. His *Letters of Peter*

queer contrast between his black coat and his snow-white head, and the equally curious contrast between the clerical amplitude of his person and the most unclerical wit, whim, and petulance of his eye. I shook hands with him very heartily; and on the Catholic question we immediately fell, regretted Evans, triumphed over Lord George Beresford,[1] and abused the Bishops. He then very kindly urged me to spend the time between the close of the assizes and the Commencement of the Sessions at his house; and was so hospitably pressing that I at last agreed to go thither on Saturday afternoon. He is to drive me over again into York on Monday Morning. I am very well pleased at having this opportunity of becoming better acquainted with a man who, in spite of innumerable affectations and eccentricities, is certainly one of the wittiest and most original write[rs of][2] our times. I shall see him indeed in [those?][2] situations in which he displays his [best and?][2] his worst peculiarities most strongly, at the head of his table and in his pulpit. How strange an instance of self-love it is that the man who possesses perhaps the finest sense of the ridiculous of any person now living, should not perceive the exquisite absurdity of his own style of preaching.

Believe me ever Yours affectionately
T B M

TO ZACHARY MACAULAY, 26 JULY 1826

MS: Trinity College. *Address:* Zachary Macaulay Esq / 16 George Street / Mansion House / London. *Partly published:* Trevelyan, I, 142–4.

Bradford. July 26. 1826.

My dear Father,

The idle people at the Temple are such indifferent correspondents that, until they improve, I shall send all my letters to you, and leave them to pick up such information of my movements as you may chuse to vouchsafe to them at second hand.

Plymley, in defense of Catholic emancipation, were published in 1807–8. TBM had met Smith, presumably for the first time, in London on 16 May 1826 at George Philips's and found him 'equally amusing and unclerical' (Selina Macaulay, Diary, 17 May 1826). In writing about Sydney Smith to Zachary Macaulay TBM had to keep in mind that Smith was a mocker of Evangelical piety and an enemy to its dogmatic righteousness. *Peter Plymley* speaks of the 'patent Christians of Clapham' (Letter 3), and in 1808, when Zachary Macaulay was still its editor, Smith had written of the *Christian Observer* that it was 'a publication which appears to have no other method of discussing a question fairly open to discussion, than that of accusing their antagonists of infidelity. No art can be more unmanly, or, if its consequences are foreseen, more wicked' ('Indian Missions,' *Works of the Rev. Sydney Smith*, 2nd edn, 1840, I, 151).

[1] Beresford (1773–1862: *DNB*), Primate of Ireland since 1822, was an opponent of Catholic relief.   [2] Paper torn away with seal.

On Saturday I went to Sydney Smith's. His parish lies three or four
miles out of any frequented road. He is, however, most pleasantly situated.
"Fifteen years ago," said he to me when I alighted at the gate of his
shrubbery, "I was taken up in Piccadilly and set down here. There was no
house, and no garden, nothing but a bare field." One service this eccentric
divine has certainly rendered to the Church. He has built the very neatest,
most commodious, and most appropriate rectory that I ever saw. All
its decorations are in a peculiarly clerical style, grave, simple, and
Gothic. The bed chambers are excellent, and excellently fitted up, the
sitting rooms handsome, and the grounds sufficiently pretty. Tindal[1]
and Parke,[2] not the judge[3] of course, two of the best lawyers, best
scholars, and best men in England, were there. We passed an extremely
pleasant evening, had a very good dinner, and many amusing anecdotes.
Mrs. Sydney Smith was very hospitable, and seems to be very accomplished. Their daughters[4] are two very pleasant girls, one of them
very handsome, in my judgment, though dark enough for a Queen of
the Gypsies.

After breakfast the next morning I walked to Church with Sydney
Smith. The ladies came in the Carriage. The edifice is not at all in keeping
with the rectory, a miserable little hovel with a wooden belfry. It was
however very well filled and with very decent people, who seemed to take
very much to their pastor. I understand that he is a very respectable
apothecary; and most liberal of his skill, his medecine, his soup, and his
wine, among the sick. He preached a very queer sermon – the former half
too familiar and the latter half too florid, but not without some ingenuity
both of thought and expression. It was on the duty of good will to our
neighbours, and, for aught I know, may have been the same that opened

---

[1] (Sir) Nicholas Tindal (1776–1846: *DNB*), on the Northern Circuit since 1809; one of
   the counsel for Queen Caroline in 1820; M.P., 1824–7; appointed Solicitor-General and
   knighted, September 1826; Chief Justice of the Court of Common Pleas, 1829–46. Two
   months after this dinner TBM was admitted, on 25 September 1826, to the British Museum
   on the recommendation of Tindal (Coleman O. Parsons, 'Pilgrims of Research,' *Quarterly
   Review*, 305 [1967], 65).

[2] James Parke (1782–1868: *DNB*), afterwards first Baron Wensleydale, a member of the
   Northern Circuit since 1813 and one of the counsel for the prosecution in the trial
   of Queen Caroline. Judge in the Court of King's Bench, 1828; in the Court of Exchequer
   from 1834; created Baron Wensleydale, 1856. 'He is a man of most agreeable manners,
   and tells or hears a good story at the convivial board, with infinite zest' ([James
   Grant], *The Bench and the Bar*, 1838, I, 240). Both Parke and Tindal had been Fellows
   of Trinity.

[3] Sir James Alan Park (1763–1838: *DNB*), long on the Northern Circuit before being made
   judge of the Court of Common Pleas, 1816. Though respected as a judge, the absurdity of
   his manner was the source of innumerable anecdotes. Park was one of the judges at this
   summer's assizes on the Northern Circuit.

[4] Saba (1802–66), married Sir Henry Holland; Emily (1807–74), married Nathaniel Hibbert.
   The dark one was Emily: see 20 September 1832.

Beaumont's eyes to the depravity of Lady Swinburne.[1] For it certainly was open to the same charge with that.

He drove me through the magnificent woods of Castle Howard. Lord Carlisle, whom he knows very well, was at Paris; but I caught a glimpse of this celebrated structure, one of the finest works of Vanbrugh, and contrived to see the three Maries, the most renowned ornament of the Orleans Gallery, and the glory of Caracci. It is indeed a wonderful picture. The Magdalene, the Virgin, and the dead body of Christ are superior to any thing which I remember to have seen.[2]

Sydney Smith brought me to York on Monday Morning in time for the stage-coach which runs to Skipton. We parted with many assurances of good will.[3] I have really taken a great liking to him. He is full of wit, humour, and shrewdness. He is not one of those shew-talkers who keep all their good things for great occasions. It seems to be his greatest luxury to keep his wife and daughters laughing two or three hours every day. His notions of law, government, and [   ][4] are surprisingly clear and just. His misfo[rtune][4] is to have chosen a profession at once above and below him. Zeal would have made him a prodigy. Formality and bigotry would have made him a bishop. But he could neither rise to the duties of his order, nor stoop to its degradations.

He praised my articles in the Edinburgh Review with a warmth which I

---

[1] A letter from Thomas Wentworth Beaumont (1792–1848: *DNB*) to Lord Grey, written in 1823, charging that Lady Swinburne, wife of Sir John Swinburne (the poet's grandfather) was guilty of adultery with Grey, with his brother, General Grey, and with her butler, had just been made public. Beaumont, M.P. for Northumberland from 1818, had been defeated in the general election and had publicly charged that the opposition to him had been acting maliciously. In response to this, his correspondence with Grey and others in 1823–4 on the subject of Lady Swinburne was published as evidence of his unsoundness of mind. Beaumont gave no evidence for his accusation but said that he was moved to make it by 'some prayers ...selected from a book of Bishop Hoadley's, and in which, as well as in a sermon of Sydney Smith's, I was struck by the absence of all acknowledgement of the atonement of our Saviour, and the misrepresentation of the principal object of his coming upon the earth, to die for the sins of mankind' (*The Times*, 22 July).

[2] Purchased from the Orleans collection by Lord Carlisle, the picture was the acknowledged showpiece of Castle Howard. The enthusiastic Thomas Frognall Dibdin, writing of a visit in 1836, begins his account: 'There is THE picture....the ANNIBAL CARACCI,...one of the *four greatest pictures in the world*. It is *here* that you may go down *at once* upon your knees....' He goes on thus for another two pages (*A Bibliographical, Antiquarian, and Picturesque Tour in the Northern Counties of England and in Scotland*, 1838, I, 237–9). TBM saw the picture again at the British Gallery in 1851: 'I went at once to the Three Maries – unseen for a quarter of a century; – it almost brought tears into my eyes' (Journal, IV, 126–7: 10 June 1851).

[3] In his review of Trevelyan, Lord Houghton says of TBM's first visit to Sydney Smith that 'one still living, present at that interview, remembers the look of ludicrous relief with which the host shut the door after his guest, exclaiming, "I am now like Zacharias, my mouth is opened"' (*Academy*, IX [29 April 1876], 398). Neither Tindal nor Parke was still living in 1876, nor did TBM and Sydney Smith part at Foston, but the story is at least *ben trovato*.

[4] Paper torn away with seal.

am willing to believe sincere, because he qualified his compliments with several very sensible cautions. My great danger, he said, was that of taking a tone of too much asperity and contempt in controversy. I believe that he is right, and I shall try to mend.

I reached Skipton on Monday evening late. Yesterday the Sessions took place and closed at eleven in the evening. This morning I came in a chaise with two other barristers to the filthiest and most inconvenient town in the West-Riding. I am, however, tolerably lodged by comparison; and I expect to escape to Leeds by Saturday.

Ever affectionately yours
T B M

P.S. Of course nothing that I have said about Sydney Smith must get abroad.

TO HENRY MACAULAY, 15 MARCH 1827

MS: University of Texas.

Lancaster March 15. 1827

My dear Henry,

I am really very sorry that I must forego the pleasure of seeing you this circuit.[1] I assure you that nothing but poverty prevented me from going to Liverpool. The same poverty, I am afraid, must prevent me from bringing you to Lancaster. I shall not be able[2] to go through the circuit without a fresh remittance from London – I would gladly have avoided the necessity of sending for it at all; and, even for your company, I do not like to make it larger. In the summer I hope to be richer and more fortunate.

Ever yours affectionately
T B M.

TO HANNAH MACAULAY, 20 MARCH 1827

MS: Trinity College.

Lancaster March 20. 1827

My dear Hannah,

I cannot in gratitude delay to answer your very pleasant letter, which, for a large school hand, is not ill written, and really deserves good penmanship. I heard from my mother by the same frank; and am much

---

[1] The spring assizes were held at Lancaster, 10–24 March; at York, 24 March–12 April.
[2] MS reads 'I shall not be able, I shall not be able.'

obliged to her for her epistle. But as she is an older correspondent and does not require encouragement, I think it best to inscribe my reply to you. From my mother's letter I infer, though she does not actually say so, that her eyes are quite recovered. I hope that it is so.

On Thursday Wakefield[1] is to be tried. On Friday Ellis[2] and I leave Lancaster in a chaise,[3] and sleep at Bolton, the most beautiful spot on the road and the scene of a silly poem of Wordsworth's, the White Doe. I caught a glance at it last year. It is indeed a place in which nature and art strive for the mastery, a beautiful ruin in a beautiful situation, not equal to Tintern, but superior to anything else of the kind that ever I saw. On Saturday we shall proceed to York. All your letters therefore from the time that you receive this ought to be directed thither.

I always thought your hero Sibthorpe[4] a goose. But the excellent story you tell me of him puts the matter out of all doubt. I hope that Miss Edgeworth's Harrington[5] will never fall in his way. If it should he will infallibly turn Jew, nourish his beard, and eat the Passover while his congregation is waiting for a Good Friday Sermon. Mr. Lewis Way and Wolfe[6] will have to reconvert him. By bribing him with a pipe of the real

---

[1] Edward Gibbon Wakefield (1796–1862: *DNB*), later famous for his work in colonial matters, was on trial with his brother William for the abduction of the heiress Ellen Turner, whom Wakefield had married in 1826. The trial was put back until Friday on account of the illness of Scarlett, one of the counsel. The newspapers in the last week of March are filled with long accounts of the trial, which excited great popular interest and ended with the Wakefields sentenced to three years' imprisonment.

[2] For Ellis, see Introduction. Trevelyan, I, 177, says that TBM and Ellis did not meet until 1827, but according to Perry, *Contributions to an Amateur Magazine*, pp. 309–10, Ellis was in residence as a senior bachelor at Trinity when TBM came up in 1818, and the statement agrees with the dates of Ellis's academic career: B.A., 1818; Fellow, 1819. Hannah Trevelyan's Memoir of TBM, p. 16, says that TBM loved to 'talk of the college struggles between [Stainforth] and Mr. Ellis, 'suggesting that he knew of Ellis from college days. In any case they met in March 1826, on TBM's first circuit. Ellis wrote to his wife then that 'Macaulay has joined, and is a very amusing person – somewhat boyish in manner, but very original' (Memoir of Ellis [by Louisa or Marian Ellis]: MS, Trinity).

[3] 'A barrister may join or leave the circuit per coach, but he must travel from one circuit town to another in a private conveyance of some sort. . . . It is simply a rule of delicacy, it being deemed improper for counsel to be mixed up with parties and witnesses' (*Law Magazine*, XXII [November 1839], 380).

[4] Richard Waldo Sibthorp (1792–1879: *DNB*), at this time evening lecturer at St John's Chapel, Bedford Row; the brother of Col. Charles Sibthorp (see 8 August 1832: to Lord Mahon). He had while in college attempted to join the Catholic church; in 1841 he was received into it and was ordained priest in 1842; the next year he returned to the established church; in 1857 he was readmitted to the Anglican ministry, but he returned to the Catholic priesthood in 1865. At his burial, 'in accordance with his express desire, the English service was read over his grave' (*DNB*).

[5] *Harrington, A Tale*, 1817: the hero, a young English gentleman, becomes a champion of the Jews.

[6] The Rev. Lewis Way (1772–1840: *DNB*), the leading spirit of the London Society for Promoting Christianity Amongst the Jews. Joseph Wolff (1795–1862: *DNB*), a converted Jew who had studied at Cambridge during TBM's years there, was the Society's most active missionary.

Hockheimer, and taking him to see the Merchant of Venice acted he may perhaps be reclaimed.

I wish that I knew where my old friend Mrs. Meeke[1] lives. I would certainly send her intelligence of the blessed effects of her writings. I grieve to think how carelessly I have read them, and how little I have considered them in a theological light. Mr. Elliott,[2] you know, boasts that he read St Paul's Epistles over in a geographical point of view, and found them very useful in that respect. I shall read over Mrs. Meeke's hundred and one novels in a theological point of view; I hope with equal benefit.

A new edition of Laughton Priory[3] ought certainly to be published cheap for distribution among the poor Irish. It would aid Lord Farnham[4] in the mighty work which he is performing in Cavan. He would be the very person to preside over the British and Foreign Laughton Priory Association. I will certainly attend Freemasons hall, and perhaps favour the Ladies and Gentlemen with a speech.

So the Jesuits kept Sibthorpe in hiding. Alas, my dear Carolina Wilhelmina Amelia, I must like Sir William Thornhill, pronounce your anecdote in that respect fudge.[5] I suspect that, having experienced the good effects of fictitious narrative in his own case, he intends to try the same experiment on other people and to pass himself off for Juliano Algernon,[6] I suppose. If he really were, like Juliano, confined as insane, I cannot much blame his keepers. – But enough of Mr. Sibthorpe.

I am rather pleased than otherwise at the event of the Leicester petition.[7] Success was not to be expected; and, considering the strong and, indeed, discreditable tone which Peel adopted, I was agreably surprised to find the minority so respectable.

But I must stop and go back to court. There is a highwayman to be tried for his life who interests the ladies very much;[8] a stout handsome

---

[1] Mrs Mary Meeke (d. 1816?: *DNB*), TBM's favorite bad novelist; beginning with *The Abbey of Clugny* in 1795, published twenty-eight novels from the Minerva Press under her own name and the pseudonym of 'Gabrielli.'

[2] Henry Venn Elliott travelled in the eastern Mediterranean countries, 1817–20; after his return he was in residence at Trinity, 1821–3, when TBM very likely heard the remark about St Paul. Elliott prepared a MS account of his travels which was not published (Josiah Bateman, *The Life of the Rev. Henry Venn Elliott, M.A.*, 1868, p. 100).

[3] 'Gabrielli' [Mrs Meeke], *Laughton Priory*, 4 vols., 1809. This work is not in the British Museum, and no copy is located in Dorothy Blakey, *The Minerva Press, 1790–1820*, 1939.

[4] The fifth Baron Farnham (1767–1838), of county Cavan, where he had estates worth £30,000 a year. I cannot explain the reference to his 'mighty work.'

[5] See Goldsmith, *The Vicar of Wakefield*, ch. 11.   [6] Perhaps the hero of *Laughton Priory?*

[7] A petition for redress against the proceedings of the corporation in the Leicester election (see 31 May 1826) was made the subject of a motion for a committee of inquiry in the House of Commons, 15 March 1827. Peel spoke against the motion, which was lost, ninety-two to sixty-eight: see *Annual Register*, 1827, pp. [177–9].

[8] The trial of John Macdonald for highway robbery at Lancaster assizes is reported in *The Times*, 23 March. Macdonald, 'a young man of remarkably fine and athletic appearance,' was acquitted.

swaggering fellow, the very image of Macheath. He has been twice tried since we came hither and has got off by alibi both times. If he is convicted the Lancashire witches[1] will be inconsolable – "such a nice gentleman; – and if he did rob the folks, why, it is hard to hang such a pretty young man for that. It is a shame, so it is, to hang a fellow-creature for a few sovereigns. They would not have such a thing to answer for, not if you would give them the whole world." Pretty creatures! But in spite of their prettiness and of their pity I would not give two pence for the life of this Adonis if he should be convicted. Love to every body at home.

Ever your affectionate Brother
T B M

TO ZACHARY MACAULAY, 29 MARCH 1827

MS: Trinity College. *Address:* Z Macaulay Esq. / 16 George Street / Mansion House / London. *Partly published:* Trevelyan, I, 110.

York March 29th. 1827

My dear Father,

I have this instant seen the report in the New and Old Times of the proceedings before the Lords.[2] It seems, if those concise accounts can be trusted that no hope of reversing the judgment can rationally be entertained. For this indeed I was prepared. But from the small space which the business occupies in the two papers I mentioned, the only papers which, as far as I have been able to discover, allude to the business, it must be inferred that the public interest in the question is at an end, – that the storm has blown over. When the case was argued before the Chancellor whole columns were devoted to it in every journal. This seems to prove that you may take whatever course shall be thought advisable without apprehension of misconstruction.

---

[1] *The Famous History of the Lancashire Witches*, [1780?], an anonymous chapbook; or the trial of 1613; or Shadwell's comedy, 1681.

[2] Zachary Macaulay's appeal to the House of Lords against the decision in the Court of Chancery in the *John Bull* case (see 4 August 1824) was heard on 26 and 27 March by Lord Eldon, who thus sat in judgment on his own decision. Eldon reserved his opinion until he had consulted Lord Redesdale, and on 3 April gave judgment affirming the Court of Chancery's decision; in summing up he remarked that among the 'Legion' of his anonymous correspondents he had one who had written that 'all the men of eminence at the bar think that this decision is wrong, and that it is produced by the affection which the Lord Chancellor is supposed to have had for some Mr. Shackell, or some such gentleman,' but this, Eldon said, was a base slander (Richard Bligh, *New Reports of Cases Heard in the House of Lords* . . . *1827–8*, I, [1829], 136; a full report is in Bligh, pp. 96–137). Since Macaulay had no hope that a commission could obtain fair testimony in the West Indies he must have dropped the suit. In a letter of 28 November 1827 Wilberforce says that Macaulay's legal expenses were already 'more than two thousand pounds' and that his friends are raising a subscription to meet them (William Wilberforce, *Correspondence*, 1840, II, 511).

Till yesterday I was not aware that the crisis was so near. The lines which you enclosed to me under cover to Brougham did not find their way to me till they had been 48 hours in York. His Clerk kept them for a day, and then gave them to a stupid messenger who took them to Alderson's[1] lodgings instead of mine. Sending any thing under cover to a person so busy as Brougham at present is, will turn out to be a very dear œconomy.

I hope to be at home by Monday Week, or at least very soon after. In the mean time I hope to be punctually informed of every thing relating to your business, which does not find its way into the newspapers; I am rather glad that I was not in London, if your advisers[2] thought it right that I should have appeared as your Counsel. Whether it be contrary to professional ettiquette I do not know. But I am sure that it would be shocking to publick feeling; and particularly imprudent against adversaries whose main strength lies in detecting and exposing indecorum or eccentricity. It would have been difficult to avoid a quarrel with Sugden,[3] with Wetherell,[4] and with old Lord Eldon himself. Then John Bull would have been upon us with every advantage. The personal part of the consideration it would have been my duty, and my pleasure and pride also, to overlook. But your interests must have suffered. Love to my Mother and all at home. Thanks to H[annah] M[ore Macaulay] for her letter. Nothing from Edinburgh.[5]

Yours most affectionately
T B M.

---

[1] (Sir) Edward Hall Alderson (1787–1857: *DNB*), on the Northern Circuit since 1811; judge of the Common Pleas, and knighted, 1830; Baron of the Exchequer, 1834–57. After meeting him years later TBM called him 'a solemn humbug now as he was a pert humbug formerly' (Journal, IV, 93: 14 May 1851).

[2] Zachary Macaulay's lawyers in the appeal were Sir Lancelot Shadwell (1779–1850: *DNB*), who became in this year Vice-Chancellor, and Christopher Pepys (1781–1851: *DNB*), afterwards first Earl of Cottenham, who was Lord Chancellor under Melbourne, 1836–41, and under Lord John Russell, 1850–1.

[3] Edward Burtenshaw Sugden (1781–1875: *DNB*), afterwards first Baron St Leonards. A lawyer of almost unrivalled professional success, he was one of the counsel for Shackell before the Lord Chancellor and in the appeal to the Lords. Sugden was Lord Chancellor of Ireland in Peel's first and second administrations, and Lord Chancellor in Derby's, 1852, when he was raised to the peerage.

[4] Sir Charles Wetherell (1770–1846: *DNB*), a leading Chancery lawyer, one of the counsel for Shackell. He was Solicitor-General in 1824, when the case was heard in Chancery, and Attorney-General in 1827, when the appeal was heard in the Lords. Wetherell had also been opposed to Zachary Macaulay in his earlier libel suit against Robert Thorpe. Tory M.P., 1812–32, Wetherell earned such great unpopularity by his opposition to parliamentary reform that his official visit to Bristol in his capacity of Recorder, October 1831, set off the riot in which a large part of the city was burned.

[5] The reference is probably to TBM's article on 'Major Moody's Reports: Social and Industrial Capacities of Negroes,' *ER*, XLV (March 1827), 383–423, a review no doubt written at Zachary Macaulay's instance. The same number of the *ER*, which did not appear until 19 April, also contained TBM's 'Machiavelli,' pp. 259–95.

TO ZACHARY MACAULAY, 3 AUGUST 1827

MS: Trinity College. *Address:* Z Macaulay Esq / 16 George Street / Mansion House / London.

York[1] August 3rd. 1827

My dear Father,

I am much obliged to you for your letters. I was curious to see the Times because I supposed that it might express the opinions of the Government.[2] As to the abuse of our opponents – particularly of Macqueen,[3] I have not even the slightest curiosity about it.

The article[4] is very well printed, without a fault, I think. The alterations are, in all essential points, judicious; but I wish that Jeffrey[5] would take a little more pains with the expression of the passages which he inserts. They do not fit in well. He is fond of omitting his *thats* and *whiches*, a thing which I never do. All this however is of very little consequence.

[1] TBM had been at the Midsummer quarter sessions of the West Riding, Skipton, 9 July; Bradford, 11–14 July; Rotherham, 18 July. The York assizes did not open until 28 July and closed 9 August. Perhaps TBM spent the interval between the close of the sessions and the opening of the York assizes at Rothley Temple, as he did the interval between the York and Lancaster assizes; he went to Rothley Temple on 13 August and did not arrive in Lancaster until 30 August, the day after the opening of the assizes.

[2] This seems to refer to some object of the abolitionists, but there is nothing about them in *The Times* of this period.

[3] James MacQueen (1778–1870: *DNB*), geographer and editor of the Glasgow *Courier*, had published various articles and pamphlets in defense of the West Indian interests. In December 1826, he began a series of eleven articles in *Blackwood's* that ran through 1833, attacking the abolitionists, the African Institution, the Sierra Leone colony, and, in particular, Zachary Macaulay. MacQueen 'is now known to have been subsidized by the Society of West India Planters and Merchants of London' (Lowell J. Ragatz, *A Guide for the Study of British Caribbean History, 1763–1834*, Washington, D.C., 1932, p. 532).

[4] 'The Present Administration,' *ER*, XLVI (June 1827), 245–65. This article, which is not included in TBM's collected works and is therefore usually omitted from the list of his writings, was widely and correctly attributed to him at the time. A note summarizing most of the evidence for the attribution to TBM is in Stuart M. Tave, *New Essays of De Quincey*, Princeton, 1966, pp. 27–8. Further evidence is in Selina Macaulay's Diary, which reports on 6 June 1827 that Jeffrey has asked for an article 'on the new administration' which 'Tom has promised to do' and on 16 June that 'Tom was very busy the whole of yesterday in writing his article on the present ministry.'

[5] Francis Jeffrey (1773–1850: *DNB*), lawyer and critic; one of the founders of the *ER*, he had been its editor since 1803 and wrote regularly for it himself. Long held back by the handicap of his Whig politics, Jeffrey had by this time achieved a good legal practice and was soon to come into political rewards. He was elected Dean of the Faculty of Advocates, 1829; appointed Lord Advocate, 1830, when he entered Parliament; judge of the Court of Session as Lord Jeffrey, 1834–50. He retired from the editorship of the *ER* in 1829, but continued to advise his successor, Macvey Napier (see 15 April 1828). TBM had an unswervingly high opinion of Jeffrey both as person and as writer. Trevelyan says that 'the only commendation of his literary talent which even in the innermost domestic circle [TBM] was ever known to repeat, – was the sentence with which Jeffrey acknowledged the receipt of his manuscript: "The more I think the less I can conceive where you picked up that style"' (I, 117–18). In 1843 TBM dedicated his *Essays* to Jeffrey, 'in token of the esteem, admiration, and affection of his friend.'

Brougham is so busy that I have not been able to exchange a word with him. I have at length myself received a brief[1] – the first, and perhaps the last. It is of no great consequence. I am junior to Pollock, and shall have only to take notes, and perhaps to examine a single witness.

I have been trying, since the commencement of the Assizes has brought so many men to York, to ascertain whether the feeling respecting the Cambridge election[2] which I remarked at the Sessions, could be considered as general. I am fully convinced that Robert Grant[3] will receive very strong support, if he avoids the error into which he fell in 1822.[4] He must speak out. His conduct then has left something of an unfavourable impression on many who are, on the whole, well inclined to him. He not only shrunk from explanation about the Catholic Question but in his Circular letter of resignation he absolutely complained of being considered as a supporter of the Claims and represented the unfairness of attacking, on that ground, a person who had never spoken on the subject, and who had merely given one silent vote on it some years before. Whether this representation of his co[uld][5] be just or not I cannot determine[. But][5] such is the impression of the Whigs who took a part in that contest. Their universal language is: Let him act a manly part. Let him put the Catholic claims forward – and he may command all our votes. This, with all delicacy, should be hinted to him or to his friends. It concerns his character as well as his success at Cambridge.[6] I would sooner see him or any other person whom I value defeated like Evans than victorious like Cave.[7]

I shall be in want of a fresh supply of money before I leave York. Two and twenty pounds of the last 50 which I received went in bills and for rent before I left London. I should therefore be obliged to you to advance

---

1 Of the cases reported from this term's assizes, the one that seems most likely to be that in which TBM figured is the suit of a timber merchant named Watson brought to recover £19 17s 6d from a wheelwright named Walker. The defendant produced a receipt signed by one of the plaintiff's partners who had since died, but the signature was suspected to be a forgery. The jury found for the plaintiff and assigned costs of 40s (York *Herald*, 11 August 1827). See 8 August 1827.

2 In May Sir Nicholas Tindal defeated William John Bankes at Cambridge on the issue of Catholic relief. TBM voted for Tindal in this election (Selina Macaulay, Diary, 10 May 1827), which he celebrated in his verses on 'The Country Clergyman's Trip to Cambridge. Part the First,' published anonymously in *The Times*, 14 May 1827.

3 Robert Grant (1779–1838: *DNB*), second son of Charles Grant of the East India Company and Clapham, was M.P. for various constituencies, 1818–34; Commissioner of the Board of Control, 1830–4, when his brother Charles was President of the Board; Governor of Bombay, 1834–8; died in India. Grant took the lead in the unsuccessful effort to remove the civil disabilities of the Jews, 1830–4. He spoke only once on the question of Catholic relief, and then not until the end of the debates, in 1829.

4 In the election for Cambridge of that year: see 26 October 1822.

5 Paper torn away with seal.

6 There was no election for Cambridge after that of Tindal in May 1827 until June 1829. Grant was M.P. for Inverness Burghs, 1826–30.

7 The loser and winner in the Leicester election, 1826: see 31 May 1826.

me 50 more. I forgot to say when I left town that my clerk will be put to shifts if he is not paid till I return in Septr. – I have generally paid him weekly. Will you be so kind as to settle with him from time to time and add it to my account. I have scarce left myself room to thank Selina and Hannah for their very agreable letters.

Ever yours affectionately

T B M.

TO ZACHARY MACAULAY, 8 AUGUST 1827

MS: Trinity College. *Address:* Z Macaulay Esq / 16 George Street / Mansion House / London. *Partly published:* Knutsford, *Zachary Macaulay*, p. 443.

York August 8th. 1827

My dear Father,

Many thanks for your letter and its inclosure. I am extremely shocked about Canning;[1] not that I think the administration endangered by his death; but the event is in itself most affecting. The death of the Princess Charlotte herself was less so. To fall at the very moment of reaching the very highest pinnacle of human ambition! The whole work of thirty chequered years of glory and obloquy struck down in a moment! The noblest prize that industry, dexterity, wit and eloquence ever obtained vanishing into nothing in the very instant in which it had been grasped. Vanity of vanities – all is vanity.

Brougham has been very unwell too, but he is now pretty well recovered – and the only effect of his indisposition is to give a milder and more subdued manner to his speaking, which, in ordinary cases, is an improvement. He has heard from the Marquess of Lansdowne[2] who speaks, he tells me, highly of my article.[3]

---

[1] George Canning died on 8 August 1827, four months after becoming Prime Minister.

[2] Henry Petty-Fitzmaurice (1780–1863: *DNB*), third Marquess of Lansdowne, Whig politician and a figure of decisive importance in TBM's life as the means by which, in 1830, he was introduced into Parliament. It is worth noting that, as TBM dedicated his *Essays* to Jeffrey, he dedicated his *Speeches* to Lansdowne; the two dedications thus acknowledge his most important literary and political patrons. Lord Lansdowne had been associated with every Whig notable in politics and literature since the end of the eighteenth century, when he was a student at Edinburgh with Palmerston, Brougham, Jeffrey, Cockburn, Horner, and Sydney Smith, and he faithfully supported the succession of Whig causes in the House of Lords for over fifty years. 'There is no man,' wrote Sydney Smith, 'who performs the duties of life better, or fills a high station in a more becoming manner. He is full of knowledge, and eager for its acquisition. His remarkable politeness is the result of good-nature, regulated by good sense. He looks for talents and qualities among all ranks of men, and adds them to his stock of society, as a botanist does his plants; and while other aristocrats are yawning among Stars and Garters, Lansdowne is refreshing his soul with the fancy and genius which he has found in odd places, and gathered to the marbles of his palace. Then he is an honest politician, a wise statesman, and has a philosophic mind; he is very agreeable in conversation, and is a man of unblemished life. I shall take care of him in my Memoirs!' (*Letters*, II, 784: 4 June 1843). 　　　　　　　　　　　　　　　　[3] 'The Present Administration.'

I shall be probably at Rothley Temple on Saturday. None of our West Riding men go to Durham, for the best of all reasons. It is not in our power to go more than once in four years or thereabouts;[1] and to go to an assize-town is merely throwing money away unless we go regularly.

I discharged my duty, I hope properly, to my client; but nothing could be of use in his case. It was a fraudulent defence – bolstered up, I strongly suspect, by a forged document. So at lea[st][2] the Judge and the Jury thought; and all that Pollock or I could do was in vain.

Love to all at Highwood.[3] I expect to see Henry before I reach Lancaster. But there will be ample time to make arrangements on that head.

Ever yours affectionately

T B M.

TO ZACHARY MACAULAY, 14 AUGUST 1827

MS: Trinity College. *Address:* Z Macaulay Esq. / 16 George Street / Mansion House / London. *Extract published:* Trevelyan, I, 145.

Rothley Temple August 14. 1827

My dear Father,

I came hither on Monday, and received your letter yesterday.[4] I have in consequence written to Evans to say that if it suits him, I will pay him a visit on my way to Lancaster.[5] My movements will depend on his answer.

I received the Edinburgh Paper which you sent me. Silly and spiteful as it is, there is a little truth in it.[6] In such cases I always remember those excellent lines of Boileau –

---

[1] Presumably because the summer assizes at Durham and the midsummer session of the West Riding usually fell at the same time.

[2] Paper torn away with seal.

[3] Highwood Hill, Wilberforce's house near Mill Hill from 1825. TBM's sisters were regular visitors there.

[4] TBM may have misdated this letter, for he writes as though Monday were the day before yesterday; Monday was 13 August.

[5] The visit was made: see 1 September 1827.

[6] In 1826 the Edinburgh branch of the British and Foreign Bible Society seceded from the parent organization in protest against the Society's inclusion of the Apocrypha in the bibles it circulated. Andrew Thomson (1779–1831: *DNB*), minister of St George's, Edinburgh, and, according to Carlyle, the 'famous *malleus* of Theology in that time' (*Reminiscences*, 1887, II, 61) led the secession. In his address to the annual meeting of the Edinburgh Society, 9 July 1827, he had renewed his quarrel with the officials of the London Society, who included Zachary Macaulay, charging, e.g., that 'their careful concealment of their sinful conduct is a great aggravation of their error in the sight of God.' He also said that they had been slow to acknowledge the opposition to the Apocrypha, which was true (Edinburgh *Evening Courant*, 14 July 1827; see 14 April 1828, and Knutsford, *Zachary Macaulay*, pp. 437–9).

"Moi, qu'une humeur trop libre, un esprit peu soumis
De bonne heure a pourvu d'utiles ennemis,
Je dois plus à leur haine; il faut que je l'avoue,
Qu'au faible et vain talent dont la France me loue,
Sitôt que sur un vice ils pensent me confondre,
C'est en me guérissant que je sais leur repondre."[1]

I am glad to find that there seems to be no chance of a change of administration.[2] Indeed I have all along been convinced that there was none, and that the death of Canning, a melancholy event doubtless, would rather strengthen than weaken the new government. Most of the abuse had fallen to his share; whatever suspicion attached to the manner in which the ministry had been formed, was directed to him. He carries with him to the grave the whole obloquy of the cabinet. His death too has evidently softened the public mind, and disposed the country to look with kindness on his colleagues. Besides this, it is lucky for the ministers that they have been in so very short a time. They have not enjoyed power long enough to abuse it. They have not been able to forfeit one pledge, or to disappoint one hope. It was easy to upset Fox in 84 when he had brought in his India Bill. The Whigs in 1807 had rendered themselves unpopular by abandoning or appearing to abandon the principles which they had avowed in opposition. But if the present ministers were now to be dismissed they would go out with immense public favour, with highly raised expectations which a few months will, in all probability, shew to be fallacious. They would therefore form an opposition most dangerous to the fee[ble][3] Cabinet which would succeed them.

But though I do not apprehend evil consequences from poor Canning's death, it is impossible not to be deeply affected by it. I learned an anecdote of him yesterday from a clergyman which you will be pleased to hear. This Clergyman has a medical friend who was lately called in to attend a servant in Canning's family. He found his patient in great danger. As soon as Canning heard it he himself took a Bible to the sick man, and pressed upon him the propriety of seeing a clergyman. Considering his avocations, the story is highly creditable to him in every point of view.[4] Love to all.

Ever yours most affectionately
T B M

[1] *Épitres*, VII, 57–60; 67–8.
[2] The coalition ministry formed by Canning continued under Lord Goderich only until January 1828.
[3] Paper torn away with seal.
[4] Zachary Macaulay repeats this story in his letter to Hannah More, 24 August 1827 (Knutsford, *Zachary Macaulay*, p. 444).

TO HENRY MACAULAY, 30 AUGUST 1827

MS: University of Texas.

Lancaster Augt. 30 – 1827

My dear H[enr]y,

I have this moment reached Lancaster where I have found three letters from you. I am sorry for the trouble which I have given you and for the delay which my absence has occasioned – for other sorrow there seems to be no occasion. For the lines appear to be well printed.[1] I hope to snatch a few hours with you at Liverpool towards the close of next week or the beginning of the week after. I shall be glad to shew every civility to Sr. Panizzi.[2]

Yours affectionately

T B Macaulay –

TO ZACHARY MACAULAY, 1 SEPTEMBER 1827

MS: Trinity College. *Address:* Z Macaulay Esq / 16 George Street / Mansion House / London. *Partly published:* Trevelyan, I, 144–6.

Lancaster September 1st. 1827

My dear Father,

Thank Hannah from me for her pleasant letter. I would answer it if I had anything equally amusing to say in return. But here we have no news, except what comes from London, and is as stale as inland fish before it reaches us. We have circuit anecdotes to be sure. And perhaps you will be pleased to hear that Brougham has been rising through the whole of this struggle. At York Pollock decidedly took the lead. At Durham Brougham overtook him, passed him at Newcastle, and got immensely ahead of him at Carlisle and Appleby, which, to be sure, are the places where his own connections lie. We have not been here quite long enough to determine how he will succeed with the Lancastrians. This has always hitherto been

---

[1] Perhaps some contribution by TBM to Henry's *Olaides*: see 4 January 1823: to Henry Macaulay.

[2] (Sir) Anthony Panizzi (1797–1879: *DNB*), later Principal Librarian of the British Museum, where his monument is the reading room, had fled his native Italy in 1822 and had subsequently been condemned to death for his activities as a Carbonaro. He was at this time residing in Liverpool as a teacher of Italian; Professor of Italian at the London University, 1828, and Assistant Librarian, British Museum, 1831, becoming Principal Librarian in 1856; K.C.B., 1869. TBM may have met him as early as March 1827, when Brougham brought Panizzi, a graduate in law from the University of Parma, to the Wakefield trial (see 20 March 1827) as a consultant on points of continental marriage law. Soon after Panizzi moved to London he was introduced to TBM's family: 'Mr. Panizzi dined with us and interested us very much, he is evidently an exceedingly clever man' (Selina Macaulay, Diary, 7 November 1828).

his least favourable place. He appears to improve in industry and prudence. He learns his story more thoroughly and tells it more clearly than
formerly. If he continues to manage causes as well as he has done of late he
must rise to the summit of the profession. I cannot say quite so much for
his temper, which this close and constant rivalry does not improve. – He
squabbles with Pollock more than, in generosity or in policy, he ought to
do. I have heard several of our younger men wondering that he does not
shew more magnanimity. He yawns while Pollock is speaking – a sign of
weariness which every body else gives pretty frequently, but which
Brougham, in their present relation to each other, would do well to suppress. He has said some very good but very bitter things. There was a case
of a lead-mine. Pollock was for the proprietors, and complained bitterly
of the encroachments which Brougham's clients had made upon this
property, which he represented as of immense value. Brougham said that
the estimate which his Learned Friend formed of the property was vastly
exaggerated – but that it was no wonder that a person who found it so
easy to get gold in exchange for his lead should appreciate that heavy
metal so highly. I was in the other Court when this was said – but I
believe that I give at least the general turn of the observation. The other
day Pollock laid down a point of law rather dogmatically. "Mr. Pollock;"
said Brougham, "perhaps before you rule the point, you wi[ll][1] suffer his
Lordship to submit a few obser[va][1]tions on it to your consideration." –
Do not circulate these stories. Both the parties have been so kind to me
that I see their sparring with some regret.

I have read the Translation of Machiavelli[2] – which is very well executed. Your pamphlet[3] I have not read – Evans took it to his bed-room at
Allestree, and I was off the next morning before he was stirring. We are all
pleased here at the new arrangements.[4] Brougham learned them by a letter
which he received this morning. This place disagrees so much with me
that I shall leave it as soon as the dispersion of the circuit commences –

[1] Obscured by seal.
[2] No English translation of Machiavelli near this date appears in the British Museum Catalogue
or in the *English Catalogue of Books, 1801–1836.*
[3] Not certainly identified. Almost all of Zachary Macaulay's contributions to the pamphlet
literature of his time were anonymous, and doubtless many remain unidentified. He was at
this time editing, and largely writing unassisted, the *Anti-Slavery Monthly Reporter*, but it is
unlikely that TBM would call this a pamphlet. It may possibly be 'The Colony of Sierra
Leone Vindicated from the Misrepresentations of Mr. Macqueen of Glasgow,' 1827. This
bears Kenneth Macaulay's name on the title page, but MacQueen, in a postscript to his
article on Sierra Leone in *Blackwood's*, XXI (May 1827), 619, says 'Kenneth Macaulay has
put his name to it, but I believe it is just as much his writing as it is the Grand Seignior's.'
The formidable array of official information in the pamphlet makes the implied ascription
to Zachary Macaulay plausible; however, the preface is dated 28 March 1827, so that TBM
might be supposed to have read it well before September.
[4] The changes in the cabinet under Lord Goderich, of which the appointment of John Charles
Herries (see 19 January 1828) was the most important.

that is after the delivery of the last batch of briefs; – always supposing, which may be supposed, without much risk of mistake, that I receive no brief myself. In that case I shall be forced to linger to the close of the proceedings, with no company but the King's Counsel, and two or three other men in high practice. You may possibly see me on Saturday night. But I shall not, most likely, be in London till the Tuesday. All depends on the quantity of business which the court may be able to dispatch during the earlier half of the next week.[1]

Ever yours affectionately
T B M.

P S. The safest way to send any thing not of great urgency after you receive this will be to send it to Liverpool – either to Henry or to the Post-Office. Love to all.

TO HENRY MACAULAY, 4 OCTOBER 1827

MS: University of Texas.

London Octr. 4th. 1827

My dear Henry,

Let Panizzi have the accompanying letter. Send me the book with my wig and Gown – and remember to send those as soon as you have done with them.[2] Nothing stirring here. I shall send off an article on Dryden[3] to Jeffrey in a few days.

Yours very truly
T B M.

TO ANTHONY PANIZZI, 4 OCTOBER 1827

Text: Louis Fagan, *Life of Sir Anthony Panizzi,* 2nd edn, 1880, I, 71.

[London] October 4, 1827.

Your letter was acceptable to me as a mark of kind remembrance, but it is quite unnecessary as an apology. I assure you that I considered myself, and not you, as the offending person on the occasion to which you refer.

---

[1] The Lancaster assizes, 'which have been of an uncommon length,' closed 15 September: 'there were no less than one hundred and sixteen Barristers attending these assizes, exclusive of Sir James Scarlett, the Attorney General' (Lancaster *Gazette,* 15 September 1827).

[2] TBM may have meant to attend the Michaelmas sessions of the West Riding: Knaresborough, 16 October; Leeds, 18–20 October; Sheffield, 24–6 October.

[3] 'Dryden,' *ER,* XLVII (January 1828), 1–36.

I hope, however, that either here or in Liverpool we shall hereafter enjoy many meetings without any such cross accident.

I have not yet found time to read your kind present, poor Foscolo's book.[1] I hope soon to be able to study it, which I shall do with additional interest on his account and on yours.

Yours, etc., etc.,

T. B. Macaulay.

TO ZACHARY MACAULAY, 19 JANUARY 1828

MS: Trinity College. *Address:* Z Macaulay Esq / 16 George Street / Mansion House / London. *Extract published:* Trevelyan, 1, 139.

Leeds[2] Jany. 19. 1828

My dear Father,

I have just received your letters here. The commission[3] is welcome; and I am particularly glad that it has been given at a time when the acceptance of it implies no political obligation; at a time when there is no ministry.[4] To Lord Lyndhurst I of course feel under some personal obligation; and I shall always take care how I speak of him. The condition annexed to the gift of course decides me for the Sessions.

I do not know whether any answer is necessary. Still less do I know what answer may be proper; and I am here by myself without a single ad-

---

[1] Ugo Foscolo (1778–1827), the Italian poet, lived in exile in England from 1816. In printing this letter Fagan adds that after Foscolo's death on 10 September 1827 'the few books he left behind were purchased by some of his remaining friends; Panizzi bought as many as his means allowed him, and these he distributed among the most distinguished admirers of the deceased, one of whom was Mr. Macaulay' (1, 70–1). TBM's reference, however, seems to be to a book by Foscolo rather than to one merely belonging to him.

[2] The Christmas quarter sessions for the West Riding were held at Wetherby, 15 January; Wakefield, 17–19 January; Doncaster, 23 January.

[3] The Lord Chancellor, Lyndhurst, had just appointed TBM a Commissioner of Bankrupts. The appointment had been in prospect since 5 May 1827, when, at Brougham's urging, Lyndhurst sent for TBM to promise him the third vacancy among the commissioners (Selina Macaulay, Diary, 7 May 1827). TBM was reluctant to allow much credit to Brougham for his appointment. In a conversation with his sister Margaret, 27 November [1831], he told her that he should never have got the place had Brougham 'had anything more to do with it than the mere asking it from a person who keeps his promises, which *he* does not' (Margaret Macaulay, *Recollections*, London, privately printed, 1864, p. 55). TBM's disparagement of Brougham's efforts in his behalf is certainly unjust, as are many of his remarks about Brougham after their quarrels in 1830. Lyndhurst himself told Dean Milman that he appointed TBM 'solely on the strong recommendation of Lord Brougham. I was wholly unacquainted with Macaulay and knew only that he was the son of Zachary. It is true that I have ever since congratulated myself upon the appointment' (29 November [1861]: MS, Dr A. N. L. Munby). See also Brougham to Lyndhurst, 1827, in Knutsford, *Zachary Macaulay*, p. 442. The official return of the fees received by the Commissioners of Bankrupts (*Parliamentary Papers*, 1831, xv, 73) shows that TBM made the following sums from his office: to 1 March 1829, £110; to 1 March 1830, £355; to 1 March 1831, £295 – an average of £253 6s 8d.

[4] Goderich resigned on 8 January; Wellington became Prime Minister on 25 January.

viser. I have however, as you seem to think that there ought to be some acknowledgement, enclosed a letter which may probably be extremely absurd. Do not send it in[1] without satisfying yourself that it is unobjectionable.

Hardy[2] lives near Wakefield, at a very fine place which has been engraved for the Vitruvius Britannicus.[3] I did not dine with him after all. One of his daughters was taken ill;[4] and he was unable to receive us. Maude[5] pressed me to take all my meals with him: but I was particularly desirous to get a few days of solitary study in order to complete an article on history for the Edinburgh Review.[6] So I returned hither, took possession of my old room; and spent eight hours to-day in writing. I think, though I may be flattering myself, that there is more thought and depth in this article than in any thing that I have written. Jeffrey put me on my mettle by telling me that he wished to compare it with the paper on the same subject which Mackintosh[7] is writing for the Library of useful knowledge.

[1] See next letter.
[2] John Hardy (1773–1855: *Boase*), a member of the Northern Circuit, and Recorder of Leeds, 1806–33; M.P. for Bradford, 1832–7; 1841–7. He acquired great wealth through his ownership of the Lowmoor ironworks. An anti-slavery man and president of the Leeds branch of the British and Foreign Bible Society, he was no doubt known to Zachary Macaulay.
[3] The *Law List*, until 1830, gives Hardy's address as simply Bradford. In 1830 he is listed as of Heath, near Wakefield. This is probably Heath House by James Paine, illustrated not in the *Vitruvius Britannicus* but in Paine's *Plans, Elevations and Sections of Noblemen and Gentlemen's Houses*, 1767–83. I owe this information to Major T. L. Ingram. Hardy's son, Lord Cranbrook, says only that after his father married 'he became a provincial barrister, living first at the Bradford Manor House, now gone...and secondly at Woodhouse near Leeds, now a part of it' (A. E. Gathorne-Hardy, *Gathorne Hardy*, I, 12).
[4] 'Mr Hardy was prevented from attending the Court to-day [19 January], by the demise of one of his infant children the preceding night' (Leeds *Mercury*, 26 January).
[5] Francis Maude (1768–1842), of Hatfield Hall, Yorkshire. On the Northern Circuit, a bencher of Gray's Inn, and Recorder of Doncaster, he shared with Hardy the largest practice at the West Riding sessions.
[6] 'History,' *ER*, XLVII (May 1828), 331–67, ostensibly a review of Henry Neele, *The Romance of History: England*, 3 vols., 1828, of which it says not one word. W. H. French and G. D. Sanders, eds., *The Reader's Macaulay*, New York [1936], p. 121, suggest plausibly that the essay has been 'beheaded' out of respect to the memory of Neele, who committed suicide on 7 February 1828, aged thirty.
[7] Sir James Mackintosh (1765–1832: *DNB*), historical writer and the philosopher of the Whig party. Though the two men were entirely unlike, the life of Mackintosh presented many parallels to TBM's, of which TBM seemed later to be uneasily aware: both were Anglicized Scots; both were barristers; both interrupted their careers to take up lucrative appointments in India, obtained through their connections with Whig patrons; both were famous talkers and both noted for speaking essays in their parliamentary oratory; both were ornaments of Holland House; both set their hearts on writing that history of the revolution of 1688 which should answer Hume, and both allowed parliamentary activity to divert them from their object. TBM's sense that he was in some degree looked to as rival and heir to Mackintosh is already evident in this letter. Mackintosh had been commissioned by Brougham to write the *Preliminary Discourse on History* for the 'Library of Useful Knowledge' series of the Society for the Diffusion of Useful Knowledge that began publication in 1827 (see [August ?] 1828). Mackintosh apparently never finished it, though it was still expected as late as May 1828 (T. F. Ellis to Thomas Coates, 28 May 1828: MS, University College).

As to politics, I see all the papers. The reading rooms – all over the riding – are opened with the utmost liberality to barristers. We are also a tolerably well informed circle of ourselves, having a member of parliament,[1] and several highly connected men among us, a son of Lord Harewood's for example.[2] It seems here to be the universal opinion that none but a coalition ministry can stand or can deserve to stand – that the best ministry would be one which should include, as its extreme points, Lord Lansdowne and Mr. Peel; that the Tories and Whigs ought to make considerable sacrifices for the purpose of forming a strong government; that Lord Goderich is a fool, and Mr. Herries[3] a rogue; that if Huskisson[4] and the Whigs stand by each other they may do everything, that if they separate they will be able to do nothing. Wood the Member for Preston [wants][5] to have an Ultra Administration. He [thinks?][5] it would not have a majority at starting in the house of Commons, that an Election would make matters worse, and that the attempt would end in utter discomfiture.

Love to my Mother and all at home.

Ever yours affectionately
T B Macaulay

P S I never supposed that the account in the Newspapers related to our friend H Drummond.[6] The place, the circumstances, the epilepsy, and all the rest of the story seemed to me irreconcileable with what we knew of him. I had heard that H More was unwell – but not that the attack was so serious. Let me hear of her as soon as possible. I shall be at Doncaster on Tuesday night.

---

1 John Wood.

2 Probably William Saunders Sebright Lascelles (1798–1851), third son of Lord Harewood; M.P. for Northallerton, 1820–6; for Wakefield, 1837–47; for Knaresborough, 1847–51. He was a member of the London Debating Society in 1826 with TBM.

3 John Charles Herries (1788–1855: *DNB*), Tory M.P., 1823–41; 1847–53, specializing in matters of finance; financial secretary to the Treasury, 1823–7; appointed Chancellor of the Exchequer under Goderich, but his quarrel with Goderich and Huskisson over appointments led to Goderich's resignation. Herries was accused at the time of having conspired with the Tories to bring about the downfall of the coalition ministry.

4 William Huskisson (1770–1830: *DNB*), M.P. almost continuously, 1796–1830; a Canningite, regarded as the leading financial expert in politics; President of the Board of Trade, 1823–7; Colonial Secretary and leader of the House of Commons under Goderich, he did not stand by the Whigs but continued in office under Wellington until May 1828.

5 Paper torn away with seal.

6 *The Times*, 16 January, reports the death from epilepsy of a young man named Henry Drummond. The family friend was Henry Drummond (1786–1860: *DNB*), a wealthy banker, religious eccentric, politician, and genealogist. Drummond is best-remembered now as one of the founders and officials of the Catholic Apostolic ('Irvingite') Church; he also sat in Parliament as an independent member, 1810–13; 1847–60. Zachary Macaulay had long known him through their common interest in various religious societies.

TO FRANCIS BARLOW,[1] 19 JANUARY 1828

MS: Trinity College.

Leeds January 19th. 1828

Sir,

During the last week I have been attending the Sessions for the West Riding of Yorkshire. I did not therefore receive your letter till this evening.

Have the goodness to assure the Lord Chancellor that I shall always entertain a strong sense of his kindness to me, and that I most cheerfully acquiesce in the propriety of the intimation by which the appointment is accompanied. / I have the honour to be / Sir

Your Obedient and Humble Servant

T B Macaulay.

F. Barlow Esq
etc. etc. etc.

TO ZACHARY MACAULAY, 8 APRIL 1828

MS: Trinity College. *Address:* Z. Macaulay Esq / 16 George Street / Mansion House / London.

Edinburgh April 8. 1828

My dear Father,

Here I am; and just on the point of setting out for Craigcrook.[2] I have improved in health by my journey northward. My cold is pretty well – but I have not yet regained the sense of smelling – no great loss, you will say, unless the streets of the Good Town have very materially changed their old character.

I have taken a walk of two hours through the principal streets: and I do not know that ever in my life I looked about me with more interest. I was not only pleased by the spectacle itself –: but this sudden return after eleven years of absence[3] to a place in which I had formerly stayed long enough to become pretty familiar with it, gave an attraction to every object. It is only by meeting with old acquaintances after long separations

---

[1] Barlow (1799–1887: *Boase*), a barrister, was at this time the Lord Chancellor's Secretary of Bankrupts. Since this letter is among the Lyndhurst papers at Trinity it was evidently sent.

[2] Francis Jeffrey's country house, on the Corstorphine Hill, near Edinburgh. TBM passed up the spring assizes on the Northern Circuit this year, held at Lancaster, 8–22 March, and at York, 22 March–4 April. On 15 March he was in London, where he attended Lord Lyndhurst's levee, and on 17 March he went to Eton to spend two days with Praed (Selina Macaulay, Diary, 17 March 1828).

[3] TBM was in Edinburgh with his parents in the summer of 1817.

that we are able to measure the degree in which our tastes and feelings have changed. While we live in the same places and in the same circles the alteration is as imperceptible as that which, according to the physiologists, is constantly taking place in our bodies. I seem to myself here another being from what I was. Between me and the schoolboy of sixteen who came here in 1817 there is nothing in common – absolutely nothing; except indeed disgust at the hideous thing called Lord Nelson's Monument.[1]

I will not however begin to criticise because I shall never have done. I will only say that what strikes me most in Edinburgh is that it has, what no other Town in the island except London has, the air of a capital city. Manchester, Leeds and Sheffield are merely manufacturing towns. In Liverpool it is impossible for a moment to forget that we are in a sea-port. But about Edinburgh there is no such character. It has been very well said that a professional air is [g]²entlemanly. A perfectly well bred m[an]² will not say or do [any]²thing which marks him out for a lawyer, a doctor, or a sailor. There is the same difference in towns. Cambridge and Oxford can no more be mistaken than a dignified clergyman in a shovel hat who is always talking against the Catholics and the Bible Society. Bristol and Birmingham are like fat sleek traders whose jokes and metaphors are all drawn from their warehouses and counters. Brighton, Cheltenham, and those places, if I may carry on such a fanciful parallel, are mere Bond Street Loungers – utterly idle and empty. But London and Edinburgh resemble real gentlemen – who are highly educated – yet do not carry pedant written in their faces – who have much business to transact and who transact it well, yet whose talk does not smell of the shop – who indulge freely in pleasure and amusement, yet do not make pleasure and amusement a toil instead of a relaxation. For remarks on the details you must wait till you see me in London, where, if every thing goes right, I hope to be in about a fortnight. Love to all.

Yours ever

T B M

TO ZACHARY MACAULAY, 14 APRIL 1828

MS: Trinity College.

Court House Pomfret[3] April 14 / 1828

My dear Father,

I am glad that J Preston[4] does not expect me in London. I think that in any case it would have been inexpedient to go. All the considerations

---

[1] On the Calton Hill; erected 1806–16.   [2] Paper torn away with seal.
[3] The Easter quarter sessions of the West Riding, in Pontefract, were held 14–18 April.
[4] John Preston, Matthew's brother, a London attorney, of 10 Tokenhouse Yard, Lothbury (*Law List*, 1828).

which induce me to sacrifice so large a portion of the advantages of my Commissionership to the chance of hereafter leading on the W[est] R[iding] Sessions would apply, I think, still more strongly to this case.

I shall never end if I once begin writing about my Scotch expedition. Nothing could be more kind than the reception which I met at Craig Crook. I was in Edinburgh every day; and saw the town to as much advantage as if I had been lodged there. I saw Mrs. Grant of Laggan[1] and found her, as Jeffrey foretold, surrounded by a circle of low people, mere flatterers apparently, who administer a daily dram of adulation, as indispensably necessary to her as Mr. Wilberforce's two pills of opium are to him. Her understanding seems to have decayed, and her perception of propriety in conversation to have become rather obtuse. She said some very queer things to me and to others. Jeffrey would not go with me. He laughs at her, I understand; and she abominates him. I found out Gray,[2] not without considerable trouble: for he has lately changed his residence. I did not see him – his person I mean; for in effigy he is to be seen every where. The print shops are full of caricatures in which his long chin and tall lank form are the principal objects. I knocked at his door – and was told by his servant – a most primitive old person – and as strictly veracious as a quaker, – that Mr. Gray could see nobody. "Well," said I; "if he is engaged." "No Sir, not engaged," said this true Puritan; "he is studying." – I left my card, and walked off – hoping that he was not studying the composition of a new pamphlet. – Jeffrey says that the violence of Andrew T[homso]n was unpardonable; but that Gray has unfortunately committed what the world considers as much less excusable than violence – a breach of veracity. He declared it seems that he had nothing whatever to do with the letters which have made so much noise. This declaration was not drawn from him by impertinent questions. Had that been the case, much casuistry might have been employed *pro* and *con.* It was a voluntary affirmation. It now appears that he corrected the proof-

<hr/>

[1] Anne Grant (1755–1838: *DNB*), author of *Letters from the Mountains*, 3 vols., 1807, and *Essays on the Superstitions of the Highlanders of Scotland*, 1811. Scott politely calls her 'the respectable and ingenious Mrs. Grant of Laggan' (*Waverley*, last chapter); TMB's judgment differed: 'Tom called on Mrs. Grant of Laggan while he was in Edinburgh and disliked her extremely; he thought her full of conceit and pretension and also very deficient in propriety in conversation; she said some very impertinent things to him' (Selina Macaulay, Diary, 22 April 1828).

[2] Henry Grey (1778–1859: *DNB*), minister of St Mary's, Edinburgh, took the side of the British and Foreign Bible Society in the controversy over the Apocrypha (see 14 August 1827). To Andrew Thomson's speech attacking Grey and others, 9 July 1827, Grey's wife replied in a series of letters signed 'Anglicanus' appearing in the *Caledonian Mercury* from 12 July and published as a pamphlet in October 1827. Grey edited the letters, but was able to deny Thomson's accusation in the *Christian Instructor* for January 1828, that he had written them. Both men appeared before the Edinburgh Presbytery later in 1828 to answer charges of defamation.

sheets with his own hand. Thomson and a brother of Gray's[1] are bringing actions against each other. Jeffrey has retainers on both sides; and is doing his best, he tells me, to make up matters.

Campbell[2] I could not find. The Edinburgh Directory contained the names of twenty Campbells Writers to the Signet – and I fell in with nobody to give me his direction. Jeffrey had a sort of notion that he lived in a particular street, Heriot Street I think; and I called at a house there which was occupied[3]

.   .   .   .

say about H More; – not that her servants should have pillaged her – but that she should have found them out, and should have mustered spirit to emancipate herself.[4]

Ever yours affectionately

T B M

TO SELINA MILLS MACAULAY, 15 APRIL 1828

MS: Trinity College. *Address:*[5] Mrs. Macaulay. / 50 Gt. Ormond St. / London. *Frank:* Ponte-fract April fifteen 1828. / John Wood. *Partly published:* Trevelyan, I, 146–50.

Court House Pomfret April 15. 1828

My dear Mother,

My father is, I suppose, on his way to Bristol by this time; or at least will be so before this epistle reaches London. I therefore address it to you as the least undeserving of a very undeserving family. You, I think, have sent me one letter since I left London; My sisters none at all. My father has sometimes favoured me with two or three in the day when franks were plentiful.

I have nothing here to do but to write letters, and, what is not very

---

[1] John Grey of Dilston; Thomson was compelled to retract his charge that John Grey had any part in the letters of 'Anglicanus.' Grey published a 'Letter from J. Grey Esq. in Reply to the Calumnies of the Rev. A. Thomson, in His Christian Instructor for January, 1828,' Edinburgh, 1828.

[2] John Campbell of Carbrook, Writer to the Signet, 29 Heriot Row. Campbell was on the committee of the Edinburgh Bible Society and was thus drawn into the Thomson–Grey controversy. He had acted for Zachary Macaulay in 1823 in the case of an estate left by Michael Macmillan, agent of Macaulay and Babington in Sierra Leone.

[3] The last sheet of the letter is missing; TBM's conclusion is written at the top of the first page.

[4] The friends of the aged Hannah More had persuaded her to leave Barley Wood, where her servants were defrauding her, and to remove to Clifton: 'both Mr. and Mrs. Macaulay came to assist in the arrangements, and to see her settled in her new abode' (Knutsford, *Zachary Macaulay*, p. 449).

[5] TBM has written the address on the back of the cover; it was then copied on the front cover by John Wood, under whose frank the letter was sent.

often the case, I have members of parliament in abundance to frank them, and abundance of matter to fill them with. My Edinburgh expedition has given me so much to say that, unless I write off some of it before I come home, I shall talk you all to death, and be voted a bore in every house which I visit. Oh for the indefatigable pens of Richardson's heroes and heroines! – Oh for the accurate memory of Belford and Miss Byron![1] Then would I relate word for word all my dialogue with Mr. Macculloch[2] about the poor laws, and my dispute with Macvey Napier[3] about Porson,[4] and the talk in which Jeffrey and I lingered every night till between two and three. Which will you have? Or shall I begin as Richardson's heroine does, by full length characters of every body – and describe my companions as she describes Miss Allestree and Miss Cantillon.[5] Well then. I will commence with Jeffrey himself. I had almost forgotten his person: and indeed I should not wonder if even now I were to forget it again. He has twenty faces almost as unlike to each other as my father's to Mr. Wilberforce's, and infinitely more unlike to each other than those of near relatives often are, infinitely more unlike for example than those of the two Grants[6] or of Matthew and John Preston. When absolutely quiescent, reading a paper for example, or hearing a conversation in which he takes no interest, he looks very much like my old master Preston, – with rather more colour to be sure, and not quite so grey. There is no indication whatever of intellectual superiority of any kind. But as soon as he is interested, and opens his eyes upon you, the change is like magic. There is a flash in his glance, a violent contortion in his frown, an exquisite humour in his sneer, and a sweetness and brilliancy in his smile beyond any thing that

---

[1] Jack Belford and Harriet Byron are the hero's confidant and the heroine of *Clarissa* and *Sir Charles Grandison*, respectively.

[2] John Ramsay McCulloch (1789–1864: *DNB*), political economist; published *Principles of Political Economy*, Edinburgh, 1825; Professor of Political Economy, London University, 1828–32; wrote for the Society for the Diffusion of Useful Knowledge and contributed seventy-nine articles on his subject to the *ER*, 1818–37.

[3] Napier (1776–1847: *DNB*), soon to be editor of the *ER*, was librarian to the Writers to the Signet, 1805–37; editor of the Supplement to the *Encyclopaedia Britannica*, 1814–24; Lecturer on, and subsequently Professor of, conveyancing, University of Edinburgh, 1816–47; editor of the seventh edition, *Encyclopaedia Britannica*, 1824–42; succeeded Jeffrey as editor of the *ER*, 1829; Clerk of the Court of Session, 1837–47. Napier's remarkable diligence is evident from his having kept up simultaneously for the last ten years of his life his professorship, his clerkship, and the editorship of both the *ER* and the *Encyclopaedia Britannica*. Cockburn says that Napier 'was not generally popular. This was entirely owing to a hard air and manner, and a foolish notion of his own importance. For in reality he was an excellent man, with a warm, true heart, and a taste for kindness' (*Journal*, 1874, II, 168: 14 February 1847).

[4] Richard Porson (1759–1808: *DNB*), second, after Bentley, among Trinity College's classical scholars.

[5] Harriet Byron's first description of Miss Allestree appears in Letter 5; of Miss Cantillon, in Letter 10, *Sir Charles Grandison*.

[6] Robert and Charles Grant: see 3 August 1827 and 23 June 1832.

ever I saw. A person who had seen him in only one state would not know him if he saw him in another. For he has not, like Brougham, marked features which in all moods of mind remain unaltered. The mere outline of his face is insignificant – much like that of the Prestons, as I said before. The expression is every thing; and such power and variety of expression I never saw in any human countenance, not even in that of the most celebrated actors. I can conceive that Garrick may have been like him. I have seen several pictures of Garrick – none resembling another; and I have heard Hannah More speak of the extraordinary variety of countenance by which he was distinguished, and of the unequalled radiance and penetration of his eye.[1] The voice and delivery of Jeffrey resemble his face. He possesses considerable power of mimicry; and rarely tells a story without imitating several different accents. His familiar tone, his declamatory tone, and his pathetic tone are quite different things. Sometimes Scotch predominates in his pronunciation, sometimes it is imperceptible. Sometimes his utterance is snappish and quick to the last degree – sometimes it is remarkable for rotundity and mellowness. I can easily conceive that two people who had seen him on different days might dispute about him as the travellers in the fa[ble][2] disputed about the cameleon; and both, if they were to see him again, would probably find themselves equally deceived.

In one thing, as far as I observed, he is always the same; and that is the warmth of his domestic affections. Neither Mr. Wilberforce nor my uncle Babington, come up to him in this respect. The flow of his kindness is quite inexhaustible. Not five minutes pass without some fond expression or caressing gesture to his wife or his daughter. He has fitted up a study for himself: but he never goes into it. Law-papers, reviews, whatever he has to write, he writes in the drawing-room or in his wife's boudoir. When he goes to other parts of the country on a retainer he takes them in the carriage with him. I do not wonder that he should be a good husband: for his wife, bating her unfortunate nervous malady, which by the bye is by no means so bad as it was, is a very amiable woman. But I was surprised to see a man so keen and sarcastic, so much of a scoffer, pouring himself out with such simplicity and tenderness in all sorts of affectionate nonsense. Through our whole journey to Perth he kept up a sort of mock quarrel, like mine with Hannah and Margaret; attacked his daughter about novel-reading, laughed her into a pet, kissed her out of it, and laughed her into it again. She and her mother absolutely idolise him: and I do not wonder at it.

His conversation is very much like his countenance and his voice – of immense variety, sometimes plain and unpretending even to flatness,

---

[1] Hannah More lived in close friendship with David Garrick and his wife after her introduction to them in 1774.   [2] Paper torn away with seal.

sometimes whimsically brilliant and rhetorical almost beyond the license of private discourse. He has many very interesting anecdotes, and tells them very well. He is a very shrewd observer; and so fastidious that I am not surprised at the awe in which many people seem to stand when in his company. Though not altogether free from affectation himself – as indeed nobody seems to be when very closely watched, he has a peculiar loathing for it in other people, and a great talent for discovering and exposing it. He has a particular contempt, in which I most heartily concur with him, for the *fadaises* of bluestocking literature, for the mutual flatteries of coteries, the handing about of vers de societé, the albums, the conversaziones, and all the other nauseous trickeries of the Sewards, Hayleys, and Sothebys.[1] Such people as Professor Smyth, Chancy Townsend, and my poor old hostess Lydia White,[2] are objects of his especial aversion. I am not quite sure that he has escaped the opposite extreme, and that he is not a little too desirous to appear rather a man of the world, an active lawyer, or an easy careless gentleman, than a distinguished writer. Congreve, you probably know, was devoured by this affectation. He could not bear the least allusion to his plays: and liked to be considered as an independant man of fashion who had never dirtied his fingers with ink. When Voltaire called on him and complimented him on the excellence of his comedies he said, with some pettishness, that he wished to be treated merely as a gentleman like his neighbours. Voltaire told him that if he had been merely a gentleman like his neighbours, he would not have been troubled with the visits of a literary foreigner.[3]

I rather suspect myself of unfairness, I must own, in this critique. For when Jeffrey and I were by ourselves, he talked much and very well on literary topics. His kindness and hospitality to me were, indeed, beyond description: and his wife was as pleasant and friendly as possible. I liked everything but the hours. We were never up till ten and never retired till two hours at least after midnight. Jeffrey indeed never goes to bed till sleep comes on him overpoweringly, and never rises till forced up by business or hunger. He is extremely well in health, so well that I could not help suspecting him of being very hypochondriac: for all his late letters to me

---

[1] Anna Seward (1747–1809: *DNB*), the 'Swan of Lichfield'; friend of William Hayley (1745–1820: *DNB*), minor poet, biographer of Cowper and patron of Blake. William Sotheby (1757–1833: *DNB*), minor poet, translator, and host in London literary society.

[2] Lydia White (d. 1827), a literary hostess in London for many years. Selina Macaulay, Diary, 10 May 1826, notes that Miss White, 'a celebrated bas bleu has expressed to Mr. Geo. Phillips a great desire to see Tom,' and on 17 May that 'Mr. Phillips is to take Tom to dine there...Thursday week.' When TBM met her she had long been in bad health but continued to entertain frequently. Sir Walter Scott, calling on her on 13 November 1826, 'found her extended on a couch, frightfully swelled, unable to stir, rouged, jesting, and dying' ([David Douglas], ed., *The Journal of Sir Walter Scott*, Edinburgh, 1891, 1, 305).

[3] *Lettres Philosophiques*, 1734, Lettre 19: TBM tells this anecdote in 'Comic Dramatists of the Restoration,' *ER*, LXXII (January 1841), 526.

have been filled with lamentations about his various maladies. His wife told me when I congratulated her on his recovery that I must not absolutely rely on all his accounts of his own diseases. I really think that he is, on the whole, the youngest looking man of fifty[1] that I know, at least when he is animated.

I have little more at present to tell you about him. Small traits of his conversation will come out, one by one, as I talk over this visit with you. I will only add that his table is very elegant, his wine remarkably choice and old, and his whiskey so good that I drank a glass of it every day. One circumstance struck me as odd; though in Scotland I suppose it is common. While I was with him he had two large parties, of rather high people. The dinners were even splendid, the wines of the best sort and of the best quality, champagne, hock, Constantia. But there was no dessert whatever – not so much as an orange or a spunge-cake.

His house in Edinburgh is most magnificent. He has just taken it; and several rooms are still unfurnished. It is in Moray place – the newest pile of buildings in the town; looking out to the Forth on one side and to a green garden on the other. It is really equal to the houses in Grosvenor Square – superior to any in Portman Square that I have seen. There is a very fine dining room, three large drawing rooms and a library; and all this not mere fillagree work like the new habitations which are run up at Brighton or in the Regent's Park, but of massive stone – the masonry and the wood-work of extraordinary stability. When I told Jeffrey of the condition into which the occupants of the new houses about Russell Square are compelled to enter, that they will have no dancing on the upper floor, he laughed and said that if the Elephant who danced at Covent Garden-Theatre[2] could be got up to caper in his drawing room he should have no objection. I understand however that the furniture of these fine houses is by no means suited to the spaciousness and elegance of the rooms. The fact is that instead of wondering at the extent of the town-houses of the Scotch gentry, we ought rather to wonder at the smallness of those in which the aristocracy of London box themselves up. An Italian noble with an annual income of perhaps 800 or 1000 pounds sterling a year lives in a palace as large as Northumberland House.[3] A writer in India, I understand, has four or five rooms fifty feet long each. The materials for building are cheap. Very little furniture is wanted, and the principal article of expense is the mere skeleton of the house itself. In London the case is quite different. A nobleman like Lord Fitzwilliam or Lord Carlisle who in the

[1] Jeffrey was born in 1773.
[2] The elephant called Chunee, exhibited in London for many years until its death in 1826, was introduced into the pantomime at Covent Garden in 1811: [John Genest], *Some Account of the English Stage*, Bath, 1832, VIII, 287.
[3] On the southeast side of Trafalgar Square, where it stood until 1874.

country has a mansion six-hundred feet in length,[1] when he comes to London, shuts himself up in a house three or four windows wide, – in a house which he might put into one of the pavilions of his seat.

Fine as these new buildings are in some respects, I decidedly prefer the High Street in the Old Town. There is nothing like it in the island. The ancient parts of London were consumed by the great fire; and, even if that fire had never happened, would probably have perished of themselves. They were of wood or, at best, of brick. There is such a profusion of the best stone about Edinburgh that from the earliest times all the streets have been built of that material in a very solid manner; they therefore remain such as they were centuries ago. Conceive walking between huge masses of dark smoky stone, eight or nine windows high, down the ridge of a hill, with the Castle on its summit, and the venerable, though irregular palace of Holyrood at its foot. You have been there. But you have not seen the town – and no lady ever sees a town. It is only by walking on foot through all sorts of crowded streets at all hours that a town can be really studied to good purpose.

There is a new pillar to the memory of Lord Melville[2] – very elegant and much better than the man deserved. His statue is at the top with a wreath on the head very like a nightcap drawn over the eyes. It is impossible to look on it without being reminded of the fate which the original most richly deserved. There is an imitation of the Temple at Pæstum[3] fitted up for an exhibition of pictures. The pictures are poor – not much worse than those at Somerset House to be sure. The building is handsome, though very ill placed. The observatory[4] I think detestable. These are the most remarkable public edifices which have been erected at Edinburgh since we were there last. But there are several handsome streets and squares. Moray Place is well built but its shape is strangely irregular. Sir Walter Scott calls it a circle in hysterics.

But my letter will overflow even the ample limits of a frank, if I do not conclude. I hope that you will be properly penitent for neglecting such a correspondent when you receive so long a dispatch written amidst the bellowing of justices, lawyers, criers, witnesses, prisoners, prisoners' wives and mothers, and spectators. If you write after the receipt of this, direct to Leeds. I shall be there, probably on Saturday, at the latest on Monday.[5] Love to my Father, if he is at home – to my sisters – and to yourself.

Ever yours affectionately
T B M.

---

[1] I.e., Wentworth Woodhouse and Castle Howard.
[2] His monument in St Andrew's Square was completed in 1827.
[3] The building of the Royal Scottish Institution, begun in 1823.
[4] Built 1818, on the Calton Hill.
[5] TBM probably meant to attend the Leeds Borough sessions, 21–2 April, but changed his plans; he was in London on Sunday, 20 April (Selina Macaulay, Diary, 22 April 1828).

TO LEONARD HORNER,[1] [MAY? 1828]

MS: University College, London. *Address:* L Horner Esq / Percy Street.

[London] Monday Evening.
Dear Sir,
   I have scrawled a few lines which will give you a notion of the course which I think advisable.[2] The greater part of the paper[3] which I send you is transcribed from Long's. I have attempted to frame it in such a manner as to give a general idea of his plan, and to evade, at the same time, all the matters on which there is likely to be any difference of opinion.
   But the more I think on the subject the more fully convinced I am that Homer is the book with which the lectures ought to begin.

Yours very truly
T B Macaulay

[Enclosure]

   I think that Long should begin with Homer on every principle. If he wishes to follow the course of Greek history, Homer is the earliest of Greek historians as well as of Greek poets. If he wishes to teach his pupils to trace the progress of the language it is in the Iliad and Odyssey that the

---

[1] Horner (1785–1864: *DNB*), brother of the Edinburgh Reviewer and Whig politician Francis Horner, was the first Warden of the London University, which held its opening classes in October 1828. Horner very soon quarrelled with his faculty and resigned in 1831. The London University (now University College), organized in 1826, was an enterprise in which reformers, dissenters, Evangelicals, and Whigs of all descriptions cooperated. The poet Thomas Campbell, Brougham, and Isaac Goldsmid were most prominent in its founding; Zachary Macaulay was on its first council, with such men as Grote, Joseph Hume, Lansdowne, Mackintosh, and James Mill. TBM's 'The London University,' *ER*, XLIII (February 1826), 315–41, was written in defense of the plan for the University against the hostility of Churchmen and Tories.

[2] TBM's letter is part of a bundle including the prospectus, dated from the University of Virginia, 31 March [1828], of the course in 'Greek Language, Literature, and Antiquities' which George Long (see 6 March 1821) proposed to give as Professor of Greek at the London University. In a course of readings and lectures lasting two years, Long intended to begin with the first four books of Herodotus and to pass through Thucydides, Xenophon, Aristotle's *Politics*, the Attic orators, Arrian, Aeschylus, Sophocles, and Aristophanes. The Homeric poems, he thought, should wait till the end of the second year: 'the student will then be better prepared to examine the language and the structure of these antient poems.' Horner submitted Long's prospectus to several judges; with the bundle of MSS including TBM's letter is one from B. H. Malkin to Horner, 21 May 1828, commenting on the plan and promising that 'you will hear from Ellis with respect to the subdivision of it.' On 5 November 1828 Selina Macaulay records in her Diary that 'Mr. Long the Greek professor gave his introductory lecture in the afternoon. Papa and Tom were there and were much pleased.'

[3] This, evidently something other than the remarks accompanying TBM's note, has not been found.

language has its fountains. It is true, as he says, that the student will be better able to understand Homer after two years of Greek reading than before. But this is the case with every other book. Something must be first; and must be read under those disadvantages to which a beginner is necessarily subject.

Long proposes to read those parts of the first four books of Herodotus which relate to Greek history; and to give a cursory glance to the last five. Now I should just have reversed the scheme. The first four books are neither very interesting nor much to be depended on. The last five contain the best written history that ever existed of the most important war that the world ever saw. Besides the history of Thucydides joins on so close to that of Herodotus that the student ought immediately to pass from the end of one to the beginning of the other.

I think you have noticed every thing else that occurs to me. Some of Plato ought undoubtedly to be read – some of Theocritus – perhaps a little of Pindar. His odes are very curious in a historical point of view. They illustrate the more romantic parts of Herodotus better than any thing else in the language.

T B Macaulay

TO ZACHARY MACAULAY, 24 JULY 1828

Text: From MS in possession of Mr C. S. Menell, who furnished transcript. *Address:* Z. Macaulay Esq. / 16 George Street / Mansion House / London. *Frank:* York. July twenty four 1828. / John Wood. *Mostly published:* Knutsford, *Zachary Macaulay,* p. 449.

York[1] / July 24, 1828.

My dear Father,

I have nothing or next to nothing to tell you. We have no causes here of any interest. Brougham seems to be much better.[2] On Monday I dine

---

[1] TBM left for the circuit *via* Rothley Temple, 9 July (Selina Macaulay, Diary, 11 July); he first attended the midsummer quarter sessions at Skipton, 15 July, and Bradford, 17 July. The sessions were then interrupted by the York assizes, 19 July–2 August. These were followed by the Leeds borough sessions, 4–5 August, and by the resumed West Riding sessions, Rotherham, 6–7 August. TBM then went to Rothley Temple until the opening of the Lancaster assizes, held 20–30 August.

[2] Brougham had been ill in some unspecified way through much of 1828; Zachary Macaulay and Buxton were also in bad health then, so that the three leaders of the abolitionists were unable to act as usual. Zachary Macaulay wrote to Brougham, 16 July 1828, saying that his greatest prayer was that God 'may restore to you your capacity of usefulness and strength for the various services to mankind which seem almost to hang on your influence and exertion' (Chester New, *Life of Henry Brougham to 1830,* Oxford, 1961, p. 304). The Leeds *Intelligencer* (Tory, and hostile to Brougham) reported, 24 July, that Brougham, 'notwithstanding the ominous paragraphs which have appeared in the Times...as to the state of the Learned Gentleman's health...looked not the least worse since last assizes.'

with Sydney Smith and take a bed at Foston. I am getting on rapidly and on the whole satisfactorily with Hallam.[1]

I think the Duke of Wellington's speech[2] as bad as possible. But as a general matter of policy I would never have any discussion in the Lords except in case of necessity. The strength of the abolitionists lies in the Commons, and the ministers there are more inclined to be civil and conceding.

By the bye I met the other day with a curious trial in the French Causes Celebres. A negro – this was before the Somerset cause in England[3] – maintained before the parliament of Paris that his master had no right to his service in France – and the Court decided in favour of his liberty.

Send the enclosed, if you please, to your secretary Pringle.[4] He has written to ask me for some poetry towards a volume which he is editing. I would gladly be of use to him, but I have so much to do at present that I have sent him a civil refusal. Let me hear of George and Sarah Anne[5] – of Margaret's movements – for I know nothing of them – and of the circumstances and probable consequences of old Parker's death[6] of which I have just heard from the Temple.

Love to all.

Ever yours affectionately,

T B Macaulay

[1] 'Hallam's Constitutional History,' *ER*, xlviii (September 1828), 96–169. A review of *The Constitutional History of England, from the Accession of Henry VII. to the Death of George II.*, 2 vols., 1827, by Henry Hallam (1777–1859: *DNB*), the Whig historian. When the Macaulay family attended the inaugural classes of the London University, 'Mr. Hallam who was also there expressed himself to Papa as much gratified by the manner in which Tom has spoken of his work in his last article; Papa afterwards introduced Tom to him' (Selina Macaulay, Diary, 5 November 1828).

[2] Wellington had said in the House of Lords, 23 June, that 'it was more wonderful to behold the progress already made, than to express any strong censure for what remained to be done' towards the abolition of slavery in the West Indies (*Hansard*, New Series, xix, 1465–7).

[3] In 1772: see [29 April 1814].

[4] Thomas Pringle (1789–1834: *DNB*), secretary of the Anti-Slavery Society since 1827. Pringle had spent six years in South Africa; an article by him on the slave trade there brought him to Zachary Macaulay's notice and led to his appointment with the Anti-Slavery Society. He edited the literary annual *Friendship's Offering* from its first issue, 1826, until his death. TBM's 'The Armada' appeared in *Friendship's Offering*, 1833.

[5] Wife of George Babington.

[6] Charles Stewart Parker, a Glasgow merchant in the West India trade. His son James (see 11 March 1830) had been engaged to Mary Babington since 1825, but the elder Parker, who owned slaves, was opposed to any connection with the Saints, and the Babingtons were scandalized by the guilt of Parker, so that the marriage was obstructed from both sides; it took place in June 1829 (Sketch of the Life of Sir James Parker: typescript, Mrs Lancelot Errington).

TO ZACHARY MACAULAY, 31 JULY 1828

MS: Trinity College.

York July 31. 1828

My dear Father,

I passed a very pleasant day at Sydney Smith's. He has called on me since here. And this morning I met him in the reading room and took a drive in his gig to Bishops Thorpe – the Archbishop's Palace. I liked him even better than before. To be sure his conversational talents are prodigious. He is the only man of much celebrity who bears a very close inspection without suffering by it. Brougham, when you come to know him, is superficial and uncertain. Jeffrey is as pleasant as man can be. But his talk has no very eminent intellectual power. Sydney Smith is inexhaustible. He pours out for an hour together without intermission good things on which any other professed wit would live for a fortnight. And his humour, even when most wild and whimsical, is always bottomed on a strong foundation of good sense. He is a most hearty friend to the abolition – a regular speaker at the York society. He introduced me to Tuke[1] the Quaker with whom I had some talk about the compulsory manumission clause.[2] Sydney, who no doubt has heard much on the subject from his son in law,[3] took both sides of the question and argued both very well.

By the bye Hibbert tells me that he thinks the Duke's speech a very foolish and improper one – and that he has completely overshot the mark. But Hibbert who is very independent in his views probably does not speak the sentiments of his family. However on the whole I think the West Indians gained less in the Lords than they lost in the Commons.[4]

[1] Samuel Hack Tuke (1784–1857: *DNB*), tea and coffee merchant of York. Tuke had made a special study of mental diseases and the reform of their treatment. His book on the Quaker insane asylum at York, *Description of the Retreat*, York, 1813, had been favorably reviewed by Sydney Smith in the *ER*. Tuke was active in the York branch of the Anti-Slavery Society.

[2] An Order in Council for the crown colony of Trinidad, 16 March 1824, provided that if a slave wished to buy his freedom or that of other slaves the owner must allow the sale. This ordinance was meant to be a model for both chartered and crown colonies in the West Indies, but was so fiercely opposed there that the government never succeeded in enforcing it.

[3] Nathaniel Hibbert (1794–1865), married Sydney Smith's younger daughter Emily in January, 1828. Hibbert was on the Northern Circuit with TBM. He was the son of George Hibbert, a West India merchant and a prominent defender of the West Indian interest.

[4] In response to Wellington's speech (see 24 July 1828) Sir James Mackintosh stated in the House of Commons, 25 July, that unless the government acted the abolitionists would propose measures of their own in the next session of Parliament (*Hansard*, New Series, XIX, 1779). Sir George Murray, the Colonial Secretary, replied that the government meant to maintain the principle embodied in the resolutions passed by the Commons in 1823 for the mitigation and gradual abolition of slavery. The successful resistance of the West Indian legislatures to such measures as the compulsory manumission clause, and Wellington's remarks on 23 June, had made the abolitionists fear that the government would make no

I shall leave York, I think, on Saturday night – on Monday Morning very early at the latest for the Sessions at Leeds. On Tuesday I shall go from Leeds to Rotherham and on the Friday or Saturday from Rotherham to Rothley Temple. I will if possible contrive to escort Margaret home. Why do not My Mother and sisters write me a line now and then. I will not quarrel with Selina on account of her head, or with my mother on account of her eyes. But the chits have no excuse. Love to them all notwithstanding.

Ever yours very affectionately
T B Macaulay.

TO ZACHARY MACAULAY, 7 AUGUST 1828

MS: Trinity College. *Address:*[1] Z: Macauley, Esqre. / 16: George Street / Mansion House / London. *Frank:* Rotherham August Seven 1828. / John Wood.

Rotherham August 7. 1828

My dear Father,

I am deeply – most deeply concerned for Empson.[2] I am here surrounded by friends of his – all of whom are very anxious for him. Wrightson[3] – the chairman of our Sessions when Lord Wharncliffe[4] is away, – has heard from him. His report is a little, and but a little more

strong effort towards abolition. The 'gradualism' of the 1823 resolutions was the real issue between the ministry and the abolitionists; the latter finally succeeded in persuading the country that immediate and total abolition was the only realistic policy, though even the Act of 1833 stopped short of that.

[1] TBM has written the address on the back of the cover; it was then copied on the front cover by John Wood, under whose frank the letter was sent.

[2] William Empson (1791–1852: *DNB*), one of TBM's closest friends in the years between TBM's leaving the university and his going to India. Empson, a graduate of Trinity College and a barrister, succeeded Mackintosh in the professorship of 'general polity and the laws of England' at the East India College, Haileybury, 1824, where he remained until his death. In 1838 he married Lord Jeffrey's daughter, Charlotte; he was editor of the *ER*, 1847–52. TBM's correspondence with Empson, apart from a few fragments, has not survived. There is no record of when their acquaintance began, but Empson was, with TBM, on the original committee of the Anti-Slavery Society in 1823, and was secretary to the African Institution in 1827. He had been a contributor to the *ER* from at least as early as 1825, and he acted as an unofficial agent in London for the editor, Macvey Napier, suggesting topics, reporting on contributors, and gathering opinion for Napier's service. Empson's health seems never to have been strong: Selina Macaulay's Diary, 17 May 1826, notes that Empson is going to Italy for his health; and in the 1830s and later he spent long periods at Wiesbaden on the advice of his physicians.

[3] William Battie Wrightson (1789–1879: *Boase*), of Cusworth, near Rotherham; M.P., East Retford, 1826–30; Hull, 1830–2; Northallerton, 1835–65.

[4] James Stuart-Wortley-Mackenzie (1776–1845: *DNB*), first Baron Wharncliffe; a moderate Tory, Wharncliffe mediated between the parties in the Lords during the Reform Bill crisis. He held office in Peel's first and second administrations. 'He had made a special study of criminal jurisprudence, and as a chairman of quarter sessions is said to have been unequalled' (*DNB*). He presided over these midsummer sessions at Rotherham.

favourable than yours. The malady, as far as I can learn, has certainly not affected the lungs.

What are Margaret's movements. If she goes to York, which it is a pity she should not do, having so good an opportunity, I shall scarcely be able to escort her back – I must be in London according to agreement with my brother Commissioners by the beginning of September[1] – so that I shall have to leave Lancaster about a week after I reach it. To morrow I set off for the Temple.

You are too hard on Sydney Smith. His sermons are to be sure wretched things – but they are wretched as Brougham's hydrostatics[2] are wretched – or as the Duke of Wellington's speculations on slavery are wretched – not from want of mental power, but from ignorance of theology – both in its general principles as a science – and in its application to particular cases. The taste is also very false – and this extends to all that he writes. But on every question of policy or jurisprudence, it is astonishing how just and precise his notions are, how quickly he disentangles a question – how fully and fairly he hits a sophism. My opinion about his powers for such investigations is by no means singular – at least among those who know him. I have heard Jeffrey say the same in even stronger words. And his son in law Hibbert – who talks of him freely, and who is rather a cynical observer, admires his reasoning powers even more than his humour.

I have had a letter from my mother – and another from Hannah – for both which I am properly grateful. Love to all.

Ever yours very affectionately

T B Macaulay.

[1] The account of 'Public and Private Meetings before Commissioners of Bankrupts' (*Parliamentary Papers*, 1830, XXIX, 65) shows nine meetings on 5 September 1828 before the first list of commissioners, which included TBM. There are no further meetings of this group until 31 October.

[2] *Hydrostatics*, 1827, in the 'Natural Philosophy' series of the Society for the Diffusion of Useful Knowledge. Sir Frederick Pollock recalled that T. F. Ellis induced him to exchange a copy of the first edition for a revised one because Brougham had made 'the strange mistake of confusing the weight and pressure of water, confirmed by a diagram, in explaining the hydrostatic paradox. . . . It was speedily discovered and set right, and Ellis, as a member of the Committee of the Society for the Promotion [*sic*] of Useful Knowledge, was bound to do all he could to suppress and withdraw the number containing this absurd blunder' (*Personal Remembrances*, I, 101–2). In Peacock's *Crotchet Castle*, ch. 2, the cook is reading Brougham's *Hydrostatics*.

TO HENRY MACAULAY, 21 AUGUST 1828

MS: University of Texas. *Address:*[1] H: Macauley Esqre. / Messrs: Cropper Benson and Co. / Liverpool. *Frank:* Lancaster August twenty one / 1828. / John Wood.

Lancaster Augt. 21. 1828

Dear Hal,

I got a letter from Meg this morning dated three weeks back. I do not know where she is – whether at Liverpool – at Sedgewick[2] or in London. You doubtless know. Forward the enclosed to her as soon as possible.

I wish to know whether I can be of any use to her. If her plans are formed and you are acquainted with them let me know them – and I will, if possible, arrange mine so as to meet them. It depends partly on her movements and partly on business here whether I shall be able to see you at Liverpool. You may be sure that I shall come if possible.

Yours very truly and affectionately

T B M

TO HENRY MACAULAY, 26 AUGUST [1828]

MS: University of Texas.

My dear Hal,

A line to say that it will be out of my power, as I shall be of no use to Meg, to see you at Liverpool. I am glad that she has so pleasant a jaunt and you the hope of a holiday.

Yours most affectionately

T B M

Lancaster Augt 26.

---

[1] TBM has written the address on the back of the cover; it was then copied on the front cover by John Wood, under whose frank the letter was sent.

[2] Sedgewick House, near Kendal, was the home of the Wakefield family. The sons of James Cropper, Edward and John, married two Wakefield sisters, Isabella and Anne. Margaret Macaulay had spent this summer in a long visit to the home of the Cropper family at Dingle Bank, Liverpool, varied by trips in the company of the Croppers to Rothley Temple (Margaret to Selina Mills Macaulay, 5 June 1828: MS, Huntington) and to the Lake District, where she stayed with the Wakefields (Selina Macaulay, Diary, 17 June 1828). By 1 August Margaret was back in London (Margaret to Frances Macaulay, 1 August 1828: MS, Huntington).

TO THOMAS FLOWER ELLIS, [AUGUST? 1828][1]

Text: Extract in Ellis to Henry Brougham, 14 September 1828: MS, University College, London.

Malden has written to me to say that he likes the scheme,[2] and that, if he can be secure not to be hurried in the execution, he will begin forthwith. But his time is much occupied, and his habits of research and slow labour in composition will require consideration. As soon as I hear from you I will answer him. I will set to work as soon as I get to London.[3]

TO THOMAS FLOWER ELLIS, [SEPTEMBER? 1828?]

MS: Trinity College.

[London]

My dear Ellis,

I am forced to go to Basinghall Street[4] early this morning and I therefore shall not have time to go attentively through your article.[5] This is of less consequence as I read it at York. I have looked over the parts which you mentioned yesterday; and I observe nothing which requires alteration.

I leave Malkin's pamphlet[6] with you. It has considerable merit. But I confess that I see some objections to it more serious than any errors as to

---

[1] Since TBM expected to be in London at the beginning of September (see 7 August) this was presumably written in late August.

[2] A proposal that Malden write a history of Rome for the Society for the Diffusion of Useful Knowledge. The work was published in five parts, 1830–2 as *History of Rome* in the 'Library of Useful Knowledge' of the SDUK. Both TBM and Dr Thomas Arnold read and corrected the MS of part one of the *History* (Minutes of Publication Committee, SDUK, 17 June 1830: MS, University College). The work was apparently first offered to TBM, for James Mill writes to the secretary of the Society, [5 July 1827], of the proposed Roman history, that 'I understood it was engaged for by Mr T. Macaulay' (MS, University College).

[3] See Appendix.

[4] The Commissioners of Bankrupts met in an office on the west side of Basinghall Street, 'at the back of the Law Courts, in Guildhall-yard....The court is a plain useful building, erected in 1820' (James Elmes, *A Topographical Dictionary of London*, 1831).

[5] Not identified, though it may just possibly be the first part of Ellis's *Outline of General History* in the 'Library of Useful Knowledge' of the SDUK, published in 1828. A second part appeared in 1830, but the work, designed to accompany the various histories published by the Society, was never finished. Part 1 is dated 31 May 1828, but Ellis was still correcting proofs for this on 28 May (Ellis to Thomas Coates: MS, University College).

[6] Frederick Malkin, *History of Greece*, Society for the Diffusion of Useful Knowledge, 1829. Ellis was revising this in September 1828 (Ellis to Thomas Coates, 23 September: MS, University College). Malkin (1800?–30), younger brother of Benjamin Heath Malkin, was at Trinity with TBM, where he was elected Scholar, 1821; B.A., Senior Classic and Chancellor's Medallist, 1824; Fellow, 1825. He died at Cambridge, May 1830.

particular facts, and far less likely to be removed. There is, I think, a general obscurity and confusion about it – not perplexing to myself of course or to any body acquainted with the subject, – but likely to repel and puzzle a mere English reader. The absence of all dates whatever in the earlier part of it increases the perplexity. You have yourself noticed, I see in the margin, that Troy, Polemarch, and I think one or two other names and offices are spoken of without any previous explanation or definition, as if the reader were familiar with them: – I think something of the same fault runs through the whole narration.

As to the rest, the faults of detail are comparatively trivial. I do not think that the nature or extent of the authority exercised by the Argian Kings is justly estimated. But this is merely a difference of opinion: and Malkin is as likely to be in the right as I am. I think that far – very far too little is said of the manners of the Homeric age – for which we have such excellent authority – and too much on the other hand about the hair-breadth escapes of Aristomenes – stories for which there is really no authority at all – and fit only for the travels of Sinbad the Sailor.[1]

I may very likely be fastidious: but do you just read over the first 20 pages placing yourself as far as you can in the situation of a mere English reader – who knows no more of the subject than he has picked up from Goldsmith[2] – and consider whether you should carry away any clear notion of early Grecian history from this account. Do not tell Malkin all this – but if you concur in my objections, tell him as much of it as you think will be useful. The work is certainly so good that I should be very glad to see it better. A few slight criticisms have occurred to me on style etc. but I have not time to mention them.

Yours truly
T B M

TO ZACHARY MACAULAY, 20 OCTOBER 1828

MS: Trinity College. *Address:* Z Macaulay Esq / 16 George Street / Mansion House / London.

Wakefield Octr. 20. 1828

My dear Father,

Your letter followed me hither where I am spending the interval between the Leeds and Sheffield Sessions.[3] Maude had no bed for me; but has overpowered me with his hospitality, in other respects. I dined with him

[1] See Malkin, *History of Greece*, pp. 3, 9, 16–18.
[2] *Grecian History*, 2 vols., 1774.
[3] TBM left for the Michaelmas sessions on 7 October (Selina Macaulay, Diary, 7 October); they were held at Knaresborough, 14 October; Leeds, 16–18 October; Sheffield, 22–4 October.

yesterday. To day I dine with Hardy. To morrow I breakfast with Maude and proceed with him to Sheffield, stopping to dine at Wentworth.[1] I may possibly be in London on Friday. But you must not absolutely count on my coming before Saturday.[2] I think that you had better not write to Sheffield.

I like the Reporter[3] much. *Ad homines* it is unanswerable. But I think it tells more against the Conversion Society than against the W[est] I[ndian] system. That men should be compelled to work at all for the benefit of others is an evil. But it is an evil which will not appear to many persons to be much aggravated by their being compelled to work on Sunday as well as on other days; and that for this reason, that what the Slaves do by compulsion three fourths of the Xtn world do by choice – and that it is not considered in any part of Europe, Catholic or Protestant, this country and the U S alone excepted, as either matter of hardship or matter of scruple – I suspect that the Sunday is more a day of rest – more a day of religious instruction among the slaves on many West Indian estates than among the freemen of France, Italy, Spain, Portugal, or indeed even Germany. It cannot, by all accounts, be less so. I think that in a system abounding with evils to which no European state furnishes any thing similar it is rather imprudent to dwell much on a practice which, – however censurable in itself, – is well known to exist in the most thriving, most moral and best governed communities of the continent and with respect to which the scrupulous are in a minority at least of the professors of the Xtn Religion. As to the Missionaries and their Society you have certainly done their business.[4] Love to all.

Ever yours affectionately

T B M

---

[1] Lord Fitzwilliam's seat. Selina Macaulay's Diary, 27 October, reports that TBM dined there 'with about thirty of his brethren of the circuit on one of the public days when a general invitation is given to all the lawyers on the northern circuit; he describes every thing as having been on the most magnificent scale.'

[2] TBM arrived in London on Friday, 24 October (Selina Macaulay, Diary, 27 October).

[3] *The Anti-Slavery Monthly Reporter*, a publication of the Anti-Slavery Society which first appeared in June 1825, was largely the work of Zachary Macaulay. The issue for October 1828 has as its text the 1827 report of 'The Incorporated Society for the Conversion and Religious Instruction and Education of the Negro Slaves in the British West India Islands.' The *Reporter* charged that the slaves had no 'Christian Sabbath' and that the Conversion Society had failed to 'vindicate the *right* of the negro to the Sabbath, of which he is iniquitously deprived' (p. 313).

[4] The *Reporter*, pp. 322–6, shows in detail the falsity of the Conversion Society's claim to provide effective religious instruction.

TO ZACHARY MACAULAY, 14 MARCH 1829

Text: Trevelyan, I, 150–1.

Lancaster:[1] March 14, 1829.

My dear Father, –

A single line to say that I am at Lancaster. Where you all are I have not the very slightest notion. Pray let me hear. That dispersion of the Gentiles which our friends the prophets[2] foretell seems to have commenced with our family.

Everything here is going on in the common routine. The only things of peculiar interest are those which we get from the London papers. All minds seem to be perfectly made up as to the certainty of Catholic Emancipation having come at last.[3] The feeling of approbation among the barristers is all but unanimous. The quiet townspeople here, as far as I can see, are very well contented. As soon as I arrived I was asked by my landlady how things had gone. I told her the division, which I had learned from Brougham at Garstang. She seemed surprised at the majority. I asked her if she was against the measure. "No; she only wished that all Christians would live in peace and charity together." A very sensible speech, and better than one at least of the members for the county ever made in his life.[4]

I implore you above everything, my dear Father, to keep up your health and spirits.[5] Come what may, the conveniences of life, indepen-

---

[1] The Spring assizes were held at Lancaster, 7–21 March; at York, 21 March–4 April. TBM had also attended the Christmas quarter sessions of the West Riding, Wetherby, 13 January; Wakefield, 15–19 January; Doncaster, 21–2 January (Selina Mills Macaulay to Henry Thatcher, 22 January [1829]: MS, University of London).

[2] I.e., such men as Henry Drummond, Edward Irving, Spencer Perceval, and other adepts in the foretelling of the apocalypse. For Irving, see 23 July 1831. The so-called Irvingite church did not yet exist in 1829, but Irving and Drummond were already giving scandal by their interpretation of biblical prophecy. Spencer Perceval (1795–1859), eldest son of the assassinated prime minister and well known in the Evangelical circles of the Macaulay family, came under the influence of Drummond and Irving; his position in society made his religious eccentricities conspicuous.

[3] Peel's motion for a committee of the whole House to consider the subject of Catholic disabilities passed by a majority of one hundred and eighty-eight on 6 March. The bill which was then brought in passed its third reading in the Commons on 30 March, in the Lords on 10 April, and received the royal assent on 13 April.

[4] The members for Lancashire were Lord Stanley (afterwards thirteenth Earl of Derby) and John Blackburne. The remark may be a joke, for Stanley, who supported Catholic relief, spoke little, and Blackburne, member for the county for forty-six years, hardly at all. A portrait of Blackburne hung in the county sessions hall at Lancaster; perhaps TBM was looking at it as he wrote.

[5] The firm of Macaulay and Babington, under the management of Thomas Gisborne Babington since 1823, had overextended itself and, as early as 1826, was unable to meet its engagements. The firm avoided bankruptcy, but the partnership was dissolved on 23 December 1828, the *Gazette* notice stating that 'all debts owing to and by the said firm will be received and paid by the said Zachary Macaulay, who will carry on business as before' (*London Gazette*, 2 January 1829, p. 9). The name of Zachary Macaulay, merchant, appears in the

dence, our personal respectability, and the exercise of the intellect and the affections, we are almost certain of retaining: and everything else is a mere superfluity, to be enjoyed, but not to be missed. But I ought to be ashamed of reading you a lecture on qualities which you are so much more competent to teach than myself.

Ever yours very affectionately
T. B. M.

TO MACVEY NAPIER, 16 SEPTEMBER 1829

MS: British Museum. *Address:* Macvey Napier Esq / Edinburgh.

50 Great Ormond Street London / Septr. 16. 1829

Dear Sir,

On my return from the Northern Circuit,[1] I found your letter waiting for me. As you have already communicated with Empson about the business to which it refers, you must be aware that neither his scruples nor mine originated in any personal feeling towards yourself.[2] I have not seen

Post Office London Directory from 1830 to 1834. Zachary Macaulay, who in 1818 had reckoned his fortune at £100,000 (Trevelyan, 1, 125), lost all that he had. Writing to Lord Grey, 2 May 1834, for appointment to the Poor Law Commission, Macaulay explained that 'in the year 1826...I shared in the calamities of that period of commercial disaster and a large property and income were suddenly swept away, leaving, after I had discharged the pecuniary obligations under which I had come, a large mass of outstanding debts which have hitherto proved irrecoverable' (copy, Brougham MSS, University College). There is a summary account of Macaulay's business failure in Knutsford, *Zachary Macaulay*, pp. 395–406; further details are given in Christopher Fyfe, *A History of Sierra Leone*, Oxford, 1962, pp. 166–7. TBM's income from his Trinity fellowship, his Commissionership of Bankrupts, and his writing for the *ER* – a total of perhaps £700 in 1829 – was now the support of the family. TBM's attendance on the Northern Circuit and at the West Riding sessions was an expense rather than a source of income. Of his brothers, Henry, at Liverpool, was probably self-supporting by this time. John had just taken his B.A. at Cambridge; he was not ordained to his first living until January 1830. Charles was at the London University, of which he was the first registered student. The five girls were all at home, though frequent visitors for long stays at Rothley Temple, and at the homes of such friends as Wilberforce, James Stephen, and James Cropper.

1 The Summer assizes were held at York, 1–15 August; at Lancaster, 29 August–14 September. Probably TBM spent the interval between assizes at Rothley Temple. Since he says that he left London 'about six weeks ago' he seems to have passed up the Midsummer quarter sessions of the West Riding, held at Skipton, Bradford, and Rotherham, 14–24 July.

2 On the prospect of being made Dean of the Faculty of Advocates, Jeffrey had resigned the editorship of the *ER*. Napier (see 15 April 1828) succeeded him in June 1829, the October issue being the first under his editorship. TBM and Empson both hesitated about continuing their connection with the *ER* under Napier, but through Jeffrey's intermediation they quickly came to a good understanding with Napier (Empson to Napier, 9 August [1829]: MS, British Museum). In his letter to Napier, 16 September 1830, TBM says that his reason for wishing to withdraw from the *ER* was his fear that Brougham would domineer over it. Empson was also on doubtful terms with Brougham, who called him a 'bad imitator of

him since I left London about six weeks ago. But he has written to tell me in general terms that his difficulties are removed.¹ And his assurances and Jeffrey's ought, I feel, to be perfectly satisfactory to me.

I cannot as yet absolutely promise an article for the next number. But as soon as I can judge with certainty whether some other avocation which it is impossible for me to neglect,² will leave me leisure for that purpose, you shall hear from me again. / Believe me, dear Sir,

Yours very truly

T B Macaulay

TO MACVEY NAPIER, 3 OCTOBER 1829

MS: British Museum. *Address:* Macvey Napier Esq / Edinburgh. *Partly published:* Macvey Napier, ed., *Selection from the Correspondence of the Late Macvey Napier*, 1879, p. 66.

50 Great Ormond Street London / Octr. 3. 1829

Dear Sir,

Empson is in London, and begs me to tell you that he will immediately set to work about Turkey.³ The Westminster Review has put forth another attack on us;⁴ and both Empson and I think that, as the contro-

Macaulay' (*DNB*), and probably agreed with TBM that Napier would not be able to meet Brougham with the same authority that Jeffrey had. According to TBM, Jeffrey had first offered the editorship of the *ER* to him but Brougham had protested. 'The truth was, [Brougham] felt that his power over it diminished as mine increased, and he saw that he should have little indeed if I were the editor' (Margaret Macaulay, *Recollections*, 27 November [1831], in Trevelyan, I, 186).

¹ 'I wrote to Macaulay some time ago: and had a letter from him so entirely favorable that I have no doubt that you will find him ready to comply with your request' (Empson to Napier, 5 September [1829]: MS, British Museum).

² TBM was in Cambridge on 19 September (Zachary Macaulay to Selina Mills Macaulay, 19 September 1829: MS, Huntington).

³ 'The Ottoman Empire,' *ER*, L (January 1830), 437–85.

⁴ TBM had attacked the rigidly theoretical approach to politics of James Mill and the Utilitarians in 'Mill's Essay on Government: Utilitarian Logic and Politics,' *ER*, XLIX (March 1829), 159–89. Bentham himself was asked to write an answer, and obliged with forty pages of manuscript, but 'this turned out to be purely a history of his own thought and no reply at all to the Edinburgh' (George L. Nesbitt, *Benthamite Reviewing: The First Twelve Years of the Westminster Review, 1824–1836*, New York, 1934, p. 140). Accordingly, the editor, Major (later General) T. Perronet Thompson, 'wrote four pages of reply to the *Edinburgh*, and appended thereto the Bentham history of his own thought condensed to ten pages' (*ibid.*). The result appeared as '"Greatest Happiness" Principle,' *Westminster Review*, XI (July 1829), 254–68. TBM responded with 'Bentham's Defence of Mill: Utilitarian System of Philosophy,' *ER*, XLIX (June 1829), 273–99 (the June number of the *ER* appearing after the July number of the *Westminster*). Thompson answered with 'Edinburgh Review and the "Greatest Happiness Principle",' *Westminster Review*, XI (October 1829), 526–36 – the 'attack' mentioned in this letter. TBM's final article in the controversy was 'Utilitarian Theory of Government, and "the Greatest Happiness Principle",' *ER*, L (October 1829), 99–125. Thompson had the last word in 'Edinburgh Review and the "Greatest Happiness Principle",' *Westminster Review*, XII (January 1830), 246–62, but the general opinion was

versy has certainly attracted much notice in London, and as this new article of the Benthamites is more absurd than any thing that they have yet published, one more paper ought to appear on our side. I hope to have one ready in a week or a little more – I could indeed finish it much sooner. But we have abundance of time before us, and I am rather more busy than usual.[1] – I hope and trust that this will be the last blow. Believe me

Ever yours very truly
T B Macaulay

TO MACVEY NAPIER, 14 OCTOBER 1829

MS: British Museum. *Address:* Macvey Napier Esq / Edinburgh.

50 Great Ormond Street London / Octr. 14. 1829

Dear Sir,

I send off by the Edinburgh Mail of to-night the article which I promised you. It has been hastily written, and you may perhaps think it here and there too sharply expressed. If so, of course you will soften it down.

I shall be obliged to you to send me the proof-sheets. You shall receive them again by return of post. In a very short time you will, I imagine, receive Empson's article, so that we shall, I hope, be out in November.[2]

Ever yours very truly
T B Macaulay

TO MACVEY NAPIER, 23 OCTOBER 1829

MS: British Museum. *Address:* Macvey Napier Esq / Edinburgh. *Mostly published:* Napier, *Correspondence,* p. 66.

50 Great Ormond Street London / Octr. 23. 1829

My dear Sir,

By the mail of to-morrow I shall dispatch the proofs. I shall not have time to finish looking them over to-night. I have re-written the two first

---

that TBM had seriously damaged Benthamite orthodoxy: the impact of his attack upon the Utilitarians is made clear in Nesbitt, pp. 139–43. John Stuart Mill wrote that 'I saw that Macaulay's conception of the logic of politics was erroneous,' but also that 'there was truth in several of his strictures on my father's treatment of the subject; that my father's premises were really too narrow....I was not at all satisfied with the mode in which my father met the criticisms of Macaulay' (*Autobiography,* 1873, pp. 157–8). James Mill in fact made no effort to answer TBM, but treated the articles as unworthy of notice. TBM did not reprint these articles in his lifetime, being 'unwilling to offer what might be regarded as an affront to the memory of one from whose opinions he still widely dissents, but to whose talents and virtues he admits that he formerly did not do justice' ('Preface,' *Critical and Historical Essays,* 1, 1843, viii). They were, however, included in the *Miscellaneous Writings,* 2 vols., 1860, edited by T. F. Ellis, and thereafter in the *Works,* 8 vols., 1866, edited by Hannah Trevelyan.

[1] Perhaps with the 'long and complicated parliamentary case' mentioned in 1 December 1829.   [2] With the October number.

paragraphs which were, I must own, indecorously violent. I have softened some other passages. If you think any further mitigation desirable, I hope that you will not scruple to exercise your prerogative. You will not find me a refractory subject.[1]

I have not time even to allude to any of the subjects treated of in your very kind and interesting letter. / Believe me ever

Yours very faithfully

T B Macaulay

TO MACVEY NAPIER, 1 DECEMBER 1829

MS: British Museum. *Address:* Macvey Napier Esq / Edinburgh. *Mostly published:* Napier, *Correspondence*, p. 71.

50 Great Ormond St. London / Decr. 1. 1829

My dear Sir,

I have just received your letter and the inclosed draft.[2] I ought before this time to have answered more at length the kind letter which I had from you some weeks back. I have been busy with a long and complicated parliamentary case of which I have at last got rid; and I hope that I shall be able to do something for the next Number. I will try my hand again on Southey's Book.[3] What is your latest day? I should like to have the last place, if possible.

I have not spoken to any body about Niebuhr;[4] or rather I have not made any agreement on the subject. I mentioned it to a man of great knowledge and abilities,[5] who declined it, because he was not sufficiently intimate with the original German. He will however write an article on Lord Redesdale's new Edition of Mitford's History;[6] and I really expect from him an elegant, learned, and popular, essay on Greek history and literature.

[1] 'Do not blame me for inserting another blow at the *Utilitarians*. I have softened its severity, and I am bound to say that Macaulay has behaved handsomely' (Napier to J. R. McCulloch, 28 October 1829, in Macvey Napier, ed., *Selection from the Correspondence of the Late Macvey Napier*, 1879, p. 68). But for the aftermath see 25 January 1830.
[2] Jeffrey had paid TBM £84 for the two preceding articles on the Utilitarians (Selina Macaulay, Diary, 8 October 1829); presumably Napier adhered to the same scale.
[3] Robert Southey, *Sir Thomas More; or Colloquies on the Progress and Prospects of Society*, 2 vols., 1829; reviewed by TBM in 'Southey's *Colloquies on Society*,' *ER*, L (January 1830), 528–65. There is no record of TBM's having attempted this subject earlier.
[4] Vol. 1 of the English translation of Barthold Niebuhr, *History of Rome*, Cambridge, 1828.
[5] T. F. Ellis; Empson wrote to Napier on 10 November [1829] that 'when I last saw Macaulay I was talking with him about a Review of Niebuhr by one of his Trinity Friends' (MS, British Museum). That this was Ellis appears from 11 and 22 March 1830.
[6] William Mitford, *History of Greece*, 8 vols., 1829, with a memoir of the author by his brother, Lord Redesdale. It was not reviewed in the *ER*. In calling the edition 'stupid' TBM may have been influenced by the knowledge that Redesdale's opinion had strengthened Lord Eldon's decision against Zachary Macaulay in the *John Bull* case: see 29 March 1827.

I am glad that the new Number is well spoken of at Edinburgh. It is not yet out here. I cannot say that I am quite satisfied with it. For, though very respectable in general, it seems to me rather deficient in energy and animation.

Ever yours very truly
T B Macaulay

P S. I suppose that Lord Redesdale's stupid Edition of Mitford can hardly be pre-occupied. If it should be so, we can find some other book on Greek history lately published, – the History edited by the Society for the Diff[usio]n of Useful Knowledge[1] for example.

TO MACVEY NAPIER, 15 DECEMBER 1829

MS: British Museum. *Address:* Macvey Napier Esq / Edinburgh.

50 Great Ormond Street London / Decr. 15. 1829

My dear Sir,

I have just received your letter. It had not occurred to me that the voyage by sea could have been so long,[2] – as I supposed that the steam-communication between Edinburgh and London was constant. Curiously enough, I walked into a large bookseller's shop in the city last Saturday, and asked whether the Review was out yet. The bookseller said that it had not yet appeared, and he could not conceive why. A gentleman who was standing by suggested that it might be detained by foul winds. But the bookseller affirmed that to be impossible in these days of steam; and one of the people who were reading in the shop told us that, as he was informed, the Review had been stopped for the purpose of cancelling some sheets which had given great dissatisfaction.

If the evil be unavoidable, we must bear it, and attempt to counterbalance the peculiar disadvantages under which the Review labours by peculiar excellence. But I cannot doubt that there really is an evil in this delay; – if it were only that, at a time so critical as this,[3] it gives rise to such absurd reports and surmises among the literary quidnuncs. Notices in

---

[1] Frederick Malkin, *History of Greece*, 1829: see [September? 1828?].

[2] The October number of the *ER* had not yet appeared in London. It was finally published on 19 December, when Longmans, the London publisher of the *ER*, explained that the number had been 'long delayed at sea by contrary winds; however they hope to make such arrangements as will prevent similar occurrence for the future' (*The Times*, 28 December). Charles Knight says that as early as 1821 the voyage by steam between Edinburgh, and London took only sixty hours (*Passages of a Working Life*, I, 270).

[3] Presumably TBM means a critical time for the *ER*, following the change of editorship.

newspapers and journals are useful – whether hostile or friendly – if they appear a day or two before the review. But an interval of a month is far – very far – too long. The public overstays its appetite.

At all events it would be desirable that the review should not be advertised until the time of its appearance can be predicted with tolerable certainty. The present Number was advertised on Saturday the 20th of November.[1] It was then announced for the following week. It should therefore have appeared – at latest – on the 27th. This is the 15th of December, and it is not yet out. With regard to this number you have had all the labour and merit of great punctuality. And it is hard therefore that you should appear to the public to have so grievously transgressed it.

I hope that you do not imagine from what I said about Southey that I am at all dispos[ed][2] to take up a greater portion of the Review th[an][2] falls to my share. Most of my articles have bee[n][2] under two sheets – and I never but once exceeded three.[3] But I think it really essential to the success of the Review that, where a subject is treated which branches out into many heads and admits of very various illustration, those who write should not have any fears of exceeding a particular number of pages. The size of a number gives ample room for ten or twelve short and lively articles, even if there should be two or three very long ones. Of the importance of variety I am fully sensible. It had occurred to me indeed that it might be useful to end every number with a lively apperçu – concisely and neatly written, – of the works which had appeared during the quarter, and which were not of sufficient importance to deserve separate articles. The Monthly Review has always done this; and I really believe that it is now the only part of the Monthly Review which any body reads. I am sure that if it were done as it might be done, – with taste, spirit, gentlemanly and candid feeling, yet with a certain squeezing of acid, we should beat all the monthly magazines on their own ground. There would however be considerable difficulties and objections to get over. – Believe me

Ever yours truly,

T B Macaulay

[1] Saturday was the twenty-first; the *ER* was advertised for 'next week' in the *Examiner*, 22 November; *Morning Chronicle*, 24 November; *The Times*, 27 November.
[2] Paper torn away with seal.
[3] Articles in the *ER* were measured in 'sheets' of sixteen pages each; the article of TBM's exceeding three sheets is 'Hallam's Constitutional History,' which runs to seventy-four pages.

M.P. FOR CALNE, 1830

1830 January 25
Finishes 'Southey's *Colloquies on Society*' (*ER*, January)

– February 8
Goes to Bowood, to stand for election at Calne on Lord Lansdowne's invitation

– February 15
Elected M.P. for Calne

– February 18
Takes seat in Parliament

– March 6–early April
On circuit for last time

– April 5
Maiden speech, on Jewish disabilities

– April 29
Returns proofs of 'Montgomery's *Poems*' (*ER*, April)

– June 12
Elected to Athenaeum

– July 10
Returns proofs of 'Sadler's *Law of Population*' (*ER*, July)

– August 2
Re-elected for Calne, following dissolution of Parliament

– September 1
Leaves for Paris

– September 22
Death of sister, Jane

— September 30
Leaves Paris for London

— December 17
Finishes 'Civil Disabilities of the Jews' (*ER*, January 1831)

— December 18
Elected to Brooks's

— December 25
Finishes 'Sadler's *Refutation*, Refuted' (*ER*, January 1831)

TO MACVEY NAPIER, 25 JANUARY 1830

MS: British Museum. *Address:* Macvey Napier Esq / Edinburgh. *Mostly published:* Trevelyan, I, 151–2.

50 Great Ormond Street London / January 25. 1830

My dear Sir,

I send off by the mail of to day an article on Southey – too long I fear to meet your wishes, but as short as I could make it. If it does not suit you for the present number, I shall not have the least objection to your keeping it for the next. If you will send me the proof-sheets, you shall have them again by return of post.

There were, by the bye, in my last article a few omissions made, of no great consequence in themselves, – the longest, I think, a paragraph of twelve or fourteen lines. I should scarcely have thought this worth mentioning, – as it certainly by no means exceeds the limits of that Editorial prerogative which I most willingly recognize, – but that the omissions seemed to me and to one or two persons who had seen the article in its original state, to be made on a principle which, however sound in itself, does not, I think, apply to compositions of this description.[1] The passages omitted were the most pointed and ornamented sentences in the review. Now for high and grave works, a history for example or a system of political or moral philosophy, Doctor Johnson's rule – that every sentence which the writer thinks fine, ought to be struck out,[2] – is excellent. But periodical works like ours, which unless they strike at the first reading are not likely to strike at all, – whose whole life is a month or two, – may, I think, be allowed to be sometimes even viciously florid. Probably, in estimating the real value of any tinsel which I may put upon my articles, you and I should not materially differ. But it is not by his own taste, but by the taste of the fish, that the angler is determined in his choice of bait.

Perhaps after all I am ascribing to system what is mere accident. Be

---

[1] Jeffrey wrote to Napier, 13 December [1829], reporting that 'Macaulay . . . is vexed, I find, at your alterations on his paper – and says (according to Empson's report), that you have broken off the points of his best paragraphs'; he added that 'any new cause of offence may distaste him altogether' (MS, British Museum). On 20 December Empson wrote to Napier saying that TBM was 'chagrined by some of the alterations . . . which he found in his published article. He repeated some of them to me, saying, "they are more numerous in this one article than in all the 13 I wrote for Jeffrey during our whole connexion."' Empson suggested that 'a little management is required in such a case as with a favorite Actor on the Stage' (MS, British Museum). Apparently some part of TBM's text had been omitted by the printers – the 'accident' mentioned in 3 February 1830 – as well as blue-pencilled by Napier. The mildness of TBM's remarks on the subject to Napier does not accurately express his feeling, but, as Empson wrote in the letter already quoted, 'he would not write to you himself, lest you should think him jealous and captious, and seeking for an offence.' If Empson is accurate in reporting TBM as having said that he wrote thirteen articles for Jeffrey, then there are two of his articles yet unidentified for the period 1825–9.

[2] See Boswell, *Life of Johnson*, 30 April 1773.

assured at all events that what I have said is said in perfect good humour, and indicates no mutinous disposition.

The Jews are about to petition parliament for relief from the absurd restrictions which lie on them[1] – the last relique of the old system of intolerance.[2] I have been applied to by some of them in the name of the managers of the scheme to write for them in the Edinburgh Review. I would gladly serve a cause so good – and you, I think, could have no objection. But I doubt whether the next Number will be out in time to serve them in the approaching Session of Parliament. What are your arrangements?

> Ever yours truly
> T B Macaulay

TO MACVEY NAPIER, 3 FEBRUARY 1830

MS: British Museum. *Address:* Macvey Napier Esq / Edinburgh.

> 50 Great Ormond Street London / Feby. 3. 1830

My dear Sir,

I send you the proof-sheets by the mail of this evening. I have made several corrections, and I should be much obliged to you to look after the printing of them. The quotation from old Holinshed[3] has been dreadfully disfigured.

I have tried to alter what I said about the butchers.[4] If you are not satisfied, change it to your mind. I have left the passage about Mr. Shannon[5] for you to alter, – as you know who and what he is, and with what degree of civility it may be proper to speak of him.

I am sorry that my last letter has hurt your feelings. It was by no means

---

[1] The petition was presented by Robert Grant, 22 February, who said that it was 'the first application that had for the last eighty years been made by the collective body of the Jewish community to that House, for the purpose of being restored to their rights as British subjects' (*Hansard*, 2nd Series, XXII, 796).

[2] After the repeal of the Test and Corporation Acts in 1828 and of Catholic disabilities in 1829, the Jews were the only religious group still affected by the form of oath required of M.P.s. See 16 October 1830.

[3] TBM quotes from the printer John Harrison's introduction to Holinshed's *Chronicles*, 1577, in the review of Southey, *ER*, L, 557–8.

[4] After quoting a passage from Southey in which Sir Thomas More states that the butcher's trade must brutalize those employed in it, TBM accuses Southey of detesting butchers but, in his poems, of admiring soldiers and even of 'delight in snuffing up carnage....Mr. Southey's feeling, however, is easily explained. A butcher's knife is by no means so elegant as a sabre, and a calf does not bleed with half the grace of a poor wounded hussar' (*ibid.*, pp. 537–8). This part of the review was particularly attacked by William Maginn in his 'Mr. Thomas Babington Macauley and Mr. Southey,' *Fraser's*, 1 (June 1830), 593–7, and by John Wilson ('Christopher North') in *Blackwood's*, XXVII (April 1830), 683–4. TBM omitted the passage when he reprinted the review in his *Essays*.

[5] No reference to Mr Shannon appears in the published essay.

my intention to do so. I was very far from intending the least reflection when I hinted that I thought you too much inclined to prune my writing of its ornamental parts. My own taste has changed greatly, and is changing. I write less floridly than I did some years ago. In any extensive work I should write less floridly than in the Edinburgh Review. I did not mean to say more than that you might probably think of what I write at twenty-nine as I myself think of what I wrote at twenty-four, – that you might blame in a Review what I should myself blame in a history or a large treatise. I had not the least intention of insinuating any thing disrespectful towards you.

The omissions in the former article were trifling in themselves, and I attached no importance to them my self – though one or two other people differed from me on this point, – except as indications of a difference of opinion which, I am glad to find, does not exist. I am really sorry to have plagued you so much about an accident with which you had nothing to do. I hope, however, that you will not conclude from what has passed between us that I am an irritable or unreasonable person. I am impatient for the appearance of the Number. I hope the winds will be kinder this time than the last. / Believe me

Ever yours truly

T B Macaulay

TO THOMAS FLOWER ELLIS, 10 FEBRUARY 1830

MS: Trinity College. *Address:* T F Ellis Esq / 15 Bedford Place[1] / London.

Bowood[2] Feby. 10. 1830

Dear Ellis,

Every thing seems to be quite certain. All the votes have been promised to me. On Monday I expect to have my election dinner, and on Tuesday

---

[1] Ellis lived until his death at 15 Bedford Place, then a favored place of residence for lawyers.

[2] The seat of Lord Lansdowne, near Calne, Wiltshire. About the middle of January 1830 Lansdowne wrote to TBM to offer him the seat in Parliament for Lansdowne's borough of Calne, vacated by James Abercromby on his appointment as Chief Baron of the Exchequer of Scotland. Lansdowne is said to have told TBM that he made the offer because he had been impressed by TBM's series of articles in the *ER* on the Utilitarians and by TBM's 'high moral and private character' (Trevelyan, I, 139; see also Lansdowne's earlier commendation of TBM's article on 'The Present Administration,' 8 August 1827). Since Lansdowne was connected with some of Zachary Macaulay's enterprises – he was, for example, a vice-president of the Anti-Slavery Society – he had many opportunities to hear about TBM. Lord Houghton suggests that Lansdowne's intimacy with the Austins, Charles and John, and Sarah, John's wife, had some influence on Lansdowne's decision (*Academy*, 29 April 1876, p. 398). Since they were avowed Benthamites, their effect, as Alexander Bain has suggested, would seem to cancel that of TBM's articles on Mill (*James Mill*, pp. 331–2).

evening to take my seat.[1] I am living in this magnificent palace with Lord Kerry[2] – an extremely amiable and intelligent young man – and his tutor Guthrie[3] of Trin[ity] who inveighs fiercely against the Duke of Cumberland[4] – " Clodius accusat mœchas"[5] I had a great mind to quote to him. If there is any thing stirring worth writing I should be obliged to you for a letter. For we see no newspaper but the Sun. Lord and Lady Lansdowne and all the establishment except about a poor dozen of servants or so are in London. The library is delightful and the Collection of pictures still better. The grounds pretty – the apartments more comfortable by far than any apartments equally large and splendid that I ever saw.

Remember me kindly to Mrs. Ellis,[6] and tell her that I will contrive some day or other to get her a place in the ventilator of our House[7] – that is to say if she is as fond of heat, headache, hunger, bad speaking, late hours, and the smell of chandeliers as other ladies.

Ever yours faithfully

T B Macaulay

TO ZACHARY MACAULAY, 10 FEBRUARY 1830

Text: Trevelyan, I, 152–3.

Bowood: February 10, 1830.

My dear Father, –

I am here in a very nice room, with perfect liberty, and a splendid library at my command. It seems to be thought desirable that I should stay in the neighbourhood and pay my compliments to my future constituents every other day.

---

[1] TBM was elected on Monday, 15 February, but did not return to London until Wednesday, 17 February (Selina Macaulay, Diary, 18 February). He took his seat in the House of Commons on 18 February, being sworn in at the same time with Brougham.

[2] Lord Lansdowne's eldest son William (1811–36), styled Earl of Kerry. He sat for Calne, 1832–6.

[3] John Guthrie (1794?–1865: *Boase*), B.A., Trinity, 1817; chaplain to Lord Lansdowne in 1834 and Vicar of Calne, 1835–65. At Bowood in 1851 TBM wrote that 'Guthrie read ill and preached worse, as usual' (Journal, IV, 342: 28 December 1851).

[4] Ernest Augustus (1771–1851: *DNB*), fifth son of George III, reactionary and highly unpopular.

[5] Juvenal, *Satires*, II, 27.

[6] Ellis married Susan McTaggart in 1820; Hannah Trevelyan describes her as 'a most superior charming woman' (Memoir of TBM).

[7] The only ladies' gallery in the old House of Commons was 'a circular ventilator, in the roof' (Trevelyan, I, 269n), also described as 'a kind of loft above the roof of the chamber,' where the ladies could listen to the debates 'through the ventilator' (G. W. E. Russell, *Collections and Recollections*, Series II [1909], p. 317). Maria Edgeworth gives a good description of listening to the Commons through the ventilator on a visit in 1822: Christina Colvin, ed., *Maria Edgeworth: Letters from England 1813–1844*, Oxford, 1971, pp. 369–70.

The house is splendid and elegant, yet more remarkable for comfort than for either elegance or splendour. I never saw any great place so thoroughly desirable for a residence. Lord Kerry tells me that his uncle[1] left everything in ruin, – trees cut down, and rooms unfurnished, – and sold the library, which was extremely fine. Every book and picture in Bowood has been bought by the present Lord, and certainly the collection does him great honour.

I am glad that I stayed here. A burgess of some influence, who, at the last election, attempted to get up an opposition to the Lansdowne interest, has just arrived. I called on him this morning, and, though he was a little ungracious at first, succeeded in obtaining his promise. Without him, indeed, my return would have been secure; but both from motives of interest and from a sense of gratitude I think it best to leave nothing undone which may tend to keep Lord Lansdowne's influence here unimpaired against future elections.[2]

Lord Kerry seems to me to be going on well. He has been in very good condition, he says, this week; and hopes to be at the election, and at the subsequent dinner. I do not know when I have taken so much to so young a man. In general my intimacies have been with my seniors: but Lord Kerry is really quite a favourite of mine, – kind, lively, intelligent, modest, with the gentle manners which indicate a long intimacy with the best society, and yet without the least affectation. We have oceans of beer and mountains of potatoes for dinner. Indeed, Lady Lansdowne drank beer most heartily on the only day which she passed with us, and, when I told her laughing that she set me at ease on a point which had given me much trouble, she said that she would never suffer any dandy novelist to rob her of her beer or her cheese.

The question between law and politics is a momentous one. As far as I am myself concerned, I should not hesitate: but the interest of my family is also to be considered. We shall see, however, before long what my chance of success as a public man may prove to be. At present it would clearly be wrong in me to show any disposition to quit my profession.

I hope that you will be on your guard as to what you may say to Brougham about this business. He is so angry at it that he cannot keep his

---

[1] John Henry Petty (1765–1809), second Marquess of Lansdowne, half-brother of the third: 'after a youth of considerable promise, he became somewhat eccentric in his habits and amusements, and proved a great disappointment to his father' (GEC, *Complete Peerage*). He sold his father's library and collections of maps, prints, pamphlets, manuscripts, coins, and pictures.

[2] TBM was merely holding Calne for Lord Kerry. Lansdowne wrote to William Smith about TBM, 1 March 1830, that 'I have been able to promise him but a short lease (as far as I am concerned) of his parliamentary existence, as my eldest son will probably be of age to come in when there is another dissolution' (MS, Duke University). There were only twenty-four electors at Calne (*Royal Kalendar*, 1830).

anger to himself.[1] I know that he has blamed Lord Lansdowne in the robing-room of the Court of King's Bench. The seat ought, he says, to have been given to another man. If he means Denman,[2] I can forgive, and even respect him, for the feeling which he entertains.

Believe me ever yours most affectionately

T. B. M.

TO MARGARET MACAULAY, 11 MARCH 1830

MS: Morgan Library. *Address:* Miss Margaret Macaulay / 50 Great Ormond Street / London. *Frank:* Lancaster March eleven 1830 / T B Macaulay.

Lancaster[3] March 11. 1830

My darling Margaret,

Thanks, loves, and kisses without end, for your kind letter. I shall have a great deal to chat about with you all, but particularly with you and Hannah who were away during our great events, when I come back to London. But in the mean time I have not very much to write to you about. Lancaster is enlivened only by the absurdities of Judge Park – whom you must not confound with my friend Judge James Parke, – though they are both Jameses. Judge Park began a charge to the jury yesterday as follows. "Gentlemen, sitting here as a Christian Judge, in all my robes, I am bound to direct you etc. etc. etc." I shall have many other anecdotes equally absurd before we leave York.

I do not suppose that you will care much to know that Brougham is going down in practice, and that Alderson is climbing rapidly. – I have not exchanged a single word with Brougham;[4] – indeed we have not been placed in any situation which rendered it necessary that any communication should take place between us.

My franking privilege, I assure you, is not suffered to lie dormant here. Every body is writing letters; and the four members of parliament on the

---

[1] Brougham said that Denman (see next note) ought to have had the seat for Calne rather than TBM, but TBM attributed Brougham's annoyance to a jealousy that he was unable to keep from showing. TBM told Margaret Macaulay that, when he took his seat, 'as I turned from the table at which I had been taking the oaths, [Brougham] stood as near to me as you do now, and cut me dead' (Trevelyan, I, 187; see also the extract from Selina Macaulay's Diary, Knutsford, *Zachary Macaulay*, p. 450).

[2] Thomas Denman (1779–1854: *DNB*), first Baron Denman, Lord Chief Justice, 1832–50. Denman was a close friend of Brougham and had been associated with him in the defense of Queen Caroline. He was also a loyal Whig politician.

[3] The Spring assizes were held at Lancaster, 6–19 March; at York, 20 March–10 April. TBM left the circuit early, in time to make his maiden speech in Parliament, 5 April.

[4] TBM and Brougham must have had to speak to each other later, for both were among the counsel for the plaintiff in *The Society of Apothecaries* v. *Greenwood*, and *The Society of Apothecaries* v. *Wharton* at the York assizes, 1 April 1830 (York *Herald*, 3 April 1830).

circuit[1] have scarcely any of their franks left for themselves. John Wood was drawn dry to day, and came to beg for one from me. – I had only one – and that I kept – though I did not tell him so – for my little Margaret.

Parker[2] will be here in a day or two, I suppose. Tell Mary[3] that she can write through me if she likes. Mrs. Ellis's letters come under cover to me; and I have found out that they are much more numerous than those which my family vouchsafe to me. Pretty encouragement to remain a bachelor! Unless you exert yourselves more, ladies, I shall certainly when I come back in April introduce some smart Yorkshire damsel to you as Mrs. T B Macaulay – in hope that I may receive when I next go the circuit letters for myself as well as for my friends.

So you like my last article.[4] I am glad to hear it. It is, as far as I can learn, popular enough. Denman says that it is my best; and Alderson spoke civilly to me about it the other day. I must write for the next Number – because Ellis's article,[5] for which I encouraged Napier to hope, will not be ready. I scarcely know what subject to take. But I think of giving a little wholesome correction to a bad poet. I have sent for his poems; and if they are as bad as the extracts which I have seen, I will see whether I cannot do unto him as Jeffrey did unto similar offenders twenty years ago. The man is that Robert Montgomery[6] – not the Sheffield

[1] There seem to have been at least six M.P.s on the Northern Circuit: TBM, Brougham, William Marshall, M.P. for Petersfield, Lawrence Peel, M.P. for Cockermouth, John Williams, just elected for Winchelsea on Brougham's vacating that seat for Knaresborough, and John Wood.

[2] (Sir) James Parker (1803–52: *DNB*), married Mary, third daughter of Thomas Babington, in 1829. Parker, a graduate of Trinity College, joined the Northern Circuit in 1829; Q.C., 1844; Vice-Chancellor and knighted, 1851. At the time of his death Parker was the owner of Rothley Temple, which he bought from Thomas Gisborne Babington, in distress through the failure of his partnership with Zachary Macaulay.

[3] Mary Babington Parker; Eliza Conybeare, her niece, says that TBM once 'laid himself out, with all his powers, to captivate Aunt Mary. She was a year or two older [she was born 1799], and did not take the matter seriously, and very likely he never meant it seriously, but they carried on largely, and the folk present then say he never through life was so brilliant as during those few months' ('Aunt Eliza's Story'): Mrs Conybeare puts this episode when TBM was 'a young man of twenty-one,' but TBM in his Journal for 21 July 1858, on the death of Mary Parker, says that 'when I was seventeen or eighteen I was half in love with her. But her conversation soon healed the wound made by her eyes' (XI, 347).

[4] The review of Southey.

[5] See 1 December 1829. The article must be 'Müller's *History of the Dorians*,' *ER*, LIII (March 1831), 119–42. Though this is not certainly attributed to Ellis in Walter Houghton, ed., *The Wellesley Index to Victorian Periodicals*, 1 (1966), 474, no other article in the *ER* fits the known evidence.

[6] Montgomery (1807–55: *DNB*), whose *The Omnipresence of the Deity, A Poem*, 11th edn, 1830, and *Satan, A Poem*, 2nd edn, 1830 (published 30 December 1829), were reviewed by TBM in 'Mr Robert Montgomery's Poems, and the Modern Practice of Puffing,' *ER*, LI (April 1830), 193–210. Montgomery, the illegitimate son of a clown at the Bath theater named Gomery, had partly drawn this attack on himself for his lines on Zachary Macaulay and TBM in his anonymous satire, *The Age Reviewed*, 1827, pp. 111–12: 'Sweet Afrique saints, our sour sectarian foes, / Whose common heart with holy humbug glows, – / . . . .

poet,[1] – whom Chancy Townsend, if you remember, envied so much. He has been puffed into a sort of repute which renders him worth correction. Puffing of all sorts is my aversion; and I think this an excellent opportunity for exposing claims founded on puffing and on nothing else. – Love to all.

Ever yours affectionately
T B M

TO MACVEY NAPIER, 22 MARCH 1830

MS: British Museum. *Address:* Macvey Napier Esq / Edinburgh. *Frank:* York March twenty-two / 1830 / T B Macaulay. *Mostly published:* Napier, *Correspondence*, pp. 79–80.

York March 22. 1830

My dear Sir,

I have just found your letter here. It has, as I infer from the date, been awaiting my arrival for some days. I ought to have written to you before in answer to your kind letter of congratulation: but I was in some doubt as to what I should be able to do for Number 101; and I deferred writing till I could make up my mind. If my friend Ellis's article on Greek history, of which I have formed high expectations, could have been ready, I should have taken a holiday. But as there is no chance of that for the next Number, I ought, I think to consider myself as his bail, and to surrender myself to your disposal in his stead.

I have been thinking of a subject, light and trifling enough, but perhaps not the worse for our purpose on that account. – We seldom want a sufficient quantity of heavy matter. There is a wretched poetaster of the name of Robert Montgomery who has written some volumes of detestable verses on religious subjects, which by mere puffing in magazines and newspapers have had an immense sale, and some of which are now in their tenth or twelfth editions. I have for some time past thought that the trick of puffing as it is now practised both by authors and publishers, is likely to degrade the literary character and to deprave the public taste in a frightful degree. I really think that we ought to try what effect satire will

---

Then pert Macaulay bawls – "They *shall* be free," / While Stephen squeaks – "No sugar, Sir, for me!" / . . . . No Scotch Review – no Clarkson's Bedlam rant, / No Suffield tales of heav'n blaspheming cant, – / Excuse the fulsome meanness of a lie, / Though babe Macaulay fetch'd it from the sky!' He had also been unwise enough to publish a poem called *The Puffiad*, 1828. The popularity of his religious poems among the Evangelicals made him an especially attractive target to TBM, who was, however, by no means the only reviewer who treated poor Montgomery roughly, though without affecting the sales of the poems. Montgomery published a foolish reply to the *ER* (apparently without knowing the identity of the reviewer) in a note to his *Oxford, A Poem*, 1831, pp. 218–21.

[1] James Montgomery (1771–1854: *DNB*), editor of the Sheffield *Iris* and a poet then much esteemed in Evangelical circles.

have upon this nuisance; and I doubt whether we can ever find a better opportunity.

Let me know what you think of this plan of mine; and what arrangements you have made with respect to time and space. I shall be here for the next ten days.

I think that the last Number was on the whole very good; and I believe that the public is of the same opinion; but I am not very competent to judge of the public opinion on the subject, as I left London on the day on which the Review appeared.[1] / Believe me ever, / My dear Sir,

Yours very faithfully
T B Macaulay

TO MACVEY NAPIER, 27 MARCH 1830

MS: British Museum. *Address:* Macvey Napier Esq / Edinburgh. *Frank:* York March twenty seven 1830 / T B Macaulay.

York March 27. 1830

My dear Sir,

I have received your letter and the inclosed draft.[2] I shall return to London before the close of next week, and as soon as we adjourn for the Easter holidays, which will be, I suppose, in less than a fortnight, I will give three or four days to the Review. I shall be able, I trust, to send you an article by the middle of April. It will certainly be under two sheets, and probably a good deal under that quantity. But about this, of course, I cannot as yet positively judge. Ellis's article will, I believe, be ready for Number 102.

I am very glad to hear that you intend to visit London at a time when I shall be there. / Believe me ever,

Yours very faithfully,
T B Macaulay

P.S. As to Sir H Davy I have not read his book.[3] But I knew him, and did not by any means like him or admire him; – in society of course I mean.

---

[1] I.e., 5 March (Empson to Napier, 12 March [1830]: MS, British Museum).

[2] In payment for the review of Southey.

[3] Sir Humphry Davy's posthumous *Consolations in Travel, or the Last Days of a Philosopher* appeared in February 1830. Davy (1778–1829: *DNB*) was Professor of Chemistry at the Royal Institution, 1801–13, and was knighted, 1812, for his contributions to chemistry; baronet, 1818; President of the Royal Society, 1820–7. He spent the last year of his life abroad, and on his final journey, from Rome to Geneva, stayed six days at Genoa, where he suffered 'a serious relapse' (Anne Treneer, *The Mercurial Chemist*, 1963, p. 249). No review of Davy's book appears in the *ER*. TBM had dined with Lady Davy, 13 June 1827 (Selina Macaulay, Diary, 14 June 1827), but Sir Humphry was then abroad. He returned to England for a few months later in 1827, and TBM may have met him then. For Lady Davy, see 6 August 1832.

His own last days were a curious instance of the triumph of disease over the consolations of philosophy. His irritability amounted to absolute madness. At Genoa, I understand, he beat the waiters and threw the dishes about the rooms. I should not chuse to write an unfavourable article on his posthumous work; and I should hardly write his eulogy *con amore.*

TO SELINA MACAULAY, 27 MARCH 1830

MS: Trinity College. *Address:* Miss Macaulay / 50 Great Ormond Street / London. *Frank:* York March twenty seven 1830 / T B Macaulay.

York March 27. 1830

My dearest Selina,

I was quite sorry to receive your letter; – because, though I am always glad to hear from you, I know that writing does not agree with you; and I by no means intended that my jocose reprehensions[1] should produce such an effect. On the whole my sisters have been very good this circuit, though very far inferior in punctuality to my friend's wives. You would laugh to see what a number of elegant female hands are sometimes heaped on my breakfast table at once. The postman must think me, I am sure, a man of most extraordinary gallantry.

I have heard from Empson. He tells me that my father expressed himself satisfied with the tone of his article on providence; and seems to be very much gratified at having such an authority to oppose to objectors.[2] I do not see how any moderate or judicious man can think that article presumptuous or indecent, nor, delicate as the subject is, have I heard a whisper against it. I am glad that my father approves of it.

I had a letter from Napier this morning inclosing sixty pounds, and filled with all sorts of compliments on my article which, he says, is the most attractive that has for a long time appeared. Two writers, he says, both men of talents, who had applied to him for leave to review Southey, and had been rather mortified at his refusal, have written to express their satisfaction, and to confess that my performance is better than theirs would

---

[1] See 11 March.

[2] 'Providential and Prophetical Histories,' *ER*, L (January 1830), 287–344, a review of George Miller, *Lectures on the Philosophy of Modern History,* 8 vols., Dublin, 1816–28, and Charles Forster, *Mahomadanism Unveiled,* 3 vols., 1829. Empson wrote to Napier, [12 March 1830], that 'you will be glad to hear that Macaulay the Father, who is a great Authority in the serious world, has just called on me: assured me that he has read the *providence* article over twice with great attention: that he subscribes to every word of it etc.: that it is very powerful: that he is very glad to see such Articles in the Edinburgh Review. This is great Authority for its Effect upon the Saints' (MS, British Museum).

have been.[1] I shall not tell him in my answer that, if these men of talents are writers in the Edinburgh Review, I do not take their confession for a very high compliment. We are miserably off – that is the truth. I liked the Number pretty well at first. I have since looked over it again and am dissatisfied. Rice's article[2] is goo[d][3] and pleasant. I am sick of defendin[g][3] Empson, and finding nobody else of my opinion. Defoe[4] is a noble subject wretchedly ill treated. It is a comfort to think that the Quarterly Review is worse still.

I shall be in London, I hope, next Friday. I am sorry to hear of my father's cold. But this glorious weather, I hope, has already set all your maladies to rights. We have not seen such skies or inhaled such air for ten months or more. Love to all.

Ever yours most affectionately
T B Macaulay

I thank Hannah and Margaret for their letters most heartily. I have put off my marriage till next circuit in consequence of their improved regularity.

TO [FRANCIS BARLOW], 27 MARCH 1830

MS: Trinity College.

York March 27. 1830

Sir,

In answer to the questions which the Lord Chancellor has directed you to propose,[5] I have to state that I was appointed a Commissioner of Bankrupts in January 1828.

[1] One of these was William Hazlitt. He had suggested Southey's book as a possible subject on 13 July 1829; on 19 March 1830 he wrote to Napier that 'I am not sorry I had not *Southey* as it is so ably done' (MS, British Museum). The letter from the other writer is not in the Napier correspondence.

[2] 'Mr Sadler's School – Italian Economists,' *ER*, L (January 1830), 344–63. Thomas Spring-Rice (1790–1866: *DNB*), afterwards first Baron Monteagle; Whig M.P. for Limerick, 1820–32; for the town of Cambridge, 1832–9; raised to the peerage, 1839. From 1830 to 1839 Spring-Rice held various offices in the successive Whig ministries, notably the Chancellorship of the Exchequer, 1835–9. He was not a success in this office, and his peerage was a means of retirement from politics. An Irishman, Spring-Rice was personally very popular. He contributed eighteen articles to the *ER* between 1825 and 1852.

[3] Edge of sheet torn away.

[4] 'Wilson's *Life and Times of Daniel Defoe*,' *ER*, L (January 1830), 397–425, was by William Hazlitt.

[5] Under the pressure of Brougham's speech on law reform, 7 February 1828, and with the cooperation of the Chancellor, Lord Lyndhurst, the government was undertaking a number of legal reforms, including that of the procedure in bankruptcy. The reform was not accomplished, however, until 1831, under Lord Grey's administration, when the old bank-

I am a barrister and generally practice as such in the court of King's Bench. I go on the Northern Circuit. I do not hold nor have I ever held any other office of any kind; nor am I entitled to any office in reversion. / I have the honour to be, / Sir,

Your most obedient humble Servant

T B Macaulay

To the Lord Chancellor's⎫
Secretary of Bankrupts ⎭

TO UNIDENTIFIED RECIPIENT, [8 APRIL 1830][1]

MS: Trinity College.

My dear Sir,

I need not, I hope, tell you how much I am obliged to you for the kind interest which you have taken in my success.[2] As far as I can learn, the impression which I made was much more favourable than I at all anticipated, as I carefully abstained from every thing like display. Your advice has been of great use to me. I hope that you will continue to give it with perfect freedom, – and that you will let me know what faults of matter or manner[3] you have heard noticed in my speech of Monday. Any body can

ruptcy commission was abolished by 2 William IV, c. 56, and ceased to act on 11 January 1832. TBM did not qualify for the pension of £200 per annum granted to the senior commissioners in consequence of the abolition of their office. The information elicited by the questions TBM here answers appears in *Parliamentary Papers*, 1830, XXIX, 54.

[1] Endorsed, in unknown hand, 'April 1830.' The letter clearly refers to TBM's speech of Monday, 5 April: see next note. The recipient of the letter was perhaps one of the friends in Parliament of Zachary Macaulay – for example, William Smith (see 25 August 1814), who as an old friend of the family, a veteran of Parliament, and a Nonconformist, might naturally take an interest in both TBM and in his subject. Smith spoke in support of the Jewish disabilities bill in the debate of 5 April. The tone of the letter, however, suggests that TBM may be writing to Richard Sharp (see [31 July 1830]).

[2] TBM's maiden speech in the House of Commons, 5 April, on Robert Grant's motion for leave to introduce his bill for the removal of Jewish disabilities (*Hansard*, 2nd Series, XXIII, 1308–14). Margaret Macaulay writes that 'we did not know beforehand that he was going to speak, when he made his debut in the House; and the next morning he came before breakfast to tell us, with half a dozen newspapers in his pocket' (*Recollections*, p. 193). Hannah Macaulay says, expressing the family partiality, that 'the report in the Times though a good abstract gives no idea...of its spirit and power' (to Thomas Gisborne Babington, 8 April 1830: MS, Mrs Humphry Trevelyan). The motion passed by a majority of eighteen.

[3] 'His speech was very well received, though his friends found fault with his voice that it was too thick, and his manner for being too easy and conversational' (Margaret Macaulay, *Recollections*, p. 193). But TBM's notable fault of manner was a too-rapid delivery; the honest reporter for *Hansard* begins by saying that '*Mr. Macauley* proceded to address the House *nearly as follows*' (2nd Series, XXIII, 1308: second italics mine). The spelling 'Macauley' is, for the first few years of TBM's public life, almost standard: see, e.g., the title of Maginn's article, cited under 3 February 1830, note.

praise and congratulate. But it is only from friends so kind and judicious as yourself that I can expect correction. / Believe me ever, / My dear Sir,

Yours most truly

T B Macaulay

Gray's Inn[1] / Thursday Morning

TO MACVEY NAPIER, 29 APRIL 1830

MS: British Museum. *Address:* Macvey Napier Esq / Edinburgh. *Frank:* London April twenty nine 1830 / T B Macaulay. *Mostly published:* Napier, *Correspondence,* p. 80.

London April 29. 1830

My dear Sir,

I send back the proofs. I quite approve of all your alterations. But I doubt as to the first paragraph. I think that to dash into the fable at once would have rather too flippant a look;[2] and I would rather err on the other side.

There are two subjects on which I think of writing for the next Number. The Romantic Poetry of the Italians is one of them. A book on the subject has just been published by my friend Panizzi[3] – Professor in the London University – which will afford a good opportunity. I have long had this project in my head.

If, as I rather fear, we should be beaten in Parliament this year about the Jews,[4] a short, pungent, article on that question might be useful and taking.[5] It ought to come within the compass of a single sheet.

Let me know what you think of these two subjects.

Ever yours truly

T B M

P S   Jeffrey is here – quacking himself and amusing us all as usual. I am most happy to learn that we shall soon see you among us.

[1] Either late in 1829 (Trevelyan, I, 129; 138) or early in January 1830 (Selina Macaulay, Diary, 15 January 1830), TBM had left the family home in Great Ormond Street for chambers at 8 South Square, Gray's Inn. He remained there until his departure for India in 1834. The obscure and starving junior barrister on Pickwick's side in *Bardell* v. *Pickwick,* a Mr Phunkey, lived in Holborn Court, Gray's Inn – 'Holborn Court, by the bye, is South Square now' (Dickens, *Pickwick Papers,* ch. 31, *ad fin.*). The building in which TBM resided was in poor condition and was pulled down to make room for additions, completed in 1842, to the Gray's Inn Library.

[2] The review of Montgomery begins with a paragraph apologizing for the fable that follows – a story of how three rogues collaborated to persuade a Brahmin that a lame, blind dog was in fact a sheep fit for sacrifice.

[3] Anthony Panizzi, ed., *Orlando Innamorato di Bojardo; Orlando Furioso di Ariosto: with an Essay on the Romantic Narrative Poetry of the Italians,* 9 vols., 1830–4. The subject was evidently a favorite of TBM's, but he never succeeded in writing on it: see 10 December 1834 and 8 October 1838.

[4] The Jewish disabilities bill was defeated on its second reading by a majority of sixty-three, 17 May.   [5] The suggestion was carried out later in the year: see 16 October.

TO HANNAH MACAULAY, 16 JUNE 1830

MS: Trinity College. *Address:* Miss H Macaulay / Rothley Temple / Mount Sorrel / Leicestershire. *Frank:* London June sixteen 1830 / T B Macaulay.

[London]

Miss,

Sister Fanny says, says she, "If you will but write a few lines to little Hannay here she will be so pleased." "Blow me light," says I, "y[ou do]¹n't say so. Well then I wil[l."]¹ So down I sits to write a knowing Epistle – quite up to any thing. But lauk o' me, here's the end of the paper. Well I wish it was larger. But all's one for that. I don't like it so I shall lump it.

Yours

T B M.²

TO HANNAH MACAULAY, 28 JUNE 1830

MS: Mrs Humphry Trevelyan.

London June 28. 1830

My dear Hannah,

I will tell you a story. There was a naughty girl who was always grumbling and honing and moaning for letters. And it was from morning to night – "Write to me. Only write. I am letter-sick. Nobody cares for me. I will never write again." This young lady had a brother who, in the midst of many literary, professional, and political, engagements, contrived to find time to write an affectionate and simple epistle to her. Immediately Miss Shrew – for that was her name – began to murmur again. "Such letters are only fit for a footman to write. You must ask pardon on your bended knees." – So her brother never wrote to her again.

Moral –

Young ladies who wish for letters very much should receive them when they come very civilly.³

So the King is dead.⁴ And all London is in a stir with the business of

---

¹ Paper torn away with seal.
² Below the signature Fanny Macaulay has written: 'An elegant epistle from the member for Calne!!!'
³ This hardly seems fair to Hannah, who on 19 April 1830 had written to her cousin Thomas Gisborne Babington after hearing a sermon intended to show that nothing on earth should be idolized, how she 'felt that there was one I idolized, one I loved more than God, one on whom I depended alone for happiness, and in one moment we might be separated for ever. And yet I cannot endure the thought of ever loving him less than I do at this moment, though I feel how criminal it is' (MS, Mrs Humphry Trevelyan).
⁴ George IV died on 26 June.

proclaiming William the fourth. The members of parliament are being sworn in again. I vowed all sorts of things and smacked the calf-skin 6 or 7 times. Peel was there in a dress not much unlike my Uncle Babington's liveries. They call it the Windsor Uniform[1] – a great deal of gilding and lace. He looked like a good boy's beau ideal of human happiness – the reward of doing as you are bid and shutting the door after you. We are to go to court soon in a body. I shall not go unless I can go without a sword and a fool's coat.

A word of consolation, and I have done. Pray, my dear, do not take on so about the poor old King. Exert your excellent sense, and bear up against this calamity. I know how you feel it. So do I. The paper is blistered with my tears – to say nothing of Fanny's and Selina's which are falling fast on each side.

Ever yours most affectionately

T B M.

TO MACVEY NAPIER, 10 JULY 1830

MS: British Museum. *Address:* Macvey Napier Esq / Edinburgh. *Frank:* London July ten 1830 / T B Macaulay. *Partly published:* Trevelyan, I, 125.

July 10. 1830

My dear Sir,

I send back the proofs.[2] Be so kind as to look carefully to the printing. I have altered the numbers in the passage about the peerage, so as to take in the Royal Dukes and the births and marriages mentioned in the Appendix.[3] It now stands thus –

---

[1] 'A uniform introduced by King George III, consisting of a blue coat with a red collar and cuffs, and a blue or white waistcoat' (*OED*).

[2] Of 'Sadler's Law of Population, and Disproof of Human Superfecundity,' *ER*, LI (July 1830), 297–321. Michael Thomas Sadler (1780–1835: *DNB*), partner in a Leeds firm of linen merchants, is remembered as the champion of the factory children through his sponsorship in Parliament of the Ten Hours' Bill, 1831–2. He was chairman of the parliamentary committee of inquiry into child labor whose report in 1832 roused public opinion on the subject. Sadler was a strong Tory, and entered the House of Commons in 1829 as the nominee of the Duke of Newcastle to oppose Catholic emancipation. His concern with the necessity for social legislation inspired his attack on Malthus, whose theory of population was used to prove the inutility of all efforts to improve the condition of the poor, in *The Law of Population: A Treatise in Six Books; in Disproof of the Superfecundity of Human Beings, and Developing the Real Principle of Their Increase*, 2 vols., 1830. These two volumes contain only four books; no more were published, presumably as a result of TBM's destructive review. Sadler owed TBM a heavy debt of ill-will as the man who both overthrew his theory of population and, two years later, put an end to his parliamentary career by defeating him at Leeds.

[3] To the 1828 edition of *Debrett*. TBM was refuting Sadler's argument that the peers were, as a class, comparatively barren. See *ER*, LI, 316.

Married peers	287
Marriages	333
Births	1437

The other calculations are not affected by the change. So much depends, in an argument of this sort, on the correctness of the figures that they ought to be particularly attended to.

I have re-written the last paragraph as you [desi]¹re, and I send it in the envelope with some of the other sheets. If y[ou]¹ do not like it now, alter it as you please.

I am off for Calne² on Monday. I shall be in London again on Wednesday, and shall not go down again till the Election. There is no doubt of our³ return – and next to no doubt I think of our success before an Election Committee.⁴ I have been very hard worked of late; so hard worked that I have not found time to answer a very kind letter of Jeffrey's. I hope he has something in our new Number.

Ever yours truly

T B Macaulay

(Turn over –)

I think it best on the whole to leave the theological part of the question as it stands.⁵ Much more might be said certainly. But the position which I have now taken is absolutely impregnable, and if we were to quit it, though we might win a more splendid victory, we should expose ourselves to some risk. My rule in controversy has always been that to which the Lacedæm[onians]⁶ adhered in war, – never to break the ranks for the purpose of pursuing a beaten enemy.

T B M

¹ Obscured by stain from seal.
² Following the death of George IV, Parliament was to be dissolved. TBM visited Calne, 12–14 July, and returned for the election, which took place on 2 August.
³ The other member for Calne was Sir James Macdonald (1784–1832), second Baronet, who was first elected for the borough in 1812; Commissioner of the Board of Control, 1830–2; on account of ill health he accepted the High Commissionership of the Ionian Islands, but died of cholera, June 1832.
⁴ The election was to be contested by a Mr Edmund Hopkinson and Col. Edward Cheney, a Waterloo veteran, 'in order to give the inhabitants an opportunity of endeavouring to recover their right of having a voice in the choice of their representatives' (*Devizes and Wiltshire Gazette*, 29 July 1830). The issue was whether the right of election lay in all the ninety-three inhabitant householders of the borough, or was restricted to the twenty-four members of the corporation. The question would require a petition to the House of Commons, which Hopkinson and Cheney duly presented: see *to* Napier, 27 November 1830. At the election the votes were eighteen for TBM and Macdonald and seventy-seven for their opponents, but the majority votes were all disqualified.
⁵ In reply to Sadler's argument that the Malthusian theory impugns the goodness of God TBM asks whether there is 'any difference between the particular form of evil which would be produced by over-population, and other forms of evil which we know to exist in the world?' (*ER*, LI, 300).
⁶ Cut off by mounting of MS.

TO HANNAH MACAULAY, 16 JULY 1830

MS: Trinity College. *Address:* Miss H M Macaulay / T Babington's Esq / Bank / Leicester.
Frank: London July sixteen 1830 / T B Macaulay.

London July 16. 1830.

My dear little girl, –

I shall be coming to the Temple, I hope, if they can give me a bed, in
three weeks or less; and I hope to be able to stay there some time.[1] The
election will interfere with my going to York and the bankrupt-business
with my going to Lancaster.[2]

I have been to Calne, and must go there again. I shall probably proceed
from thence to Clifton – look in at the godmother, and then cross the
country to see the god-daughter.[3] Tell Erskine[4] to have some very short
sermons in readiness for my arrival, and Matthew to put on his best wig.
But seriously let me know whether my visit will be perfectly convenient to
my Uncle and Aunt.

There is a talk that the Cow Keeper[5] is going to stand for Hull. William

---

[1] TBM must have intended to be at the Temple following his election at Calne on 2 August.
He was at Rothley Temple between 19 August, when he writes from London, and 30 August,
when he left London on his way to France, but whether he was there between 2 and 19
August is not recorded. His uncle Babington wrote on 20 July that they were 'glad, that we
are soon to see you for some time' (MS, Huntington).

[2] The Spring circuit of 1830 was the last that TBM attended.

[3] I.e., Hannah More, now residing at Clifton, and Hannah More Macaulay. TBM did visit
Hannah More after his election. It was his last visit to her, and in the event a costly one.
Roberts, *Letters of Hannah More to Zachary Macaulay*, pp. 207–8, says that 'some relations
of mine were present on the occasion . . . soon after the general election. He then entered her
apartment, attended by Mr. Protheroe, the triumphant candidate for Bristol [Protheroe was
not elected for Bristol until 1831], whose appearance was a rather striking contrast to the
heavy and somewhat corpulent figure of the friend who introduced him. Macaulay was then
full of spirit and vivacity, and spoke with all his customary flow; but it was, on that occasion,
notwithstanding, that some sentiments he broached were combated, and combated successfully, in the opinion of the company, by a female disputant who was strong with the majesty
of truth.' Hannah More had for years intended to leave her library to TBM – the plan is
mentioned as early as 24 August 1816 (Selina Mills Macaulay to Zachary Macaulay: MS,
Huntington), but his Whiggish politics as they appeared on this visit and in his subsequent
career in the House of Commons changed her mind. TBM knew what effect he was producing on the old lady. When his mother wished to send Hannah More his speech on the
Reform Bill, 2 March 1831, '"Oh, no," he said, "don't send it; if you do, she'll cut me off
with a Prayer-book"' (Margaret Macaulay, *Recollections*, p. 207). By a codicil dated 11 August 1832 she revoked 'the legacy of the residue of my books left in my will to Thomas
Babington Macaulay': they went, instead, to Charles Popham Miles, identified by Roberts
as 'an excellent relation of her own' (*ibid.*, p. xiv). Miles (1810–91: *DNB*), after serving as a
midshipman in the East India Company's navy, was ordained in 1838; Principal of the
Malta Protestant College, 1858–67; Vicar of Monk Wearmouth, 1867–83.

[4] Henry David Erskine (1786–1869: *DNB*), second son of Lord Erskine; Rector of Swith-
land, Leicestershire (near Rothley), 1817–41; of Kirby Underdale, Yorkshire, 1840–7; Dean
of Ripon, 1847–59. Selina Macaulay, Diary, 5 June 1826, notes 'a very long and dull sermon' from Erskine.

[5] William Wilberforce the younger, after an unsatisfactory career at Cambridge, which he
left without taking a degree, had been established by his father as a dairy farmer at St John's

Smith will no longer be encircled by the halo which his parliamentary dignity threw round him.[1] Lushington[2] will have a hard fight for it at Reading. An accomplished young man whose name particular reasons prevent me from mentioning is certain of his return for Calne. I am glad to hear of Evans's favourable chances.[3] Love to every body at the Temple. Remember me kindly to Evans. Best regards [   ][4]

T B M

TO HANNAH MACAULAY, 21 JULY 1830

MS: Trinity College. *Address:* Miss H M Macaulay.

London July 21. 1830

My darling Hannah,

We are to be prorogued the day after to-morrow[5] – and my franks will be of no more value than so much waste paper – a sermon of Mr. Erskine's for example. But only think – I shall go to the House of Lords, and there the King will sit on his throne – so grand – with his crown of gold on his head, and his sceptre in his hand, and all his royal robes. And he will make a speech to us – and he will call us his faithful Commons, and say " Gentlemen of the House of Commons, I thank you for voting me such handsome supplies."[6] Only think of a brother of yours being thanked for his munificence by a King in all his glory. And there will be the Lords – bless their hearts – all in their best – red velvet, gold, ermine and so forth. And we of the Commons shall not be so shabby neither as you may think, Miss – pursing up your quality mouth at us as you always do – a proud stuck-up swan! – No. Not so bad as all that comes to, neither. The speaker will have his long black gown all flowered with gold; and the

---

Wood, and, as 'the Cow Keeper,' had become one of the favorite butts of the *John Bull.* About February, 1830, the enterprise, which Lord Teignmouth described as 'a herd of 360 cows and a regiment of milkmaids' (*Reminiscences*, I, 249), failed, involving the elder Wilberforce in a 'very heavy loss of nearly all the capital which had been invested in the business' (Robert and Samuel Wilberforce, *The Life of William Wilberforce*, 1838, V, 314). The younger Wilberforce did not stand for Hull in 1830 (he was elected for Hull in 1837 and unseated on petition, 1838); in consequence of his losses, he left for the continent in 1831 (Selina Macaulay, Diary, 31 March 1831).

[1] Smith retired from the House of Commons after the dissolution of 1830.

[2] Stephen Lushington (1782–1873: *DNB*), barrister, judge, and Whig M.P., one of the most important and active of the anti-slavery men in Parliament. Lushington, who supported parliamentary reform, was defeated at Reading in 1830 but was returned for Winchelsea shortly afterwards.

[3] William Evans was returned for Leicester in the general election.

[4] TBM's concluding words have been written over and thus obscured.

[5] Parliament was prorogued by William IV in person, 23 July, and dissolved the next day.

[6] 'Gentlemen of the House of Commons; I thank you for the supplies which you have granted' (speech from the throne, *Annual Register*, 1830, p. [140]).

members who are officers will have their uniforms – the soldiers red – the sailors blue – as it is written

> "Some men get coats of red and blue
> To shew their Sovereign honour due."[1]

And the ministers who are not in the army or the navy will wear the Windsor Uniform – a very dashing costume I can tell you. So don't you wish to be there? – What would you give? A ring worth five shillings? Or would you tell me what it was that Madge and you talked about, if I would take you? Lauk o' me – what a little sheet of paper. Quite big enough for you though.

T B M

TO [RICHARD SHARP, 31 JULY 1830][2]

MS: Mr F. R. Cowell.

My dear Sir,

I send back Allen's book,[3] with many thanks. I have tried to see you three or four times without success to thank you for the other little volume[4] which you were so kind as to send me, and which will always be valuable to me both for its own sake, and for the sake of the giver.

I start for Calne this evening. There is no doubt about my return, and very little, I apprehend, about my success on petition. I hope that your

---

[1] See TBM's juvenile hymn, *c.* 1808, the second stanza of which begins 'Some men make Gods of red and blue / And rob their Sovereign of his due' (MS, Huntington: facsimile in *London Scottish Regimental Gazette*, II [1897], 7–9).

[2] The MS is accompanied by a card identifying Sharp as the recipient and stating that the letter was 'written on the day that Louis Phillipe was embraced by Lafayette and proclaimed King of the French.' Sharp (1759–1835: *DNB*), called 'Conversation' Sharp, was a long-time friend of Samuel Rogers, an intimate of Holland House and of Whig society generally, an eminently clubbable man. He made a fortune as a West India merchant, entertained all the distinguished members of the Whig literary and political world, and published *Letters and Essays in Prose and Verse*, 1834; M.P., 1806–12; 1816–19. Sharp was a bachelor; his ward, Maria Kinnaird (see 28 May 1831) was for a time thought to be the object of TBM's affections. Lord Dudley wrote [19 February 1830] of what must have been TBM's introduction to Sharp that 'this Macaulay that Lord L[ansdowne] has brought into Parliament, where I think he will cut some considerable figure, is a *very* clever, *very* educated, and *very* disagreeable man. Sharpe, in his capacity of dry-nurse to rising men of talents, is about to give him a dinner, to which in memory of ancient times he has asked me. Poor old gentleman! – Macaulay is just the kind of fellow to undervalue him. Stern and unsparing, he will have no mercy upon a little vanity and twaddle' (*Letters to "Ivy"*, ed. S. H. Romilly, 1905, pp. 347–8). But TBM felt very kindly towards Sharp.

[3] John Allen, *Inquiry into the Rise and Growth of the Royal Prerogative in England*, 1830. For Allen, see 30 May 1831.

[4] Perhaps Sharp's privately printed *Epistles in Verse*, 1828.

projects have taken some definite form. I should like to serve a parliamentary campaign or two in your company and under your eye.[1]

What news this from France.[2] It throws even our general election into the shade.

Ever yours truly

T B Macaulay

Gray's Inn / Saturday Morning

TO MACVEY NAPIER, 19 AUGUST 1830

MS: British Museum. *Address:* Macvey Napier Esq / Edinburgh. *Frank:* London August nineteen 1830 / T B Macaulay. *Mostly published:* Napier, *Correspondence*, pp. 82–3.

London August 19. 1830

My dear Sir,

The new number appeared this morning in the shop windows. It is certainly respectable; but I do not think that it is eminently good. The article on Niebuhr[3] contains much that is very sensible; but it is not such an article as so noble a subject required. I am not like Ellis Niebuhr-mad;[4] and I agree with many of the remarks which the reviewer has made both on this work and on the school of German critics and historians. But surely the Reviewer ought to have given an account of the system of exposition which Niebuhr has adopted and of the theory which he advances respecting the institutions of Rome. Some of the notions of the German are I think extremely just – some false and extravagant. But true or false they all indicate a vigourous and cultivated mind and will all find favourable acceptance with a large party in the literary world. The appearance of the book is really an æra in the intellectual history of Europe; and I think that the Edinburgh Review ought at least to have given a luminous abstract of it. The very circumstance that Niebuhr's own arrangement and style are obscure, and that his translators have need of translators to make them intelligible to the multitude, rendered it more desirable that a clear and neat statement of the points in controversy should be laid before the

---

[1] Sharp did not sit in Parliament after 1827.

[2] The revolution broke out on 27 July.

[3] 'Niebuhr's History of Rome,' *ER*, LI (July 1830), 358–96, was by Thomas Jefferson Hogg, the friend and biographer of Shelley.

[4] As early as 1828 Ellis says that he is 'working at Niebuhr for my General History' (to Brougham, 14 September 1828: MS, University College); a note at the beginning of part two of his *Outline of General History*, published 1 November 1830 in the 'Library of Useful Knowledge' of the Society for the Diffusion of Useful Knowledge, acknowledges that 'in the following summary we have been guided with scarcely an exception by the introductory chapters of the third edition of Niebuhr (Berlin, 1828).'

public. But it is useless to talk of what cannot be mended. The best editors cannot always have good writers, and the best writers cannot always write their best.[1]

Brougham must be out of his wits. I heard that his triumph in York-shire[2] had turned his brains or something very near it. I have no notion on what ground he imagines that I am going to review his speech.[3] He never said a word to me on the subject. Nor did I ever say either to him or to any one else a single syllable to that effect. I do remember, indeed, what till to day I had quite forgotten, that a friend of mine begged me, some time ago, to write an article on slavery.[4] I said that I thought it impossible that parliament could do any thing on the subject before Christmas, and that the beginning of next year would be a fitter time than the autumn of this. At all events I shall not make Brougham's speech my text. We have had quite enough of puffing and flattering each other in the E[dinburgh] R[eview]. It is in vile taste for men united in one literary undertaking to exchange these favours.

I have a plan of which I wish to know your opinion. In ten days or thereabouts I set off for France where I hope to pass six weeks. I shall be in the best society, that of the Duc de Broglie,[5] Guizot,[6] and so on. I think

---

[1] The second volume of the English translation of Niebuhr was reviewed by Henry Malden instead of Hogg: see 21 March 1832.

[2] Brougham had been returned for Yorkshire in the general election after an energetic cam-paign on the issues of abolition and parliamentary reform. Before Brougham's election 'no one who was not a resident of the county had been elected to represent Yorkshire in Parlia-ment since the Reformation and no lawyer since the Commonwealth. . . . Everyone said that his Yorkshire triumph "intoxicated" Brougham' (New, *Brougham*, pp. 407; 410). Writing anonymously just after his election, Brougham said of it that it 'is assuredly the most extraordinary event in the history of party politics' ('The Ministry, and the State of Parties,' *ER*, LI [July 1830], 582n.).

[3] On 13 July Brougham made a long speech against slavery on his motion for the House to take up the subject of abolition in its next session. Brougham wrote to Napier, [23 July 1830], that 'I had meant today to send you my Colonial Slavery Speech. . . . T. Macaulay is to prepare a leading article on it and the subject for the next Number' (Napier, *Correspon-dence*, p. 80). In the same letter Brougham asked Napier to insert a notice of the speech, promising a review of it for the next number. Napier printed a notice, *ER*, LI (July 1830), 583–4, but this made only a vague promise, and the speech was not reviewed in the *ER*.

[4] 'Macaulay is under engagement to his father and me to write a paper this No. [of the *ER*] on W[est] I[ndian] Slavery' (Brougham to Napier, 8 September 1830: MS, British Museum). The anti-slavery campaign had languished in 1828, when its leaders were in bad health, and in 1829, when the question of Catholic relief was paramount; it was intended to revive it in 1830, a plan in which Brougham's speech of 13 July was the first step. It is at least very likely that Zachary Macaulay had asked TBM to contribute to the effort.

[5] Victor, third Duc de Broglie (1785–1870), *juste-milieu* statesman, at this time minister of education; prime minister, 1835–6; ambassador to England, 1847. Zachary Macaulay had long known de Broglie as one of his most useful supporters in the effort to put down the French slave trade.

[6] François Guizot (1787–1874), historian and statesman, was minister of the interior in the new government. Zachary Macaulay met him in 1823, and reported that he was 'one of the very ablest men, I do believe, in France' (Knutsford, *Zachary Macaulay*, p. 412).

of writing an article on the politics of France since the Restoration,[1] with characters of the principal public men, and a parallel between the present state of France and that of England. I think that this might be made an article of extraordinary interest. I do not say that I could make it so. It must, you will perceive, be a long paper, however concise I may try to be. But as the subject is important, and I am not generally diffuse, you must not stint me. If you like this scheme let me know as soon as possible. The Italian poets must stand over, – that is if you approve of my plan. I am glad to hear that Ellis found so good a Cicerone, or, as Mr. Shepherd of Liverpool always calls it in his travels, – so good a *Cicisbeo*.[2] John Mill[3] is gone to France on a mission to preach up the republic and the physical check,[4] I suppose.

Ever yours truly

T B Macaulay

TO MARGARET MACAULAY, 26 AUGUST 1830

MS: Mrs Lancelot Errington. *Address:* Miss Macaulay / E Cropper's Esq / Dingle Bank[5] / Liverpool. *Frank:* Leicester August twenty six / 1830 / T B Macaulay.

Temple Thursday.

My darling Margaret, –

I have little or nothing to say to you. But as I am franking a letter to you, I will just write one line to say how much I love you – and how

---

[1] See Appendix.

[2] William Shepherd, *Paris in Eighteen Hundred and Two and Eighteen Hundred and Fourteen*, 1814; the only instance of the word that I find in the book is on p. 106: 'The person who acted as our cicisbeo.' The *OED* defines '*cicisbeo*' as 'the name formerly given in Italy to the recognized gallant or *cavalier servente* of a married woman.' TBM was probably pleased to think that the blunder was made by a friend of Brougham's.

[3] John Stuart Mill (1806–73: *DNB*), the philosopher and publicist. He went to Paris in the week of 8 August and remained until the first week of September (Mineka, ed., *The Earlier Letters of John Stuart Mill*, I, 54). TBM, together with other young Cambridge graduates, had been one of the original members of the London Debating Society, founded by Mill in 1826; but TBM's name is not in the Society's list of members for 1830, and there is no indication in the Society's published records that he ever spoke at its meetings.

[4] I.e., a contraceptive method. Mill had in 1823 been arrested for distributing a pamphlet on birth control, and though the episode is only imperfectly documented, London gossip always remembered it.

[5] A thirty-acre field on the banks of the Mersey, two miles upriver from Liverpool, where James Cropper and his two sons, Edward and John, had each built a house and where they lived as a family community: see F. A. Conybeare, *Dingle Bank, the Home of the Croppers*, Cambridge, 1925. Harriet Beecher Stowe was entertained there in 1853 and described it in her *Sunny Memories from Foreign Lands*, 1854, Letter 2. Dingle Bank reappears as a footnote to literary history as the place where Matthew Arnold, whose sister Susan married into the Cropper family, was staying on the day he died.

heartily I sympathise [w]¹ith all that you have had to s[uffe]r.² I am off for Paris next week; and you shall have such a journal as was never seen. I intend to breakfast every day on frogs and to marry a French wife, and to come back all begrimed with snuff and as filthy as M. Simond.

Yours ever dearest
T B M

Kind remembrances to the Croppers.

TO MACVEY NAPIER, 27 AUGUST 1830

MS: British Museum. *Address:* Macvey Napier Esq / Edinburgh. *Frank:* Leicester August twenty seven 1830 / T B Macaulay. *Partly published:* Napier, *Correspondence*, pp. 83–4.

Rothley Temple Leicestershire / August 27. 1830

My dear Sir,

I have just received your letter and the inclosed bill.³ To morrow or on Monday I set off for London – on Wednesday for France. I will take into full consideration your hint about dividing my article.

The paper on the State of Parties⁴ – Brougham's of course – has made considerable noise. The general opinion is that the craving for place appears in it too undisguisedly; and I think that, considering how strongly the Whigs have always censured the attacks on female character in the John Bull, the allusion to the women of fashion who support the Duke might have been spared with advantage.⁵ The reviewer says that, if he could, he should have no more scruple in exposing these ladies to ridicule than in attacking Peel or Goulburn.⁶ Now surely the ladies who visited the Queen⁷ must, if this be a proper way of looking at the subject, have been fair objects of satire.

Ellis has written to me. He speaks in the warmest terms of your kindness and of the pleasure which he had in his visit to Edinburgh.

¹ Paper here and in next line torn away with seal.
² Edward Cropper's wife Isabella suffered a paralytic stroke on 24 July; Margaret Macaulay nursed her until her death, 27 September 1830.
³ In payment for 'Sadler's *Law of Population.*'
⁴ Henry Brougham, 'The Ministry, and the State of Parties,' *ER*, LI (July 1830), 564–82. One of three articles by Brougham in this number of the *ER*.
⁵ In a note at the end of the review Brougham says that Wellington, though abandoned by the newspapers, is supported by 'the talk of several women of fashion' (*ER*, LI, 582).
⁶ Henry Goulburn (1784–1856: *DNB*), M.P., 1808–56; for Cambridge University from 1831. An intimate friend and loyal supporter of Peel, he was Chancellor of the Exchequer in Wellington's ministry, Home Secretary in Peel's first administration, and Chancellor of the Exchequer in his second.
⁷ I cannot explain this reference.

You shall hear from me as soon as I see my way about these French affairs clear before me.

Ever yours truly

T B Macaulay

Empson's article about Jefferson[1] is pleasant and by no means, I think, too long.

TO THOMAS FLOWER ELLIS, 28 AUGUST 1830

MS: Trinity College. *Extract published:* Trevelyan, I, 164.

Rothley Temple Leicestershire / August 28. 1830

My dear Ellis,

On Monday I go to London; on Wednesday, nothing unforeseen preventing, I set off for Brighton. On Thursday I proceed by steam to Dieppe; on Friday by the *diligence* to Rouen where I shall sleep, and look at the Cathedral and other curiosities. On Saturday night I hope to be at Meurice's Hotel in the Rue St Honoré.

I will, if I find your book[2] at my chambers, or can procure it from your Society's Office, carry it with me, and read it on the Steam-boat. I shall hardly have time during the few hours of my stay in London, what with bankrupt commissions, and what with travelling preparations, to look over it critically. I hope to have access to the Ambassador's bag at Paris; and if so I shall correspond gratis. If you have any thing to say, send a letter to Great Ormond Street. It will be forwarded, wherever I shall then be in France. I hope to see Orléans, Blois, and Tours, Versailles of course, possibly Fontainebleau, and I may perhaps return by Ghent and Antwerp. My travelling books and maps are bought; and I have a bag of seventy five as good looking Napoleons and Louis d'or's as you would wish to see. There is much that I am impatient to see – but two things specially, – the Palais Royal, and the man who called me the Aristarchus of Edinburgh.

So you have seen the exquisite compliment paid me by the Sun.[3] Jeffrey tells me that I have triumphed too much over Sadler's blunder in

---

[1] 'Jefferson's *Memoirs and Correspondence*,' *ER*, LI (July 1830), 496–526.

[2] Part two of Ellis's *Outline of General History* for the SDUK.

[3] The *Sun*, 23 August, reviewing the July *ER*, said that 'We do not recognise the vigorous and elegant pen of Macauley, unless it be in the analysis of "Niebuhr's Roman History," and we here trace it rather in the choice of subject than from any internal evidence that the style puts forth.' As to the essay on Sadler, it is 'sensible and satisfactory,' but the reviewer possesses no powers of 'humour and sarcasm.'

mathematical nomenclature;[1] – and that it would, in his opinion, have been more dignified to pass over that inaccuracy lightly, as the real meaning of the doctrine was obvious. I differ from him. Sadler's personal influence does as much harm as his theory is likely to do. And it is, I think, of quite as much importance to shew that he is ignorant as that his principle is false. Jeffrey is, as to the rest, very complimentary. He says that he much regrets having missed you, and desires me to tell you that he hopes to be more lucky another time.

I pity Adolphus[2] from my soul. All his old Tory friends are turning radicals, – not from principle, for they never had any, – but from spite and folly: – and he will find himself like an owl in the desert. A man must have been very short sighted who could not always perceive the Jacobinism through the chinks and cracks of Milner's[3] Churchmanship and loyalty. I wish you would write a poem in imitation of Campbell's last man,[4] and entitle it the last Tory. If you add the best Tory, you will not be much out.

Mr. Dunn[5] is no stranger to me. I was in the Court of K[ings] B[ench] one morning when he came to make a motion. The ground which he took was that you might have a writ of Error because an arbitrator before whom the accounts had gone had refused to hear certain evidence. Lord Tenterden[6] was half an hour trying to understand what he meant. He could not suppose that any thing under a gown and wig could be so stupid. "What," said the gentleman connected, with great rhetorical vehemence. "Shall an arbitrator be in a better condition than your Lordships. If your Lordship gives a wrong charge or asks a wrong question error will lie." "Indeed Sir," said Lord T, "but it won't." "Good God,

---

[1] Sadler had argued that 'the prolificness of human beings, otherwise similarly circumstanced, varies inversely as their numbers'; TBM concluded that 'Mr Sadler does not know what inverse proportion means' (*ER*, LI, 302; 304). Sadler evidently meant only to say that the less dense the population the greater the prolificness, and vice versa, but TBM holds him strictly to his unlucky use of 'inverse proportion.'

[2] John Leycester Adolphus (1795–1862: *DNB*), the son of the historian and himself the author of the able, anonymous *Letters to Richard Heber*, 1821, identifying Scott as the author of the Waverley novels, and of a parody entitled 'The Circuiteers,' which TBM is said to have called 'the best imitation he ever read' (*Notes and Queries*, 2 January 1864, p. 6). He had been on the Northern Circuit since 1822 but without marked success; Pollock, *Personal Remembrances*, I, 100, describes him as 'modest and retiring.' He was a close friend of Ellis's, and collaborated with him in a series of *Reports* of cases in the Court of King's and Queen's Bench, 1835–52. From 1852 Adolphus was a judge of the Marylebone County Court.

[3] Charles Milner (1790–1837), a barrister on the Northern Circuit, was at this time deputy Recorder of Leeds and one of the leading counsel at the West Riding sessions. He succeeded Hardy as Recorder of Leeds in 1833; the Leeds *Mercury*, 23 March 1833, says that Milner is 'well known to be a determined and even a warm Tory.'

[4] Thomas Campbell, 'The Last Man,' 1823.

[5] Probably the James Dunn who was admitted to the University of Dublin, aged fifteen, 1789; Lincoln's Inn, 1792; Irish bar, 1795. The *Law List*, 1828–30, names a J. Dunn, 45 Marsham Street, of the Northern Circuit and Lancashire sessions.

[6] Charles Abbott (1762–1832: *DNB*), first Baron Tenterden, Lord Chief Justice.

my Lord," said the best public instructor, "do you mean to say that wrong decisions can be pronounced, and that there is no remedy." Lord Tenterden laughed and told Mr. Dunn to sit down. "Really, really, Sir, there are first principles." I remember the youth — a black, little, ugly, Irishman. – Drinky,[1] you say, is gone to Kendal for his portmanteau. Are you sure that he is not gone to fight Mr. Dunn?

Brougham is evidently out of his wits or very near it.[2] What a pity that every crisis which particularly calls for prudence and self-command should throw him into so violent a state of excitement! Àpropos of his Greek. The Morning Herald has taken up the classical line and seems likely to rival the Standard. There were three pieces of Greek in the last Number, that I saw. What do you think of "that virtuous and eminent class of Athenian citizens to whom the great Pericles gave the appellation of πολλοι or many" – ?[3]

The ministry are clearly in a scrape. I do not think that they can possibly stand till Xmas. They have certainly been making overtures to Lord Melbourne,[4] and, I think from some hints that I have had, to Lord Goderich too. They have certainly obtained no favourable answers as yet from any quarter. The elections have put them in a worse position than that in which they were last year – and, God knows, that was bad enough. Every one of the Peels has had a beating except the Sec.[5] He had enough last year to last him his life, I should think. Dawson, Peel's brother in law, had two beatings, or rather ran away twice without fighting. Is not Wodehouse[6] as Croker?[7] Is not Lord Charles Manners[8] as Gaffer Gooch?[9]

---

[1] John Drinkwater (1801–51: *DNB*), later Drinkwater Bethune, a graduate of Trinity and on the Northern Circuit with TBM. In 1848 he was appointed to the post on the Supreme Council of India that TBM had once held; he died in India.

[2] See 19 August 1830. Brougham was, however, still useful to TBM. On 1 September Zachary Macaulay wrote to Brougham that 'Tom sets off in an hour or two for Paris laden with kind introductions from you and his other friends particularly Lansdowne and Mackintosh. He carries with him your letter to La Fayette' (Brougham MSS, University College).

[3] 'The mass of people – οι πολλοι, as Pericles called the multitude, when addressing the gallant and accomplished "men of Athen" [*sic*]' (*Morning Herald*, 27 August).

[4] William Lamb (1779–1848: *DNB*), second Viscount Melbourne, Prime Minister, 1834; 1835–41.

[5] Not every one: William Peel came in for Yarmouth in this election. But Edmund and Jonathan Peel were defeated, and Sir Robert's brother-in-law, George Dawson, who had sat for Londonderry since 1815, was forced to find a seat in England, being returned for Harwich. Sir Robert, Wellington's Home Secretary, was returned for Tamworth.

[6] Edmond Wodehouse (1784–1855: *Boase*), a Norfolk landowner and Tory M.P., defeated in this election for Norfolk.

[7] John Wilson Croker (1780–1857: *DNB*), Tory M.P., 1807–32; Secretary of the Admiralty, 1809–30; opponent of the Reform Bill; most influential of the contributors to the *Quarterly Review*; and editor of a useful edition of Boswell's *Life of Johnson*, 1831; he provoked a more virulent hatred in TBM than any other public man, for reasons that are by no means clear. The earliest reference of TBM's to Croker occurs in 'The London University,' where the tone is already hostile: 'We have observed that, since Mr Croker, in the last session of Parliament, declared himself ignorant of the site of Russell Square, the plan of forming an

I hope that the sixth child[1] has been added to your fecundity, which is certainly that of a man who has lived on a very thinly peopled spot of ground.[2] And I hope that you have had such an accession of briefs as may lead you to think this increase of population no evil. Remember [. . . .][3]

JOURNAL LETTER, 2–[13] SEPTEMBER 1830

MS: Trinity College. *Extracts published:* Trevelyan, I, 163–4.

[Paris]

Journal

Thursday Septr. 2. 1830

At ten in the morning I was on the pier at Brighton. The day was beautiful; the sea slightly agitated, the scene extremely lively, the crowd great. On the pier I met Gurney[4] the King's Counsel and his wife, with whom I chatted while the baggage was put on board. At a quarter after ten I went into the packet and commenced my first voyage. It was really delightful. Some of the passengers were very sick. I suffered from nothing but hunger. The sea-air excited my appetite, and the sea-fare was not such as I liked. If any thing could have made me sick it would have been the aspect of the sandwiches which the Ship's Steward served out.

We lost sight of Brighton at about twelve o'clock, the English coast faded from our sight rapidly, except one point – Beachy Head, the white scalp of which my eyes could distinguish – though mine alone in the ship – till near four o'clock. A few minutes after five, a faint streak began to appear in the opposite quarter of the sky – the coast of France. It was night

University in so inelegant a neighbourhood has excited much contempt' (*ER*, XLIII, 319). By 1830, though no particular provocation is known, TBM's feeling was so strong against Croker that he went out of his way to defend Brougham, for whom he had no love, for the sake of attacking Croker in a speech in the Commons, 23 November, so violent as to result in his being called to order. The bitterness of their opposition over the Reform Bill deepened but did not originate the malevolent feeling between the two men. It is possible that TBM saw and resented in Croker too many resemblances to himself; both were barristers who, without rank, had imposed themselves upon politics and society through their gifts as speakers and writers. That, with his origins, Croker, besides being a Tory, should adopt an air of patronizing superiority seems exactly calculated to call out all of TBM's hostility.

[8] Son of the fourth Duke of Rutland, defeated for Cambridgeshire, 1830.

[9] Cobbett's name for Sir Thomas Sherlock Gooch (1767–1851: *Boase*), M.P. for Suffolk, 1806–30. (*From opposite page.*)

[1] The Ellises' child was still-born, 27 August.

[2] A joke at the expense of Sadler's law of population.

[3] The rest is missing.

[4] (Sir) John Gurney (1768–1845: *DNB*), one of the leading counsel in the Court of King's Bench, where TBM attended without practice; K.C., 1816; appointed Baron of the Court of Exchequer and knighted, 1832.

however before we reached land. I love coming to a new town or a new country by night. There is something in the indistinctness of the objects which at once piques and gratifies curiosity. The sounds from the coast, the lights, the hallooing of the fishermen, the figures moving up and down the shore in the moonlight made the approach much more interesting than it would have been by day.

We were close to land. Yet I could see no houses. The pilot however directed our course round a kind of promontory; and we were at once in still water – in a sort of dock, – surrounded by the town of Dieppe. The houses are all of stone, coloured and decorated in a manner which, if not perfectly graceful, is extremely lively. The whole was in a blaze of light. Hundreds of people were running along the quays, with lanthorns and torches, bawling to each other – pushing each other, – and eager to receive us from the steam-boat.

We stopped at the quay, close to the houses, in the middle, in fact, of a square of smart shops, which is built round the bason of the harbour. An officer and two soldiers instantly came on board, to examine our passports and prevent us from smuggling. We were permitted to take out the few things which might be necessary for our night's rest and the next morning's toilette. The rest was left on board under a guard.

The Master of the York Hotel at Brighton had recommended the Hotel Royal at Dieppe. People from that Hotel, – and from every hotel in the place, were in waiting on the quay; and at nine o'clock I found myself taking my ease, as Falstaff says, in mine own inn.[1] The people spoke English; but the room was eminently French; – a bed in an alcove which was hidden by glass folding doors, – silk curtains, – a gilded cornice, – and a brick floor.

I called stoutly for something to eat; and was asked whether I should like a beef-steak. By all means – and out came something very good, but no more entitled to be called a beef steak than a raspberry cream. They brought me a partridge for second course – plenty of excellent bread and a bottle of light wine which cost about eighteen pence of our money. After dining, I went to bed heartily fatigued, but not till I had written a line to tell you of my safe arrival. I gave it to my land lord, who ten to one has not sent it; as I did not remember that it was necessary to pay to the frontier. I fell fast asleep as soon as I was in bed.

Friday Sept 3.

As soon as I had dressed myself and washed myself with some soap with which no English farmer would have washed a sheep after shearing, I went down to the custom house. The people were civil. The only

---

[1] *1 Henry IV*, III, iii, 91.

article in my baggage which excited suspicion was Lord Lansdowne's parcel for the Duc de Broglie. Naturally enough, the officers of the douane might think that this was cover for some smuggling transaction of mine. They made several inquiries. But at last they returned the parcel unopened; and my baggage was carried to the Hotel Royal. I breakfasted and went to the Prefet to change my passport for another. I then tried to procure a place in the diligence. But the diligence was full for that and the next day. I was therefore forced to travel post. My land lord had a stout though not very handsome calèche which he wished to send to Meurice's at Paris. So that I made a very reasonable bargain; and as post-horses are much cheaper here than in England, I had, I think, my money's worth for my money.

Dieppe is a lively town – I know no English town which gives any idea of it. The houses are not high – they are of stone – generally streaked, and painted. They have almost all balconies. There is an air of antiquity and ruggedness – yet at the same time of smartness and gaiety about the aspect of the streets which is extremely peculiar. It shared little in the late agitation. The Duchess of Berri[1] had been its principal patron. It was her watering-place – and the inhabitants were in consequence more favourable to the Bourbons than the people of France generally are. Then too the constant resort of English had tended to diminish the national feeling among them. They are half English in their manners and even in their language – and our money passes among them with ease.

I left Dieppe soon after ten. In about half an hour I passed the diligence, and certainly did not at that moment envy those who had forestalled me in procuring places. Imagine a cabriolet mounted as high as a house, with two old hackney coaches awkwardly fastened to it behind, the whole harness composed of ropes. This machine is drawn by a kind of drove of horses, – not placed two and two, but running backward and forward, sometimes two sometimes three abreast. The whole is directed by a queer fellow who looks like an old soldier turned beggar, or a strolling player in the part of a King, in an embroidered coat falling to pieces, with a whip as long as a ship's cable fastened to a handle as short as a hoop-stick. Instead of sitting, like a Christian Coachman, on his box, this conducteur was bestriding one of his horses, talking to them in the strangest tones, and grinning so sentimentally that I thought I should have died with laughing. My postillion, I must own, was almost as queer a person; and my harness also was of ropes. The road was excellent. It is, I am told, the best in France, and has been an object of especial attention on account of the frequent journeys of the Duchess of Berri and the Duke of Bordeaux.[2]

[1] Daughter-in-law of Charles X.
[2] The Duchess's son: in 1832 she made an abortive attempt to regain the throne for him.

The hills are not cut down nor the vallies filled up, as in the best roads of England, but there cannot be a smoother or a stronger path underfoot, than I found this. The aspect of the country was on the whole cheerful. The want of inclosures and hedges is a disadvantage. But the numerous woods which are scattered amongst the cornfields redeem the country from the reproach of nakedness. Pleasant villages lie upon the road at short distances from each other. At all the churches the tricoloured flag was flying. At Dieppe I had seen few signs of zeal for the late revolution. The lilies which have been effaced every where else were still visible in every part of that town.

The road became more and more interesting as I proceeded. For some miles before I reached Rouen there was an almost constant succession of houses, like that in the neighbourhood of London – not such good houses indeed; but still good enough to indicate great prosperity. Many new buildings are rising along this part of the road. At last through a magnificent avenue of trees I entered Rouen; and drove to the Hotel de France, as my host at Dieppe had advised.

I was shewn into a very comfortable sitting room – as comfortable as a sitting room without a carpet can be. I ordered dinner to be ready at half past six. It was then four; and I set out to look about me.

Rouen is indeed an interesting city. I could be willing to pass a week there. The general aspect of the town is even more remarkable than the splendour of particular edifices. I have seen nothing like it. Bristol perhaps is the English city which resembles it most. Both are old towns, – both are seats of bishops, – both are commercial towns, – both are situated in beautiful landscapes. But Bristol is far – very far – inferior to Rouen both in its old and in its new part. Its cathedral is not to be named in the same day with that of Rouen – and the Church of St Mary Redcliff, though very fine, is far inferior to the Church of St Ouen. The river at Bristol is a mere brook compared to the noble Seine. Yet the Seine disappointed me a little. It is not by any means so wide as the Thames at London.

At Rouen I was most struck with what I have already mentioned as the thing which struck me at Dieppe; – I mean the union of venerable and gloomy antiquity with extreme liveliness and gaiety. We have nothing of the sort in England. We have indeed very few old towns. Till the time of James I, I imagine, our houses were almost all of wood. They have in consequence disappeared. In York there are some very old streets; but they are abandoned to the lowest people, and the gay shops are in the newly built part of the town. The same may be said of Edinburgh. In London, what with the fire of 1666, and what with the natural progress of demolition and rebuilding, I doubt whether there are fifty houses as old as the reformation. Rouen is for the most part, I should think, as old as the colleges of Oxford and Cambridge; or older. Imagine to yourselves street after street of high, dark, stern looking masses of stone, with Gothic carvings. The buildings are so high and the streets so narrow that the sun can scarcely reach the pavements. The houses are rugged and dark with old age. Yet in these streets, so monastic in their aspect, you have all the glitter of Regent Street or the Burlington arcade. It is a blaze of ribbands, gowns, watches, trinkets, artificial flowers, – peaches such as Covent Garden does not furnish – grapes, melons, filling the windows of the fruiterers; [   ]¹ It is the Soho Bazaar² transplanted into one of the gloomy cloisters of Oxford.

The Cathedral is fine; but it has suffered dreadfully from fire. The Church of St Ouen is, I think, finer. It reminded me – and it is the first building that ever reminded me – of the Chapel of King's College. It is indeed inferior to that incomparable edifice. But there is something of the same Grecian unity of conception which, when combined with the Gothic richness of detail, produces the highest miracles of architecture.

At half past six I went back to my inn, and dined very well. I ordered horses at six the next morning; and went to bed.

Saturday Sept 4.

I was up in time, breakfasted on café au lait and an excellent loaf, and set off by the light of a brilliant sun. The road was very beautiful, and the view of the rich valley of the Seine from the Hills that overlook Rouen was as fine as any thing of the kind that I have ever seen. The whole day I travelled through a country – well inhabited and well cultivated, – with a sufficient variety of hill and valley to be picturesque, yet by no means mountainous. The towns were all alive. The national guards were to be seen every where. The tricoloured flag was flying on every steeple and on every public building.

I did not see much beggary excepting at the places where I changed horses. There is a beggar regularly stationed at every post to plague the travellers. I could hardly help suspecting that the government provides these hideous old wretches as it provides the post horses, and receives the proceeds of their supplications. The instant that the postillion cracks his whip at the door of the post house out comes a man with a wen or a wooden leg, and stands by the carriage till the horses are put in, repeating

¹ Three lines have here been heavily overscored in the MS. The extract in Trevelyan, I, 164, reads: 'showy women swimming smoothly over the uneasy stones, and stared at by national guards swaggering by in full uniform.'

² The Soho Bazaar, on Soho Square, opened in 1816 as a place where the widows and dependants of British soldiers might sell wares of their own manufacture. The building is now occupied by the publishers A. and C. Black; an account of the bazaar is given in the firm's history, *Adam and Charles Black, 1807–1957*, 1957, pp. 51–3.

"Pour l'amour de Dieu, mon brave Monsieur, ayez quelque compassion de ma misère" – or "Mon cher Monsieur, prenez pitié d'un pauvre miserable estropié, qui se reccommand a vos humanités." I was half enraged and half inclined to laugh at this ceremony which was regularly repeated at every stage, without one omission. At Louvieres indeed when I heard the whining begin, and turned round with some impatience, I was agreably surprised to see two very pretty little girls, instead of the horrible paralytic old wretch whom I had expected – and whom I on no other occasion expected in vain. I gave them a couple of sous a piece, and was amply repaid by the ludicrous scene which followed. "Ah, Monsieur," they had been crying, "ayez pitié d'une pauvre pétite fille, qui n'a ni père ni mére, qui n'a rien mangé, depuis hier." – The moment they touched the money, they began skipping like rope dancers, shouting, laughing, clapping their hands, riding on each other's backs – (they could not have been more than ten years old) and they followed me half through the town crying "Bon voyage, milord." The postillion could hardly keep his seat for laughing, – I suppose to see how the Englishman had been taken in.

I had been told that there were very few country houses in France. Certainly this is by no means the case on the road from Dieppe to Paris. There are few seats which in England we should call large – and I saw none which I should call fine. But there were many with large pleasure grounds and avenues. Some of these houses are of staring red brick, – a strange defect of taste in a country which abounds with stone. I did not see one seat which was not either formal or slovenly – which did not look like a tea-garden or like a farmyard.

I dined at Nantes – at a bad inn – and had a bad dinner. What I ate I leave on the conscience of the cook – for it was like no food that I ever ate before; and may have been a fricassee of cats and dogs for any thing that I know to the contrary. I then re-entered my vehicle; and set off as usual amidst the howling of an old beggar with a swelling on his neck as big as his head.

The sun was setting as I rode through the forest of St. Germains – a place which may almost be called a part of England – so many English recollections are connected with it.[1] The moon rose with great brilliancy. At a little after nine I passed the arch at the top of the avenue of Neuilly and was in the midst of a blaze of lamps. Nothing can be finer than a moonlight entrance into Paris by this noble road. Palace after palace rises and sinks as you pass – the gilded dome of the Invalides, the Portico of the Palais Bourbon, the statues – too white by day light, but beautiful in the moon, – which line the Pont de Louis Quinze, the magnificent Place de Louis Seize, the Thuilleries, the arcades of the Rue Rivoli the

---

[1] James II held his court in exile and died at St Germain-en-Laye.

Pillar of Austerlitz – you catch a glimpse of all, before you are buried in the Rue St Honoré. No city, I imagine, can boast of so noble an approach, nor could I have seen this noble approach under more favourable circumstances.

I have now brought myself to Paris. You shall hear in my next packet what I think of Paris. – Sir Robert Inglis goes to morrow, and I must give him my narrative. I assure you that I rose at five this morning to write it.

T B M

TO ZACHARY MACAULAY, 13 SEPTEMBER 1830

MS: Trinity College. *Address:* Z Macaulay Esq / 50 Great Ormond Street / London.

Paris Septr. 13. 1830

My dear Father,

Sir R Inglis sets off for London to morrow. I will charge him with a long narrative of my adventures. I agree in the main with what you say about politics. But I do not think that Huskisson and his friends will or can join the present administration[1] – at least without such changes both of men and of measures as would be very humiliating both to the Duke and to Peel. Kind love to all. I suppose that Henry must be in England by this time.[2]

T B M.

JOURNAL LETTER, 14 SEPTEMBER 1830

MS: Trinity College. *Extracts published:* Trevelyan, I, 164–5.

Paris Septr. 14. 1830. Tuesday.

Sir R Inglis does not I find go till to morrow. So that I have time to carry my story further. But where shall I begin or leave off. Though I have

---

[1] The Tory party, following the crisis of Catholic emancipation and in face of the pressure for reform, was divided among the extreme Tories, resentful of what had already been done, the supporters of the administration, and the Canningites under Huskisson. Wellington's government, which refused to consider any measure of parliamentary reform, resigned on 16 November 1830.

[2] On the death of Kenneth Macaulay in 1829 Zachary Macaulay sent Henry to Sierra Leone to superintend the closing out of Macaulay and Babington's business there (Knutsford, *Zachary Macaulay*, p. 405). Henry left England in January 1830 with instructions to return by June; he stayed, however, until the beginning of the rainy season and fell seriously ill for five weeks (Selina Macaulay, Diary, 15 January; 30 December 1830). He was evidently back in England by late September; in January 1831 he returned to Sierra Leone (*ibid.*, 15 January 1831). Henry made a long report on the tangled affairs of his father's business in a letter of 16 August–7 September 1830 (MS, Huntington).

been ten days in this great city there are large districts and interesting sights which I have not yet visited. Take however the best account which I can give of the impression which Paris has produced on me.

As to public buildings, I doubt whether the advantage be with Paris or London. On the whole I lean to London. The Pantheon is fine, but immeasurably inferior to St Paul's. Notre Dame is pretty well – but not to be compared with Westminster abbey. St Roch is well enough. But not equal to several of Sir Christopher Wren's Churches. The Hotel des Invalides is very magnificent – but hardly, I think, so fine as Greenwich Hospital, either within or without. As to bridges it would be absurd to institute a comparison. Three arches of the Waterloo Bridge would span the Seine in the broadest part of its course through Paris. And there is nothing like those gigantic masses of warehouses and those vast docks which line the Thames at the East of London.

On the other hand we have not, I think, in London any architectural compositions so beautiful – so correct and at the same time so magnificent – as the Palace of the Deputies, – the Place Louis Seize, – and, above all, the Eastern facade of the Louvre. The monument, though a fine pillar and twice as large, I should think, in every dimension, as the column of Austerlitz, is by no means equal to that column in beauty. None of our public offices – not even the Post Office,[1] is equal to the Bourse: and though the architecture of the Thuilleries and of the galleries which run between the Thuilleries and the Louvre, is by no means pure, there is certainly great splendour in the general effect. When the whole plan is completed the circumference of this vast palace will be, I should think, considerably upwards of a mile.

Above all we have nothing in London like the Palais Royal. If I were to select the spot in all the earth in which the good and evil of civilisation are most strikingly exhibited, in which the arts of life are carried to the highest perfection, in which all pleasures, high and low, intellectual and sensual, are collected in the smallest space, I should certainly chuse the Palais Royal. It is the Covent Garden Piazza, the Pater-Noster Row, the Vauxhall, the Albion Tavern,[2] the Burlington Arcade, the Crockford's, the Finish,[3] the Athenæum,[4] of Paris, all in one. Even now, when the first

---

[1] Built 1825–9.

[2] In Aldersgate Street; famous for the best and most expensive dinners in London. The East India Company typically feasted each new Governor-General there, and extended the courtesy to TBM on his Indian appointment (see 8 January 1834). In anticipation of TBM's return to England in 1838 Ellis wrote to Napier that 'I hope you will be in London in the summer: we will have another Albion dinner out of Macaulay' (26 February 1838: MS, British Museum).

[3] A disreputable night house in Covent Garden, closed in 1829.

[4] Founded by John Wilson Croker in 1824; TBM was elected to membership on 12 June 1830. The club in that year took in two hundred new members, half of whom were chosen

dazzling effect has passed by, I never pass through it without feeling bewildered by its magnificent variety.

I will try to give you an idea of it. My father can illustrate, if my description is obscure. Fronting the Rue St Honoré is a modest looking building – not much unlike the front of Somerset House towards the Strand, but far inferior. This is the part of the Palais Royal inhabited by the present King. He will probably soon remove. The ground floor, as you can see through glass doors, is constantly occupied by national guards. Above is a suite of apartments, which seems to be splendidly furnished, where his majesty resides. Behind this residence, – a splendid one for the Duke of Orléans,[1] but hardly fit for the King of the French, lies a small but brilliant square of shops. After traversing this square you reach the great court of the Palais Royal.

Imagine a space as large as Portman square, planted with trees, a fountain in the centre, and a continued range of lofty buildings, of the most florid architecture, running round it. The whole ground-floor consists of the most brilliant shops, cafés, and taverns, that you can conceive. Books, jewellery, millinery, fruit, pastry, china, glass, prints, all in the most rapid succession. An arcade runs along all these shops, and this arcade is full from morning to night of all the gayest people – as far as dress at least is a sign of gaiety, in Paris. I have passed at eight in the morning. I have passed at eleven at night, and always found it swarming with people, and in a constant buz of voices. At night it is gorgeously lighted up with lamps. Among the trees in the middle of the court are cabinets, neatly painted, where newspapers are to be seen, and where ices and lemonade are sold. Pedlars run about from morning to night with their boxes, flower-women with baskets of nosegays, little Italian boys with squirrels and monkeys, national guards hurrying to and from the palace; – singing in one cabinet, smoking in another – women staring at the shops, dandies staring at the women, and Englishmen staring at every thing.

by a special committee and half by the club at large. Admission by election of the special committee was, according to Sir Henry Holland, regarded as a distinction for which there was 'eager struggle' (*Recollections of Past Life*, 1872, p. 265). TBM was among those honored by the committee, as were John Stuart Mill, Charles Austin, and the younger James Stephen (Humphry Ward, *History of the Athenaeum, 1824–1925*, 1926, pp. 41–4). Theodore Hook was also among the new members; it would be interesting to know how TBM conducted himself towards Hook, the man responsible for the *John Bull*'s libels on Zachary Macaulay, and towards the club's founder, Croker, whom TBM apparently already despised (see 28 August 1830). But Bulwer's remark may explain the situation: 'A charming place the Athenaeum. The people are so informed; it is a pity they do not know each other. And so very entertaining; it is a pity they never converse' (Michael Sadleir, *Bulwer: A Panorama*, 1931, p. 218n.). According to the club's records, TBM's name was proposed by Empson and seconded by W. H. Ord. Ord (1781–1855), then M.P. for Morpeth, was a graduate of Trinity.

[1] As Louis Philippe was before the revolution.

Here are the restaurateurs of the greatest fame. Here are Vefour and Very. Here is the Café des Mille Colonnes.[1] Of a French Café you can have no conception. A splendidly dressed and often a handsome woman presides instead of a dirty servile waiter. You take off your hat and make your bow on entering. During the morning dejeuners à la fourchette are going on, – during the middle of the day people are drinking lemonade and eating grapes and peaches, at night they are playing cards. The news-papers attract many people to these places. It is not the fashion to take in a paper here. You go to a café – call for a cup of coffee – a glass of liqueur or lemonade, and dawdle over the Constitutionel. I have not adopted this course much, as I subscribe to Galignani's.[2]

But not only are there these brilliant shops and coffee-houses in the Palais Royal. Low flash-houses are intermingled with them. While you are dining above with ladies of the highest character, – for Ladies dine here at the respectable Restaurateurs, – underneath in the cellarage there is a dance of the lowest thieves and blackguards in Paris at the Café des Aveugles – or du Sauvage. A man dressed in skins beats a drum and yells in a frightful manner for the diversion of these gentry; – above your head is probably a gaming house; – and still higher in the attics of this vast building sharpers, swindlers, and all the wretched creatures who live on the follies and vices of a great metropolis have their lodgings. The Palais Royal is perhaps the spot in all the world in which the extremes of the social system are brought together within the smallest compass. As a great capital is a country in miniature, the Palais Royal is a capital in minia-ture, an abstract and epitome of a vast civilised community, exhibiting at one glance the politeness which adorns its higher ranks, – the coarseness of its populace – the arts which embellish, the wealth which enriches, the knowledge which enlightens it, the vices and the misery which lie under-neath its brilliant exterior. – Every thing is there – and every body – Statesmen, wits, philosophers, beauties, dandies, blacklegs, adventurers, artists, idlers, King Louis Philippe and his court, beggars with matches crying for charity, wretched creatures dying of disease and want in garrets. There is no condition of life, I believe, which is not to be found in this gorgeous and fantastic Fairy land.

The general aspect of Paris is certainly superior to what I had expected – yet by no means equal to that of London. London is larger than Paris in still greater proportion than I should have expected from the difference of population. Set out in what direction you will in Paris, a vigorous walk of

[1] On his visits to Paris TBM frequently returned to these restaurants in the Palais Royal, particularly to Véfour and Véry's, as well as to the Trois Frères Provençaux, all among the city's most famous. Brillat-Savarin mentions Véry's, and a meal there is described in Bulwer Lytton's *Pelham*, 1828, ch. 12.

[2] The English reading room opened by the publisher Giovanni Galignani in 1800.

three quarters of an hour brings you to green trees and open country. The streets are much higher and much narrower than ours; few of them have pavements for the walkers and a gutter runs foaming down the middle, so deep that children have been drowned there. To compensate the want of accommodation for walkers in the streets they have numerous arcades. This fashion is recent; but has been carried very far. There are now probably twelve or fifteen arcades in different parts of Paris the poorest of which is far broader – and more brilliant – than our only arcades – that by Burlington House and that behind the Opera House. The principal shops are in these places – the shops at the Palais Royal which are the finest in Paris always excepted. I do not mind walking even through their worst streets. Thames Street is worse than the worst, and I have many a time fought my way through the carts of Thames Street.

There is scarcely a square or open Place in Paris. The most remarkable is the Place Vendôme. It is as like one of the Bath circuses and Hexagons as possible – the stone of the same colour – the architecture in the same style. You might fancy yourself at Bath, but for the pillar in the middle, cast of brass from the cannon taken in the war against Austria and Russia in 1805. I went up to the top of this pillar by a winding staircase in utter darkness, and had a view of Paris. No cloud of smoke as in London. The view was as clear as that from Richmond hill. An honest labouring man in a smock frock had climbed just before me – for nothing is paid at the sights here. We entered into chat. "Ah Monsieur il avoit du génie – le garçon qui a bâti ceci." "Et di qui donc parlez-vous?" said I. I thought he meant the architect. "Eh, mais c'étoit Napoleon," said he. He pointed out the Pantheon and told me that it was by Soufflot.[1] I wonder how many English carters know that St Paul's was built by Wren.

But I must stop. I have a great deal more to say – The Fauxbourg St Germain – the Chamber of Deputies – the Duke and Duchess de Broglie etc. etc.

Ever yours affectionately

T B M.

---

[1] Jacques Germain Soufflot (1713–80); the Panthéon, begun in 1764, was incomplete at the time of Soufflot's death.

TO MACVEY NAPIER, 16 SEPTEMBER 1830

MS: British Museum. *Address:* Macvey Napier Esq / Edinburgh / Great Britain. *Mostly published:* Trevelyan, I, 197–200.

Paris September 16. 1830

My dear Sir,

I have just received your letter; and I cannot deny that I am much vexed at what has happened.[1] It is not very agreable to me to find that I have thrown away the labour, – the not unsuccessful labour as I thought, – of a month; particularly as I have not many months of perfect leisure. This would not have happened if Brougham had notified his intentions to you earlier, as he ought in courtesy to you and to every body connected with the Review, to have done. He must have known that this French Question was one on which many people would be desirous to write.

What I have written will be utterly useless for your December Number. It is true that at first I thought of giving a view of French affairs since the Restoration. But you may remember that you yourself desired me to separate the article into two, – and in the earlier of the two to confine myself to the late transactions. I had done my best to meet your wishes in this respect.

I ought to tell you that I had scarcely reached Paris when I received a letter containing a very urgent application from a very respectable quarter.[2] I was desired to write a sketch, in one volume, of the late revolution here. Now I really hesitated whether I should not make my excuses to you, and accept this proposal; not on account of the pecuniary terms, for about those I have never much troubled myself; – but because I should have had ampler space for this noble subject than the Edinburgh Review would have afforded. I thought however that this would not be a fair or friendly course towards you. I accordingly told the applicants that I had promised you an article, and that I could not well write twice in one month on the same subject without repeating myself. I therefore declined; and recommended a person whom I thought quite capable of producing an attractive book on these events. To that person my correspondent has probably applied. At all events I cannot revive the negotiation. I cannot hawk my rejected articles up and down Paternoster Row.

I am, therefore, a good deal vexed at this affair. But I am not in the least surprised at it. I see all the difficulties of your situation. Indeed I have long foreseen them. I always knew that in every association, literary or political,

---

[1] See 19 August 1830 and Appendix. Napier's letter to TBM would have reported the substance of Brougham to Napier, 8 September, that 'I must beg, and indeed, make a point of giving you my thoughts on the Revolution, and, therefore, pray send off your countermand to Macaulay' (Napier, *Correspondence*, p. 88).

[2] Dionysius Lardner: see 16 October 1830.

Brougham would wish to domineer. I knew, also, that no Editor of the Edinburgh Review could, without risking the ruin of the publication, resolutely oppose the demands of a man so able and powerful. It was because I was certain that he would exact submissions which I am not disposed to make that I wished, last year, to give up writing for the Review. I had long been meditating a retreat. I thought Jeffrey's abdication a favourable time for effecting it; not, as I hope you are well assured, from any unkind feeling towards you but because I knew that, under any editor, mishaps such as that which has now occurred would be constantly taking place. I remember that I predicted to Jeffrey what has now come to pass, almost to the letter.

My expectations have been exactly realised. The present constitution of the Edinburgh Review is this, – that at whatever time Brougham may be pleased to notify his intention of writing on any subject, all previous engagements are to be considered as annulled by that notification. His language translated into plain English is this. "I must write about this French revolution and I will write about it. If you have told Macaulay to do it, you may tell him to let it alone. If he has written an article, he may throw it behind the grate. He would not himself have the assurance to compare his own claims with mine. I am a man who act a prominent part in the world: he is nobody. If he must be reviewing, there is my speech about the West Indies. Set him to write a puff on that. What have people like him to do, except to eulogise people like me?" No man likes to be reminded of his inferiority in such a way: and there are some particular circumstances in this case which render the admonition more unpleasant than it would otherwise be. I know that Brougham dislikes me; and I have not the slightest doubt that he feels great pleasure at having taken this subject out of my hands, and at having made me understand, – as I do most clearly understand, – how far my services are rated below his.

I do not blame you in the least. I do not see how you could have acted otherwise. But on the other hand I do not see why I should make any efforts or sacrifices for a review which lies under an intolerable dictation. Whatever my writings may be worth, it is not for want of strong solicitations and tempting offers from other quarters that I have continued to send them to the Edinburgh Review. I adhered to the connection solely because I took pride and pleasure in it. It has now become a source of humiliation and mortification.

I again repeat, my dear Sir, that I do not blame you in the least. This however only makes matters worse. If you had used me ill, I might complain and might hope to be better treated another time. Unhappily you are in a situation in which it is proper for you to do what it would be improper in me to endure. What has happened now may happen next quarter, and must happen before long, unless I altogether refrain from writing for the Review.[1] I hope you will forgive me if I say that I feel what has now passed too strongly to be inclined to expose myself to a recurrence of the same vexations. / Believe me ever, / My dear Sir,

Yours most truly

T B Macaulay

JOURNAL LETTER, [21–2 SEPTEMBER 1830]

MS: Trinity College. *Extracts published:* Trevelyan, 1, 165–7.

[Paris]

You will probably think that you have had enough of the buildings of Paris – for some time at least. I will therefore come to my personal adventures. I have been several times at the Duc de Broglie's. I left Lord Lansdowne's parcel, my father's letter for the Duchess and my card on the Monday after my arrival. I received next day an invitation to dinner, and, at the appointed hour, 6 o'clock, I went to the table of the Prime Minister.[2]

He lives in the Fauxbourg St Germain – the aristocratical quarter of Paris, – corresponding to our Grosvenor Square and Berkeley Square, as the Chaussée d'Antin, the Rue des Mathurias and other places in that neighbourhood correspond to our Russel Square. There is this difference however that the hotels of the great bankers and manufacturers are finer and newer in their painting and furniture than those of the old noblesse.

The great houses of Paris are quite unlike those of London. The British Museum[3] may give you a notion of them, except that it is very much larger than any of them that I have seen, and that it is built of brick, whereas they are all of stone. Fronting the street there is generally a low dull looking range of building, the windows grated with iron. This last indeed is an almost necessary precaution, for there is not such a thing as an area from one end of Paris to the other. In the middle of this low building is a gate like that of an inn with an archway. Indeed the whole look is not unlike that of an inn kept in good repair, but of which the custom has fallen off. When you pass the archway, you find yourself in a small square court built all round, sometimes with wretchedly mean architecture, – sometimes with great taste and neatness, – but never, as far as I have seen, with any thing like magnificence.

---

[1] In place of 'for the Review' TBM first wrote and then overscored: 'on questions to which Brougham may by possibility take a fancy.'

[2] De Broglie was not Prime Minister but Minister of Education. I cannot explain TBM's mistake.

[3] In Montagu House, which stood till 1845.

The aspect of the Fauxbourg St Germain is very melancholy. The houses of the great nobles are most of them portioned out into lodgings. There are very few fortunes in France since the Revolution which could keep them up. The general effect of that great change has been most salutary. A vast and thriving middle class has risen on the ruins of an exclusive and oppressive aristocracy. But the Fauxbourg St Germain is not the better for the alteration. Imagine Grosvenor Square and St James's Square turned into Hotels and lodging houses, with "Rooms to let," – "a convenient office to be had here," painted on half the doors and you will have some notion of the effect which a walk through these ancient abodes of the French nobles produced on me.

There are still however some streets which are exclusively inhabited by rich people and generally by people who under the old regime were noble. The Duc de Broglie's house stands in one of these select parts. You must not fancy that a French Duke and Peer is by any means so great a person as an English nobleman. The majority of the French chamber of Peers have less, I believe, than eight hundred a year. The Duc de Broglie may have about three thousand, besides the emoluments of his place, which are probably considerably greater than his private income. I went at 6 o'clock in a fiacre to dine with his Excellency. I walked into the court, found nobody there, marched in at the first door that I saw. Still nobody appeared. I put a bold face on the matter, ascended the marble staircase, and entered the first open room. There were two or three servants in waiting. I gave my name; and, after traversing a small ante room was ushered into the Duke's salon.

The room has a very pleasant look-out into a small garden, not unlike those which we sometimes see at the West End of London, – large enough for two or three trees, a grass plot and a flower-bed. But the room is not very magnificent – certainly not larger than our front drawing-room. There was little ornamental furniture, and that little, though extremely neat, was not sumptuous, – a pier-glass, a clock on the chimney piece, a sofa and chairs covered with silk streaked white and green, a table with pamphlets and newspapers, green silk window-curtains. And voilà tout. I believe that I have given the inventory of every article in the room. There is no carpet; the floor is of oak very handsomely dovetailed and carved; – but not so handsome, I think, as a velvet hearth rug or a fine Brussels tissue. You will think that I have some intention of turning upholsterer.

The Duchess[1] received me very kindly. We were a large party – and I could not find out that any of us had ever seen any of the others before. The Duke, a lively clever little man, with less gracefulness than I expected from a Frenchman of rank, and much more animation and frankness than

---

[1] Albertine (1797–1838), daughter of Mme de Staël, married the Duc de Broglie in 1816.

I expected from a minister of any country, talked about politics very freely, and enlivened all his observations with "Eh ma foi!" and "Comment diable." We then went to dinner. The children – very nice children, from six to eleven years old, – dined at the side-table, and were very merry, though not so as to interrupt the conversation of the grown up people. We had of course a French dinner. I ate whatever was brought me, not having the least knowledge by the sight of any thing that was on the table. We had no drinking of healths. A bottle of common wine was at each person's side, and the rarer sorts were frequently handed round. I was surprised at one thing. At every French dinner at which I have been, a glass of Madeira is always presented after the soup. I thought that this wine had been unknown on the continent.

As soon as we had dined, we rose and adjourned to the salon. There we were joined before long by crowds of people who came to do homage to the Prime Minister's lady. The Duke himself, as soon as dinner was over, went to the council at the Palais Royal. Lord Haddington[1] was the only Englishman of the party besides myself, and we struck up a sort of acquaintance.

Before I went away the Duchess asked me to breakfast there the next day, and promised to procure me a good seat in the chamber of Deputies and to send me thither in good company. Her Excellency's breakfast-hour did not exactly suit me, – half-after-eleven. She complained herself that the Duke's duties deranged all the habits of the family.

I was forced next morning to stay my stomach with a noble bunch of grapes for which I gave a penny – two sous. At half after eleven I reached the Duke's Hotel in the Rue d'Universite. The Duke was out on business. The Duchess, her children, a mad-looking English woman, dressed like a scare-crow, who is, it seems, a great friend of the family, and an extremely intelligent, pleasant, young man who seems to be a sort of half-secretary, half-tutor, but who is treated in such a manner that I supposed him for some time to be a brother or nephew of the Duke, made up our party.

But what made up our breakfast? If I give you twenty guesses you will never find out. Roast mutton, – stewed spinach, green gages – an oyster patty, – and a bottle of Burgundy. I was so ravenously hungry that I could have eaten the Duchess's excellency and her three children; so that I fell on the mutton without much ceremony. But lo! after I had replenished myself therewith, came a second course of café-au-lait – cakes – bread and butter – eggs, – and other things fit for a Christian's breakfast. What think you, ladies, of a French family meal?

[1] Thomas Hamilton (1780–1858: *DNB*), ninth Earl of Haddington; Tory M.P. before succeeding to the title in 1828; a Canningite but afterwards loyal to Peel; Lord Lieutenant of Ireland in Peel's first administration; First Lord of the Admiralty and then Lord Privy Seal in Peel's second administration.

Well, this strange breakfast was finished, and the Duchess gave me an order for the Diplomatic Gallery at the Chamber of Deputies. Thither I went, and found myself seated side by side with the Earl of Haddington, with whom, during the intervals of the debate, I had some very amusing conversation. He was, you know, one of the most intimate friends of Canning and Huskisson. Poor Huskisson![1] – But of him in due season.

The chamber of deputies is in the form of a semicircle, with benches rising one above another to a considerable height. The members sit on these benches – the liberals on the left – the aristocrats on the right. The further left or the further right you sit, the stronger are your opinions supposed to be. This distinction has been kept up ever since the meeting of the Constituent assembly forty one years ago. The present hall is of wood and only temporary, but I believe it is, in its general arrangement, like that which is being erected for the permanent use of the chamber.[2] The benches of the Honourable deputies, are covered with cloth, and their floor is the only well carpeted floor which I have seen in France.

The President has a high seat in the middle of the side of the Hall fronting the semi-circle. Underneath him is the stand from which the speakers address the chamber – called the tribune. So that when there is an orator speaking, the president and he look not unlike a parson taking his ease in the reading desk while the clerk underneath him is giving out the psalm. The president has two ways of keeping order which seem to our English apprehensions rather comical. In common cases, he rings a bell most furiously till the members become quiet; but when the disorder is too great to be appeased by this remedy, he puts his hat on. M. Laffitte[3] seemed to me to discharge his functions with good sense and vigour, but not with much dignity.

The proceedings were of no very great interest. But I had the pleasure of hearing Benjamin Constant[4] speak; – and he spoke very well, – quite without preparation, – and with much more force and feeling than I had expected. I saw Casimir Périer,[5] and one or two other public men of some note. But the day was not one of particular interest. I shall go again.

I have since been to the Duchess de Broglie's soirée, and have again dined there. It was on Saturday last that I dined there the second time.

---

[1] Huskisson was killed by being run over by a locomotive at the opening of the Liverpool and Manchester railway, 15 September.

[2] The Chamber of Deputies in the Palais Bourbon was extensively remodelled between 1828 and 1835.

[3] Jacques Laffitte (1767–1844), banker and politician, then President of the Chamber of Deputies.

[4] Constant, Vice-President of the Council of State after the revolution, died on 8 December 1830.

[5] Périer (1777–1832), banker and politician, rival of Laffitte in the state of parties following the revolution; Premier from March 1831. Died of cholera during the epidemic of 1832.

Lord Haddington came in the evening. A French Lady who made her
appearance at about ten o'clock told us of Huskisson's death. I was
shocked – Lord Haddington extremely agitated. I proposed to go to
Galignani's and see if we could learn any thing. We went in his carriage;
but the London Papers of Thursday evening containing nothing, and we
were in high hopes that the whole was false. The next day Lord H sent
me a note to say that he had seen the Ambassador and that it was too true.
It has been much felt here – both by English and French.

I wrote the above yesterday Tuesday Septr. 21. I take up my pen again
to day to tell you of my visiting news. In the evening of yesterday I went
to General De La Fayette's[1] soirée. He is so overwhelmed with business I
scarcely knew how to deliver even Brougham's letter to him – which was
a letter of business, – and I should have thought [it] absurd to send him
Macintosh's[2] which was a mere letter of introduction. I fell in with an
English acquaintance of mine who told me that he had an appointment
with La Fayette on business and would undertake to deliver them both.
This I thought the best course. If I had left them with the porter ten to
one they would never have been opened. I hear that hundreds of letters
are lying there. Every Wednesday Morning from nine to eleven La Fayette
gives audience to anybody who wishes to speak to him. But about ten
thousand people generally attend on these occasions and fill all the court-
yard and half the street as well as the house. La Fayette, you are aware, is
commander in Chief of the national guard of France. The number of these
troops in Paris alone is upwards of forty thousand. – I believe it is fifty
thousand. You go nowhere without seeing them. They guard every
public place. They perform all the functions of our police officers – of our
watchmen – of our beadles. All the shop-keepers of Paris are inrolled; and
I cannot sufficiently admire their disinterestedness and patriotism. The
government finds them a musket and bayonet. But the uniform, which
costs about ten Napoleons, they provide themselves. They have serious
work to do – not mere marching about like our volunteers on Sunday.
My land lord Meurice, a man, I suppose, who has realised a million of
francs or more – forty or fifty thousand pounds, is up one night in four
with his firelock doing the duty of a common watchman in the street. You
cannot imagine how gay the presence of the national guard makes Paris.
The frequented streets are all in a blaze with uniforms, – and all new uni-

---

[1] The Marquis de La Fayette (1757–1834), commanded the National Guard during the
revolution; by the end of the year he had withdrawn his support from Louis Philippe.
In the Chamber of Deputies he supported the abolition of the slave trade and of slavery.
Brougham's letter may very well have referred to those subjects.

[2] Thus in MS. TBM often spells the name in this way.

forms – for the force has only been organised since the downfal of the tyrant on the 29th of July.

As an explanation of the zeal with which the *bourgeoisie* here give their time and money for the public this is to be said. The army received so tremendous a check, and so painful a humiliation from the people in the battles of July, that it is by no means inclined to serve the new system faithfully. The mere rabble behaved nobly during the conflict – and have since behaved with rare humanity and moderation. Yet those who re-member the former revolution feel, naturally, an extreme dread of the ascendancy of mere multitude; – and there have been little signs – trifling in themselves – but such as may naturally alarm people of property. Work-men have struck for wages; – others have attacked machinery; – inflam-matory hand bills have appeared on the walls. At present every thing is quiet – and at no time has the great body of the working class shown any tendency to disorder. Still the thing may happen – particularly if Polignac and Peyronnet[1] should not be put to death. The peers wish to save them. The lower orders who have had five or six thousand of their friends and kinsmen butchered by the frantic wickedness of these men will hardly submit. "Eh," said a fierce old soldier of Napoleon to me the other day – he was a cabriolet driver and had fought at the taking of the Louvre – "Eh – pardonner! – Non! Non! – Eh – Coupez-leur le cou. Non – Sacre! Ça ne passera pas comme ça."

But I did not mean to go at present into a long political disquisition. Understand this, however, that the army is discontented, and that the multitude may become discontented. Such a crisis would be, as you must see, full of danger to property, and might bring back the worst scenes of the former revolution. The best security against this danger is to organise the whole middle class of France as a military force. This is the great work with which La Fayette has been intrusted. In a few weeks a national guard of a million of men will render this fine country, I fervently hope, per-fectly secure against all danger from within or from without.

This long digression will explain to you why M. De La Fayette is so busy. He has more to do than all the ministers together. However my letters were presented, and he told my friend to say that he had a soirée every Tuesday, and should be most happy to see me there.

On Tuesday the 14th I was engaged elsewhere. But yesterday night I went to General De La Fayette's, at the État Major of the National Guard in the Rue de la Chausée d'Antin. It is a fine house. But of the crowd you can have no conception. – I mean the crowd of well-dressed people, for

---

[1] Jules, Prince de Polignac (1780–1847), Charles X's Prime Minister, and Charles, Comte de Peyronnet (1778–1854), the minister who promulgated the ordinances which set off the revolution, were both sentenced to life imprisonment in 1831, released but banished, 1836, and allowed to return to France, 1845.

the guards kept the court yard free from the intrusion of those who had no business there. Of the feeling of the lower orders of Paris and of the interest which they take in politics you may judge by this. I told my cabriolet driver – not the same whom I mentioned a little while ago – to wait for me, and asked his number. "Ah, Monsieur, c'est un beau numéro, c'est un brave numéro – c'est 221." You may remember that the number of deputies who voted the intrepid address to Charles X which irritated him into his absurd coup d'état, was 221.[1]

Well I walked into La Fayette's hotel through a crowd of men in uniforms, and up the stair case into the reception rooms. They were as full as they could hold. I saw four of them; – they are handsome and well lighted. I could not make my way to La Fayette. But I was glad to see him. He looks like the brave, honest, good-natured, simple, man that he is.

From La Fayette's I went to the Duc de Broglie's. But the Duke had that day changed his house. He had gone to live in the Hotel belonging to his department. Thither I pursued him, and found him much more magnificently lodged than in his former habitation. His new residence is very handsome, and the salon in which I was received blazes with crimson satin and velvet – but still no carpet.

Here I met the Questeur – as they call him – pedantically enough – of the chamber of deputies.[2] He gave me a general order for the gallery occupied by retired members, – so that I shall go whenever an interesting discussion is expected.

I have seen something of the commercial as well as of the aristocratical grandees. I dined with M. Delessert,[3] the great banker, at his villa a Passy. Besides this villa he has a most splendid Hotel in the Rue Montmartre.

His villa is extremely luxurious, glasses, pictures and billiard tables within, a flower-garden without, and a noble view from the windows over Paris and its neighbourhood. I was very much pleased with the family.

But here I must stop for the present. On Tuesday next I may perhaps be able to send an account of the cemetery of Père La Chaise and some other curious sights which I have seen.

T B M

[1] In April, the address declaring that there was no concurrence between ministers and the people.
[2] The officer charged with the finances and administration of the Assembly itself.
[3] Benjamin, Baron Delessert (1773–1847), banker, politician, and philanthropist.

TO ZACHARY MACAULAY, [26 SEPTEMBER 1830][1]

MS: Trinity College. *Address:* Z Macaulay Esq / 50 Great Ormond Street / London. *Published:* Trevelyan, I, 200–1.

Paris

My dear Father,

This news has broken my heart.[2] I am fit neither to go nor to stay. I can do nothing but sit in my room and think of poor dear Jane's kindness and affection. – When I am calmer, I will let you know my intentions. There will be neither use nor pleasure in remaining here. My present purpose, as far as I can form one, is to set off in two or three days for England, and in the mean time to see nobody, if I can help it, but Dumont,[3] who has been very kind to me. Love to all – to all who are left me to love. We must love each other better.

T B M

TO ZACHARY MACAULAY, 28 SEPTEMBER 1830

MS: Trinity College. *Address:* Z Macaulay Esq / 50 Great Ormond Street / London.

Paris Septr. 28. 1830

My dear Father,

I wrote a few lines to you the day before yesterday, when I was in much distress. The first bitterness of this great sorrow is now over; and I have had time to think over the many alleviating circumstances; – how gently the stroke has fallen on the dear girl,[4] – from what a life of suffering it has released her, – and to how sublime and happy a mode of existence it has, as I hope, introduced her. To grieve as I have grieved is mere selfishness. Soon I hope nothing will remain of the feeling with which I received the tidings – except that affectionate remembrance of dear Jane's many ex-

---

[1] Postmarked 26 and 28 September 1830.

[2] Jean Macaulay died on 22 September. 'We had been so accustomed to see dearest Jean suffer from illness that the idea of approaching danger in her case never presented itself to us, and when the blow fell were at first quite overwhelmed by it' (Selina Macaulay, Diary, 14 October 1830).

[3] Louis Dumont, a friend of Zachary Macaulay's through his participation in the anti-slavery movement, was 'a permanent official in the Ministry of Foreign Affairs' (Knutsford, *Zachary Macaulay*, p. 385). Just after TBM's departure from Paris Dumont wrote to Zachary Macaulay, 1 October [1830], complimenting him upon his son and assuring him that TBM will be a great source of comfort (MS, Huntington).

[4] A note (by Fanny Macaulay?) at the end of this letter describes Jean's death in language taken over by Trevelyan, I, 200: 'She was found in the morning lying as though still asleep, having passed away so peacefully as not to disturb a sister who had spent the night in the next room, with a door open between them.'

cellent qualities which my mind must retain, as long as it retains any thing.

I feel all the kindness which prompted the advice given me by my mother and you respecting my stay here. But, though my spirits have risen from their extreme depression, I am in no humour for seeing sights and going to soirées. I pine for my home like a schoolboy. I shall leave Paris by the diligence for Boulogne on Thursday morning. I hope to be in London on Saturday night. Will you be so kind as to give my people notice to expect me? Do not be uneasy however if I should not make my appearance. My movements will depend on wind, weather, and my own sensations after thirty hours of jolting on a paved road.

Love to all. I hope to find Henry well; and Margaret, who is almost as great a stranger as Henry, returned.[1]

Ever yours most affectionately

T B M

TO MARGARET MACAULAY, [9][2] OCTOBER 1830

MS: Mrs Lancelot Errington. *Address:* Miss M Macaulay / Rothley Temple / Mountsorrel / Leicestershire. *Frank:* London October nine 1830 / T B Macaulay.

London October 8 – 1830

My dearest Margaret,

I cannot frank this cover for Hannah without putting into it a single line from myself – to tell you how much I have felt for you, in all your distresses,[3] and how heartily I rejoice at the thought of seeing you again. We must love each other better and better, my darling, that, when these inevitable separations come, we may have nothing to reproach ourselves with, and that no remorse may mingle with our sorrow. Between you and me, dearest, there has been as little ground for such remorse as between any two people in the world. I am sure that there will be none. I am sure that no change of situation or lapse of time can alter a love like that which I bear to you and which you have always shewn to me. I pine for your society; and so do we all. Give my kindest love to all at the Temple and the Vicarage.[4] Ever, my sweet sister, yours most affectionately

T B Macaulay.

---

[1] Margaret was either still with the Croppers at Liverpool or at Rothley Temple (next letter).
[2] Postmark and frank agree on 9 October.
[3] Isabella Cropper and Jean Macaulay died within a week of each other.
[4] Lydia Babington Rose (see 8 May 1813) and her seven children lived there; her husband, Joseph Rose, Vicar of Rothley, died in 1822. Thomas Babington then presented the living to his son John, who already held another family living as Rector of Cossington. John provided a curate for Rothley, so that Lydia and her children were able to remain at the vicarage, close to Rothley Temple.

TO MACVEY NAPIER, 16 OCTOBER 1830

MS: British Museum. *Address:* Macvey Napier Esq / Edinburgh. *Frank:* London October sixteen 1830 / T B Macaulay. *Mostly published:* Napier, *Correspondence*, pp. 91–4.

London October 16. 1830

My dear Sir,

Your letter of the 24th of Septr. reached Paris just after I had been re-called from thence, by a very melancholy event in my family. After much delay and many mistakes it has at last arrived in London. I have just received it from the Foreign Office. I have had some correspondence and conversation with Empson on the subject to which it refers, and he has, I believe, told you what has passed between us.[1] – I am extremely sorry to find that my letter gave you pain. The precise expressions which I used I cannot remember. I certainly wrote in haste and warmth. Yet I must have expressed myself very ill if I led you to think that, even in the first moment of irritation, I felt any personal resentment towards you, or that I considered my secession from the Review as a punishment – to use your own phrase. I considered it as a measure not of punishment, but of precaution. If the whole question had been between you and me, the expressions of kindness and regret which you employed would have much more than satisfied me. But there was another person concerned, the person of all persons on earth to whose dictation I feel least inclined to stoop. Your intentions towards me, I know, are perfectly kind and fair. I have no such confidence with respect to his. I would sacrifice much to your convenience. But I cannot tell you how my whole heart and soul rise up against the thought of sacrificing any thing to his love of domination.

My reason for thinking that in the present case B[rougham] was exercising an unjustifiable dictation was a very simple one. The transaction was, as you say, and as I could not but feel, one which required very special circumstances to justify it. Now I could see no special circumstance except B's will and pleasure.[2] Nor do I yet see any. I have been a very anxious observer of French politics. I have talked with very intelligent men on both sides of the channel; and I solemnly declare to you that I am utterly unable to imagine how it can be a matter of necessity or of pressing expediency that a Whig manifesto about the late Revolution should appear

---

[1] 'Macaulay is back on his Sister's death. I shall see him on Saturday and he will write to you as soon as he gets your Letter back from Paris. Meantime he says to me "I acquiesce in your award" etc. But concludes by saying "I have made up my mind immutably to this – that my first concession is my last." Therefore we must mind our *ps* and *qs*' (Empson to Napier, 7 October [1830]: MS, British Museum).

[2] In announcing that he must write the article on the July revolution Brougham told Napier that 'the reason is this: all our movements next session turn on that pivot, and I can trust no one but myself with it, either in or out of Parliament' (Napier, *Correspondence*, p. 88).

before the meeting of Parliament. Of course it is desirable that just views of so important an event should be entertained throughout the country: but nobody, I believe, expects that any propositions directly relating to the changes in France will be brought forward during the next Session by any party. Brougham chose, however, to persist in his demand. That circumstance, I think and always thought, fully justified you. His talents are not, I think, displayed to most advantage in the Edinburgh Review. But his withdrawing, and his direct hostility which would assuredly follow his withdrawing, might do immense injury. Without disputing whether his articles are better than mine, I am sure that his secession would do you more harm than mine. These considerations seemed to me to exculpate you completely. What it might be advisable for me to do was, as I think you must allow, a very different question. I never doubted that your intentions towards me were perfectly friendly. But I thought that you would find it impossible to carry them into effect. The difficulties of your situation, justified, as I could not deny, your proceedings with regard to me. But they also, I thought, justified my secession. I have no right to expect that you or any editor will risk the ruin of a review in order to spare me a little mortification. But I have a perfect right to keep as much as I can out of all connection with a review which can be saved from ruin only by measures mortifying to me.

Perhaps I have said more about the past than is proper in a letter of reconciliation. But reconciliation is scarcely the word. For there has been no interruption of personal kindness and esteem; and I really wished to explain clearly the principle on which I have acted. As for the future, I require no pledge. When any such case as that which has now occurred shall present itself, act as you think best for the Review. If you decide against me, I shall not, I assure you, think myself ill-used, at least by you. I shall attribute whatever may happen to the extreme difficulty of your situation. On the other hand you must not think hardly of me if I should then put into execution the purpose which I at present relinquish; – if I should, without the least anger towards you, and with real regret for any inconvenience which you may sustain, withdraw from a connection which, I sincerely assure you, has never, as far as you are personally concerned, given me any thing but pleasure.

And now, my dear Sir, let us finally dismiss this unpleasant topic. Yet I should wish for a few lines from you to say that the conduct which, without the least unkind or suspicious feeling towards you, and purely, as I intended, in self-defence, I have adopted on this occasion, has not diminished that personal regard which I flattered myself that you felt for me, and which will, I hope, be proof against any of the occurrences which may disturb our literary connection.

A day or two after I had written to you from Paris I heard again from Dr. Lardner[1][, who][2] mentioned his application to you. The [fact?][2] need no longer be a secret. I have ag[reed][2] to write an account of the political changes of France since the Restoration and of this late revolution for his Cabinet Cyclopædia. I hope to have finished this task by Xtmas. My article on the Italian Poets must be postponed till the spring. But I can easily find time for a short paper in the Winter Number.[3] The Jews have been urging me to say something about their claims.[4] And I really think that the question might be discussed, both on general and on particular grounds, in a very attractive manner. What do you think of this plan? But I must absolutely stop. / Believe me ever, / My dear Sir,

Yours most truly

T B Macaulay

TO LORD LANSDOWNE, [16 OCTOBER 1830][5]

MS: Fragment, The Marquess of Lansdowne. *Address:* The Marquess of Lansdowne / etc. etc. etc.

[London]

[. . .] subject perfectly mild and reasonable. He praised the King and La Fayette to the skies, and spoke very civilly of the chambers.

I am afraid that you will think me presumptuous and tedious into the bargain. It is but little that can be learned of a great nation in three weeks. During my three weeks in Paris, however, I made ample use of my eyes

---

[1] Dionysius Lardner (1793–1859: *DNB*), a graduate of Trinity College, Dublin, having made a name as a writer on scientific subjects, was appointed in 1827 to the chair of Natural Philosophy and Astronomy in the London University. In 1829 the 'Cabinet Cyclopaedia' began publication under his editorship; it was completed in 133 volumes by 1849. Lardner also edited 'Lardner's Cabinet Library,' 9 vols., 1830–2, and the 'Edinburgh Cabinet Library,' 38 vols., 1830–44: these were all notable pioneer efforts in the popular publishing of 'enlightening' literature.

[2] Paper torn away with seal.

[3] 'Civil Disabilities of the Jews,' *ER*, LII (January 1831), 363–74.

[4] The repeal of the Test and Corporation Acts in 1828, restoring full civil freedom to Dissenters, put the Jews in worse case than before by providing a new form of oath for those taking public office which included the words 'on the true faith of a Christian.' The removal of Catholic disabilities in 1829, however, encouraged the Jews to hope for a change in their situation, and a campaign for emancipation was organized in 1830 by Isaac Lyon Goldsmid and his son Francis, whose anonymous 'Statement of the Civil Disabilities and Privations affecting Jews in England,' 1829, is the title prefixed to TBM's essay (see [D. W. Marks], *Memoir of Sir Francis Henry Goldsmid*, Part 1, 1879, p. 23; and I. Abrahams and S. Levy, eds., *Essay and Speech on Jewish Disabilities by Lord Macaulay*, 2nd edn, Edinburgh, 1910, p. 63). Isaac Lyon Goldsmid (1778–1859: *DNB*), a banker and philanthropist, was known to Zachary Macaulay as a supporter of the Anti-Slavery Society and a principal founder of the London University. He was created baronet in 1841, the first Jew to receive the distinction.

[5] Postmarked 16 October 1830. Only the last page of the letter remains.

and ears, and most of the correspondents of our English newspapers seem to me to have used neither.

I am sorry to say that I cannot learn anywhere on what precise day the King's speech will be delivered.[1] / Believe me ever, / My dear Lord,

Your Lordship's faithful Servant

T B Macaulay

TO MACVEY NAPIER, 27 NOVEMBER 1830

MS: British Museum. *Address:* Macvey Napier Esq / Edinburgh. *Frank:* London November twenty seven / 1830 / T B Macaulay. *Mostly published:* Napier, *Correspondence*, pp. 97–8.

[London]

My dear Sir,

I have only a minute to write. I will send you an article on the Jews next week – Sadler[2] as soon as he comes out. He does not know what a reason is. And all his boasts and anticipations of victory[3] only prove that he does not.

I do most earnestly hope that Jeffrey will take office.[4] I am best as I am.

You will be glad to hear, I am sure, that the Calne petition[5] was decided in my favour yesterday. Charles Wynne[6] who presided over our Committee was of opinion that the petition ought to have been declared frivolous and vexatious.[7]

You will see that I gave Croker a dressing the other night in B[roug-

---

[1] Parliament met on 26 October but William IV's speech from the throne was not given until 2 November.

[2] Sadler's 'A Refutation of an Article in the Edinburgh Review No. CII.,' is advertised as 'just published,' *The Times*, 16 December 1830.

[3] The full title of Sadler's pamphlet appeared in, e.g., the *Literary Gazette*, 20 November 1830, p. 758, and is itself a kind of boast, offering 'additional Proofs of the Principle at issue' and incorporating a motto from Locke; in his review TBM calls the implied parallel thus established between Sadler and Locke 'exquisitely laughable' (*ER*, LII, 504).

[4] Jeffrey was appointed Lord Advocate in Grey's administration, 2 December.

[5] The committee appointed to consider the petition of Cheney and Hopkinson (see 10 July 1830) against the election of TBM and Macdonald heard the arguments of both sides on 26 November and reported on 30 November. The petitioners unsuccessfully maintained that all the householders of Calne enjoyed the right of election, not just the members of the corporation. See *Commons Journals*, LXXXVI, Part I, 131; 135.

[6] Charles Watkin Williams Wynn (1775–1850: *DNB*), entered Parliament in 1797 and remained there until his death, by which time he had become 'father' of the House. An authority on parliamentary procedure, he was unsuccessful candidate for the speakership, 1817. President of the Board of Control, 1822–8; joined the opposition to Wellington, 1828, and was Secretary at War and member of the Board of Control in Grey's administration, but resigned and voted against the Reform Bill.

[7] In which case the petitioners would have had to bear the whole costs of the hearing.

ham]'s defence.¹ I was in no good humour with B. But the insufferable impertinence and poltroonery of Croker exasperated me beyond all patience. I am thought to have had the best of the battle by our critics here. The newspapers are not very correct.

As to the *ballot*,² I have not yet absolutely made up my own mind. Much nonsense is talked for it and much against it. I am sorry that you have nothing this month from Jeffrey. Our Lord Chancellor will do little more for us, I suspect.³

Ever yours

T B M.

TO [RICHARD SHARP?,⁴ 2 DECEMBER 1830]

MS: Mr W. Hugh Peal.

My dear Sir,

I cannot tell you how much ashamed and vexed I was when, this evening, it flashed upon my mind that I had forgotten my engagement to breakfast with you yesterday. To say the truth, my election committee, and my apprehensions that an attempt would be made on Tuesday evening, however hopelessly, to set aside the decision,⁵ put every thing else out of my head.

Tell me that you forgive my want of thought, and that you will not punish it by witholding the advice which you promised me.

Ever yours truly

T B Macaulay

Gray's Inn / Thursday Evening

¹ Brougham accepted the Lord Chancellorship, 22 November, after having stated in the House of Commons that he would not join the new government and that he was determined to remain in the Commons. Croker, 23 November, charged that Brougham's talk of keeping clear of office was simply 'shuffling intrigue' (*Hansard*, 3rd Series, I, 637). To this TBM replied that Croker, had Brougham been present to answer, 'would sooner have burned his tongue than have made such an attack' (*ibid.*, 648). He was called to order for the remark.

² Now that reform was to be taken up by the government the question whether voting by ballot should be part of the measure was much debated. TBM at length decided in favor of it (see 2 September 1831), though the ballot was regarded as a peculiarly Radical measure and most of the Whigs were opposed to it.

³ Brougham nevertheless contributed fifteen articles to the *ER* in the four years that he was Lord Chancellor.

⁴ The letter is endorsed (in a contemporary hand?) 'To R Sharp.'

⁵ TBM's election committee reported on Tuesday, 30 November. There is no evidence that any protest against its decision was made.

TO MACVEY NAPIER, 17 DECEMBER 1830

MS: British Museum. *Address:* Macvey Napier Esq / Edinburgh. *Frank:* London December seventeen 1830 / T B Macaulay. *Mostly published:* Napier, *Correspondence*, pp. 98–9.

London December 17 1830

My dear Sir,

I send you an article on the Jews. Sadler's Book is out; but I have not seen it yet. When I have read it, I will let you know whether I think it worth an answer. If I do, I suppose there will be time to prepare it for this number. I am very busy or I should have sent you this Jew article before. It is short, and carelessly written, – perhaps as to style, – but certainly as to penmanship. Be so kind, if it is convenient, as to send me the proofs.

I am in hourly expectation of hearing what arrangement is made for bringing Jeffrey into Parliament.[1] I am most impatient to hear him there.

My French History, the House of Commons, and the Bankrupts, have almost killed me between them. I have not the Chancellor's[2] Encyclopædic mind. He is indeed a kind of Semi Solomon. He *half knows* every thing from the cedar to the hyssop.[3] You see that he is coming out with a treatise on Natural Theology to be prefixed to Paley's Book on that subject.[4]

I am in good humour with him. He has given my brother a living of £300 a year in Warwickshire without the least solicitation direct or indirect.[5] It was the first living that he had to give, and nothing could be

---

[1] Jeffrey came into Parliament on 13 January 1831 for the Forfarshire Burghs but was unseated in March through a flaw in the proceedings; on 6 April he came in for Lord Fitzwilliam's borough of Malton.

[2] Brougham's.   [3] See 1 Kings 4: 33.

[4] *The Times*, 16 December 1830, advertised an edition of Paley's *Natural Theology*, 1802, by Brougham and Sir Charles Bell for the Society for the Diffusion of Useful Knowledge, to be accompanied by a 'preliminary discourse' by Brougham. The Society then withdrew from the work owing to its rule 'excluding theological matter' (Monica Grobel, 'The Society for the Diffusion of Useful Knowledge, 1826–1846,' unpublished M.A. thesis, University of London, 1933, p. 116). Charles Knight tells of being summoned by Brougham to the House of Lords where Brougham, surrounded by the Lord Chancellor's anxious attendants and on the point of going into the House, exclaimed '"I can only stay to say a word...advertise Paley to-morrow morning."' Knight went away, he says, 'meditating... upon a new example of the versatility of discourse' (*Passages of a Working Life*, II, 156). The edition finally appeared in the following form: Brougham, *A Discourse of Natural Theology, Showing the Nature of the Evidence and the Advantages of the Study*, 1835; Paley, *Natural Theology, with Illustrative Notes by Henry Lord Brougham...and Sir Charles Bell...to Which Are Added Supplementary Dissertations by Sir Charles Bell*, 2 vols., 1836; Brougham, *Dissertations on Subjects of Science Connected with Natural Theology, Being the Concluding Volumes of the New Edition of Paley's Work*, 2 vols., 1839.

[5] Brougham appointed John Macaulay, since January 1830 Curate of Tilstone, Cheshire, to the living of Alderminster, Warwickshire. There was a delay of the gift, however, and John was still waiting to take possession of the living in November 1831 (Margaret Macaulay, *Recollections*, 1864 edn, p. 64).

done more handsomely. He speaks civilly of me: but I have not met him since his elevation.

I ought to say that my article goes by the mail to night.

Ever yours truly
T B Macaulay

TO MACVEY NAPIER, 25 DECEMBER 1830

MS: British Museum. *Published:* Napier, *Correspondence*, pp. 99–100.

London Dec 25. 1830

My dear Sir,

I send you to day an answer to Sadler.[1] I think I have completely settled the question, by my calculations on his own tables. If you do not think it a satisfactory answer, do not print it. I will be absolutely governed in this matter by you, as it has taken something of a personal shape, from the tone of Sadler's pamphlet; and I have no wish to bring the review into a scrape on my account.

If you have seen his pamphlet you will not wonder at the occasional sharpness of expression which I have employed.[2]

Let me have the proof sheets. It is absolutely necessary that I should look again over the numbers.

Ever yours most truly
T B Macaulay

[1] 'Sadler's Refutation, Refuted,' *ER*, LII (January 1831), 504–29.
[2] Sadler knew, what was doubtless common knowledge, that the review of his *The Law of Population* in the *ER* was TBM's. In retaliation for TBM's remarks on a verse passage in his book Sadler quotes a couple of lines from 'Pompeii'; he then urges TBM to weed out of his writings 'the towering and noxious plant of a conceited and contemptuous self-sufficiency, which always grows most luxuriantly upon the meanest soils' ('A Refutation of an Article in the Edinburgh Review,' p. 6). Throughout the pamphlet he accuses TBM both of invincible ignorance and of deliberate falsification. In reply TBM says that Sadler's 'anger is the most grotesque exhibition that we ever saw. He foams at the mouth with the love of truth, and vindicates the Divine benevolence with a most edifying heartiness of hatred' (*ER*, LII, 529).

TO MACVEY NAPIER, II JANUARY 1831

MS: British Museum. *Address:* Macvey Napier Esq / Edinburgh. *Frank:* London January eleven 1831 / T B Macaulay. *Mostly published:* Napier, *Correspondence*, p. 100.

London Jany. 11. 1831

My dear Napier,

I send back the proofs. Your story is excellent and excellently told.[1] I have a little altered the structure of the first paragraph in order that the patch may not be discernible. I hope that my corrections will not confuse the printer's devil. I have, as you will see, substituted a new table for one which I sent you. The case is a stronger one. I have written my addition in a most clerk-like hand. I have cut out the last sentence as you desired. If anything in the way of per[sonality][2] offends you, blot it out with[out][2] scruple. I had much rather that in a case [of][2] private provocation you should judge for me than that I should judge for myself.

If you could, I should very much wish that you would revise a second proof before the article goes finally to press. Much depends on the accuracy of the printing. If you will guarantee that, I guarantee the arithmetic.

I am worked to death with writing and reading – and have not had a day of rest at Christmas. I am excessively mortified at Jeffrey's failure.[3]

Ever yours

T B Macaulay

I have struck out some sentences about the verbal dispute.[4] If people think that we had too much of that last time, we had better be concise now.

TO WILLIAM WHEWELL,[5] 5 FEBRUARY 1831

MS: Trinity College. *Address:* Rev W Whewell / Trinity College / Cambridge. *Frank:* London February five 1831 / T B Macaulay. *Partly published:* Trevelyan, I, 173–4.

London Feby. 5. 1831

Dear Whewell,

I received your letter and the inclosure this morning. You will see what I have to say about Sadler, or part of it, in the new Number of the Edin-

---

[1] 'My father gave Macaulay the anecdote of Heron, with which he commences the article on Sadler' (Napier, *Correspondence*, p. 100).   [2] Paper torn away with seal.

[3] Jeffrey had been defeated at the Cupar election, 29 December.

[4] Sadler's use of the term 'inverse proportion': see 28 August 1830.

[5] Whewell (1794–1866: *DNB*), B.A., Trinity, 1816; Fellow, 1817; Tutor, 1823–39; Master of Trinity from 1841, the greatest of the nineteenth-century Masters and during his tenure the most prominent personality in the university. Whewell wrote voluminously on many

burgh. I am fully resolved to come and take up my quarters for a month or two in College as soon as I can.[1] I love it the more, the more I see the men whom it sends out. They beat the world before them. But I cannot say much for our recent appearance on the Tripos.[2]

I suppose Malden is regular in settling with you. We think highly in London of his Roman History.[3] Tell him, when you see him, that Hallam, the most fastidious and one of the most competent judges that I know, praises it to the skies.

We are admiring another production of a great Cambridge man – Herschel's Treatise in Lardner's Cyclopædia.[4] A very little physical science would make me admire. But the vigour and propriety of the style, of which I can judge better, are very remarkable. Herschel must be a man of letters as well as a man of science.

I am impatient for Praed's debut.[5] The House of Commons is a place in which I would not promise success to any man. I have great doubts even about Jeffrey. It is the most peculiar audience in the world. I should say that a man's being a good writer, a good orator at the bar, a good mob-orator, or a good orator in debating-clubs, was rather a reason for expecting him to fail than for expecting him to succeed in the House of

---

subjects, especially mathematics and philosophy, his major works being a *History of the Inductive Sciences*, 2 vols., 1837, and *Philosophy of the Inductive Sciences*, 2 vols., 1840. An aggressive, domineering man, it was Whewell of whom the prize fighter said, 'what a man was lost when they made you a parson' (Leslie Stephen's memoir in *DNB*), and of whom Sydney Smith said that 'science is his forte and omniscience his foible' (*ibid.*). TBM and Whewell must have been known to each other from the beginning of TBM's Cambridge career. Though their relations were always polite, it is unlikely that two such assertive men could ever have enjoyed each other thoroughly. Hannah Trevelyan observes in her Memoir that 'I do not think that [Whewell] ever cordially liked your uncle' (Trevelyan, I, 178). Whewell, who admitted Thorwaldsen's statue of Byron to the Trinity library after its long exclusion, refused to allow Woolner's statue of TBM (1863) to be placed in the ante-chapel of Trinity, for which it had been originally designed and where it was set up only after Whewell's death.   [1] He never did.

[2] Of the eight Trinity men among the thirty-one wranglers, the highest stood fourth.

[3] Malden was then resident at Cambridge, but in this year he succeeded George Long as Professor of Greek at the London University. Part 1 of his *History of Rome* (see [August?] 1828) was published on 15 December 1830; part 2 on 1 January 1831.

[4] John Frederick William Herschel, *A Preliminary Discourse on the Study of Natural Philosophy*, 1831. Herschel (1792–1871: *DNB*), son of Sir William Herschel, graduated from St John's College, Cambridge, 1813, and was a close friend of Whewell, who reviewed his *Preliminary Discourse* in the *Quarterly Review*, July 1831.

[5] Praed, now a declared Tory after his Radical youth, was elected for the pocket borough of St Germans, for which he paid £1,000, in December 1830 (Derek Hudson, *A Poet in Parliament, the Life of Winthrop Mackworth Praed, 1802–1839*, 1939, pp. 167–9). The current gossip was that Praed had been hired to oppose TBM, but Praed wrote, in a letter to a friend, 14 January 1831, that 'the scandal vexes me, because wherever I have any name or connexion I ought to be known as being under great obligations to Macaulay, his warmest admirer, and most zealous friend. Any man who believes such a story as that I allude to must believe me half rascal and half lunatic' (Hudson, p. 172). Praed's maiden speech, on the cotton duties, delivered 14 February, was 'extremely successful' (Hudson, p. 173).

Commons. A place where Walpole succeeded and Addison failed, – where Dundas succeeded and Burke failed, – where Peel now succeeds and where Macintosh fails – where Erskine[1] and Scarlet[2] were dinner-bells, where Lawrence[3] and Jekyll[4] – the two witti[est][5] men or nearly so of their time, were thought bores, – is surely a very strange place. And yet I feel the whole character of the place growing upon me. I begin to like what others about me like, and to disapprove what they disapprove. –

Canning used to say that the House, as a Body, had better taste than the man of best taste in it; and I am very much inclined to think that Canning was in the right.

Ever yours

T B Macaulay

TO MACVEY NAPIER, 12 FEBRUARY 1831

MS: British Museum. *Address:* Macvey Napier Esq / Castle Street / Edinburgh. *Frank:* London February twelve 1831 / T B Macaulay. *Mostly published:* Napier, *Correspondence,* pp. 100–1.

London February 12. 1831

My dear Sir,

I have received your letters and the inclosures. Empson is in London. He shall have your note directly. People here think that I have answered Sadler completely[6] – at least those who have spoken to me on the subject think so: – and if no fault in the arithmetic can be discovered, I do not see how any doubt can exist on the matter. – Empson tells me that Malthus[7] is well pleased, which is a good sign. As to Blackwood's trash,[8] I could

---

[1] Thomas, Lord Erskine (1750–1823: *DNB*), Lord Chancellor.

[2] James Scarlett (1769–1844: *DNB*), first Baron Abinger, had unparalleled success as a barrister but was not notable as a speaker in the House of Commons.

[3] Probably French Laurence (1757–1809: *DNB*), like Erskine and Scarlett a lawyer whose professional reputation was not sustained by his performance in the House of Commons.

[4] Joseph Jekyll (d. 1837: *DNB*), more famous as a wit than as a politician, sat for Calne, 1787–1816. TBM met him early in 1832: 'on Sunday Tom dined at Mr. Rogers's, and met Sir J. Mackintosh, Mr. Sharpe, and Mr. Jekyll, *the Yorick*, as Mr. Rogers calls him, of our time. He is very old, and seemed, during a great part of the time, half asleep, but sometimes revived to tell his story' (Margaret Macaulay, *Recollections*, p. 226).

[5] Paper torn away with seal.

[6] Sadler published 'A Reply to an Article in the "Edinburgh Review" Entitled "Sadler's Refutation Refuted",' 1831, but the controversy was dead.

[7] The Reverend Thomas Robert Malthus (1766–1834: *DNB*), whose *Essay on Population*, 1798, was the object of attack in Sadler's *Law of Population*. Malthus was Professor of History and Political Economy at Haileybury, where he remained from 1805 until death, and where Empson was his colleague.

[8] 'Mr Sadler and the Edinburgh Reviewer. A Prolusion in Three Chapters. By Christopher North,' *Blackwood's*, XXIX (February 1831), 392–428, undertakes to vindicate Sadler 'from one of the basest attacks ever made by ignorance and folly on learning and wisdom' (p. 402), retorts on TBM that his own writings are 'a tawdry bedizenment of flower, froth,

not get through it. It bore the same relation to Sadler's pamphlet that a bad hash bears to a bad joint. It is too much, after being nauseated with such an odious dish to have it served up again in such a *rifacciamento*. As far as I looked at it, I saw nothing original, – nothing that was not in Sadler's pamphlet. – Is it possible that such stuff can be Wilson's?[1]

I shall not, I fear, be able to do much for the next Number. But I will try to do something. I do not like to review Moore[2] – in the first place because I am no great admirer of his hero; and in the next place because the topic is a little hackneyed. I cannot well imagine from what quarter you can have heard that I thought of reviewing Lardner's Cyclopædia. I do not remember that any body ever mentioned it to me. Lardner, I recollect, spoke to me warmly of Herschel's treatise on Natural Philosophy, and expressed a wish that it were well reviewed. But I never dreamed that he could mean to propose it to me who know nothing about natural philosophy. It is, as far as I can judge, a very able performance: but I am a mere child in such matters.

Suppose that I were to write an article on Reform, after the Ministers have developed their plan.[3] Jeffrey, I understand, has drawn the Scotch Bill.[4] But he is, as in duty bound, as close as Lord Burleigh himself. I think he must succeed. I do not see how he can fail. Yet he is nervous: and I am, I own, a little nervous for him.

I see that the Age[5] charges me with the article on England and

---

fume, foam, flash, flutter, and feather of speech' (p. 405), accuses him of having 'narrowly escaped the fate of Wooden Spoon' in the Cambridge examinations (p. 408), and, referring to TBM's remarks on the slave population in the United States in the article on Sadler, says 'who knows but he may become himself a Slave Proprietor, and crack his finger and thumb at the Anti-Slavery Reporter, the African Institution, and at all that his friend Thomas Babington Macauley has written and spoken against all sorts of slavery, and in favour of all sorts of liberty all over the world ?' (p. 427).

[1] John Wilson (1785–1854: *DNB*), Professor of Moral Philosophy in the University of Edinburgh, wrote for many years for *Blackwood's* under the pseudonym of 'Christopher North,' especially the series called 'Noctes Ambrosianae,' 1822–35.

[2] The second volume of Thomas Moore's *Letters and Journals of Lord Byron, with Notices of His Life*, 2 vols., 1830-1, appeared in January. The work provided the text for TBM's 'Moore's Life of Lord Byron,' *ER*, LIII (June 1831), 544–72. Moore (1779–1852: *DNB*), the Irish poet, was an intimate of Whig society; he lived in a cottage on Lord Lansdowne's estate, and in London was a fixture at Holland House. TBM apparently knew him already; the time of their first meeting is not recorded but it cannot have been long before the date of this letter.

[3] The suggestion was not acted on. The Reform Bill was introduced on 1 March.

[4] The Scottish Reform Bill was Jeffrey's responsibility as Lord Advocate and was brought in on 15 March.

[5] 'The fifth article in the last *Edinburgh Review* contains a furious philippic against the Exclusives. Would our readers like to know the reason why? Because Tom Macaulay, the scribe, has tried in vain to get a ticket for Almack's' (*Age*, 6 February 1831). The *Age* under Charles Westmacott (see 17 October 1831) was a Tory scandal sheet specializing in blackmail of the fashionable.

France.[1] I do not wish to pry into secrets: but I think that it is Bulwer's from internal evidence.

Goldsmidt told me that the Jews want to print my article as a separate pamphlet. I told him that, if the publishers had no objection, I had none.[2] But I declined interfering in the matter. He means to apply to Longman[3] whom he knows. I think his solicitude quite superfluous. The Jews cannot, I imagine, be kept out of parliament longer.[4]

Ever yours truly

T B Macaulay

[1] Bulwer wrote 'Spirit of Society in England and France,' *ER*, LII (January 1831), 374–87, a comparison much to the disadvantage of 'fashion' in England. Edward Lytton Bulwer-Lytton (1803–73: *DNB*), later first Baron Lytton, the novelist and politician, was still known in 1831 as Edward Bulwer. He came up to Trinity College in 1822 when TBM was in residence but migrated to Trinity Hall in October; he was a member of the Cambridge Union in the days of TBM's success there, and among the contributors to *Knight's Quarterly Magazine*. Bulwer at this time was contributing to many periodicals, writing novels in rapid succession, and on the point of entering Parliament, to which he was first returned in April; later in the year he added the editorship of the *New Monthly Magazine* to his activities.

[2] No such reprinting is known.

[3] Thomas Norton Longman (1771–1842: *DNB*), head of the publishing firm, which, since 1826, had been sole proprietor of the *ER*.

[4] They were in fact excluded until 1858, when Baron Lionel de Rothschild took his seat as M.P. for the City of London.

APPENDIX:
BIBLIOGRAPHICAL NOTES

13 July 1814, note 3

Several writers have stated that Zachary Macaulay discouraged TBM's eagerness to contribute to the *Christian Observer*, but this letter is the only definite evidence that he did. Roberts, *Letters of Hannah More to Zachary Macaulay*, pp. xix–xx, says that TBM was 'often baffled' in his efforts to publish. An anonymous source quoted in [Eliza Rennie], *Traits of Character*, 1860, II, 12, says that when TBM submitted an article signed with his initials Zachary Macaulay sent it back and published a note addressed to 'TBM' in the next issue. Henry Thornton remembered that Zachary Macaulay, though publishing a contribution from TBM signed 'Juvenis,' accompanied it with a note instructing Juvenis to think more and write less (Alston, 'Recollections of Macaulay,' p. 59). I have not found either of these notes in the *Christian Observer*. The article attributed to TBM on Thornton's authority is 'On the Deceitfulness of the Human Heart,' *Christian Observer*, XV (October 1816), 635: the attribution is not otherwise supported.

There is good evidence that the following items, at least, in the *Christian Observer* are by TBM: 'Nature of an Auto-da-Fé,' X (March 1811), 161–2 (an extract from Foxe's *Book of Martyrs* with a brief preface; according to Margaret Macaulay, *Recollections*, p. 238, this was a collaboration between TBM and his sister Selina); 'Observations on Novel Reading,' XV (December 1816), 784–7 (Zachary Macaulay to Kenneth Macaulay, 1 January 1821: MS, University of London; Trevelyan, I, 60); 'Remarks on A.A. and Candidus on Novel Reading,' XVI (April 1817), 230–1 (Zachary Macaulay to Kenneth Macaulay, 1 January 1821); 'Paraphrase of the Prophecy of Nahum,' XIX (March 1820), 169–70 (Zachary Macaulay to Hannah More, 30 March 1820, in Knutsford, *Zachary Macaulay*, p. 352); 'The Lamentation of the Virgins of Israel for the Daughter of Jephthah: A Hebrew Eclogue,' XIX (September 1820), 587–8 (see [19?] August 1820). These are in addition to the indexes that TBM compiled for volumes 13 and 14 of the *Christian Observer*: see 16 January 1815 and 14 May 1816. One of the peculiarities of the *Christian Observer* is that it has no volume 21, an intended general index never published. T. Mozley, *Reminiscences*, 1882, I, 107, says that TBM described to Robert and Samuel Wilberforce 'his father Zachary's extreme disappointment when he declined the important service for which he had been destined and educated, the long desired Index of the "Missionary Register," or whatever the name of the father's periodical.' The story may be true, although Zachary Macaulay was not the editor of the *Christian Observer* in 1822, the year in which the index volume ought to have appeared, nor is it likely that he would have imposed such a discipline on a son who had reached his majority. Moreover, a note to the preface of the *Christian Observer*, XXII (1822), states that the index is 'in a considerable state of forwardness, and may be expected in a very few months,' implying that someone was at work on it. A note on the letter of 9 September 1816 in which Zachary Macaulay offers the editorship of the *Christian Observer* to the Rev. S. C. Wilks states, more probably, that Zachary Macaulay intended to offer the editorship to TBM four years from the date of the letter (MS, Mrs Humphry Trevelyan). Probably he had authority enough in the affairs of the *Christian Observer* to make such plans, for the terms of his proposal to Wilks make it clear that the editorship of the *Christian Observer* is entirely at his disposal.

[August? 1828], note 3

On a history of the Stuarts for the SDUK. In the letter to Brougham of 14 September 1828 in which the extract from TBM's letter is quoted, Ellis writes that 'I cannot think what made me forget to mention to you that I had several conversations with him [TBM] on the subject, both at York and Lancaster. He is very much in earnest on the matter, and stipulates only that he may not be confined within too narrow limits as to the number of sheets which he is to occupy with his history of the Stewarts. You probably know that, in consequence of his attention having been drawn lately to reviewing Hallam's Constitutional History, he has become very familiar with the details of the Events of the times of the Stewarts; and, as this is beyond comparison the most important history which we shall publish, I took it upon myself to assure him that we should not quarrel with him for diffuseness. He proposes to begin with an introductory view of the state in which society and opinions were left at the death of Elizabeth. In the body of the history, he intends to introduce, wherever he can do so with perfect security as to truth, characteristic anecdotes and speeches – giving for instance King James's broad Scotch verbatim....I wrote to Macauley, on receiving your note; and the following is an extract from his answer [the extract given above is here quoted]. I shall write by this post to say that we will (subject to the approbation of the Publication Committee, as to which there can be no doubt) take his assistance on his own terms, begging him to lose no time, as we shall publish it as soon after Xtmas as we can get it, and shall have no other history after that time till Rome is ready. If you think this is going too far, write word directly to me, or to Macauley (whose letter will be forwarded from Great Ormond Street), qualifying what I have said as far as you think fit.' The Society's minutes contain no record of any agreement with TBM for this work, and there is no evidence that he ever wrote any of it. A letter from Thomas Coates, secretary of the Society, to George Waddington, 7 March 1834, says that 'the Committee have long been desirous of having a history of England, and the subject was at the commencement of the Society parcelled out among Mr. Southern, Mr. Macaulay and Lord John Russell: all of whom are prevented from fulfilling the task' (MS, University College). Monica Grobel, 'The Society for the Diffusion of Useful Knowledge, 1826–1846,' unpublished M.A. thesis, University of London, 1933, p. 280n., says that the arrangement was for Southern to write the history up to the Stuarts, TBM to do the Stuarts, and Russell the years from 1688.

The Society for the Diffusion of Useful Knowledge, remembered as an early enterprise in popular education, was founded by Brougham in 1826 and published its first treatises in 1827. On the Committee of the Society were many of those who were associated in the same year with the founding of the London University, and Society and University shared the same secretary. The works published by the Society appeared in fortnightly numbers for sale at sixpence; to an original 'Library of Useful Knowledge' series were added a 'Library of Entertaining Knowledge,' the popular *Penny Magazine* and *British Almanac*, and such ambitious publications as the *Penny Cyclopaedia*. The Society continued in operation until 1846, but, though well publicized, does not seem to have been a practical success. See Charles Knight, *Passages of a Working Life*, II, *passim*; and R. K. Webb, *The British Working Class Reader*, 1955, pp. 66–73. Ellis was one of the most active members of the Committee, serving on the publication sub-committee, recruiting writers from among his Cambridge acquaintance, correcting treatises in mathematics and history, and himself contributing an *Outline of History* (see [September? 1828?]). For his many services he was made an honorary life member of the Society. Zachary Macaulay was appointed to the Committee in 1830; TBM had no official connection with the Society, though he was evidently interested in it (its office in 1830–1 was at 4 South Square, Gray's Inn; TBM's chambers were at 8 South Square). Knight, *Passages of a Working Life*, III, 30, says that TBM 'took no part' in the work of the SDUK, but this is not quite true. From the papers of the Society, now in University College, London, it appears that TBM read and commented on, besides the treatises of Malden and Ellis, the MSS of Malkin's *History of Greece* (see [September? 1828?]), of E. P. Burke's unpublished *History of France* (Minutes of Publication Committee, 4 June 1829), and perhaps of William Shepherd's *History of the American Revolution*, 1830 (Minutes of Publication Committee, 19 August 1830). A letter from Thomas Coates to Thomas Denman, 13 August 1830, says of Shepherd's work that 'Mr. Macaulay will add either by way of note or of appendix the little dissertation upon the nature of the connection between Colonies and the Mother Country. This note Mr. Brougham will revise' (MS, University College); such a note appears on p. 64 of the *History of the American Revolution*, but it bears no resemblance to TBM's style. 'Mr. Macaulay' may well have been Zachary.

19 August 1830, note 1, p. 282

The fate of the article thus proposed is very complex and may be conveniently summarized here. It was designed in two parts, the first to cover the revolution; the second, French politics from the restoration to the revolution. The first part TBM seems actually to have written (see 16 September 1830). On 8 September Brougham wrote to Napier saying that TBM's article must be called off, for Brougham himself meant to write on the subject of the revolution (Napier,

Correspondence, p. 88). Napier and TBM were obliged to submit to Brougham's dictation, and his article, 'The Late Revolution in France,' duly appeared in the *ER*, LII (October 1830), 1–25. Before Brougham's interference, TBM had been invited by Dionysius Lardner to write a sketch of the 1830 revolution; the invitation was afterwards renewed, and on 16 October TBM reported to Napier that he had agreed to write a survey of French politics from the restoration for Lardner's series of popular surveys and guides called the 'Cabinet Cyclopaedia,' begun in 1829. This work would certainly have embodied not only what he had already written but what he had intended to write as the second part of his *ER* article; it was never published, however, though much of it seems to have been written and it has generated two bibliographical ghosts. TBM thought that he could finish by Christmas (see 16 October), and he worked hard at the book with that object in mind. Jeffrey wrote to Empson on 31 January 1831 that 'I hope [TBM's] history is done, and that he will soon be restored to his disconsolate friends' (Lord Cockburn, *Life of Jeffrey*, 1852, II, 234), but he was still at work on it as late as 29 October 1831. It was advertised for publication on 1 March 1831 as *French Revolution of 1830* (Leeds *Mercury*, 8 January 1831); two weeks later an advertisement in the *Literary Gazette*, 22 January, p. 64, listed it for publication on 1 April under the title *View of the History of France, from the Restoration to the Revolution of 1830*; in the *Literary Gazette*, 19 February 1831, p. 128, it is advertised for publication in two volumes 'in the course of the present year'; the notice adds that 'this work will form a supplement to the History of France [by Eyre Evans Crowe], published in the Cabinet Cyclopaedia.' In the *Literary Gazette*, 13 August 1831, p. 528, it is announced for publication on 1 December, but now in *one* volume, 'Complete.' The change in plan is perhaps reflected in TBM's statement, 29 October 1831, that he hopes to finish at least part (i.e., volume?) one; his inability to finish the work as originally planned could be a reason for the final suppression of what he had written. As late as July 1833 Lardner was still advertising the book (publisher's advertisement dated 1 July 1833 in Sir Harris Nicolas, *The Chronology of History*, 'Cabinet Cyclopaedia,' 1833), and a note in Lord Mahon, 'Lord John Russell on the Causes of the French Revolution,' *Quarterly Review*, XLIX (April 1833), 163, makes sarcastic reference to the announcements of the still unpublished work (Mahon's article was revised by Croker, who may have been responsible for the note; it does not appear in the original text of the article, which Mahon published as a separate pamphlet in 1833). Finally, the *English Catalogue of Books, 1837–1849* included *View of the History of France* in its listing of books actually published. Meantime printing had begun at least by June 1831 (see 17 June 1831), but the only evidence of the extent of what was then set in type is Trevelyan's statement (I, 168) that 'ten years ago [probably 1864] proofs of the first eighty-eight pages were found in Messrs Spottiswoode's printing office, with a note on the margin to the effect that most of the type was broken up before the sheets had been pulled.' Trevelyan writes as though he had seen these proofs ('the task, as far as it went, was faithfully performed', *ibid.*); no trace of them has been found since. To perplex things further, the *English Catalogue of Books, 1835–1863* and the *London Catalogue of Books, 1816–1851* made the mistake of entering as by TBM an anonymous work entitled *Historical Memoirs of the House of Bourbon*, 2 vols., 1831 (misdated 1830 in the *English Catalogue*), in Lardner's 'Cabinet Library' (a series separate from the 'Cabinet Cyclopaedia'), and this has sometimes been taken to be identical with TBM's unpublished *View of the History of France*. It is worth noting that in 1885, when their records were still intact, Longmans, who published both the 'Cabinet Cyclopaedia' and the 'Cabinet Library,' were unable to throw any light on the authorship of the *Historical Memoirs of the House of Bourbon*: see *Book-Lore*, 1 (April 1885), 158. A copy of this work (it is not rare), identified as by TBM, was sold at Sotheby's, 18 November 1946.

INDEX

A full index will be published at the end of the work. For the convenience of the reader in the interim this list is given of TBM's contemporaries, with a reference to the place where they are first noted. Persons who clearly need no identification – e.g., Byron, Napoleon, George IV – are not included. Neither are those whom I have been unable to identify.